Jennie Churchill

Jennie Churchill

Winston's American Mother

ANNE SEBBA

JOHN MURRAY

First published in Great Britain in 2007 by John Murray (Publishers)
An Hachette Livre UK company

2

© Anne Sebba 2007

A CIP catalogue record for this title
is available from the British Library

ISBN 978-0-7195-6339-3

Typeset in Bembo by M Rules

Printed and bound in Great Britain by William Clowes Ltd, Beccles, Suffolk

Hodder Headline policy is to use papers that are natural, renewable
and recyclable products and made from wood grown in sustainable
forests. The logging and manufacturing processes are expected to
conform to the environmental regulations of the country of origin.

John Murray (Publishers)
338 Euston Road
London NW1 3BH

www.johnmurray.co.uk

To my own sister, Jane

'One must always pretend the sun is shining even when it isn't,' said
Jennie, as she had the electric light bulbs painted yellow.
Quoted in Anita Leslie, *The Gilt and the Gingerbread*

Contents

Illustrations

The author and publisher would like to thank the following for permission to reproduce illustrations: Plates 1, 7, 8, 12, 14, 15, 25 and 34, Tarka King; 2, neg. no. 79711d, Collection of The New-York Historical Society; 3, neg. no. 61054, Collection of The New-York Historical Society; 4, Booklyn Public Library–Brooklyn Collection; 5, 19, 23, 24 and 35, Jonathan Frewen; 6, neg. no. 79712d, Collection of The New-York Historical Society; 9, photograph by Peter Smith reproduced by kind permission of His Grace the Duke of Marlborough, Blenheim Palace Image Library; 10, Private Collection; 11, FremantleMedia; 13, 22 and 26, Hulton Archive/Getty Images; 19, Pethbridge; 20, Mary Evans Picture Library; 21, supplied by Churchill Archives Centre, CHAR 28/086/006 © Winston S. Churchill, Curtis Brown Ltd; 27, supplied by Churchill Archives Centre, BRDW II/15 © Winston S. Churchill, Curtis Brown Ltd; 28, National Portrait Gallery, London; 29, David R. Kilby; 30, supplied by Churchill Archives Centre, BRDW © Winston S. Churchill, Curtis Brown Ltd; 31, Sir John Leslie and Castle Leslie Trust; 32, Illustrated London News Picture Library; 33, Collection of Elaine Hirschl Ellis.

Preface

IN 1980 I moved with my husband and new baby from London to New York and settled in Brooklyn Heights. Most afternoons I walked this baby according to English habits in his pushchair to gaze idly at the boats on the East River or watch the frenzied activity in the warehouses below. Sometimes we strayed further afield and strolled into Brooklyn itself, a mere block from Pineapple Street to Henry Street.

More than a hundred years earlier another mother on fine afternoons took her small children to the area later known as Brooklyn Heights. They, too, fed the pigeons and watched the paddleboats, tugs and sailing skiffs on the East River. Sometimes a kind gentleman let them peer through his telescope so they could see right over the low roofs of Manhattan Island. Occasionally, just as I was to do later, they crossed by ferry steamer to Wall Street where the father, Leonard Jerome, self-made millionaire and stock speculator, had his office.

Every biographer craves something that will explain their fascination or obsession with their subject. Had I known then that the subject of this book was born so near the street where I lived, would I have written about her sooner? I hope not. I believe there is a time, after certain experiences have been digested, that gives a writer the confidence to understand, to make connections.

Eventually this baby that I walked in Brooklyn Heights grew up to be a soldier and, when he was sent abroad, I confess that as I packed up the occasional book to send him I was conscious that another mother of a soldier had done a lot more and arranged for many more books or hampers of food to support and comfort her son in India.

Often, as I sat buried deep in the Churchill Archives in Cambridge reading the letters from the young subaltern to his newly widowed mother, my thoughts were profoundly engaged with her and her worries. As I type this introduction today I am interrupted by some breaking news: two young British soldiers have been killed in Iraq. I can barely control my own emotions as I think of her anxieties for her two sons as they fought in the Boer War and the bloody Battle of Spion Kop, and how she bravely agonised over her elder son Winston's capture in South Africa. Exactly a hundred years later I wandered over the grassy mounds of that very mountain, scene of so much destruction and brutal loss of life. How did she cope with the days and weeks of uncertainty when this precious, special son was putting himself in the path of so much danger? But, aware of the hazards of self-identification with the subject of my biography, I do not pursue that further. Taking charge of a hospital ship is not in my sights. What remains is a clear appreciation of her steadfast faith in Winston's destiny, a faith which, crucially, she passed on to him.

Jennie Jerome, an American beauty, infused the Marlborough dynasty with vigour, courage and colour. A woman who embraced life with a passion, she was an outsider, an original, who did not live by the dusty old rules of the English aristocracy. She had, according to her son Winston, not blood but the wine of life coursing through her veins. A diamond star flashed in her hair matching the sparkle everyone reported in her dark eyes. She was tempestuous and quick tempered – 'that sudden rage, without heat, that never offends', was how one nephew put it.[1] Another described her as inflammable.

'How Churchillian,' the nieces and nephews took to remarking on occasions of outlandish daring in the twentieth-century family. Yet in saying this they were referring not to John Churchill, the first Duke of Marlborough, a brilliant strategist in battle and a clever tactician in domestic politics, nor to his descendants who lived in the fabulous Blenheim Palace, given by a grateful nation to the Marlboroughs following the battle of the same name in 1704 during the War of the Spanish Succession. It was Jennie, always at the centre of a throng, never alone, her warmth radiating through the room as all eyes turned to admire, they had in mind. For the most beguiling Churchill of them all was not born a Churchill.

Jennie was an explosive personality who fell passionately and instantly in love with the second son of a duke and never looked back. For a short while, Jennie and Randolph became the most brilliant, and extravagant, couple that ever advanced on London. How that daring love fared in the course of a turbulent twenty-year marriage and how it was transmitted to her elder son is, to an extent, the subject of this book. The cult of Winston Churchill, the Greatest Briton, the determined bulldog who saved the western world from domination by Hitler, has never been stronger. Yet Winston himself, it has been said, had few 'Churchillian' qualities, as 'the Churchills were a dreadful family'.[2] According to this admittedly partisan view expressed by his cousin Charlie Londonderry, Winston's genius and vitality were both inherited directly through the female line: the former from his grandmother, a Vane-Tempest who became Duchess of Marlborough, the latter from his American mother, a Jerome. It is the women in the Churchill family, from Sarah, the first Duchess onwards, who were the prudent housekeepers, showing the clear-eyed determination of the convert to maintain a warrior dynasty into which they had married. Among Churchill men, the most forceful was the original Sir Winston Churchill of Dorset, who died in 1688. His survival depended upon that quality. As royalists during the Civil War, he and his family were forced to endure harsh times before the restoration of the monarchy and of their own fortunes. Churchill men have often been loathed, perhaps none more virulently than Winston's own father Randolph, who prompted the vitriolic effluvium attributed to Gladstone: 'There never was a Churchill from John of Marlborough down that had either morals or principles.'[3]

At the same time, the Anglo-American 'special relationship', arguably created by the later Winston, has also never been more in evidence than it is today, in the early years of the twenty-first century. If one had to pick a single achievement that altered the course of world history it would be Churchill's success in ensuring American involvement in the Second World War. The response, therefore: *cherchez la femme*. From Jennie, his mother, Winston learnt enough New World charm and polish to soften the rougher Churchillian edges, since 'a very decided brusquerie of manner is an inseparable accident of the ducal house of Churchill'.[4] And when Jennie displayed some daring originality or eccentricity the relations would comment: 'How very American. How very Jerome.'[5]

And so this book is about Jennie Jerome, who carved out a niche for herself in history and deserves to be remembered as much more than the American mother of a future British prime minister or the wife of a would-be prime minister. She was ambitious politically in the days before women had the vote and before wives of politicians were considered an electoral asset. Jennie all but won the seat by campaigning for her husband and promoting his interests. But she was constantly in demand in her own right long after the political platform bestrode by her husband had been removed. It was a life well lived, although not as well as she had once hoped in her youth.

Jennie, while she thrived on company, returned far more vitality than she ever derived from others. She was not one who lived life vicariously. Educated mostly in Paris, she spoke French fluently and dressed with

French chic. She galvanised American women in England at a time when they did not yet see themselves as an identifiable group. She conceived, produced and edited a profoundly original literary magazine of the highest quality. She wrote plays and articles, devised entertainments and decorated houses as (more or less unsuccessful) ways of making money with innate style and skill. For pleasure, she rode, painted and played the piano to concert standard – although typically always preferring to play four-handed rather than alone. And she loved.

She married three times but neither she nor any of her husbands had enough money to fund their lifestyle and, until the end, she never managed – nor even tried – to curb her lavish tastes not least for love. Above all, she was a woman who was not afraid to fail. Women admired her but men fell in love with her – at least two hundred of them, it was said (the remark itself indicating that her animal magnetism was seen by many as sexually threatening). But the one man she loved longest and unconditionally was her firstborn, child of her youthful passion and energy. And he was deeply proud of being half American. She alone, against all the odds, never doubted that one day he would scale the heights of British political life to which she believed he was uniquely fitted. She did not live to see his triumph as prime minister. But her zest, confidence, recklessness and spirit, as well as her extravagant tastes, she bequeathed to her son.

Writing a book, Winston Churchill once told his cousin Ivor Guest, 'was like living in a strange world bounded on the north by a preface and on the south by the appendix and whose natural features consist of chapters and paragraphs'. Factual books cannot be expected to win friends, he knew, 'at any rate friends of the cheap and worthless everyday variety . . . after all, in writing, the great thing is to be honest'.[6] In the following pages that is what I have tried to be, given the flood of material that has passed across my desk and, to mix my metaphors as Winston sometimes liked to do, the mountain that is now available just beyond my desk on the internet. I know how, merely in my selection of that material, I am inevitably biased in the way I am describing the life and aspirations of a woman I came to admire and, I hope, understand. Some days in her life – and her thoughts on those days – she has still resolutely refused to yield to this nosey investigator. And she is right so to do.

Like all biographies, the following pages are inevitably subjective. They are my interpretation of the life of Jennie Jerome and of necessity they have depended upon the material that has survived. I have found rich rewards in the Churchill Archives in Cambridge, where the family has deposited large collections of papers from various sources.[7] I was lucky enough to see these as 'real' letters, with crossings out, corners cut off which had been kissed by the sender, or black bordered. Almost all have subsequently been transferred to microfilm, preserved for the next generation but now invested with an air of unreality. There are also 'real' letters to Jennie's sisters and parents, which fate and good luck have preserved, as well as some transcribed, and occasionally edited, by her literary descendants. I have discovered other treasures in South Africa, the United States, Ireland and various parts of the United Kingdom. Where it improves readability I have added accents and punctuation to quotations. Inevitably, there are gaps. Yet these, too, are revealing. No letters from Jennie to Randolph in the years 1887, 1888 and 1889 exist in the Cambridge Archives. Yet there are four files of empty envelopes addressed to Lady Randolph Churchill in the hand of Lord Randolph Churchill covering those years. And I know that what I have seen can only be a selection of what was written over a lifetime. I started keeping a note whenever I came across an instruction to burn accompanying material. Yet obviously posterity cannot know about those letters carrying an instruction that they themselves be burnt after reading – if the recipient obeyed that instruction. The diaries of others have been another useful source, but these too, with one eye trained on the reader, cannot be considered wholly reliable. Ultimately, the view of Jennie that you will discover in the following pages is a personal one, shaped not only by history and hindsight but by my own experiences in the years when I was thinking so intensely about her, as well as one drawn from the views of others and extrapolating from events.

Money, or the lack of it played an important part in Jennie Churchill's life. In the text I have always quoted the actual, contemporary amounts of money. As a guide, £1 in 2007 would have been worth £46 in 1875, increasing to £61 in 1900. In the quarter century that followed, by 1925, the equivalent value of £1 had fallen to £32 (source: Office of National Statistics).

I

Just Plain Jennie

~

'I'VE GIVEN YOU all I have,' said Leonard Jerome on his deathbed to his three daughters, Clara, Jennie and Leonie. 'Pass it on.' They knew what he meant. The fabulous riches had all been spent long before, but the unconquerable spirit that, as one grandson wrote, led Leonard Jerome up a new financial hill every time he fell down, was a much more significant and longer-lasting part of his heritage. Jennie, the daughter most like her father, had grasped this early on in life and, in time, passed it on to his grandson and namesake Winston Leonard. Winston always believed in the importance of ancestors and the need to respect the bloodline. He never missed an opportunity to recall with pride that the Jeromes were rooted for many generations in American soil and fought in Washington's armies for the independence of the American colonies and the foundation of the United States. 'I expect I was on both sides then and I must say I feel on both sides of the Atlantic Ocean now,'[1] he maintained. He was referring to the fact that he had at least two forebears who fought against the British in the American War of Independence: one great-grandfather, Samuel Jerome, served in the Berkshire County Militia, while another, Major Libbeus Ball of the 4th Massachusetts Regiment, marched and fought with George Washington's army at Valley Forge. Furthermore, Leonard Jerome's maternal grandfather, Reuben Murray, served as a lieutenant in the Connecticut and New York regiments.

Leonard Jerome was a man who inspired myths. He was famous for losing fortunes as quickly as he made them, for scandalous love affairs, for incredible parties and for driving horses ten miles through the snow without wearing gloves. Born in 1818, he was the fifth of ten children who lived in a white clapboard farmhouse on a hillside in Syracuse, western New York. There were nine boys and one girl, and Leonard was always the most rebellious, the most restless and the only musical child. His parents, Isaac Jerome and Aurora (née Murray), of Scottish descent, were of puritan stock and of a God-fearing frame of mind. Timothy Jerome, his great-great-grandfather and the first American Jerome, had sailed from the Isle of Wight in 1710 in the quest for religious freedom. His hard-working descendants retained the strong religious beliefs and the conviction that enjoyment and fun were both steps on the road to hell.

Money was scarce, but somehow there was enough for the four eldest brothers to go to Princeton. Leonard, who laboured diligently on the farm, was from the age of fourteen contributing to the family budget by working at the village store for a dollar a week. Since barter was the order of the day and Leonard had to deal with shrewd farmers always bargain hunting, he may have learnt his first financial skills at this stage.

But then an offer came from Isaac's elder brother Hiram, a judge in Palmyra, sixty miles away, for the boy to go and live with him. Hiram offered to supervise his further schooling. But he believed in austerity and hard work and was furious to discover that young Leonard had spent his savings on a violin. Naturally musical, Leonard taught himself and was soon playing any melody by ear, entertaining guests at parties. The crunch came when Leonard took his violin with him on his next visit home and dared to play on the Sabbath, thinking he would not be discovered. His father Isaac, hearing the music in the barn, burst in and smashed the instrument to pieces. Eighteen-year-old Leonard from this point on renounced any lingering religious beliefs. Nor did he ever play the violin again but poured all his musicality into singing.

By this time, 1836, his brother Aaron had made enough money in a dry-goods business to send Leonard to Princeton. According to the Princeton alumnus magazine, he was, at the end of his freshman term, well ahead of his class with an average grade of 83.6. He then leapfrogged an entire year to join the sophomore class, which he still found easy, but was to flounder in his junior year where mathematics was the main component. He took an active part in a variety of Princeton activities – especially the concert hall – but departed with some blots on his record. According to the Princeton Faculty Minutes of July 1838 he was briefly suspended for going to Trenton without permission and was caught sabotaging the test tubes so that they exploded in a chemistry class. Such high jinks, together with pressure on family finances, meant that he was compelled to complete his studies at the less expensive Union College in Schenectady, New York. But, before he could attack life, he had to spend two years learning to be a lawyer in Uncle Hiram's Rochester office. It was to prove valuable training.

In 1844 brother Lawrence, also working for Judge Jerome, married Miss Catherine Hall, a dark-eyed heiress of twenty-one with two sisters but no parents. She had been brought up by her elderly aunts in Palmyra and, spurred on to match her income, Lawrence and Leonard abandoned their legal careers. Helped by the Hall inheritance they bought a newspaper, the *Daily American*. Leonard invested everything he had in this, believing that profit would come from printing on the side. Politics was the main thrust of the paper, which quickly gained a reputation as a hard-hitting Whig organ expressly devised to attack the Democrats. Newspapers were, by the mid-nineteenth century, beginning to be profitable investments as both population and literacy rates were rising. As the circulation quickly doubled from 1,000 to 2,000 and then to nearly 3,000, an extraordinary figure for the day, the brothers became local celebrities, in great demand for parties and musical evenings, and 'very popular with the young ladies'.[2]

One of these young ladies, Miss Lillie Greenough, was a mere child. Lillie met the six-foot-tall and imposing Leonard Jerome at a grand gala banquet given by her mother, Mrs William Greenough, and was totally smitten by the older man's charm, energy and good looks. Lillie had a remarkable voice for one so young and she and Leonard often sang duets together. But Leonard, at thirty-one, was ready for marriage and had by then decided to ask the somewhat enigmatic Clara Hall, the twenty-four-year-old sister of Catherine, to be his wife. In typical Jerome style, he proposed on an expedition to Niagara Falls. Leaning dangerously over the edge he shouted: 'I won't come back till you've promised to marry me! Look I'm falling – I'm falling!' The couple were married on 5 July 1849.

Clara's parents, Ambrose and Clarissa Hall, had both died within a few weeks of each other when she was only two. The Hall parents had bequeathed plenty of money for the care of their three orphan children, who never lacked for material comfort. Although some elderly aunts had stepped in to take careful charge, a sense of insecurity seems to have been harder to eradicate. Clara (as a child, she too was known as Clarissa) and her sisters grew up believing themselves to be a quarter Iroquois – something that was talked of in hushed tones then, only to become a source of exotic pride for her descendants, including Winston Churchill. In old age Clara apparently looked so much like an Indian that a younger generation nicknamed her 'Sitting Bull'.

At all events, young Clarissa grew up being told that she must never talk openly about her Iroquois blood. If others did so it was, as Edith Wharton recognised, to be considered an insult. This belief that there was something shameful, heathen, about her origins was seared deep in her psyche. Her insecurity and her snobbish desire to rise above her origins can easily be located here.

The family story went something along the following lines: Ambrose

Hall, being a young man of some fortune, built a white colonial-type house in South Williamstown for a woman he hoped to marry, but when she declined he announced that he intended never to marry at all. However, one day while out hunting he knocked on the door of a cabin hoping for a drink and was answered by a strikingly beautiful teenager twenty-two years younger than him called Clarissa Willcox, daughter of a settler by the name of David Willcox. According to this account Clarissa's mother was one Anna Baker, who had possibly been raped by an Indian so that her daughter Clarissa was born of mixed race, half Iroquois. This could explain why she was thirty-five when she gave birth to Clarissa, rather late for the time. Ambrose could not get the girl's exquisite dark-skinned face out of his mind and therefore gave up his pledge to remain single, went back to marry her and installed her in the great white house. But she, being a child of nature, did not thrive in such majestic surroundings and, shortly after giving birth to her sixth baby, died aged thirty-one, leaving her romantic origins a mystery for her descendants to puzzle over.

More recently this story of Native American blood in the Churchill family has been disputed, and it is true that, although some of Clarissa's descendants today bear remarkable facial similarities to Native Indians, there is no genealogical evidence beyond the high cheekbones and broad noses to support the romantic story of Indian ancestry in the Jerome lineage.[3] (A DNA test, which could nowadays put an end to this discussion, has not, so far as is known, been carried out.) But the stories existed and were believed by most of the Jerome and Churchill family. As Winston Churchill, Jennie's great-grandson, said: 'If Clara's descent is other than "American Colonial of English background" . . . why, some 130 years ago, would Clara have told her daughters the story at a time when it would have been deeply unfashionable to make such a claim . . . for me, physical features speak louder than any entry in a register of births.'[4]

At all events, the new Mr and Mrs Jerome were both ambitious. Leonard plunged into working hard for a number of socially progressive causes, mostly Rochester based, which his paper promoted in editorials, directed by him, such as the Rochester Anti-Slavery Society, a campaign to build a City Library and the need to send aid for the Irish famine. There were appeals to improve city sanitation and provide new sewers, agitation for a ten-hour day for working men, and a proposal for gas to replace the oil lamps currently illuminating the city. One of the most controversial ideas was the provision of free education for all out of taxes. In March 1850, Leonard, as a reward for his services to the Whig cause through the news-

paper, was appointed US consul to Ravenna, in Italy. The Whigs, a fore-
runner of today's Republican Party, believed in a strong nation as opposed
to strong state control.

Meanwhile Clara, socially ambitious, spent her time redecorating rooms
and redirecting furniture. On 15 April 1851 the couple celebrated the
birth of their first daughter, Clarita, always known as Clara, whose blonde
hair, blue eyes and delicate features totally captivated her parents. By the
time of her birth the couple had made a break with their Rochester origins and moved closer to the new business, to Brooklyn, then a city legally
independent of New York with a population of 120,000 souls, and were
renting a fifteen-room redbrick house spread over four storeys, today called
a brownstone, closer in towards the fashionable section later known
as Brooklyn Heights. They shared this house, 426 Henry Street, with
Leonard's brother and business partner Addison, his wife and an unspeci-
fied number of black servants. It was soon littered with half-filled crates and
trunks as Clara, thrilled by her husband's Italian posting and thoughts of a
glittering diplomatic career ahead, had started packing.

But Leonard realised he had to relinquish the Ravenna appointment. He
and Addison now had their own office in Wall Street, a short ferry ride
away, and soon became well-known brokers in the brash, thrusting world
of downtown New York. There were as yet a mere nineteen official New
York millionaires – a figure which would double in ten years and rise
exponentially until it reached nearly 6,000 by 1922.[5] The brothers were
determined to add their names to the list as quickly as possible, mostly
by plunging into such risky ventures as railroad and steamship financing.
Leonard thrived on the fast pace, in sport as much as work, and was admired
for his quick wit and fashionable walrus moustaches, as well as for his habits
of hard work. According to a contemporary snapshot of Leonard: 'I never
knew him to take a drink in a bar or public place. Yet Jerome belonged to the
city with all its garish brilliance. No man ever became more completely a
New Yorker.'[6]

Part of what defined being a New Yorker for Leonard Jerome was par-
taking fully in the city's musical life. There were a few small-scale operas
and concerts which he attended, mostly without his wife. She could never
appreciate music, which to her embarrassment represented a meaningless
cacophony of sounds. The Metropolitan Opera House was not founded
until 1883, but the New York Philharmonic, the city's oldest symphony
orchestra, had been started in 1842. So when, in September 1850, Jenny
Lind, the so-called Swedish Nightingale, came to New York for her first
American concert tour, Leonard knew he had to hear her. Thanks to the

skilful publicity of P. T. Barnum, who organised her tour, excited crowds flocked to her concerts, and Lind's name was eventually tied to every kind of commodity, from songs to gloves and bonnets, from chairs to sofas and even pianos. 'Lindomania' followed her everywhere as she sang to packed concert halls around the country for nearly a year. In New York she was mobbed by 20,000 cheering fans, some of whom had paid twenty or thirty dollars to hear her crystal voice. Leonard Jerome heard her sing more than once – he described her voice as 'Like the dawn – who wants more?' – and the great opera star herself remarked that, of all her admirers, 'Mr Jerome was the best looking.'[7]

And so Clara, never as comfortable as her husband with the frenetic pace of New York life, was thrilled when, in 1852, the Senate confirmed Leonard's second diplomatic appointment. This time Trieste, a giant market-place of a seaport in the top right-hand corner of the Adriatic, was the destination. The serious and sober Clara responded by buying clothes but also by reading accounts of the history of the Austro-Hungarian Empire, 'so that I should know *something* about the place to which we were going. But what a complicated and involved story it did seem.'[8] The charm of Trieste was and still is that complicated story. Once a medieval fishing port, Trieste was an imperial creation without equal. Part of Habsburg territory since 1382, it was largely ignored until 1719 when it was transformed into a busy international free port, a tiny city state ruled by merchants who prospered from its connections between Europe and Asia. Money almost literally washed its shores.

By the 1850s, especially once the railway from Vienna was built, Trieste entered its heyday as bankers and other, more dubious financiers poured in. As Karl Marx wrote of the seaport in 1857, just a few years after the Jeromes' arrival, it was run by 'a motley crew of speculators', Italian, German, English, French, Armenian and Jewish, which meant, he said, that it was not weighed down by tradition and had the advantage, like the United States, of 'not having any past'.[9]

The Jerome family – mother, father and baby plus young Lillie Greenough – crossed the Atlantic under sail in 1852. Leonard Jerome had agreed to pay for singing lessons for young Lillie in Trieste, so the pretty girl with the delightful voice who adored Leonard became part of their entourage. Clara Jerome's irritation at the arrangement can only be guessed at. Probably she was not even consulted. But when Lillie lost her special travel papers, in the days before passports, her anger burst into the open. Once settled, however, Clara Jerome responded to the warmth of the sun as well as to that of the charming foreigners who entertained her. She soon gave up her attempt to speak their language, although not her interest in Paris gowns. It was always remembered in the family what irritation the presence of Miss Greenough had caused Mrs Jerome. But where art or music was concerned Leonard allowed no difficulty to interfere.[10]

Trieste was a formative experience for the young family. It was here that Clara, the matriarch, became determined that her children would succeed where she had failed. They would have a fluency in foreign languages and the cultural confidence that she lacked. As the family settled into a comfortable villa with a bevy of servants and well-trained cooks, Leonard soon indulged himself by buying his first boat, a small white yacht which obliged him to have sailing lessons. The trading middle classes in Trieste's boom years supported a vibrant musical life and the Jeromes would have had no difficulty in finding a singing teacher well versed in the latest operatic techniques for Lillie, as well as attending as much opera as they wished themselves at the Teatro Verdi, the city's renowned opera house and the first in the world to take its name from the great Italian composer. It is easy to imagine Leonard and Clara Jerome promenading together, as Trieste couples were wont to do, the women keen to show off their fine clothes and fine husbands, or both.

It must have been a relaxed time for them as the job of the US consul in the mid-nineteenth century seems to have been all style and little substance. Leonard Jerome kept his consular sword, with its fine steel blade decorated with a medallion of Emperor Francis Joseph and the motto 'Vive Le Roi', purchased in Trieste in 1852, all his life and passed it on to his descendants – a 'somewhat undemocratic symbol', noted his grandson Shane Leslie, to whom it was bequeathed. But then the Jeromes were always fervent monarchists. The sixteen months they spent under the influence of Italian culture made a lasting impression on them and, although Leonard soon wearied of the slow pace of life with not enough to keep him busy, this first visit to Europe had given his wife a taste for European culture which inspired her for the rest of her life. In the short term, however, the replacement of Whig President Millard Fillmore by the Democrat Franklin Pierce meant that Leonard Jerome lost his job and the family returned home to America.

When Jennie came, in middle age, to write her reminiscences she said: 'Italian skies gave me my love of heat and of the sun and a smiling dark-eyed peasant nurse tuned my baby ears to the harmony of the most melodious of all languages.' She added that until the age of six she spoke hardly anything but Italian – evidence of her mother's determination. Yet she goes on to describe her memories of the journey back from Trieste. 'I remember how,' she wrote, 'as we crossed the Mont Cenis in a *vettura*, the deep snow filled my childish mind with awe and astonishment. But this was a sight I was soon to become familiar with in my own country.'[11]

Why this whimsical opening to the book? Jennie never lived in Trieste, although she was conceived there. Yet it is perfectly possible that the stay in Trieste so coloured her parents' and elder sister's lives that Jennie felt as if she had been there with them. Had she been so, she would have been older, so it is hard to believe this was a deliberate ploy, typical of a woman trying to hide her precise age, something that Jennie was keen to do later in life. Birth certificates were not available in Brooklyn until 1866, but we know that on 9 January 1888 Jennie wrote to her mother: 'Dearest Mama, do you know that it is my birthday today? 34!!! I think for the future I will not proclaim my age.'[12]

The family returned to America in the autumn of 1853, shortly before she was born. According to the *Rochester Daily Union* of 17 November 1853, 'Our townsman Leonard Jerome Esq., late consul to Trieste, arrived in town last evening. He came a passenger in the *Baltic*. He is accompanied by his family – all of whom, we are happy to hear, are in excellent health.' The family party included Clara, now a toddler, an Italian nurse, Lillie Greenough, Leonard and a heavily pregnant Mrs Jerome.[13] They had one other permanent reminder of their time there: portraits of Leonard and Clara painted by the Italian artist Felice Schiavoni. Clara, almost beautiful, her olive-skinned, oval face accentuated by curtains of dark hair parted in the middle, looks happy enough if somewhat wistful.

They moved back to the bustle of Brooklyn, this time leasing a house on Amity Street, a tree-lined residential road near the waterfront. Number 8 Amity Street (now renumbered 197) was a handsome four-storey house built in 1849 in Greek Revival style to accommodate the new money moving into the city, with wrought ironwork at the stoop and swirling cast-iron newel posts. It was there, in January 1854, that Leonard and Clara Jerome's second daughter Jennie was born.[14]

'What, just plain Jennie?' Mrs Jerome had apparently exclaimed when Leonard suggested the name as a reminder of Jenny Lind. And thus it remained, although later it was briefly transformed into the more French-sounding, and therefore more sophisticated, Jeannette. For Leonard, it was now clear that his and his wife's tastes needed to be financed. Europe may have opened his eyes to many possibilities, but the reality – cash – required to experience these would depend on success in America. Leonard rejoined his brother Addison and, according to evidence in the Brooklyn directories, between 1854 and 1870, by which time the Jerome women had left New York for good, the former consul became first broker, then banker, then merchant, then broker again.

But the first year back in the US was not an immediate financial success and, within a few months of Jennie's birth, Leonard Jerome declared himself bankrupt. For two weeks, starting in mid-March, a daily paragraph announcing 'Notice of Application for the discharge of an insolvent from his debts . . .' appeared in the *Brooklyn Daily Eagle* naming Leonard Jerome as the insolvent. Declaring a state of bankruptcy, a much more common thing to do then, enabled him to pay off his debts and start again. What appears to have happened is that acting on a sure 'tip' from the treasurer of the Cleveland and Toledo Railroad Company he put up a margin of $2,000 on 500 shares of that stock. The stock plunged and Jerome, who had no more money to spare, discovered that his friend the treasurer had unloaded on him. Following that disaster, Jerome retired quietly for several months to lick his wounds and see how he might do better in future.

He did not struggle for very long, and the Jeromes seem to have settled easily into middle-class Brooklyn life. In spite of Leonard's antipathy to organised religion, they were one of several prominent families known to attend the South Brooklyn Presbyterian Church. This fine building, completed in 1845, was on the corner of their street at the intersection with Clinton Street. Scores of churches were being erected throughout Brooklyn, but it was to be another twenty-five years before the iconic bridge linking it with Wall Street was completed. For the first years of Jennie's life it seems as if Leonard Jerome had a lucky touch as a speculator, or gambler. His particular talent was in selling short, that is selling stock which he did not own, hoping that when the time came to buy it back the price would have gone down, to his advantage.

Then in 1857 he joined forces with William Travers, a noted financier from a Maryland family who had won and lost a fortune or two and who already had a longstanding personal as well as business relationship with Leonard's brother Lawrence. For a few years, the threesome did a flourishing business as stockbrokers on Wall Street and the partnership became famous for the boldness of their operations, as well as for the creation of an 'observatory' (this was Leonard's idea), set up to observe the movement not of the stars but of stocks. One of his tactics, once he had studied in detail all the facts of a company, was to feed these, along with an excellent lunch, to important editors in a small room on the upper floor of their building at Pine and Nassau Street. 'Under the genial influence of the lunch and the exhilarating conversation of Messrs Travers and Jerome',[15] the editors were often persuaded to write a piece which resulted in the upward or downward movement of certain stocks according to the requirements of the existing positions of Jerome and Travers. For a few steady years Jerome seemed unable to put a foot wrong and, in spite of occasional reverses, prospered so well that within a few years of returning from Trieste his wealth was estimated at around $10,000,000.

Jerome had made his first significant fortune largely from the sale of Ohio Life Insurance and Trust Company shares, before the company collapsed, precipitating a vast financial panic in which nearly 5,000 US firms eventually failed. Buoyed by this, in 1858 the family returned to Europe for a two-month vacation, which included a spell in Paris in a rented apartment on the Champs Elysées. As rich Americans they were invited to a grand ball at the Tuileries and presented to the Emperor Napoleon III and his wife, Empress Eugénie. 'It was universally conceded that Clara was the handsomest woman there. I never saw her look so well,' Leonard wrote proudly to his brother.[16]

But it was the four years of the Civil War which gave Leonard Jerome both substantial wealth and national fame. In 1860 he opened a new office in Wall Street, renamed Jerome and Riggs, buying and selling a broad range of stocks. His interest soon centred upon the Pacific Mail Steamship Company. He bought these shares at $62 and sold them a few years later in 1865 when they had reached $329, this time realising a vast fortune. He spent his money as freely as he earned it, and Fifth Avenue society was open mouthed at the social audacities of such a newcomer, who dared to ride through Central Park in his four-in-hand, the first ever seen in the city, often on a Sunday and with Jennie, his favourite daughter, in the front seat alongside him. The social chronicler Ward McAllister commented on the spectacle he created as he drove up Broadway, whip in hand, with flowers in the buttonhole of his bright-green coat and his coach loaded with beautiful women, who would shriek and giggle behind him as he took a corner at full tilt. Those who scorned Leonard Jerome referred to him as a 'bus driver' because of the carefree way he drove a stagecoach. His was the unabashed enjoyment of wealth rarely available to those who have inherited and who therefore feel they must husband resources for the next generation.

Thus Jennie's formative years were spent in a whirlwind of enormous amounts of money created and, just as easily, spent, or occasionally lost. Jennie, in her *Reminiscences*, devotes a mere three pages to what was obviously a very happy childhood. She recalled that the private lessons – and money for their education was never withheld – were interspersed with matinées at the opera to 'improve our minds', sleighing and skating for pleasure and driving in her father's coach and four. She was a natural horsewoman and, as soon as she was old enough, rode back and forth on a shaggy little pony in front of their house. Piano lessons were a priority and Jennie's first teacher was the renowned Stephen Heller, friend of Chopin. But, for all the indulgences organised by Leonard, Mrs Jerome clearly held tight on the reins of discipline, as Jennie also observed that, 'unlike most American children, we were seldom permitted to join in boy and girl dances'. But they were encouraged to display their patriotism on 4 July when celebrations with fire crackers often resulted in burnt fingers.

Summers were the best. From the late 1850s onwards these were spent at the newly fashionable resort of Newport, where Leonard had built a charming villa 'more in accordance with one's idea of a seaside residence than the gorgeous white marble palaces which are the fashion nowadays. There we were allowed to run wild and be as grubby and happy as children ought to be,'[17] Jennie wrote later, no doubt with the mythically proportioned Italian palazzo known as The Breakers in mind. This seventy-roomed mansion with its gigantic chandeliers and solid marble bathtubs was built by Cornelius Vanderbilt, the Commodore, a friend and erstwhile business associate of Leonard Jerome when both were fighting for control of the Harlem Race Road, but whose vast fortune would always far outstrip the Jeromes' meagre pile. One of the activities Jennie enjoyed most at Newport was driving around in her dog-cart, harnessed to two donkeys, Willie and Wooshey, a gift from her father's friend Mrs Ronalds. She learnt to spur them on with a stick which she called 'the Persuader'. Leonard also bought a fine new steam yacht, the *Clara Clarita*, decorated inside in the finest pale-blue silk and hammered silver, which he used to sail to Newport to visit his family there. She was reputed to have cost him $125,000.

By 1859, awash with dollars, Leonard decided the time had come to move out of Brooklyn and into a magnificent new six-storey mansion to be built on a plot of land in the centre of almost fashionable Manhattan, at 25 Madison Avenue on the corner of 26th Street. A stone's throw from the Jerome plot was a well-known, if classy, brothel. Much of Manhattan at this time was still under-developed farmland but the new money and availability of cheap labour, mostly new immigrants from Ireland and Germany, fuelled a construction boom. In 1857 there had been great excitement when the first passenger elevator was installed in the Haughtwout Department Store. But the new Jerome palace declared, with no need for false modesty, that this was a man who had succeeded in life and was determined to enjoy his success, whether in the shape of yachts, singers or new diamond necklaces for his wife. For the few years the Jeromes lived there, this house – it probably never felt like a home – and its happenings were at the forefront of fashion. He built his stables, on 26th Street, before he built his adjoining house – three storeys high filled with horses and carriages of the finest makes, black walnut panelling, plate glass and carpeted floors. The cost of this alone was $80,000.

'Except for the Emperor's Mews in Paris it is doubtful if any stable in the world is as fine,' claimed the *New York Tribune*. Jennie's love of horses can be dated from this time as, rather to her mother's concern, she spent as many hours as she could in the stables. The house itself, with its steep mansard roof, extremely tall windows and double porches of delicate ironwork fronting a park, made a bold statement as to who exactly the Jeromes were. On the second floor was a sumptuous hall for entertaining where Leonard and Clara wasted little time in hosting a lavish ball to celebrate moving in. For years afterwards guests breathlessly remembered the party for the two fountains which spouted throughout the evening: one with cologne, the other champagne.

It was on this occasion that Leonard invited Mrs Pierre Lorillard Ronalds, a beautiful young divorcee from Boston with an equally pleasing voice, to undertake the project of transforming the ballroom into a private theatre. 'Her face was perfectly divine in its loveliness, her features small and exquisitely regular. Her hair was of a dark shade of brown and very abundant,' is how one contemporary described this woman – with whom Leonard appeared deeply in love.[18] Just imagine, he suggested to her, what a stage it would provide for her to perform in front of New York high society, and thereby raise funds for sick and wounded soldiers in military hospitals. It was the quintessential Leonard Jerome scheme: glamorous and racy, involving self-promotion, singing, beautiful women and high art, and at the same time benefiting a good cause. But it takes little imagination also to see how slighted Clara Jerome must have felt, especially when Leonard took to bringing Fanny Ronalds to the Newport home with him on his yacht.

Leonard's private theatre was an innovation and a society talking point. Handsomely adorned and seating almost 600, the theatre boasted a fully equipped stage, an illuminated front and a magnificently finished interior with numerous and elegantly liveried servants who conducted patrons to their seats. It was the most luxurious playhouse in New York, where wealthy society flocked just to see who was performing. As a general rule, it was used to train young professionals. Normally there would be one famous diva or star, supported by amateur actresses or reigning beauties. But it was the radiant Mrs Ronalds who starred in the first performances there for wounded soldiers, taking the lead role in four Italian operas. Newspaper accounts hinted that occasionally she 'over-sparkled' but even 'the malicious were forced to admit she seemed to have become a dear friend of Clara's as well'.[19]

One young hopeful, Minnie Hauk, made her operatic debut there in the autumn of 1866 in Bellini's *La Sonnambula*. Minnie was a talented singer and in October 1866, still a teenager, performed at the Brooklyn Academy of Music, a performance which marked the start of a long and successful operatic career. Minnie was rumoured to be Leonard's daughter and evidently bore a strong physical resemblance to her. Even Clara had written on the back of one of Minnie's photographs, 'So like Jennie but less good looking'.[20] A few letters survive from Minnie to Leonard at the time of her debut from which it is clear that she adored and depended on him, even for such details as requesting that he send her stockings worked with blue rather than those with pink. She said in her memoirs how much she felt at home in the Jerome household, where she was treated as one of the family to such an extent that Mrs Jerome would lend her jewellery for her performances. She tried to join Jennie and Clara, who, in the habit of riding many miles before breakfast, 'rode like Amazons', she recalled. But here she was totally outclassed and after a few disastrous attempts gave up.

But in August 1866 she wrote to Leonard: 'I forgot to ask you last Friday if Mother and I should go to the farm alone but then you said you would come here but then you didn't come . . . Won't you come and take us out. You know I love to go with you better than anyone else.'[21] Perhaps Leonard, recognising her impending fame, had allowed his ardour for her mother to cool. Again, in October that year, Minnie wrote beseechingly, asking if he could not come and see her just for a few minutes before she made her debut: 'I feel very unhappy about some things before I make my debut and I should be so very happy to have my best friend.' In one of the last surviving letters she says: 'Goodbye, My Dear Friend. I should love to see you here again very much but I suppose I cannot so I must be content without seeing you . . . Kiss Jennie and Clara for me.'[22]

Leonard Jerome relished his role as a generous patron of the young, beautiful and talented. Adelina Patti was another teenage protégée whose musical career was launched by him in his private theatre. He also helped sponsor her first concert tour. Jerome understood the need and desire for wealthy women to perform an active role at a time when they had few outlets to satisfy their talents or, in the case of less wealthy women, few possibilities of earning money. And so, under the all-covering shield of a war charity, he arranged a series of brilliant tableaux vivants which several society women attended in all their glory, including one who, trying to personify winter, was hung with icicles made of pure diamonds.

While living in the city, Jennie attended a small and academically distinguished private school for the daughters of New York's elite at 1 Fifth Avenue. The school was run by Miss Lucy Green, who had previously taught at the Union Theological Seminary. Lucy and her brother Andrew Haswell Green both played significant roles in the city's history,* but Jennie does not refer to her time there in her *Reminiscences*. It was the Civil War, four of the bloodiest and most controversial years in American history, which, not surprisingly, gave Jennie one of her earliest important memories. Although she wrote in her memoirs, 'It passed our nursery unmolested,' she also recalled that 'Every little southerner I met at dancing classes was "a wicked rebel", to be pinched if possible. While the words of the bitter parody which we used to sing to the tune of "Maryland, my Maryland" come back to me today.'23 The other strong childhood memory was of President Lincoln's funeral in April 1865 when she was eleven and how the family's Madison Square mansion was draped from top to bottom in white and black and the whole of New York looked, she recalled, like one gigantic mausoleum. How extraordinary that the woman who became an intruder into British society, so closely identified with everything British, should have lived through such devastating and formative events in her native America.

From the first, Leonard Jerome, a determined admirer of Lincoln, threw his enormous energies into supporting the Northern, anti-slavery Unionist cause. When the war started he was forty-five and contributed a small fortune to a variety of war charities. One of his least successful ideas was a scheme for resettling Negroes in Haiti, a short and misconceived venture intended to bring them freedom but which brought him only expense and disappointment. For a while, almost every subscription list had his name on it. He was the founder of the Fund for the Benefit of the Families of the Killed and Wounded; he also contributed $35,000 towards construction of the *Meteor,* a war vessel built to catch the *Alabama,* the ship of the Confederacy. He gave a quarter of a million dollars to Northern causes but

* A. H. Green was president of the Board of Education and president and comptroller of the Central Park Commission. He also played a key role in establishing the New York Public Library.

after the war subscribed to Southern relief too. In March 1867 he staged a glittering fundraising event at his own theatre to raise money on behalf of the Southern Relief Society,[24] something that only a man of enormous courage and enterprise could carry off. This idea was to inspire his daughter many years later, as was the panache with which he did everything.

In September 1860 Leonard had bought himself an interest in newspapers once again, becoming consulting editor and one of three directors at the *New York Times* during a period when the strongly Republican paper was overseen by Henry J. Raymond, who became a noted war editor and friend, pro-Union and pro-Lincoln just as Leonard Jerome was. It was a position that lasted until 1870 and had some dramatic consequences. In the summer of 1863 violent draft riots broke out in the city with the mob, several thousand strong and opposed to the conscription law that fell largely on impoverished immigrants, burning houses, plundering stores and shooting policemen. While Raymond was penning editorials insisting that the mob should be defied, confronted, grappled with and crushed, the *Times* – aware that other newspapers had been attacked by the rioters – fortified itself with two Gatling guns, the very latest invention, which were mounted in the business office under the command of Leonard W. Jerome, who, in the event, was spared from firing them. There was a third Gatling gun mounted on the roof and the entire staff were armed with rifles. The mob was successfully intimidated, but the riots were the worst urban disturbance in US history.

Leonard continued to make money throughout the Civil War as he received constant information from the battle front (friends in the army were sending him coded messages) which enabled him to buy shares on a certainty, as he was ahead of the newspapers. Whether he was underwriting the Civil War for good business or high morals is a moot point. The twin demands of wheeler-dealing and civic-mindedness both exercised a strong pull. As one of his grandsons, Shane Leslie, wrote later: 'If he seemed to be trading on the blood of his fellow countrymen he set his conscience free by royally subscribing to the wounded, the widow and the orphan . . .'[25]

Yet the Jerome position in the increasingly stultifying exclusivity of nineteenth-century New York society was always somewhat uncertain. Leonard Jerome was one of many new millionaires in the so-called 'Flash Age' whose fortunes came through railroads, armaments or even preserved meats to feed the soldiers. Once rich, they mostly moved to Manhattan. But the Jeromes were never set to become equals of the Vanderbilts or Astors – Leonard was too multi-faceted, too gifted, to devote that relentless industry which acquisition and retention of a fortune demand. And the Jeromes would never, as Clara with some bitterness soon came to understand, be part of the Four Hundred – the inner sanctum of New York society famously based on the number of those who could fit into Mrs William Astor's private ballroom. Jerome's closest friends were his business associates, William Travers and August Belmont, the latter a man of German Jewish ancestry with a more rakish reputation than Jerome, who worked for the Rothschilds, his passion for horseracing rivalled only by Leonard's. Belmont, whose limp from an old pistol duel served only to add to his aura of attraction, was Jerome's rival as much as his friend, in affairs of finance as well as the heart. According to some privately printed memoirs:

> There were two outstanding men at that time who were most prominent in all social and sporting events. They both drove coaches and four and had large racing stables, both were married and in the prime of life. These two men fell desperately in love with Mrs R. L and A were rivals who kept the house of their lady filled with flowers and attempted to satisfy her every desire. She proved to be an accomplished general for she managed these two great men with much skill.[26]

Nothing reveals Jerome's maverick originality better than a competition he arranged between himself, Belmont and Travers to see who could offer the most perfect dinner ever achieved in society. All three had to be prepared by Lorenzo Delmonico, the city's top restaurateur whose establishment on Fifth Avenue and 14th Street with its fine ballroom was in danger of being swamped by too many with aspirations to join society. The competition rules stipulated that money was no object and that the dinners were to contain as many novelties as his cooks could provide. The result was a gentlemanly draw. But it was Jerome's dinner that was remembered by posterity, though not for its gastronomic magnificence. On opening her napkin each lady found inside a gold bracelet. Competitors they may have been but, as Belmont was often quoted as saying, 'One rode better, sailed better, banqueted better when Mr Jerome was of the party.'[27]

Leonard's most inspired venture, with which his name is permanently associated, was one of his last, but it was never going to endear him to the highest of high society. At the end of the war he bought a racehorse for $40,000. Kentucky was an incredibly successful horse and, almost immediately he entered the Jerome stable, won the Inauguration Stakes, the first race ever run at Saratoga Springs. Jennie, who told the world so few of her childhood stories, nonetheless remembered being hoisted upon the back of the celebrated Kentucky, whose sire Lexington and dam Magnolia by Glencoe 'were of the best blood in England'. Leonard was there along with William Travers to see Kentucky triumph at Saratoga and his intense pride and excitement as he led in his own winner triggered a decision to create a racecourse in New York City along the same lines. He was inspired for the rest of his life to raise horse-racing from the level of disrepute to which it had sunk in New York to be considered, as it was in England, the Sport of Kings.

In the mid-1860s Leonard bought the old Bathgate estate of approximately 230 acres at Fordham, a few miles outside the city, where for at least half a century the Bathgate family had privately bred and tried out their horses. Jennie, encouraged by her father, was by the age of ten an accomplished horsewoman and loved the freedom of being able to ride in the countryside there. But the place was ideally suited to her father's more grandiose plans as there was a large hill, called the bluff, standing in the centre of a natural race track. Leonard knew exactly what he wished to create – a club house and stand with the course curling around it – and he brought in his friends William Travers and August Belmont as well as brother Lawrence to help, advise and fund. They turned to Charles Wheatley, designer of the Saratoga course, and within months the men had founded the American Jockey Club, which had its first meeting in Leonard's office at 46 Exchange Place in April 1866. Its aims were 'to promote the improvement of horses, to elevate the public taste in sports of the turf and to become an authority on racing matters in the country'.

It is hard to imagine today that the long and winding Jerome Avenue with its rusting iron elevated sections, which passes derelict buildings, impoverished tenements with broken glass, homeless tramps outside cheap food marts and restaurants, could ever have been the sweeping boulevard for Manhattan socialites that it was. Few who live in the neighbourhood, now one of the poorest in the city, have any idea why the vast leisure area still known as Jerome Park was so named. But on 25 September 1866 the Jockey Club of America held its first race meeting there. According to press accounts the opening of Jerome Park 'proved the social event of all time and started a new era in the horse racing world'. Eight thousand people came to the grand opening, from the very smartest to some of the poorest. Clara had a new dress for the occasion of deep puce silk. Mrs Ronalds wore white.

Yet the occasion was not quite free of the low life that Leonard Jerome had hoped to exclude. Among the less reputable personalities present were William 'Boss' Tweed and ex-pugilist John Morissey, a professional gambler and gang leader well known for getting out the Irish vote at elections. Jerome – and even men as rich and powerful as Commodore Vanderbilt – understood that financiers could not survive without the co-operation of the politicians and the more shadowy underworld figures. The whole of New York feared Tweed, who extracted millions of dollars in bribes. Also there was Josie Woods, a well-known Manhattan madame, decked out in her finest. Clara instinctively felt uncomfortable and feared that the venture did not bode well for the reputations of her daughters, Clara and Jennie, whom Leonard insisted on taking with him to the club house. Even on this gala opening day she excused herself and left early.

From the moment it was finished Leonard, who acted as promoter rather than owner, leased Jerome Park to the new Jockey Club and volunteered to stand an annual loss of $25,000 if the expenses could not be paid. He was never called upon to do this. He built a small cottage near the race track for winter weekends and had a small area flooded and frozen for Clara and Jennie to learn skating. It was Mrs Ronalds, with whom Jennie formed a close relationship that was to last for the rest of her life, who taught the Jerome girls the rudiments of figure skating.

As contemporary newspaper accounts make plain, Leonard Jerome was becoming an important city entrepreneur, playing a major role in a variety of municipal activities and rallies. But in 1868 he suffered a serious reversal. He had held on to his Pacific Mail stock for too long and when new stock was issued he offered to take the whole issue off the company's hands at $200 a share. The offer was accepted. But the stock did not find support elsewhere and remained on his hands, a financial catastrophe that almost ruined him. Within two hours he had lost a million dollars. Those who had tutted at his Sunday drives now lost no time in pointing out the moral lesson. This was what happened to those who rode 'in a lumbering barouche decked with gay and laughing ladies as he drove through Fifth Avenue when filled with churchgoers'.[28]

But there was no widespread ill-will felt in the city for this charmer. As a *New York Times* writer put it, commenting on rumours current for the past few days of the failure of Mr Leonard Jerome: 'We have only referred to the subject . . . in order to express the hope that no such calamity as a failure will ever overtake Mr Jerome . . . wealth in the hands of a man like Leonard Jerome is a blessing to many. In his loss the many would be the losers.'[29]

Mrs Jerome scarcely rates a mention in contemporary accounts of

Leonard's heady days of success. Since Clara kept no diary and few of her letters have survived, most of what is known about her derives from family stories or gossip. What emerges is a more or less silent form of resignation to a way of life in which she felt out of her depth. She made few demands on her husband, her apparent snobbishness probably a cover for shyness. Although Leonard and Clara travelled like a prince and princess, Leonard's heart was always in New York, hers in Europe. Although they collected art treasures, Clara was insecure about her own taste meeting the highest standards of others. Although she acquiesced in Leonard's theatrical excitements, that was an alien world for her. According to great-granddaughter Anita Leslie: 'She could not understand music, horses or finance and yachting made her sick. How could a quiet motherly person amuse such a husband when all the glamorous ladies of New York went out of their way to catch his eye?'[30] She never responded to the dynamic rhythm of New York and instead retreated into memories of graceful Europe. Leonard always recognised this and later in life wrote to her rather cruelly, 'If you had any go in you, like either of the girls, and could mount your horse and keep up, we might knock about together and enjoy it. But you haven't a bit of taste that way and never had. And you couldn't stand that sort of life now even if you liked it once upon a time.'[31] The truth, as both knew, is that she never had liked it.

There was one additional sadness. In 1855, just a year after Jennie's birth, the Jeromes had had a third daughter Camille. A fourth, Leonie, was born in 1859 when Clara was thirty-five. It is interesting to note the French names given to the last two children but Leonie, a female version of Leonard, also indicates that the couple had given up on any hopes they might once have nurtured for a son. But in 1863, while the family were enjoying a summer at Newport, Camille died of a sudden fever. In pre-antibiotic days there was little that could be done to save the seven-year-old. Her body was brought back for burial in Greenwood Cemetery. The family seems to have forced itself to cope with the tragedy of Camille's death by never referring to it. But for the remainder of the war Clara hid in her villa with her three other daughters.

In 1867, prompted no doubt by the dramatic financial losses of that year, Clara, dignified as ever, decided that the time had finally come to decamp to Europe with her almost marriageable daughters. Moving to Paris was a brave decision for one who did not speak French. She had no friends nor family support in the capital. To move there alone assumes that she was sorely tested. She maintained that health reasons prompted the move, but no malady was ever mentioned – unless increasing plumpness was the cause. Leonard, it was agreed, would remain in New York but visit as often as he could. In October 1868 he left the city of his fortune and fall to visit the four women in his family. He found them comfortably ensconced in an apartment in the Boulevard Malesherbes.

2

I Love Her Better than Life Itself

~

CLARA JEROME WAS forty-two and still handsome when she moved
with her three daughters to Paris. It was not her first time in the
city but deciding to live there at first without her husband was a brave
move with consequences that, it is probably fair to say, she imagined
only too clearly.

Mid-nineteenth-century Paris, just like London, was a city marked by
pervasive poverty, alcoholism, disease and starvation. But it was also a city
of brilliance and splendour. The Emperor Napoleon III, who, together
with his Spanish-born wife Eugénie, ruled France for twenty-one years,
managed to offer his people almost full employment with steadily rising
wages. The Second Empire is often imagined through the paintings of
Winterhalter as a time when the rich danced and the poor suffered. Yet
behind a façade of military parades and masked balls was a vast reconstruc-
tion programme that created wide, well-paved, tree-lined and gas-lit
boulevards, magnificent new buildings including Les Halles, the Ecole des
Beaux-Arts and the Bibliothèque Nationale, as well as parks and a department store, the Bon Marché. Under the guidance of Georges Haussmann,
a former civil servant with determined vision, Paris was transformed
and modernised.

But the contrasts were still striking. Most girls working in dressmakers'
sweatshops were lucky if they were paid two and half francs a day to produce the frivolous creations society demanded as clothes. At the same time
the Emperor patronised and praised the wild and light-hearted operettas of
Jacques Offenbach – even though his more strait-laced Catholic wife was
often horrified at the way his stories portrayed the imperial court as a place
where pleasure and sensuality ruled supreme. Second Empire society
thrived on the lavish balls held at the Tuileries, the long narrow building in
the centre of the city which served as the Imperial Palace. These balls often
catered for 5,000 *invités*. There were also Monday evening salons, the much
duller *petits lundis*, for a mere 500, plus masked balls and other court receptions for particular occasions or for visiting dignitaries. These *fêtes impériales*

all had their own rules – for example, ladies were expected always to dress in white, their trains to be no shorter than three metres and no longer than four, guests were forbidden to arrive in cabs but had to be delivered in carriages, and dancing began at precisely 9.30 p.m., usually with the Emperor and Empress opening the proceedings by twirling around the Galerie de la Paix to the tune of a well-known Strauss waltz.

At the same time Eugénie, genuinely concerned by the widespread hardship she knew existed in the city, at least one day a week visited a hospital, an orphanage, a home for foundlings or a shelter for the destitute. The Emperor allowed her 1,200,000 francs a year of which 100,000 went on her wardrobe and the rest on presents, pensions for relations and charity. Arguably, for all their extravagance, the pair did more to help the working classes than any previous rulers of France.

It is easy to see why Eugénie, coping with a wayward husband yet always slightly disapproving, would have appealed to Clara Jerome. Marie-Eugénie Ignace Augustine de Montijo, born in Granada, Spain in 1826, was a tall, elegant woman of fire and flame when she married the short, squat Charles Louis Napoleon, a man twenty years her senior. Napoleon was well known for his many mistresses, a way of life that marriage did not impede. After two miscarriages Eugénie gave birth to her only son, the Prince Imperial, and, warned by doctors that a further pregnancy would risk her life, departed from the marital bed. Entering even the outer French royal circle gave Mrs Leonard Jerome the respectability she craved, especially now that her husband was no longer quite the millionaire he had once been. According to some estimates, Jerome's fortune of $10 million, if indeed he had ever owned that amount, had been suddenly halved. He now leased his Madison Square house to the Union League Club, which spent $50,000 adapting it for its new use. The second-floor theatre, once the scene of so much excitement and glamour, was in future to be used for meetings and lectures. Leonard Jerome slowly made his way to Paris. But Europe could never be home for him. He became an occasional visitor, his soul remaining for ever in New York, where he took to residing in his club.

In addition, both Eugénie and Clara shared an irremediable fondness for beautiful dresses along with a concern for the proprieties in life which allowed them to be admired by men mostly from afar. And both were underwhelmed by opera singing. Offenbach, whose music captures so brilliantly the charm and allure of the Second Empire, was at his height in 1867 when the Jerome women came to Paris. His triumphant piece (although rarely played today), *La Grande Duchesse de Gerolstein*, had its debut in April that year at the Exposition Universelle, the great exhibition in Paris which celebrated the strides in industry and technology made by France under Napoleon III. As far as Offenbach, and much else that her husband admired, was concerned, Eugénie was sceptical.

But, as Jennie herself recorded, 'the last flicker of the candle, the last flame of the dying fire, is ever the brightest and so it was with Paris'.[1] According to her version of events, her mother went to Paris in order to consult the celebrated American physician and gynaecologist Dr James Sims, inventor of the Sims speculum and founder of the Women's Hospital in New York. Sims, an Alabama native, was in self-imposed exile in Paris during the Civil War. But Jennie does not elaborate on what may have been the problem and in any case Sims returned to America in 1868. Apparently her mother quickly regained her health and, finding that the educational advantages were greater in Paris than New York, 'we decided to remain there'. She also reveals that her mother's beauty and American style were much commented on as an attractive novelty, an understatement that is presumably a reference to her suitors. The Duc de Persigny, one of the most colourful characters of the Second Empire and a devoted supporter of Napoleon III, paid 'constant court' to Clara, as well as 'playing the gallant to both Clarita and Jennie'.[2] During one dance the Duke's interest in Jennie was so obvious – and Jennie's responsive smile so flirtatious – that the Duchesse de Persigny walked over to her and publicly boxed her ears. 'Such was the morality of the day that, even while her ears were being boxed by the indignant wife, Jennie knew – as all the court knew – that the Duchesse herself had so many extramarital affairs that even the Emperor had felt obliged to warn Persigny about it.'[3] Jennie, in her own account, admits that the Jeromes were on intimate terms with the Persignys, that the Duchesse 'was to say the least of it eccentric', and her temper somewhat quick. 'On one occasion, at a children's dance in Paris, I have a vivid recollection of her boxing my ears because I could not dance the mazurka.'[4]

The Jeromes arrived in Paris just when the Second Empire was at its zenith. 'Never had the Empire seemed more assured, the court more brilliant, the fêtes more gorgeous. The light-hearted Parisians revelled in the daily sights of royal processions and cavalcades. The Bois de Boulogne and the Champs Elysées, where we were living at that time, were crowded with splendid equipages.'[5] The theatricality and romance of Parisian life in these years must have been mesmerising for an impressionable young American with a deep imagination. Jennie, aged just fifteen, remembered admiring the Empress Eugénie, 'the handsomest woman in Europe, driving in her Daumont, the green and gold liveries of the postilions and outriders making a brave show'. Jennie's use of the word 'brave' is revealing. At the time, the Empress had nothing to feel brave about. Yet, with hindsight, Jennie felt pity for a woman whose husband was no longer interested in her and whose place in society was clearly undermined. It was in this environment that Jennie became a woman. As an Edith Wharton character says with disdain in *The Age of Innocence*: 'At the Court of the Tuileries, such things [married men having affairs with unsuitable women] were pretty openly tolerated.'

Jennie longed to go out in the world but was compelled instead to a life of studying – she attended the fashionable school run by Miss Demler – and piano lessons. Most days she practised for four hours and was told that she was talented enough to have a career as a concert pianist if she wished. Leonard Jerome came to visit when he had some cash to bring them. 'Everyone getting tiresome here. I'll make you a little something and come across. Paris sounds delightful and a change,' he wrote to his wife.[6] But Fanny Ronalds, Clara's nemesis, came too. Once back in New York he wrote to 'Jinks', as he sometimes called Jennie, to encourage her. He told her how important it was to write a good letter, recommended three recent novels she should read to give her a better understanding of English society – an indication that this was where they planned to go soon – and insisted that her 'disposition to please those about her' would probably ensure her future success. And so Jennie reluctantly made do hearing about court life from others, including sister Clara, who was just old enough to be allowed to make her debut at one of the Tuileries balls. 'The two Claras are having a wonderful time. I leave them to it,' Leonard wrote breezily from New York.[7]

If the rigid social hierarchy of Old New York spurned new money, Paris welcomed it. Hundreds of Americans embarked full of hope on one of the many luxury liners now crossing the Atlantic, although in the late-nineteenth century the journey was far from risk free.[8] The Empress, who had an American grandfather, always had a penchant for these bold Americans, for whom it was often easier to enter high society in Paris than in Manhattan. Another young American invited by the Empress was the former Lillie Greenough, who some twenty years earlier had accompanied the Jerome family to Trieste, but was now Mrs Charles Moulton, wife of an American banker resident in Paris, and a good friend of Jennie and her sisters. Lillie had met the Empress while skating one January day in the Bois de Boulogne. An invitation to a ball followed shortly after.

Mme Moulton described the Empress on the occasion she met her as a beautiful apparition who wore a white tulle dress trimmed with red velvet

bows and gold fringes. Her crown of diamonds and pearls and her necklace
were magnificent. As soon as the Empress learnt that Lillie was a talented
singer she was invited again to perform at a Monday-evening reception.
Nervously, she sang some American songs, including 'Swanee River', and
was rousingly applauded. Leonard's encouragement and the Trieste singing
lessons had not been wasted after all. Lillie was rewarded with a bracelet of
large rubies and diamonds set in three heavy gold coils with Eugénie's
name and date engraved inside. Mme Moulton was an important social
figure for the Jeromes in 1870s Paris, giving many parties to which the
daughters were invited.

Jennie would listen, wide-eyed, to the accounts her elder sister gave her
of an evening at the Tuileries when Clara had worn her first low-cut frock,
of her confusion at having to walk up the grand staircase between the cent-
gardes (the Emperor's magnificently uniformed soldiers), of how no
procession was formed but 'when the company was assembled the doors
were flung open and "sa Majesté l'Empereur!" was announced, then after a
pause "sa Majesté l'Impératrice," who that evening appeared a resplendent
figure in green velvet with a crown of emeralds and diamonds spiked with
pearls on her small and beautifully shaped head'. Clara told Jennie about the
demands of court ceremonial and etiquette and the degrees of bowing and
curtseying required as the guests proceeded to the ballroom.

There were other celebrated beauties in Paris whose salons and dances
almost rivalled those given by the Empress. Jennie describes Mme de
Pourtales as 'a vision of beauty in a cloud of tulle', and Princesse Mathilde,
who had a fine house in the Rue de Courcelles and used to give cotillions,
as 'undoubtedly the most brilliant and intelligent woman of the Second
Empire'. It was at her glamorous salons that some of the young and pretty
Americans in Paris, including Jennie's sister, had the privilege of meeting
such men as Dumas, Sardou, Théophile Gautier and the painter Paul-
Jacques-Aimé Baudry.

How Jennie longed to be part of this. Although experiencing it all at
one remove, she nonetheless absorbed it totally. When she came, forty years
later, to write her bestselling *Reminiscences*, it was therefore largely on
Clara's account of imperial life that she relied, much to the consternation
of her elder sister, who considered she had had her own stories 'stolen'. All
Jennie says of herself in those teenage years was how she used to ride in the
Bois de Boulogne with her father and the Prince de Sagan, another older
man, a typical Parisian beau who evidently charmed the young girl with
his eyeglass, attached to a black moiré ribbon which became the fashion.
'Mounted on a seemingly fiery chestnut, I fancied myself vastly.'[9]

No one made such a vivid impression on her as the charismatic Princess Pauline Metternich, an ideal role model. The Princess, who had wit, vivacity and chic, was a muse for writers and musicians and a genuine patron of the arts; she adored the stage and, as Jennie recognised, was never so happy as when organising theatricals. She it was who championed Wagner long before others appreciated his great operas and she made all three Jeromes devoted Wagnerians. Above all, her strikingly original innate dress sense caught the imagination of everyone who attended Tuileries balls but especially that of Eugénie, who could not resist asking for the name of her dressmaker. He was Charles Worth.

This is not the place to recount the story of this imaginative and bold Englishman who not only became dressmaker – and friend – to the Empress but, with royal patronage, changed the way rich women throughout Europe dressed. He was at the height of his creativity, promoted by Pauline Metternich, just as the Jeromes arrived in Paris and his workshops in the Rue de la Paix were besieged daily by the smartest women in the city, convinced that they needed morning, afternoon and evening gowns as well as special creations for gala balls and masquerades. He pioneered slightly shorter skirts for ease of walking and then in 1868 a skirt with no crinoline or hoops at all but the rather more attractive bustle. He used live models, and stories abound of how each lady, while sitting with her maid in one of the luxurious fitting rooms, waiting for the great man to give a dress his imprimatur, would be served with a plate of *foie gras* and a glass of Sauternes. You had to be received at Worth, the way you would by a pivotal member of society. Until now, couturiers had all been female; Worth, who considered himself an artist not a dressmaker, changed all that for ever.

No two Worth dresses were alike and certainly none was ever the same as anything ordered by the Empress herself, who owned hundreds of opulent and ornate Worth gowns. His creations, using the finest and richest materials, Valenciennes lace dust ruffles, silk chenille and silver metallic trims, crystal Austrian stones and silver-lined beads as well as brocade, tulles and muslins woven with silver or gold wire and exquisite embroideries often made expressly for him, all contributed to the illusory sensation of magic surrounding the Second Empire. When the collapse finally came, Eugénie's extravagant expenditure on dresses was often cited. But many of the women who had patronised the House of Worth were in fact wealthy Americans, some of whom had their new dresses shipped back to New York by the trunkload. Others like Clara Jerome, Marietta Stevens wife of Paran Stevens, owner of the Fifth Avenue Hotel, and Ellen Yznaga, the mother of three beautiful daughters Natica, Consuelo and Emily, understood the social realities of post-Civil War New York, which required not simply that they bought Parisian dresses but that they display their daughters wearing them in the more openly welcoming circles of imperial Paris. The Jeromes were among M. Worth's most loyal customers.[10]

Over the next half-century hundreds of American women would embark on a steamer returning to the Old World in search not only of Old World customs, clothes and culture but also of Old World husbands and houses. As the landed classes in England suffered from falling revenues and insufficient income to run their estates, marrying an American heiress offered obvious attractions. According to some estimates, by 1907 more than five hundred American women – the so-called dollar princesses – had married titled foreigners and some $220 million had gone with them to Europe.[11] An American magazine, *Titled Americans: A List of American Ladies who have Married Foreigners of Rank*, published quarterly, subscription $1 a year and revised annually, catered specifically for this market. A New York newspaper published a guide for American women with ambition: 'Dukes are the loftiest kind of noblemen in England. There are only twenty-seven of them in the whole United Kingdom. Of these there are only two available for matrimonial purposes. These are the Dukes of Manchester and Roxburghe. The Duke of Hamilton is already spoken for, the Duke of Norfolk is an old widower and the Duke of Leinster only eleven years old.' One enterprising marriage broker in New Orleans even advertised for 'Dukes, Marquesses, Earls or other noblemen desirous of meeting for the purpose of marriage, young, beautiful and rich American heiresses.'[12] As the advertisement indicates only too clearly, money was just one recommendation, the acceptable one. But being young and beautiful, able to invigorate the bloodlines, counted too. Hence a number of 'unsuitable' American girls – actresses, showgirls or industrialists' daughters – also managed to squeeze under the line.

By the time Count Otto Vogelstein, a Henry James character in a short novel called *Pandora*, remarked in 1884 that 'there appeared to be a constant danger of marrying the American girl; it was something one had to reckon with, like the railway, the telegraph, the discovery of dynamite, the Chassepot rifle, the Socialist spirit; it was one of those complications of modern life', most English aristocrats would have been only too aware of the reality – and advantages – posed by such a hazard. Lord Palmerston, the British Prime Minister, declared: 'Before the century is out, those clever and pretty women from New York will pull all the strings in half the chancelleries in Europe.'

Edith Wharton, as well as Henry James, was alive to the perils and possibilities of such complications of modern life, caviare for the imagination. Wharton, who so eloquently explored the loveless marriages at the turn of the century between rich American women and titled impoverished Englishmen, articulately contrasted the manners of the New World with those of Old Europe in several of her novels. Countess Ellen Olenska, the heroine of *The Age of Innocence*, makes a disastrous continental marriage and almost has to crawl back to New York society of the 1870s with its often stifling conventions and manners and its insistence on propriety, and crave forgiveness for her 'scandalous' behaviour. But it was in Wharton's final, unfinished novel *The Buccaneers*, about five rich and undisciplined New York girls who travel to England in search of titled husbands, that she satirised so painfully and acutely the clash of cultures alongside the dovetailing of aspirations. By the time she wrote *The Buccaneers*, not published until 1938, it was easier to reflect upon the trend and draw some conclusions.

That book may have been largely based on the Cuban-American Yznaga girls, but Wharton's portrayal of the way these spirited and talented heiresses enriched the moribund British aristocracy was just as applicable to Jennie, who was one of the first of the new American brides. She was the inspiration for the fictional Lizzie Elmsworth, who married the rising MP, Hector Robinson. The brash openness of Americans yearning for new experiences seemed like a warning battlecry to those English who believed that the solidity of tradition was its own reward. Mrs Wharton was right in seeing their adventure as nothing less than an attempted conquest of British society.

Clara Jerome may not have understood the social forces in which she was swept up. After the Civil War, America was more divided than ever as the southern economy was all but destroyed and Southerners, discovering that their way of life had been overturned in the conflagration, now faced further chaos and dislocation ahead. Most of those who had profited from the bitter conflict – and enormous fortunes had been garnered – made their way to the prosperous North, where they were not always welcomed. Often dismissed as superficial, because her delight in life came from appearances – clothes, jewels and houses – Clara had sufficient intelligence to grasp that remaining in Manhattan, where the old 'Knickerbocker' society was fighting to keep out these new Civil War millionaires, could have been disastrous for the Jerome daughters. In moving to Europe, she hoped to give her girls the great gift of being able to choose their own destinies, a springboard from which she hoped they could use the talents she was ensuring they acquired. She also gave the family a French surname, adding two accents to Jerome.

In November 1869, even though the Empress herself was away in Egypt, Clara and her mother were invited to what turned out to be the last of the Emperor's famous hunting, shooting and dancing parties outside Paris at Compiègne. These were unique events which required careful advance planning. On hunting days, for example, the ladies wore special green outfits with tricorne hats, but other days were devoted to visits to nearby châteaux and magnificent banquets for the hundred or so guests. Jennie recounted how her mother was presented on this occasion with some valuable pieces of Sèvres china. 'My sister, much to my envy, was given an inkstand shaped like a knotted handkerchief filled with Napoleons upon which the Emperor remarked, "Mademoiselle, n'oubliez pas les Napoléons."'[13]

These were heady, dangerous days. The Emperor was seriously ill, yet France, believing itself strong, allowed itself to be provoked into war with the Germans. Jennie and her sisters felt as patriotically pro-French and anti-Prussian as anyone. 'Exciting incidents crowded on us,' was how she put it years later. On one occasion they went to the opera in walking dresses with hats in their hands in case they had to go home on foot – which indeed they had to do. 'It was a strange performance as the singers were constantly being interrupted and made to sing patriotic songs.' They had the greatest difficulty getting home as the streets were teeming with an angry mob chafing for war. War came soon enough.

On 4 August 1870, the Germans crossed the border into Alsace. The Prussian Chancellor, Otto von Bismarck, wanted to unite Germany and knew that war with France was a good pretext. The French were defeated at Wissembourg, and the advancing Germans then pushed further until they had forced a wedge between two main French forces, one under Marshal Bazaine, the other led by Marshal MacMahon. There were further crushing defeats for the French in mid-August at Vionville and Gravelotte. Immediately after these the Germans began their march on Paris, and on 1 September an ill-fated attempt by Napoleon III and MacMahon to rescue Bazaine led to disaster at Sedan. The Emperor and 100,000 of his men were captured. When the news of Sedan reached Paris a bloodless revolution occurred. Napoleon was deposed, a provisional Government of National Defence was formed and a gruelling siege of the capital began. Paris held out until 28 January 1871, but only after suffering several months of famine.

Clara Jerome, well aware of the sparkling effect her eldest daughter's slightly ethereal beauty was having on the French aristocracy and revelling in her proximity to royalty, was unwilling to give it all up and seek safer climes. Just as she was allowing herself the luxury of thinking she could pick and choose a suitor for Clara – it could be the Marquis de Breteuil or the Duc de Noailles, but certainly not the Marquis de Tamisier, who was keen on her daughter but had unsuitable antecedents, nor could it be a Catholic – the Prussian army invested Paris and the Second Empire fell. But Mrs Jerome was housebound with a sprained ankle.

Their house became the rendezvous of the few remaining loyal French, among whom was the white-haired Duc de Persigny, Mrs Jerome's admirer. He told them they must leave immediately as the invading Prussians were at their door, and eventually, with a few precious possessions tied up in tablecloths and sheets, they departed Paris as refugees. They instructed the maid to pack up their trunks and send the rest of their possessions after them. Mrs Jerome had to be pushed in a wheelbarrow or carried but the women managed to catch the last train out of the besieged city, bound for Deauville. They begged a place on a boat for England, arriving in a bedraggled state at Brighton. They stayed for a few days at the Hotel Norfolk and then, along with the Yznagas and Stevens, made their way to London, where Leonard Jerome, who had been summoned to come immediately from New York and rescue them, eventually met them.

At the same time Eugénie was trying to escape via Deauville too. Fully conscious that she might be put on trial or lynched by an angry mob, she had to beg her place on Sir John Burgoyne's yacht, the *Gazelle*. Faced with heavy seas and a stiff north-westerly wind, Burgoyne was far from keen to proceed. He gave in, however, and they made it, a day later, limping into Ryde Harbour on the Isle of Wight. She and the deposed Emperor shortly thereafter made their home in England, retaining for ever a fondness for the Isle.

In spite of their meagre possessions Leonard Jerome installed his family in Brown's Hotel, just off Piccadilly, in a suite of elegant rooms with a piano so that all three girls, whatever disturbances they had just endured, could continue with their musical studies. Jennie says little in her memoirs about the hardships of that first autumn and winter her family spent in London. They kept in touch with some of the Parisian refugees, especially the Duc de Persigny, now a shadow of his former glory. 'Broken-hearted, ill and penniless our poor friend was put to many straits to eke out a living.'[14] The melancholy she felt for her friends, scattered, fighting or killed at the front, was increased by the gloom and fogs of London. 'Debarred as we were from our bright little house and our household gods it was indeed a sad time.' A German governess was employed who took the girls for educative walks in Hyde Park, but they all pined for Paris, for their severely damaged house in the Boulevard Haussmann and, as far as Jennie was concerned, for the life of which she felt she had been cheated. The family returned to France within months to inspect the damage to their house, and it was on that occasion that Mrs Jerome, finding herself at an open-air auction of the imperial possessions, bid for a monogrammed dinner service with golden crowns and the unmistakable 'N'. This dinner service, which gave Clara such intense pleasure, passed eventually to her grandson, Winston Churchill, who used it with much amusement at Chartwell.

Leonard Jerome, now in his fifties, cuts an increasingly restless figure in these days. No longer making large amounts of money, possibly even bored by the attempt, he restricted his energies principally to horse-racing, which was beset by those trying to make a racket out of the sport, and buffalo-hunting with his old friends. He protected his family from hearing about his problems, and never discussed financial worries with them – arguably an attitude that led to Jennie's disastrously optimistic belief that money would always be found. But his personality still loomed large in his daughters' lives and, although he had long ago settled various trusts in his wife's name so that she would not be too buffeted by his speculations, she still needed him to pay for all the clothes his daughters required. With his family organised in London, he made a brief return visit to Paris as a temporary representative of the American Government in order to meet Bismarck in a villa at Versailles. Having pleaded vainly for the siege of Paris to be lifted, he then returned once more to London to keep an eye on his womenfolk.

In the early summer of 1871, partly in order to escape London, where they had no home, and where young Clara was mooning about both lovesick and recovering from typhoid, Leonard decided to take his wife and daughters to Cowes, on the Isle of Wight. There was presumably a certain nostalgia felt by Leonard for the small island off the south coast of England since it was from there that his ancestors had sailed to a better life in the New World in the eighteenth century. His personal familiarity with Cowes derived from 1866 when he and Lawrence had organised the first transatlantic international yacht race across the Atlantic. The two brothers were prominent members of the New York Yacht Club, and in October that year they had challenged three millionaires, Pierre Lorillard and the brothers Osgood, to a transatlantic race. In backing *Henrietta*, the 107-foot keel-schooner owned and sailed by another millionaire, James Gordon Bennett, Leonard had won himself well over $100,000. At the victory party at the Royal Yacht Squadron, the Jerome brothers made good sport pretending to be uncouth Americans who knew no better and, when a note was delivered inviting Lawrence to a dinner with Queen Victoria, so the story goes, he maintained he had a previous engagement he couldn't possibly break. He allowed himself finally, and much to the horror of the other yachtsmen, to be persuaded to accept.

Having settled his family in Cowes, by July Leonard was once again sailing back across the Atlantic just as the *New York Times*, where he was still part owner and 'consulting director' until 1870, was reaching the climax of its battle with the notorious Tweed Ring. These were momentous days. Once it was revealed that the Tweed Ring had embezzled about seventy million dollars it was clear that cheating on such a scale could not have continued without thousands of respectable New Yorkers tolerating if not actively condoning the activities of the corrupt political leader, 'Boss' Tweed. This was a story of municipal corruption writ large involving fraudulent contracts and payrolls padded with dead men's names. No one dared speak out, but the *New York Times* did. Tweed was sentenced to twelve years in prison and, although Leonard Jerome was never mentioned as one of those directly involved, he had, through his friends August Belmont and Commodore Vanderbilt, come dangerously close.

But Cowes, as Jennie wrote, was another world, in those days 'delightfully small and peaceful. The Royal Yacht Squadron lawn did not resemble a perpetual garden party nor the roadstead a perpetual regatta, as it did later. People all seemed to know one another. The Prince and Princess of Wales and many foreign royalties could walk about and amuse themselves without being photographed or mobbed.'[15] Yet, in spite of the relative freedom which the royal family had to stroll about the streets of Cowes unmolested, there were other social conventions that could not be ignored. And sport was the best route for an unknown American millionaire to buy his way into the upper echelons of British society. Leonard Jerome understood this instinctively and Cowes was a perfect place to do it almost unobtrusively. At the same time, because the Jeromes were virtually unknown, Mrs Jerome could behave with the same airs, as if she, too, were an exiled empress. Her daughters would stand or fall on their own personalities and talent, of which they had plenty.

In the 1870s, when Queen Victoria resided at Osborne House, her vast country residence on the island, her entourage needed to be accommodated close by. Then the narrow streets of Cowes bustled with an influx of English and continental nobility at play. More significantly, her son the Prince of Wales (the future King Edward VII) liked sailing and took an active part in the racing. In general it was thanks to the Prince of Wales that

London society was responsive to the American influx and did not close its doors. The warmth of the Prince's reception during his visit in 1860 to New York left him with a lifelong enthusiasm for the refreshing vitality and openness of American women, as well as for the extravagant brashness of their self-made millionaire husbands and fathers. His connection with the Royal Yacht Squadron, housed in a former sea-front castle, was the catalyst that transformed Cowes regattas from an exciting sporting event into a major social function. As soon as Goodwood was over, society decamped to the former fishing village that was now the yachting capital of the world. For two weeks in August, Cowes became one of the greatest social functions of the fashionable year. And the centre of Cowes social life was the Castle, especially the club lawn with its wicker chairs for the fairest and finest women decked out in the fairest and finest of dresses. Everyone knew everyone and gossip was rife.

'If a wife is seen without her husband everyone makes rough speeches about her and if she is always with him something is sure to be said to the effect that they don't care a bit for each other really, you know, and fight like cat and dog at home,' is how one commentator described life there. Open-work silk stockings and patent-leather shoes with the smallest possible amount of leather about them worn by people with pretty, short frocks and pretty feet were, apparently, the main physical features of the place in summer. But the chief attraction of the Castle lawn after about 1870 was the Prince. As soon as he appeared 'a flutter ensued as the pretty ladies edge insensibly towards him for the coveted notice. He disappears and the flutter ends in a comparison of frocks and success in notice.'[16]

Also staying on the Isle of Wight that summer when the Jeromes paid their first visit were the deposed Empress, her now desperately ill husband and their fourteen-year-old son, the Prince Imperial. They were staying at Beaulieu House on the Egypt Esplanade, West Cowes, a short walk from the Castle. Eugénie was fond of the Jerome family with their three cultured and talented daughters, so it was no great surprise when they received an invitation one day asking them on an expedition around the island. Twelve-year-old Leonie developed an intense crush on the Prince Imperial after that day. But the Emperor was already a broken man. The Jeromes never saw him again, and he died the following year.

By good fortune, Leonard Jerome had found for his family 'a sweet little cottage' almost next door on the Egypt Esplanade. Beaulieu House, set back from the road, may have been grander than the Jeromes' seaside villa, but Rosetta Cottage is not a house to walk past without a second glance. The cream-coloured, gothic-style Georgian cottage, with roses arching over the front door, has character and style. Built around 1770 as the house of Thomas Godsell, rope-maker, who used it as his works office, it was neither large nor dominant. To the rear was an ample garden and apple orchard. A terrace on the first floor, nestling on the roof of the turreted porch, made a spectacular viewing point from which to watch the sailing ships racing on the Solent during the two weeks of the Cowes Regatta. Southampton, clearly visible on the horizon, was in those days just a collection of low-built houses. Clara must have been delighted by the fact that they were now neighbours of her heroine, the deposed Empress.

Yet it was, of course, the trio of American girls inside the house who were much more interesting than the house itself. Leonie was not often there as she had to complete her studies at a boarding school in Wiesbaden, Germany, and so, by the third summer, it was Clara and Jennie who had established themselves at Cowes as an intriguing and beautiful pair. They saw nothing out of the ordinary in being asked to all the smartest parties and in performing piano duets after dinner, in their Worth gowns, with true professionalism and sparkle. The one fair and fey, the other dark and fiery, both concentrated on playing as magnificently as their arduous practice sessions had prepared them for. Few English girls could come near them in ability or confidence.

Leonard, back in New York and lonely, wrote to them in the first week of August 1873:

> 'Mrs Clit [his pet name for his wife], Miss Clarita and Miss Jennie,
>
> Dearly beloved, it is nearly two weeks since I had a letter. You must be sure to write me particulars of all that is going on. I have no doubt you will see many nice people and will have Cowes all to yourselves as far as Americans are concerned . . . have you secured the Villa Rosetta for another year etc? I rather like the idea of Cowes next summer and a yacht . . .'[17]

Within days there was plenty to tell him about all that was going on. He was ordered over on the next boat.

First came an invitation to be presented to the Prince and Princess of Wales. Then, on 12 August, Clara and Jennie were invited to an afternoon ball in honour of their Imperial Highnesses the Grand Duke and Grand Duchess Cesarevitch, given by the Captain and officers of HMS *Ariadne*, then lying as guard-ship in the harbour. A launch carried Jennie and Clara in their delicate white tulle dresses decorated with fresh flowers to the brightly lit naval cruiser where, as Jennie says coyly in her book, she made the acquaintance of Lord Randolph Churchill. She kept the invitation all her life and underneath the words 'To Meet' she wrote by hand the single word: 'Randolph'. The stiff card is today preserved among her papers at the Churchill Archives in Cambridge.

Lord Randolph Churchill, twenty-three-year-old second surviving son of the seventh Duke of Marlborough and the former Lady Frances Vane, eldest daughter of the third Marquis of Londonderry, may have had impeccable aristocratic credentials but he was not known for his love of dancing. Yet that night, after one dance, he fell madly and passionately in love with the nineteen-year-old Jennie, whose deep-set eyes, black brows, dark hair and naturally coloured lips made her strikingly beautiful. His lightning love was requited, no less passionately. No diary of Jennie's has survived, nor any letters in which she talks about why she fell in love with such sudden conviction. She had almost no personal experience of men, beyond her father and his circle. Reliance on later accounts of Randolph makes her decision all the harder to fathom. He was not tall, he had slightly bulging eyes, which earned him the nickname 'Gooseberry-faced Churchill' at school, and he wore his brown hair, already receding, parted in the middle. But he sported a large moustache and an equally large personality, a mixture of charm, charisma, confidence, arrogance and shyness, which to his friends was irresistible. What latent talent excited Jennie during those hot August days as he walked about the island with his pug dog Puggles?

Randolph's son was later to describe him at that time as 'a man grown markedly reserved in his manner to acquaintances, utterly unguarded to his intimate friends, something of a dandy in his dress, an earnest sportsman, an omnivorous reader, moving with a jaunty step through what were in those days the very select circles of fashion and clubland seeking the pleasures of the turf and town'.[18] Lord Rosebery, a childhood friend of Randolph's, wrote of:

> his unexpectedness, his fits of caressing humility, his impulsiveness, his tinge of violent eccentricity, his apparent daredevilry which made him a fascinating companion, while his wit, his sarcasm, his piercing personalities, his elaborate irony and his effective delivery gave astonishing popularity to his speeches. Nor were his physical attributes without their attraction. His slim and boyish figure, his moustache which had an emotion of its own and his round protruding eyes gave a compound interest to his speeches and his conversation. His laugh . . . in its very weirdness and discordance . . . was merriment itself.[19]

According to his biographer Roy Foster, his adolescent personality would remain, although more exaggerated, for the rest of his short life, one of infectious laughter tainted by appalling rudeness, theatrical seriousness coupled with a delight in embarrassing people by unexpected behaviour. 'Capable of changing from blandishing charm to withering abuse, the problem of self-control emphasized by his father was a permanent feature, so was a mental facility to which the word "genius" was often if cautiously applied in later life but which only manifested itself in erratic bouts of activity often after long periods of indolence.'[20]

At whatever level, the knowledge that Randolph was the second son of a duke with illustrious forebears cannot have had a negative impact on Jennie. She was educated with the deliberate expectation that she would make an excellent marriage. His background could hardly have been more patrician, nor more traditional. Brought up among the many splendours of Blenheim Palace, he was sent to boarding school at Eton, which was not a success. He was frequently in trouble and threatened with removal. However, after a short continental tour he then went to Merton College, Oxford, a few miles from the ancestral home, having failed the entrance to Balliol. He had no particular aim in life, beyond a deep love for his celebrated pack of hounds, the Blenheim Harriers, which he had trained and tended himself since he was a schoolboy of fourteen, with little encouragement from his father or mother, who thought it a waste of time and money. He went to Cowes with his friend Colonel Edgecumbe merely as a seeker after pleasure. Yet, noticing Jennie across the room, something melted the traditional sang-froid. He asked a mutual friend, Frank Bertie, for an introduction and together they danced a formal quadrille. Then they talked for the rest of the evening.

Her attraction for him is perhaps easier to explain. She was unlike any woman he had ever met and very different from his own six sisters. What he saw in Jennie was a woman who had a sparkling personality, was widely read,[21] enormously talented as a musician and a skilful horsewoman. She was, he could see, greatly admired and therefore something of a prize. Her formative experience of life, seeing the once great French aristocracy impoverished and humiliated, gave her a knowingness beyond her years. It is highly unlikely that she had had any serious relationships with men that went beyond flirtations. In later years, when her love life was the subject of much gossip, an affair with the French statesman Gambetta was rumoured. Winston Churchill told his last private secretary Anthony Montague Browne, '"We mustn't be irreverent to Gambetta. Some might consider it unfilial." He went on to explain that one of the many bizarre stories circulated about himself was that Gambetta was his natural father.'[22] That her father was a millionaire was considered a fact that had no need of mention.

That Leonard Jerome was at that moment in New York having suffered the effects of a serious financial crash was not known.

They talked enough for Jennie to be aware that this was an original mind and a forceful personality and to feel excited about asking her mother if they might invite Randolph and Colonel Edgecumbe to dinner the following night. Randolph sent a polite note of acceptance, the French cook was given urgent instructions and the entertainment was provided by Clara and Jennie playing piano duets. The story has often been told of how Randolph confided in his friend later that evening that he intended to make 'the dark one' his wife. The same evening Jennie rebuffed her sister, who insisted she did not care for Randolph, by declaring that he was, she believed, the man she would marry. The following day the two men were again invited for dinner and that night Randolph contrived a walk in the cottage orchard with Jennie, where he asked her to marry him. She said yes.

Randolph, due to leave Cowes on the Saturday morning, postponed his departure until after the weekend. Writing from the Marine Hotel he thanked Jennie for the photograph she had given him and told her he had missed his boat and would therefore have to stay an extra day. They agreed to meet after church, just along the road from Rosetta Cottage and opposite the Squadron. 'You see I keep turning up like a bad shilling,' he warned her.[23] The couple exchanged further promises and love tokens, and then he returned to Blenheim. Only after he had left Cowes was Mrs Jerome informed of what had gone on between them. The noble lineage appears not to have impressed her unduly. She considered such a declaration of mutual love over-hasty. She might have been concerned that nothing would materialise and her daughter would be compromised, or perhaps she was perturbed by the idea of her second daughter being betrothed before the first. Jennie broke the news to Randolph: 'Although she likes you *very* much, [she] won't hear of it. But I am sure we shall easily get her on our side later on – when we see you in London or perhaps here – God bless you darling.' She added a postscript: 'Don't smoke too much,'[24] – a hollow request that was to echo down the years.

Randolph had sent a brief farewell from the boat. Then, once he was back at home on the Tuesday, told his own mother, a formidable character who particularly adored this son, 'everything'. She, too, was very much surprised and could not understand the speed of events. Randolph wrote very lovingly to 'My own darling Jeannette' of how he was a changed man and suddenly could not bear having to listen to 'the twaddle and gossip of my mother and sisters when my heart and thoughts were elsewhere'.[25] He declared his undying love for her and spoke of all the sacrifices he was prepared to make to ensure her happiness and to protect her from wrong.

But the real battle, he knew only too well, was still to come with his father the Duke. John Winston Spencer-Churchill, the seventh Duke, was a true Victorian. The connection with the Spencers came in the mid-eighteenth century when Anne Churchill, daughter of the first and most famous Duke, married John Spencer, son of the Earl of Sunderland. After that the family became Spencer-Churchill. Having succeeded to the dukedom in 1857, the seventh Duke was equally devout in his support of Conservatism – representing at first the family borough of Woodstock – and of Anglicanism (he was responsible for an Act of Parliament which strengthened the Church of England in towns through the subdivision of larger parishes). At the time of Randolph's meeting with Jennie, the Duke had held various government positions and was considered by the Conservative leader Disraeli a competent pair of hands in the Lords who had sympathies with the more progressive tendencies of the times.

Anticipating his parents' opposition only too clearly, Randolph wrote a moving and carefully phrased letter to his father. Admitting that he had proposed to a Miss Jeanette Jerome, the daughter of an American lady who had lived for some years in Paris and whose husband lived in New York, and that she had accepted, he said he recognised that his father would find it difficult to understand how an attachment so strong could have arisen in so short a space of time, 'and really I feel it quite impossible for me to give any explanation of it that could appear reasonable to anyone practical and dispassionate . . . But all I can say is that I love her better than life itself.' Randolph asked his father to increase his allowance so that he was in a position to ask Mrs Jerome for her daughter's hand. But at the same time he told his father that Mr Jerome 'is reputed to be very well off and his daughters, I believe, have very good fortunes'.[26]

But the most important part of the letter, which he understood would touch a raw nerve with his parents, who hoped that this clever son would follow his father into politics and represent the family borough of Woodstock, was the passage where he expressed his belief that the 'idle and comparatively useless life' which he had been leading of late would end if he were married to Miss Jerome. He had understood, in a matter of hours with Jennie, a deep truth. 'If I had a companion such as she would be, I feel sure, to take an interest in one's prospects and career, and to encourage me to exertions and to do something towards making a name for myself, I think I might become, with the help of providence, all and perhaps more than you had ever wished and hoped for me.'[27] Randolph faced opposition not only from his parents but from his brother, too. George, Marquis of Blandford, a troublesome character who was unhappily married himself, now wrote to his younger brother, in a long letter of wicked cynicism, that he considered Randolph was 'mad, simply mad':

> Had you been five and thirty or forty I could have pitied you . . . I don't care if la demoiselle was the incarnation of all moral excellences and physical beauties on God's earth. My opinion is the same. Had you told me it was a married woman you wanted to go off with I should say if you can't live happily without her, go, fate calls you. Had it been a woman for whom you were ruining yourself, I should say fatality. But my friend le mariage! It is a delusion and a snare like all the rest, and in this disagreeable addition, that it is irrevocable . . .
>
> My dear Randolph, for God's sake listen to me (though of course you won't) – you are bored . . . though in fact 'vous êtes à la recherche des émotions et vous avez touché mal, très mal![28]

Blandford's irascible letter was a foretaste of the far greater trouble he was to cause the couple in the months ahead. He was just as rude and unpredictable as his brother but cleverer and with a strong interest in the sciences.

The Duke himself replied to Randolph on 31 August 1873 – a letter which offered little encouragement. He told his son that he had done some research into the Jeromes and found that Leonard was 'a sporting and I should think vulgar kind of man'. Worse, he told Randolph, he was 'of the class of speculators and had already been bankrupt once: and may be so again'. It was a connection which no man in his senses 'could think respectable'.[29] Randolph made a brief return visit to Cowes before the month was up. Since Mrs Jerome's permission would have been necessary if Randolph and Jennie were to meet, her tacit approval of the relationship is clear. Her hesitations can easily be explained as demonstrating the position she knew society required her to take. The proprieties had to be observed in case anything went wrong. It was on this occasion that Jennie was introduced by Randolph to the Prince of Wales as the woman he hoped to marry. According to Randolph, the Prince thoroughly approved and encouraged the young couple, telling Randolph what a lucky fellow he was.

Yet by the time Leonard, the parent to whom Jennie was closest, reacted to the news of an impending engagement, the couple had been sent on their separate ways. The Jeromes remained in Cowes until 13 September, when the weather had turned cold. Then Jennie, her mother and Clara went back to Paris. They travelled via London, and Jennie and Randolph were allowed to meet there briefly and not altogether happily on Monday,

15 September. Again, Mrs Jerome must have been consulted and her agreement given for this, but both, while feigning confidence, were unsure of the future.

In a letter dated 8 August but which must have been composed on 8 September and sent to Jennie in Paris – her grandson Randolph believed an explanation for the misdating perhaps lay in the emotional stress under which he was writing – Leonard disclosed that even though she had not told him who was the object of her affections since he 'waits to consult his family', he had a pretty good idea of the suitor's identity from a letter his elder daughter Clara had sent. 'I fear he is too swell according to English ideas to gain the consent of his family though he will have to look a good while among his countrywomen to find one equal to you. If anything goes wrong you will make a dreadful shipwreck of your affections,' he wrote perceptively. 'I always thought if you ever did fall in love it would be a very dangerous affair. You were never born to love lightly. It must be *Way Down* or nothing . . . Such natures if they happen to secure the right one are very happy but if disappointed they suffer untold misery.'[30]

If Jennie and her ilk were immortalised by Edith Wharton, much of Randolph's world was brilliantly captured by Trollope. Trollope may not have known the Marlboroughs or the Churchills personally; his genius was in recognising social trends and transforming them into stories. In *The Duke's Children* Silverbridge – the character most closely resembling Randolph, although he is the first son – is told by his father, the Duke of Omnium, of his responsibility to enter Parliament:

> A Member of Parliament should feel himself to be the servant of his country, and like every other servant, he should serve. If this be distasteful to a man he need not go into Parliament. If the harness gall him he need not wear it. But if he takes the trappings then he should draw the coach . . . If you cannot feel this to be your duty you should not be there at all . . .
>
> You are there as the guardian of your fellow countrymen, that they may be safe, that they may be prosperous, that they may be well governed and lightly burdened, above all that they may be free.

It was also his responsibility to marry well and appropriately, and by throwing himself away upon an 'American adventuress', whose children and grandchildren would be his heirs, he was not behaving in the way expected of a scion of the British nobility. The old Duke of Omnium's doubts might have come directly from the mouth of the Duke of Marlborough, so unready for change and so sure of the value of his family's immutable place in the world.

The Marlboroughs were not alone. There were plenty of old English country families who responded with fear and dread to what was happening. Yet in the Marlboroughs' case there was a serious financial problem which was already only too visible. As Disraeli noted, the seventh Duke was 'not rich for a Duke',[31] a position which forced him into selling many family heirlooms and assets. By the following year he had disposed of some of the Marlborough gems and sold parcels of land in Buckinghamshire to Ferdinand de Rothschild for £240,000. Such sales were to continue into the next generation. The expenses of his position as Lord Lieutenant of Oxfordshire (from 1857) had further depleted finances, and in 1882 he agreed to sell the famous Sunderland library and the Blenheim enamels. His heirs were to make further sales.

It is against this background that his letters to his son's prospective father-in-law should be read. He would have preferred to see his son marry into the sort of respectable ancient English family his daughters were so obligingly to do. But, if that became impossible, then at least, as compensation for respectability, let there be cash. Leonard Jerome did not much like the system he was expected to defer to either. The surviving letters between the Marlboroughs and Jeromes in the months of negotiating before the marriage reveal deep misgivings on both sides and set the stage for two decades of further wrangling and financial concern. The omens were not good.

3

I Have Placed All my Hopes of Future Happiness in This World on You

~

FROM NOW ONWARDS the letters were kept. Not all. Sometimes there are gaps, scarcely noticeable, to cover indiscretions, occasionally there are instructions to burn or a private note, referred to as a p.s., inserted into the more public letter. Before Winston embarked on the biography of his father he suggested in 1902 that his mother first sort through all the letters: 'they are certainly full of most valuable and interesting material . . . All your early letters which were most carefully put away . . . there emerges from these dusty records a great and vivid drama.'[1]

For it is the letters written at least daily, occasionally twice or three times a day, sometimes sent off in anger or imprudently, often in frustration, desperation or boredom, that provide the only means by which we can sense the depth of the love, or despair, between two people at such a distance. Written so often in haste, just as one might today speak or text, but in an indelible, ineradicable voice, they were often the cause of misunderstanding, repented of at leisure. If only she had retrieved it, Jennie occasionally complained, regretting her characteristic impetuosity.

Of course, letters were kept by all classes in those days, not just in aristocratic circles. Such communication before the era of the telephone was what fuelled the day. 'Yr letters are my only pleasure. I wish I could get ten a day from you,' Jennie told Randolph at a time when, in London at least, ten deliveries a day were not unusual.[2] Love letters were tied up with ribbon and carefully saved, letters from a son killed in war acquired an additional layer of emotion. And later, as Randolph travelled so much, the sheer volume of letters is damning evidence of just how much they were apart. But in 1873–4 there is no clearer indication of the significance each saw in this emerging Anglo-American alliance than the conservation of this cache of raw emotion.[3] 'Why they were all preserved, seems incredible save that Jennie *foretold* the future,' wrote Jennie's nephew Shane Leslie to his daughter, the biographer Anita Leslie.[4] At first Mrs Jerome had forbidden her middle daughter to communicate at all with Randolph, presumably fearful (as we have seen) that if the engagement, as the couple were already referring to it, did not materialise such letters could be highly compromising to any future relationship. But Jennie appears to have had a different scheme and may, quite deliberately, have leaked the news. At any rate newspapers soon linked the couple in their gossip columns. The *Court Journal* reported under 'Approaching Marriages in High Life': 'Miss Jerome, one of the prettiest young ladies that ever hailed from New York and landed at Cowes, is about to marry Lord R Churchill, the third son of the Duke of Marlborough. The young lady, who has resided for some time in Paris, will receive a splendid dower on her marriage. Mr Jerome is one of the most inveterate of American yachtsmen.' The retraction in the next issue was irrelevant. The Jerome parents now had to be on guard for the sake of their three daughters. In the stand-off between the two families, as Randolph waited for a response from Mr Jerome, who was an ocean away, as well as from his own father, who was undertaking inquiries, he begged Jennie to persuade her mother to let her accept and send letters. 'I am sure there is no harm in it and your letters are perfectly SAFE with me.'[5]

But on the first day the women arrived in Paris, as soon as Jennie had succeeded in persuading Mama to allow her to write, the letter that she despatched gave Randolph a warning that, however passionate her love for him, she was not to be trifled with, especially where her family was concerned. She had reflected on their meeting in London the day before. 'I cannot tell you how deeply hurt I felt at the insinuation you gave me as to your having heard something against my father – I was unable to answer you or defend him as you did not choose to confide in me – all I can say is that I love, admire and respect my father more than any man living and I do not think it possible for him to have an enemy.' She told him that if he was tired of all the trouble he was encountering from his parents in order to pursue marriage with her then, 'believe me – I consider you as free as if nothing had ever passed between us. Is it not much wiser to end it all before it is too late?' Of course, as Randolph recognised, she did not really want to break off. She concluded by telling him she was 'ready to do or say anything you like so long as you leave my family alone and not abuse it'.[6]

Randolph picked up the glove and scolded her for being:

so cruel and heartless, I really may almost say so wicked, as to write to me that your impression is that I am heartily sick of the whole affair and only wish myself well out of it . . . I suppose you think that the affair has gone quite far enough, that it amused you for the moment at Cowes but that you never meant to be led into a serious engagement. Well, I tell you that if it is so, you have treated me TOO badly . . . if you cast me off tho from your beauty and attractions you will have always admirers at your feet, but you will have trifled with and spurned, the truest and most honest love and devotion that man is capable of feeling. I tell you, I have placed all my hopes of future happiness in this world on you. I have voluntarily staked what one may call one's moral fortune on this game and . . . if I lose it well then I am indeed lost. I have never loved before but I have loved and do love you as even you will never be loved again.[7]

It was a long letter, well argued and ardent, which included a poem and in which he apologised for writing crossly, assuring her of his love for her family and imploring her never again to write such a cruel and painful letter.

They had each expressed themselves powerfully. It was a foretaste of things to come. Jennie replied immediately and optimistically that this must be the last misunderstanding between them. But she added that she was not altogether sorry 'for it has given me a fresh proof of yr love and has made me discover the strength and depth of mine – I did not know how much I loved you until I left England and felt that I was leaving all I love most on earth behind me'. She even insisted that she could 'leave Father, Mother – and the whole world for you – if it were necessary',[8] and urged him to make their marriage in December after all.

Randolph, a mere five years older but more experienced and under-standing, tried to explain. What had made him wretched in London was his fear that he and Jennie might have to be married without the consent of his 'practical and unsentimental' parents. But he knew now that this consent would not be withheld, 'tho they may still try to make difficulties in order to satisfy themselves they are doing their duty . . . They always pre-tend to be very stern at first about everything but they can never hold out long as they are really very kind hearted and vy fond of me (strange to say).' He recognised that this would mean a longer engagement but tried to re-assure Jennie:

Dearest, I love you better than anything on earth and shall *never* love another. Whenever you feel doubts of me, and of course I know that sometimes many horrid thoughts will force themselves unbidden on one's mind when anyone you are vy fond of is away, just read over my letters to you and I am sure you will feel convinced that no gentleman could write as I have done to you without feeling from his heart every word he said. How could you so calmly write and recommend me to marry some English girl. You have no idea how you pain me when I think you capable of imagining even for a moment that I should ever look at or speak again to any other girl after you.[9]

It is easy to imagine this beautifully written, eloquent letter being read many times by Jennie for it conveyed much of the strength, the charm and the confidence in their future together which had won him her love in the first place and continued to bind her during these testing months. Randolph had a natural turn of phrase and was not afraid to express his deepest emotions to Jennie, his 'first and only love'. He cannot envisage a life without her. When he reflects on the 'incessant friction' at home caused by 'long ponderous lectures from my father and continual complaints and bickerings with my mother' he tells her he is forced to conclude that 'a home shared with you would be a perfect heaven on earth'.[10] By comparison her letters, occasionally scolding or critical of his smoking, are responsive to his, less rapturous, more full of domestic or local news and, not surprisingly, less mature. How could she, after three days, know that this was the man she wished to spend the rest of her life with? What was the yardstick against which she could measure him?

By the end of September Randolph felt able to write to Mrs Jerome insisting that there was no longer any opposition from his parents, 'but that taking into consideration the suddenness and rapidity of the attachment formed, [his father] said he would give his consent if we were of the same mind in a year hence'.[11] The stumbling block was that there was still no formal answer from Leonard Jerome. This was crucial because, although they did not say so, the Marlboroughs needed to know the size of the 'splendid' dowry. As the second son of an already impoverished duke it was clear to contemporaries who knew him that Randolph must marry money. He had extravagant tastes, ran up high gambling debts and no resources of his own with which to satisfy these. When Leonard learnt that the Duke of Marlborough was raising objections – although it is not clear if he was ever aware that the Duke had asked for a report on him from the British envoy in Washington, Sir Edward Thornton – he too backtracked from his initial euphoric consent. But his letters were often overtaken by events, adding to the difficulties between Jennie and Randolph. Though he was proud, he was worldly enough not only to acknowledge 'the great prejudices the English have against the Americans socially', but also to recognise that until Randolph's father gave his consent his daughter risked being 'left in a very disagreeable position'.[12] Nonetheless, while admitting that the reasons the Duke gave for hesitating were 'perfectly natural and proper . . . Precisely the same thing that I wrote to you . . .' Leonard added more comfortingly:

'I have said *whom you choose* and *whom your mother approves* is certain of my consent. That is if he is English or American.' In the same letter he confided: 'Between you and I and the post and your mother etc I am delighted more than I can tell. It is magnificent. The greatest match any American has made since the Dutchess [sic] of Leeds* . . . I want you to have all the dresses etc that you wish. You ought to have a box at the opera occasionally. You should give parties and live handsomely. You will be more swell than ever now and you will be certain to have a great influence on Clara's future.'[13]

Such encouragement, when it eventually came, was comforting. But both Jennie and Randolph had decided to ignore, insofar as they could, the parental objections. 'I do not mind telling you it is all humbug about waiting a year,' Randolph wrote confidently to Jennie. 'I could and would wait a good deal more than a year but I do not mean to, as it is not the least necessary.'[14] He said he had written a long and diplomatic letter to his father, contradicting him, arguing with him and persuading him of the strength of their mutual affection. As he explained to Jennie, his parents had set their heart on him representing the family borough of Woodstock as an MP. Since he was not himself a peer, he was able to sit in the House of Commons even though he had the courtesy title of lord. Since a dissolution of Parliament and a general election was imminent they wanted him to put all his energies into that. Randolph considered he had two possible choices:

> Either to refuse to stand altogether unless they consent to my being married immediately afterwards; or else to stand, but at the last moment threaten to withdraw and leave the Radical a walkover . . . All this may appear strange to you but you have no idea how much they think of this borough and how much they have set their hearts to it – all tricks are fair in love and war and if I am crossed I can plot and intrigue like a second Machiavelli.[15]

He warned Jennie, who was anxiously watching his mood lurch from angry and low to high spirited and decisive, that, where he had once made up his mind, he would refuse to be crossed or thwarted. He was impetuous, impatient, possessive and demanding but also captivating and in love.

Six weeks after they met, which felt like six years to him, it was clear that 'our early golden dreams of being married in December' were looking decidedly unlikely. Randolph, the more patient and philosophical of

---

* The former Louisa Caton of Baltimore in 1828 married the seventh Duke of Leeds.

the two, was even suggesting May or June; being prepared to wait so long proved his constancy, he argued. However, it also appeared that ducal consent – and the crucial allowance dependent on that – would be forthcoming only once Randolph had stood, and been elected, for Woodstock. He told Jennie that while public life held little attraction for him, it would have greater appeal if 'I think it will please you and that you take an interest in it and will encourage me to keep up to the mark.'[16] He was not an unwilling participant but had already sensed the ambition of his future wife, admitting that he thought her parents might have a higher opinion of him if he were a Member of Parliament. When he remarked idly that he wanted nothing more than a peaceful, happy life with no particular occupation she shot back that she wanted him to be 'as ambitious as you are clever and I am certain you would accomplish great things'.[17]

At all events Randolph had long recognised that the family obligation to represent the interests of Woodstock constituents in Parliament would fall on him rather than on his unreliable elder brother George, Lord Blandford, who had been expelled from Eton. This had nothing to do with money. Members of Parliament received no salary at this time, performing their duties because they shared the deeply ingrained Victorian belief in duty. Such high-minded sentiments, underpinned by the glory of living at Blenheim, were all important to Randolph's parents, who feared that their prospective American daughter-in-law might need educating in this respect.

Jennie, impetuous and physical, longed for everything to be agreed and to dispense with the tight chaperoning that was obligatory for any unmarried woman. She commented years later that 'in all her wide and deep experience of London Society' there had only been two, or perhaps three, instances of girls having affairs before they married.[18] She understood that her mother would never allow her to see Randolph alone under the circumstances of an informal engagement and she longed for some independence. At the same time Randolph disapproved of her seeing anyone else. So she felt condemned to a hermit's life, where one of the few activities which relieved her boredom was three or four hours of serious piano practice a day until her fingers ached. So few of Mrs Jerome's letters survive that it is impossible not to see her through the eyes of her headstrong daughter, with whom she was often arguing. While Jennie's loyalty was strong there is also a sense that, for this child at least, the cloying protectiveness of her mother, 'who worries me half out of my life with her absurdities',[19] was deeply irksome and had been for some time.

Yet perhaps Mrs Jerome was not simply playing a nineteenth-century game and was, with a mother's intuition, truly concerned about Randolph's suitability. Certainly she never had a warm relationship with this son-in-law. He found her difficult to engage with and considered that she 'always throws cold water on our plans',[20] whereas Leonard Jerome entered into the spirit of excitement and was much more encouraging. And it cannot be without significance that when Winston later referred to his American heritage it was his mother and Leonard Jerome that he had in mind, not the anxious and bourgeois Clara Hall, who scarcely rated a mention from him. Jennie had to urge Randolph not to feel 'cross and bitter'[21] against her mother, who was clearly nervous that he might still back off, leaving her daughter tainted. Jennie must have been influenced by her mother's daily fears – occasionally a nod to these creeps into her letters. That she chose to disregard them indicates just how determined and wilful she was. As she told Randolph shortly before their marriage: 'I won't marry you if you don't let me do *exactly as I like*. Il faut vs [vous] préparer à une vie de sacrifices with me, my dear.'[22]

But then, in early October, whatever opposition had prevented a meeting evidently collapsed. Randolph came to Paris for two weeks and the young couple spent a blissfully happy fortnight in each other's company. How easily, Randolph told Jennie, he could accustom himself to a life of going every morning to spend the day with her. Immediately, they were making plans for the next visit. 'I do not think, my darling, when I do go back to Paris, that I will leave you again. It becomes harder and harder each time.'[23] Randolph told her how he wished she lived in London away from all the brilliant and attractive people in Paris, where without him her head might be so easily turned. 'I cannot help worrying as all my life depends on you now.'[24] He admitted he was jealous and told her he wanted her to drop all the other men who were still part of her circle.

To what extent Jennie was able to give her knowing mother the slip during the October visit can only be guessed at, but the couple's subsequent letters have many affectionate indiscretions indicating that the relationship had become more physical; corners of pages are now cut out where, for example, one of them has written: 'This is the place I kissed.' Early in November, Randolph crossed the Channel again, this time partly in order to meet Leonard at last but also to see his fiancée and give her a ring. 'When I am with you I feel ready to face the devil if necessary and carry you off in the teeth of friends and relatives.'[25] But the volatility of their future relationship is already in evidence. Randolph has to suggest they mutually swear not to have a single quarrel when they meet, but then tells Jennie she is the only woman he knows who looks pretty even when cross. And, as the arguments and delays dragged on through the autumn, they had some fractious moments.

> I am sorry you find my letters have nothing in them. Yours on the contrary have rather too much. I think you are rude. I told you I did not find time to write and it is the truth you are always doubting what I say and thinking that I don't care for you . . . Really Randolph, you are tiresome – do you suppose it is nothing to me to know that you are always with people who dislike me without knowing me and with people who speak badly of me . . .[26]

The Jeromes, having decided to play the same game as the Marlboroughs, were organising searches into Randolph's past. By December the intensely romantic tone of the correspondence had undergone a transformation, with Jennie writing 'letter after letter alluding mysteriously to all sorts of bad reports that keep arriving'.[27] Randolph ridiculed these reports, which chiefly referred to his drinking too much and keeping fast company, defended himself and then suggested that she 'just tell me about yourself'. He did not specifically deny the allegations, and had already admitted, rather disarmingly, that 'in my short life I have already made a great many enemies, I am afraid, for I never cared to be civil to anybody I did not like'.[28]

The Jeromes would certainly have been made aware of a much publicised incident in March 1870 when Randolph, having been involved in a fracas with two policemen following dinner at the Randolph Hotel in Oxford, was fined ten shillings for assault but acquitted of being drunk and disorderly. There the case might have rested, a local incident of students behaving in a rowdy manner, but for Randolph bringing a counter-charge against one of the policemen for perjury. This second case went badly once the waiter concerned, Alfred Wren, itemised the large quantity of champagne, hock, sherry, claret, port and punch consumed and described Churchill spilling wine and threatening him with a wine cooler. Although the charges of perjury against Constable Partridge were dropped, Wren was shortly thereafter dismissed from his job amid allegations that Churchill had threatened to stop patronising the hotel as long as he remained. It was a murky business which fizzled out soon afterwards, but not before it had been reported in various national newspapers. Such a story cannot have done his standing with his future in-laws any good.

Randolph suggested he might come to Paris on 5 January 1874, so that they could celebrate Jennie's twentieth birthday together. But he was worried that would lead to quarrels with Mrs Jerome whenever he wanted

to be alone with Jennie. Although there was still no agreement on financial settlements and no wedding date fixed, Randolph felt at liberty, in
between playing charades, to discuss his engagement freely when he went
to visit friends such as the Alphonse Rothschilds at Aston Clinton, whom
he had known since his schooldays at the Rev. Lionel Damer's school.
Damer reported his concern about the friendship with the Jewish
Rothschilds to the Duchess at the time, but conceded that 'there is really
no one else in the neighbourhood to visit'.[29] Randolph saw it differently.
'Like all Jews' places, it is a wonderful house for eating, every kind of
food. I must confess I rather like that,' he told Jennie.[30] He was aggrieved
when he heard that Jennie and her family might visit America, jealous of
an Austrian by the name of Khinenbuller who was paying court to
her – 'your hair is mine whether I am away or not'[31] – and increasingly
frustrated by his future mother-in-law. He admitted that he had always
anticipated difficulties from her. He described her as *entêtée* or obstinate,
told Jennie he thought her opposition unwise, her insistence on delays selfish, and warned that he was not going to be bullied by her. Jennie,
despite her own passionate nature, was trapped between two strong
opposing forces. 'Dearest, you need not think I am cross or bitter against
your mother,' Randolph told her,[32] adding a day later that she should
'stick up for me and really think me a good fellow and then we shall
never quarrel . . . I don't think a woman like you has any idea what she
can do for a man when he once knows that she really cares about him.
It changes all his ideas of life . . .'[33]

Two events prevented Randolph coming to Paris again in January. In
the first place his aunt, Lady Portarlington, his mother's sister, was dying
in Ireland and he was required to attend her final illness and funeral.
Secondly, the long-awaited general election was finally announced.
Jennie was bitterly disappointed by the change in plans, news conveyed
to her by her future mother-in-law, who said she grieved on Randolph's
behalf but hoped he would be rewarded for 'his self denial' in a few
days. 'The Duke and I hope to make your acquaintance under happier
circumstances ere long,' she added.[34] It was an especially difficult time for
Jennie since it coincided with gossip that their engagement had been
broken off because they found they did not suit each other. But 'how
could I be cross with you, darling,' she wrote sweetly on her birthday,
'you are always in the right.' She had made up her mind not to mope
during this period of separation, she told Randolph. She was taking a
huge interest in his political activity, was urging him to victory against
'those abominable radicals',[35] missed him desperately, could not live

without him and could not understand how she had ever been happy before they met.

Churchill had been a local magistrate for some years and was able to draw strength from a variety of local contacts for his election campaign. There was the retiring Conservative Member Henry Barnett, the local solicitor R. B. Hawkins, society friends such as the Strange Jocelyns and his own family. His sisters Rosamond and Anne, who in high aristocratic fashion canvassed the outlying areas on horseback, were more help than his irascible elder brother Blandford, who may have hindered as much as he helped. But he was not without opposition from a mixture of agricultural labourers and liberal intellectuals. Even Randolph himself, at this stage neither a confident speaker nor a conviction politician, knew that despite widespread deference to Blenheim and the ducal interest he could not take the result for granted.

But on 4 February he was able to tell Jennie of his comfortable victory and claim that he attributed his success to her. He had won by 569 votes to 404 and was now a Member of Parliament. Disraeli had won a decisive victory, defeating Gladstone's Liberals. The day after the victory Randolph went into Oxford to meet his father and, on their return to Woodstock, a crowd gathered, as was the fashion, to draw them through the town in a horseless carriage. 'There was nothing more to be done except pay the bill, which I left my father to do. I was very glad to get away as the place had got on my nerves and altogether I wanted a change of scene.'[36]

Duty done, he was free at last to visit Paris. He told Jennie that he could stay until 2 or 3 March, with nothing to prevent them being married at Easter. Without letters to guide us, there is no indication of how they spent the time in Paris. Three weeks later, on 5 March, the correspondence is renewed, with a discussion of how soon he could return. Passions aroused, he longed to be with her again but was clearly wary. 'I almost think I had better not kiss you again till I can for good.'[37]

Did something momentous happen? Quite how much freedom did Mrs Jerome allow them during this visit, when things were so nearly settled? Since Victorian parents suspected all young men of dangerous intentions, and Mrs Jerome was a particularly strict parent, it is unlikely she would have knowingly allowed her daughter to be alone with Randolph, which could have ruined her reputation. There is a sense that the couple enjoyed a game whereby they would try to give Mrs Jerome the slip. Yet, given how little could be safely committed to paper at the time, and given what it meant for a lady to be in a gentleman's hotel bedroom in 1874 – Randolph was staying at the 'Hôtel du R de R' (Rue de Rivoli?) – his written declaration in two separate letters that he longed to be back in his comfortable little room ('I like to think of you being in my room. You can't think, darling, how I long to be back . . .') was extremely daring.[38]

Assuming that their first child was born nine months later, the possibility that conception took place in Paris during this visit must be considered. Until recently, it was more or less standard practice to insist on Winston's prematurity, with some innuendo, in spite of his obviously robust health at birth. The interest here is not a prurient one. Whether or not the future Prime Minister was conceived out of wedlock is a proper concern of this biography. The significance lies in what it might reveal of his mother's confidence, physical passion, craving for excitement and sexual fearlessness. She wanted this man for her husband and lover. At one level Jennie was attracted to Randolph for his lineage and title and because she nursed an ambition for his latent political talents. But there was chemistry at work, too, and a powerful mutual physical attraction at the beginning – a *coup de foudre*. Jennie would have known all too clearly what she risked if the marriage had not come off and any intimacy at all with Randolph became known.

Meanwhile, Randolph's brother Blandford, who had so cynically warned his younger brother against this marriage, went to Paris to inspect his prospective sister-in-law. Blandford knew exactly the financial plight into which he and his family would sink without money. According to Julian Osgood Field, the then anonymous author of *Uncensored Recollections*, Blandford had had to ask the well-known moneylender Sam Lewis not to lend his brother a shilling. 'I did so although I never told Randolph or he would have slain me.'[39] Blandford seems to have behaved himself at this meeting as Jennie teased Randolph that she did not think the two brothers looked alike and 'if he wasn't your brother I should hate him. As it is I find him charming and am sure I shall like him enormously.'[40] The brothers' relationship was scarred by jealousy, from which Jennie was soon to suffer. Blandford was unquestionably bright and witty, but his meddling in Randolph's love life had increased the antipathy. Thanks to help from Francis Knollys, the Prince of Wales's private secretary, Blandford's early attempts to derail the engagement failed. Randolph, correctly, did not trust his brother and doubted that he would bother to return to Paris for the wedding, the final arrangements for which were still being disputed.[41]

After Randolph's February visit and after receiving beautiful presents of jewellery from his parents, Jennie admitted she was much more 'calme and tranquille' and a good deal more confident than she had been throughout the previous eight months. But in the last weeks before the wedding there were as many problems as ever, with both sides accusing the other of not writing often enough or complaining that the other's letters did not contain sufficient endearments. Both were capable of allowing friendly banter to deteriorate into childlike petulance. Jennie even admitted to crying over one of Randolph's letters because of his contradictory instruction to enjoy herself and then getting angry at news that she had attended dances.

> How extraordinary men are. One never knows how to take them or what they mean. It seems to me you made me promise before you left to keep in good spirits and to amuse myself . . . and now because I went to two wretched little dances where I bored myself dreadfully . . . you are furious. I have found out, though rather late, that you are now thinking me giddy and flirtatious.[42]

In mid-March, the actual date of the wedding was still in question and they fell into the time-honoured trap of pre-wedding arguments over all possible details. Some of Jennie's last-minute concerns were frivolous: should they have an English butler and a French chef? Would the monogrammed linen she had ordered be to their taste and should Randolph not buy the bridesmaids' lockets for her two sisters in Paris? 'Much nicer than London.' She had ordered twenty-five dresses as the basis of her trousseau, and these were to be sent to London. Randolph was worried there would not be nearly enough room to stow them all at the house they were intending to rent. Jennie fretted that none of his family would be at the wedding, which might look a little odd. 'Not that I care if you don't but really I think if my father crosses the Atlantic to come it seems to me some of your family might cross the channel.'[43]

Randolph had already tried to head off her worries, excusing his parents on the rather feeble grounds that 'they have a great deal to do and a great many ties and cannot run over to Paris at any moment'.[44] A few weeks later he told her rather disturbingly he was almost relieved that they were not coming to the marriage as 'what they want would only bother us.'[45] In fact they had paid a visit to Paris a few weeks beforehand, inspected Jennie and her sister Clara, and assured her parents that she would be received into their family with warmth. Yet by now, although financial negotiations were continuing, it must have been clear to the Marlboroughs that the Jeromes were not going to provide permanent salvation for the entire family and estate for which they might once have entertained hopes.

With or without the Marlboroughs present, Jennie initially wanted the ceremony to take place in a church and tried to persuade Randolph on this. But his main concern was to ensure that things were done legally, and he warned her that if a lengthy period of residence in Paris was required of him marriage there might become impossible and she would have to come to England. But if all that was necessary was the use of both embassies, then 'I don't care much.' The interminable wrangling was wearing Jennie down. She longed for the time when everything would be settled and they could be alone, married and away from everyone, she told him in a letter of gloomy foreboding. But then she announced that her father, who was due to sail from New York in three days, had had all the financial documents drawn up according to the old Duke's suggestions. 'I am sure they will all be satisfactorily arranged.' Randolph hoped to meet Leonard in London as soon as he arrived and before he went over to Paris as he was desperate to see the business of the settlements amicably completed for fear it would never be done. 'We are quite in the dark on this side of the channel as to his wishes and intentions and I don't want him and the lawyers to be at loggerheads.'[46]

Depending on what Leonard was able and prepared to give, Randolph was trying to find them somewhere to live within their budget. That very morning he had been to see one house in central London with a thirty-seven-year lease which he believed could be renewed indefinitely and which would cost them about £600, though it would need a large amount spent on decorations. In the event Randolph found a furnished house at 1 Curzon Street, just off Berkeley Square. He rented this from a Captain and Mrs Bristowe for £250 for three months until the end of July.

Randolph was not strictly accurate when he spoke of being 'in the dark' as to Leonard Jerome's intentions, although the delays and difficulties continued until the last moment and the signed settlements were not delivered into his hands until the actual morning of his wedding. On 23 January Leonard had proposed a settlement of £40,000 to yield £2,000 a year, derived from the property which had once been the magnificent family home on Madison Avenue and 26th Street and which was now leased to the Union League Club, as well as from various government and railway stocks. A month later the capital sum was increased to £50,000 because the Duke's solicitors objected that 'it is not usual to give trustees power to make investments which yield 5%'.[47]

But the grittier arguments concerned Mr Jerome's understandable but forward-thinking desire that the income from his settlement should be paid directly to his daughter. The Duke, through his solicitors, voiced his strong opposition to this, advising Randolph that as far as he was concerned such an arrangement 'cannot be considered as any settlement at all . . . Miss Jerome is made quite independent of you in a pecuniary point of view which in my experience is most unusual and I think I might add in such a case as the present, without precedent. And his Grace desires it to be distinctly understood that, in accepting Mr Jerome's proposal, you have done so in direct opposition to his views and wishes and solely upon your own responsibility.'[48] As a compromise it was suggested that he could give his daughter pin money, first £300, then £500, then £600, and that the residue of the £2,000 should be paid to her husband. In the end Leonard was prevailed upon to have half the allowance paid to Jennie and half to Randolph. 'My daughter, although not a Russian Princess, is an American and ranks precisely the same and you have doubtless seen that the Russian settlement recently published claimed everything for the bride.' This referred to the settlement that very year on behalf of the Grand Duchess Marie Alexandrovna, only daughter of Tsar Alexander II, who married Queen Victoria's second son the Duke of Edinburgh and was to become a friend of Jennie's. She was given a marriage portion of 2 million roubles which was considered her property, and the income from it was to be 'for her separate and exclusive use and enjoyment'.[49]

It was to be another eight years before the Married Women's Property Act enshrined such attitudes in England, giving married women the same right to own property as their unmarried sisters. But there were already plenty who thought like Leonard Jerome, and in the United States there had been various Acts passed since the middle of the nineteenth century giving married women effectual protection of their own property rights. But Leonard's supportive attitude was not merely about money. American fathers tended to treat their daughters as intelligent beings, worthy of support and as capable as a son of leading a wholly fulfilling life. This attitude was of vital importance to Jennie throughout her life.[50]

As soon as Leonard arrived in Paris in early April he wrote politely to 'Dear Duke', explaining his actions, which he insisted were 'governed purely by what I conceived to be in the best interests of *both* parties . . . it is quite wrong to suppose I entertain any distrust of Randolph. On the contrary, I firmly believe there is no young man in the world safer, still I can but think your English custom of making the wife so utterly dependent on the husband most unwise.' He went on:

> In the settlement as is finally arranged I have ignored American custom and waived all my American prejudices. I have conceded to your views and English custom in every point save one. That is simply a somewhat-unusual allowance of pin money to the wife. Possibly the principle may be wrong but you may be very certain my action upon it in this instance by no means arises from any distrust of Randolph.[51]

Leonard Jerome had been around women for too long to throw all his knowledge and instinct to the wind. But he was unable to hold to his original wish that any decision about the disposal of the capital sum of £50,000 in anticipation of the future Lady Randolph dying before Lord Randolph should be at her own discretion. Randolph had told his future father-in-law that unless all the dowry capital came to him in the event of his wife dying childless 'all business between us was perfectly impossible and he could do what he liked with his beastly money'.[52] However, just a few days before the wedding a compromise was reached on this point, too. If Jennie died childless before Lord Randolph then the money should be divided equally between Lord Randolph and her family. Even so, the day before his wedding Randolph found it necessary to persuade his mother not to be too angry with Mr Jerome, who was 'evidently very sorry for himself and his bad behaviour and will, I think, make amends'.[53]

While such negotiations may seem tasteless and sordid to modern ears, they differ little from today's pre-nuptial agreements. In the nineteenth century, if a woman's fortune did not belong to her husband it would look as though that man were not master in his own home. Making provision for the money of a new wife to remain within the husband's estate was common practice in England for centuries and nothing new for the Churchill family. In addition, the Duke of Marlborough settled £20,000 on Randolph, 'or rather, as you will see by and by, it must be something less which I have power to devise by will as a charge on the Blenheim estates and the interest in this at 5% will produce you £1,000 per annum which I will undertake to pay you'.[54] And, as Randolph promised Jennie, the house in Curzon Street would have a room for her sister Clara. Their eldest daughter's future was a key concern of the Jerome parents, and they were keen that Jennie's marriage should be used to help her.

On the eve of his wedding, Randolph wrote a long letter to his beloved mother Frances. It was also the eve of her birthday. His love and respect for his parents was deep and genuine and the Duchess adored this son, favouring him above her other children. But the relationship, much like his personality, was subject to wild swings and could descend into abusive criticism. This tender exchange between mother and son shows Randolph at his most thoughtful, an aspect of him that his wife was to see less and less, as he recognised that his mother's feelings were tinged with sadness at seeing her children leave. But, as ever, part of the letter was devoted to a discussion of money. He asked her if she could persuade the Duke to hand over some of the promised allowance as there were several bills outstanding, which he would like to pay off during his honeymoon. After assuring her that 'to-morrow I ensure myself a happy home and future . . . things are all going now as merrily as a marriage bell', he then told her that the Prince and Princess of Wales had sent Jennie a very pretty locket of pearls and turquoises. 'I really must protest against you continuing to be low and to say that you are losing us all. I shall be you know as near you and as much with you as ever and shall be able perhaps to be of more assistance and use than before.' He promised her that, unlike some of his siblings, who were stuck up and reserved, 'I am not in the least like that and never shall be.'[55]

The Duchess also sat at her desk writing that day and wished her beloved son on 'one of the most important days of his life . . . the commencement of a united existence of happiness . . . She is one whom you have chosen with less than usual deliberation but you adhered to your love with unwavering constancy and I cannot doubt the truth and power of your affections.' Referring to the recent arguments she said how glad she was that 'harmony is again restored and that no cloud obscures the day of sunshine but what has happened will show that the sweetest path is not without its thorns, and I must say ought not to be without its lesson to you . . .'[56]

The wedding took place on 15 April 1874. The best account of it came from fifteen-year-old Leonie, allowed out of her German boarding school. The excitement began, she explained in a letter to a girlfriend, the Monday before the wedding with the arrival in Paris of Randolph's eldest sister Cornelia and her husband Ivor Guest. His aunt Lady Camden and brother-in-law Lord George Pratt arrived from England the same day. Francis Knollys, who had played a key role in breaking the initial deadlock between the Jeromes and Marlboroughs, came bringing a charming locket and a note from the Prince and Princess. Knollys, son of General Sir William Knollys, was the Prince's most trusted servant whose importance in defusing royal scandals was paramount.

> The next day we gave a large family dinner. All the people above were present. After dinner they all went up to see Jennie's trousseau. There were 23* very pretty dresses and six or seven bonnets and some very fine linen. Were it not too long, I would describe the dresses to you. Later in the evening Lord Blandford came from Vienna and they all stayed until about half past one the next morning. We had to get up very early and be at the English embassy [sic] at 11.15. Jennie was dressed in white satin, a plain long train behind and a great many lace flounces in front. She wore a long tulle veil which covered her entirely. Clara and myself were bridesmaids and were dressed in pale blue silk with white embroidery. We received charming bridesmaids' lockets – a crystal heart with pearls and diamonds around it.[57]

* Twenty-five according to Randolph in other accounts.

Jennie was wearing a pearl necklace that her father had given her that morning. The family drove to the Embassy, a magnificent house steeped in history at 39 Rue du Faubourg St Honoré, which had belonged to Princess Borghese, sister of Napoleon, before it became the Embassy in 1814. At the time of the wedding the Ambassador was Lord Lyons, a shy, over-cautious bachelor said to keep an excellent chef and the finest carriages in Paris.

Leonard and Jennie arrived in one carriage, Mrs Jerome, wearing an elegant grey silk dress with fancy trimmings, with Clara and Leonie in another, and the ceremony was performed in the ambassadorial residence. St Michael's Church, formerly used as the Embassy chapel, had been closed fifteen years previously, but neither Jennie (for whom attendance at church had never been important) nor Randolph seems to have considered this a cause for concern. There were two distractions Jennie might have been aware of. One was from a crowd of young American women who invaded the Embassy in order to get a close look at their successful countrywoman. The other was from the second floor, which in 1874 was being used as a maternity ward for the pregnant wives of those immediately connected with the Chancellery. This was because of legislation passed in the aftermath of the Franco-Prussian War that all male children born in France were to be eligible for military service. A wave of panic followed and so the Embassy, which counted as British territory, was pressed into service as a hospital.

Jennie walked up the makeshift aisle to where Randolph and Francis Knollys, his best man, were already standing. The family were seated around the altar as the marriage was solemnised by the Rev. Edward Forbes, Chaplain to the Embassy, a man the Jeromes probably knew from their time in Paris during the siege when he acquired a reputation as a good and faithful preacher.

Then, not being quite married [Leonie's account continued], she took Papa's arm and went with him to the American Legation. The service was performed again [with the Rev. Forbes officiating again] and then Randolph and Jennie drove off together to the house where our friends came to attend the wedding breakfast. The drawing rooms were full of white flowers. Randolph and Jennie had their breakfast upstairs in a little drawing room by themselves – an Embassy custom. When everyone was present, they came down but not for long as Jennie had to change into a very pretty dark blue and white striped dress for travelling and white hat with a white feather. At two she bid us goodbye. A beautiful carriage with four grey horses and two postilions on a carriage waited to carry them off to a chateau near Paris called Petit Val. Before four, we were alone.[58]

The Château de la Petit Val had been lent to them by Mrs Charles Moulton, the former Lillie Greenough. Just before she departed Leonard gave his favourite daughter a parasol of Alençon lace with a delicate gold and tortoiseshell handle. There cannot have been much of a celebration if the first service began at 11.15 and Jennie and Randolph had left by 2 p.m. But Jennie's feelings on this day she kept to herself. Frustratingly, like so much in the letters between the sisters over the next three decades, Leonie's account of the wedding is full of details about her outfits and her parasol, even her carriage. Of her emotions, her expectations or her anxieties, of the enormous mutual love and need for each other, there is nothing.

Strangely, perhaps, the British Embassy has no written evidence, in the form of a certificate or signed book, as testimony that the marriage of Randolph Churchill and Jennie Jerome ever took place. But the Legation of the United States in Paris did keep a formal document, now retained in a bound volume of all such certificates, signed by the Envoy Extraordinary and Minister Plenipotentiary for France, Elihu Benjamin Washburne. Normally the American Legation would permit official ceremonies only if both participants were American citizens. In a case such as this, where only one participant was American, there had to be first a ceremony that would be recognised by the host country, which in this case was deemed to be Britain.

The family kept a list of the grandest presents, which included a gold Russian coffer from the Prince of Wales. The Duke and Duchess of Marlborough sent a fine ruby and diamond ornament with pearl pendant and the Marquis and Marchioness of Blandford three Queen Anne silver bowls. As Randolph had written to his mother on 14 April: 'There are some other presents coming in today but I don't know what. We have not many but they are all vy good.'[59]

4

Jennie is Quite Satisfied with
Randolph Just Now

~

JENNIE BECAME A mother when she was still a child herself. She was
to grow up in her marriage. After a two-week honeymoon in the
Moultons' beautiful château just outside Paris, she and Randolph returned
to England and, on a beautiful spring day in early May 1874, went directly
to Blenheim for a short stay. Some of the Duke's tenants and Randolph's
constituents made up a party at the station to greet the young couple, then
dragged them, once again by horseless carriage, slowly through the town
so that everyone could get a look at this unknown American bride.

Jennie had been a town dweller all her life. However hard she tried to
prepare herself, she could not have imagined the chilly rigour of daily existence in this most stunning of English palaces. The Royal Manor of
Woodstock, just outside Oxford, had been given to John, first Duke of
Marlborough, leader of the Allied forces, by a grateful Queen Anne in
1705. It was his reward for heroic services in battle, saving Vienna from a
French invasion. The Queen promised him a palace, to be built at her own
expense and called Blenheim, in honour of the site of the decisive battle.
It was intended to rival Versailles, the glorious residence of Louis XIV, the
Sun King. Work on the vast castle, as it was originally called, began with
Sir John Vanbrugh appointed chief architect and Nicholas Hawksmoor his
assistant; Capability Brown was engaged to design the magnificent land-
scaped gardens and Grinling Gibbons, chief mason, the ornamented
towers. Of course, it all took longer and cost more than anyone had originally envisaged or was prepared to provide, and it was embroiled in political
intrigue. But, once completed, the dramatic triumphal archway leading to
the Great Court, the Column of Victory with its statue of the first Duke
and the grand bridge across the lake were all without equal in the country,
as George III remarked when he visited.

More than a century later, when Randolph brought Jennie to his family
home, little had changed. 'As we passed through the entrance archway and
the lovely scenery burst upon me,' wrote Jennie in her *Reminiscences*,
'Randolph said, with pardonable pride, "this is the finest view in

England."' She went on: 'Looking at the lake, the bridge, the miles of magnificent park studded with old oaks, I found no adequate words to express my admiration and when we reached the huge and stately palace where I was to find hospitality for so many years I confess I felt awed. But my American pride forbade the admission.' Jennie, writing more than thirty years later, recalled with honesty this clash of pride, embedded deep in the marriage from its earliest days, an expression of self-knowledge that had doubtless become clearer over the years. 'I tried to conceal my feelings, asking Randolph if Pope's lines were a true description of the inside.' As she saw her new parents-in-law waiting to greet her on the magnificently broad steps, did she really recite to her new husband the sixteen lines she quotes in her *Reminiscences*?

> See, Sir, here's the grand approach:
> This way is for his grace's coach:
> There lies the bridge, and here's the clock
> Observe the lion and the cock
> The spacious court, the colonnade
> And mark how wide the hall is made!
> The chimneys are so well design'd
> They never smoke in any wind.
> This gallery's contrived for walking,
> The windows to retire and talk in;
> The council chamber for debate
> And all the rest are rooms of state
> 'Thanks, sir,' cried I, ''tis very fine,
> But where d'ye sleep and where d'ye dine?
> I find by all you have been telling,
> That 'tis a house, but not a dwelling.'[1]

But of course Pope never knew the inside of Blenheim as Jennie came to know it. Her description of life there provides some of the most entertaining passages in her book. She had already, briefly in Paris, met the Duke and Duchess as well as two of Randolph's six sisters. But living among them in the icy corridors and vast state rooms of Blenheim was the stuff of fiction. She noticed every aspect of the strange ritual that was their daily life with the fresh and quizzical eyes of an intelligent outsider and gave an understated account of their rigid formality.

In her memoir, she described Randolph's parents as 'dignified'. The Duke was 'extremely kind and had the most courteous and *grand seigneur* appearance and manner', she said. The Duke appealed to Jennie partly because of the pleasure he took in the magnificent treasures housed at

Blenheim. She even retold one of his favourite anecdotes about an earlier duke telling the French Ambassador that some stone trophies and an effigy of Louis XIV had been *taken* not *given*. His wife, Frances Anne, Duchess of Marlborough, granddaughter of the brilliant and determined Foreign Secretary and diplomat of Vienna Viscount Castlereagh, was a different matter. Jennie wrote that her mother-in-law was 'a very remarkable and intelligent woman with a warm heart, particularly for members of her family, which made up for any over-masterfulness of which she might have been accused'. But of all her children it was only Randolph whom the Duchess truly adored. It was she, according to Jennie, 'who ruled Blenheim and nearly all those in it with a firm hand. At the rustle of her silk dress the household trembled.'[2] Yet, her own marriage to the future seventh Duke, had been against the wishes of his father.

When the family was alone there was a steely, barren regularity to the day which forced Jennie to practise the piano, read or paint so assiduously:

> that I began to imagine myself back in the schoolroom. In the morning, an hour or more was devoted to the reading of newspapers, which was a necessity if one wanted to show an intelligent interest in the questions of the day for at dinner conversation invariably turned on politics. In the afternoon a drive to pay a visit to some neighbour or walk in the gardens would help to while away some part of the day. After dinner, which was a rather solemn full dress affair, we all repaired to what was called the Vandyke room. There one might read one's book or play for love a mild game of whist. Many a glance would be cast at the clock, which sometimes would be surreptitiously advanced a quarter of an hour by some sleepy member of the family. No one dared suggest bed until the sacred hour of eleven had struck. Then we would all troop out into a small anteroom and, lighting our candles, each in turn would kiss the Duke and Duchess and depart to our own rooms.[3]

With the passage of time, Jennie is able to tell this deadpan. It's not hard to imagine how this twenty-year-old free spirit was screaming inwardly.

Mealtimes, the solid pillars of each day, were of particular fascination for Jennie. 'At luncheon rows of entrée dishes adorned the table, joints beneath massive silver covers being placed before the Duke and Duchess, who each carved for the whole company and as this included governesses, tutors and children, it was no sinecure.' Jennie poked fun at the prudish governesses who, sitting primly between their charges, were, she insisted, more interested in the meat than in the heirlooms adorning the walls. Nor did any of the family seem to notice the fabulous pictures. Before leaving the dining room, 'the children filled with food small baskets kept for the purpose for poor cottagers or any who might be sick or sorry in Woodstock. These they distributed in the course of their afternoon walks.' That the tepid leftovers – savoury or sweet, gravy and custard – were all mixed together condescendingly and disgustingly into one basket, seemed of no concern to anyone.

When the house was full for a shooting party – Blenheim was known for its abundance of snipe – even breakfast, with its vast array of dishes and courses, became an occasion for ceremony; no one dreamed of beginning until all had assembled. In her memoir, Jennie admits to 'laughing immoderately' one morning when Lady Wilton, appearing in a gown of electric-blue velvet and being asked who made it, said with conscious pride, 'It's a Stratton,' as one would say, 'It's a Vandyke.'[4] For Mrs Stratton, one of the fashionable English dressmakers of the day, was no Worth.

In private, Jennie was scathing to her family not only about the fashions she encountered at Blenheim but about the whole atmosphere. Even tea was an elaborate ritual that occupied an hour or more of exchanging empty civilities until the hostess, who, Jennie says tartly, wore a lace cape if middle aged, 'gave the signal to rise, uttering the invariable formula "I am sure you must need a little rest"'. The guests, once immured within their rooms, were not to reappear until the dining hour. However little they wanted rest, however bored by their own society or disturbed by the unpacking maid, there they were supposed to remain.

One October day, she told her mother, she found the drawing room full of people taking tea. 'I escaped as soon as I could. You cannot imagine how stiff and uncomfortable the first hour of their arrivals are. No one knows each other and so content themselves with staring. Tonight I suppose will be like last night, some playing whist or billiards or working. You can't imagine what gossip and slander people talk. Really to my discreet ears it seems quite incredible – everyone is pulled to pieces and it is not only the women who back bite . . .'[5] Jennie loathed the boring aimlessness of a shooting party, which left the women in their unsuitable trailing tweeds and enormous bird's-nest hats to trample through turnip fields after the shooters with nothing to do but gossip to each other. As a protest, she would often make her appearance deliberately late. She was not alone in her dislike of shooting parties, especially when dresses got spattered with the blood of dead or wounded birds.

Jennie's lively published account of life in Blenheim was based on much more than the brief visit she paid in the immediate aftermath of her honeymoon. Although she and Randolph never made their home there, they were frequent visitors for extended periods, especially in the early days of the marriage or when money was short or when Randolph fell ill. But in May 1874 she and Randolph settled in London, in the four-storey rented house Randolph had organised in Mayfair. They were just in time for the beginning of the season, which ran until late July, at which point everyone decamped to their country estates. Jennie, a newcomer, was plunged into a 'whirl of gaieties and excitement' – her description of the frivolous side of late-Victorian society. She was the source of much admiration and gossip. Clara, approaching twenty-five, took to staying with them for weeks at a time and it is often her letters to Mrs Jerome, back in Paris, which, although intensely trivial and mostly concerned with what frocks she and her sister wore and other superficialities, give the most vivid picture of Jennie's new life. It appears as if one ball followed another, many of them lasting until five a.m., with little but tea and froth in between. Jennie always loved dancing.

The Curzon Street house was soon looking very nice, Clara thought, as Jennie found her métier 'twisting the furniture' to give it an individual look. Jennie begged her mother to send her some photographs of her own family so that the house was not entirely filled with things from Randolph's family, and she organised twice-weekly deliveries of plants and flowers.

Almost immediately, London society was vying for an opportunity to inspect her. Jennie took to hosting regular tea parties herself. One of the first to call was Lady Londonderry, a new relation by marriage, followed by Lord Grey de Wilton and Lady Grey, the Hardwickes and the Misses Cust, who all wasted little time before paying court. Invitations were received from the Countess of Derby, Lady Granville and Mr Christopher Sykes, 'who has invited us to meet H.R.H.'. But, as Clara ruefully reported, there were some they could not accept as 'Randolph does not care to.'[6]

One day in May, Randolph's mother, the Duchess, along with daughters Rosamond and Fanny, came for tea. Fanny was 'monstrously dressed . . . She is most ugly but such a get up. Imagine a green dress, rather bright, with pink accessories and cravat, as well as lots of gold ornaments and a black veil like the "araignées",' said Clara. A few weeks later she reported that even though the Duchess 'is very kind to me . . . I can see she is at times rather jealous of me and Jennie'.[7] The one guest the girls welcomed wholeheartedly that month was their father, Leonard Jerome, with whom 'we had a nice little dinner and evening'.[8]

But although Jennie talks of enjoying her first season 'with all the vigour and unjaded appetite of youth',[9] soon Clara had to attend some of the almost nightly balls on her own, which was not nearly as much fun. 'If only Jennie had been there it would have been perfect,' she told her mother, describing a magnificent ball at Chiswick House, at which she was accompanied by Clementine, Lady Camden, Randolph's newly widowed young aunt. 'Jennie was not well enough to go. It was too bad as I did not enjoy myself much without her. We stayed rather late at the ball last night. Jennie danced too much, which made her feel very tired today.'[10] Seymour Leslie, one of Jennie's nephews, annotated this later: 'Winston on the way', and it seems likely that, six weeks after her wedding, Jennie was suffering from morning sickness. Although she does not refer to that specifically she does report feeling very tired, another symptom of pregnancy.

On 2 July Clara tried to allay her mother's fears: 'you must not think that we are at all fast. In fact, we are very humdrum and stay a great deal at home. Jennie, you see, can't go out really very much.'[11] By mid-July, according to Clara, Jennie, in her grey tulle, was not dancing at all. 'She looked so funny sitting up with the Chaperones.'[12] However, she was evidently managing to hide her pregnancy well, for, as she told her mother at the end of June, 'Clara looked so pretty in her blue tulle the other night but I don't think cuirasses are becoming to her. She looked much more in the family way than I still do.'[13] Since she had been married a mere ten weeks previously, why would she expect to look 'in the family way' at all? In another undated note Clara told her mother: 'Jennie is sorry she did not have a loose *casaque* made instead of the tight fitting jacket.'[14]

Clara was soon writing to her mother about the new house, 48 Charles Street, which the Duke of Marlborough was buying for Randolph and Jennie for ten thousand pounds. But Clara suddenly interrupted her description, 'as Jennie always complains of my telling all the news and leaving nothing for her to say'.[15] Eventually Jennie filled in the details. After apologising for not having written in ages – tiredness the main reason 'and I know Clara gave you all the news' – she goes on to tell her mother all about the house:

> [It is] in a charming situation, très chic and just three houses from Berkeley Square . . . I am so delighted to have a fixed abode at last and it is such a nice house . . . although they asked £12,000 for it after a good deal of fuss they let it go for £10,000.
>
> We only mean to furnish for the present 2 bedrooms and a sitting room downstairs, which we shall also use as a dining room. I do so hope Papa will be able to give me the £2,000 he promised. I know it would be impossible for him to do it now but perhaps he might later and of course he must not send it all at once but gradually and if convenient. There is one good thing:

we have our batterie de cuisine and china, glass and plate and linen, all things which are expensive . . .

In every way this is a very good thing, buying this house. Randolph had no settlements made on him when he married and this of course makes a settlement. If anything were to happen to him, this house comes to me.

Jennie then turned to making arrangements for the rest of the summer with her mother. She had just made up her mind to spend the whole of August at Deauville, and thought they might have the new house painted and cleaned while they were away. 'Although I should be delighted to pass September in Paris with you, I think I had better be in London till after my confinement,' she added.[16] If Jennie had been expecting her baby in January, nine months from April, then her decision not to be away in September is puzzling. But it makes sound sense if the baby was actually due in the autumn.

Clara often sent rather plaintive accounts of her London life to her mother. She grumbled about not having met a single nice young man because the dinners were usually full of old men and dukes. 'En fait d'hommes [as far as men are concerned],' she remarks conspiratorially in French, 'Jennie is quite satisfied with Randolph just now. Mais cela ne me suffit pas.' She knows she ought not to complain, 'as I amuse myself a great deal more than I would at home at this time of year'.[17] Presumably her situation as the elder, unmarried sister was irksome on occasion. She was astute enough to notice the mores whereby men flirted only with married ladies, with whom an affair was acceptable. To flirt with single women was fraught with danger. Another time she is more cheerful, saying of a ball at the Duchess of Buccleuch's where the hostess asked only about 200 people, 'I know I must have looked swell as I had at least four partners, including Lord Carrington, who was very nice to me . . .'[18] Clara understood the problem clearly enough: the Duchess wanted to ensure that her own daughters found suitable husbands before she did:

The dinner last night was a dreadful bore. I can't tell you how rude the Duchess was. Of course she asked lots of nice young men, [Lord] MacDuff, Lord Cameron . . . And after dinner did not introduce a single man to me and as Jennie did not know them of course she could not introduce me so I sat with Lord Portarlington [Randolph's newly widowed uncle] and after he left I was quite alone . . . The Duchess . . . is so jealous . . . it is the very last time I ever go there although she pretends to be so proud of me.[19]

But the Duchess had her good side too, as indeed Jennie recognised when she was formally presented to Queen Victoria at a drawing room, an occasion which made her dreadfully frightened, she told her mother. The family went off together – Lady Blandford as well as Cornelia and Clementine – in the family coach with a coachman and two footmen. The Duchess 'was very kind and lent me some rubies and diamonds, which I wore in my hair [a fashion Jennie made her own] and my pearls on my neck. I also had a bouquet of gardenias.' The Duchess herself wore black with a great diamond and a tiara of black pearls. Just as Jennie was making her curtsies to the Queen, 'I reached to kiss her hand . . . she pulled me towards her and kissed me, which proceeding so bewildered me that I kissed her in return and made several little bobs to the other royalties instead of curtsies. But the prince and princess shook hands with me and all the others.'[20]

Jennie and Clara had arrived in London just as the lavish ball, often with a thousand or so guests, various entertainments and meals, reached unparalleled heights of opulence and extravagance. The Prince of Wales, in his unceasing pursuit of pleasure, lived far beyond his means at Marlborough House in the Mall. Originally built for the first Duke of Marlborough and occupied by that family until 1817, this magnificent house had been settled on the Prince of Wales to be his official residence when he reached eighteen. It ran on eighty-five servants, four of whom were permanently employed polishing silver, plus forty or so more looking after the stables, even when there were no balls. The house gave its name to the pleasure-loving set which indulged itself with the Prince. Hostesses, knowing the Prince's penchant for dressing up, vied with each other in ostentation and magnificence at the masked balls they organised.

One of these which particularly appealed to Jennie, and which she describes in *Reminiscences*, was at Holland House:

Disguised in a painted mask and a yellow wig I mystified everyone. My sister, who was staying with us, had been walking in the garden with young Lord —— who was a *parti* [a good match] and much run after by designing mothers with marriageable daughters. Introducing him to me she pretended I was her mother. Later in the evening I attacked him, saying that my daughter had just confided to me that he had proposed to her and that she had accepted him. To this day I can see his face of horror and bewilderment. Vehemently he assured me that it was not so. But I kept up the farce declaring that my husband would call on him next day and reveal our identity and that meanwhile I should consider him engaged to my charming daughter. Deficient in humour and not overburdened with brains, he could not take the joke and left home a miserable man.[21]

Jennie, with her fondness for practical jokes, found the English generally 'dull-witted' at a masked ball and took it upon herself to shake up some of the turgidity. 'They do not enter into the spirit of intrigue, which is all-important on such occasions.'

At the time of her arrival on the social scene there were very few Americans in London: Consuelo Yznaga, the Duchess of Manchester, Minnie Stevens, Lady Paget and Lady Carrington were all friends of hers. But there was enormous ignorance about American women, whose 'habits and manners were something between a Red Indian and a Gaiety Girl. Anything of an outlandish nature might be expected of her.' With London society having so little opportunity to meet Americans they were considered disagreeable and even dangerous, to be viewed with suspicion if not avoided altogether. 'Her dollars were her only recommendation,' Jennie wrote of the typical visiting heiress.

> And each was credited with the possession of them, otherwise what was her *raison d'être*? No distinction was ever made among Americans. They were all supposed to be of one uniform type. The wife and daughters of the newly-enriched Californian miner swathed in silks and satins and blazing with diamonds on the smallest provocation; the cultured, refined and retiring Bostonian; the aristocratic Virginian as full of tradition and family pride as a Percy of Northumberland or a la Rochefoucault; the cosmopolitan and up-to-date New Yorker, all were grouped in the same category and all were considered tarred with the same brush.[22]

But the influx of American brides was welcomed by the Prince of Wales. He explained that he liked American women because 'they are livelier, better educated and less hampered by etiquette . . . not as squeamish as their English sisters and better able to take care of themselves'.[23] Clara reported to her mother that 'people always seem to ask us [to parties] whenever H.R.H. goes to them. I suppose it is because Jennie is so pretty.'[24] It wasn't only that. Jennie seemed to know instinctively where to draw the line between respect and a flirtatiously witty riposte. The Prince once said, observing that the young Churchills did not have their own carriage to collect them but relied on 'a common cab', which on this occasion was extremely dilapidated, that her conscience was better than her carriage. 'It is not, sir,' Jennie shot back. 'The Queen's carriage? How can I have a better?'[25] (Public conveyances were dubbed 'the Queen's carriages'.)

In her memoir, Jennie refers neither to the balls which she was not well enough to attend that first season nor to the balls which Randolph did not wish her to attend. But the big fancy-dress ball at Marlborough House itself on 22 July 1874, for which 1,400 invitations were sent out, was one that neither of the Jerome sisters graced with their presence, a source of much upset. According to Clara:

> Jennie got a letter from Oliver Montagu yesterday saying that he was charged to arrange the Quadrille for the Fancy Dress ball and that H.R.H. wanted Jennie and I very much to dance in it. Jennie is to be Queen of Clubs according to H.R.H. and will dance with the King of Diamonds being the Duke of Atholl and I the Seven of Hearts to dance with Lord MacDuff as Seven of Spades. But Randolph is furious that the Prince should send us word through Montagu and not Francis Knollys, besides which he says it will be a great expense as the dresses cannot cost less than £15 a piece. R says he won't let us go. I think it is too bad as it would be very lovely. Only 24 ladies had he asked . . . I do hope R will change his mind but he is so obstinate . . . Tomorrow night we are all dining at Lady de Rothschild's grand dinner . . . they say there are going to be three other fancy balls, but if we don't go to Marlborough House we shan't be able to go to any.[26]

Clara's fears that the invitations would dry up if they did not attend Marlborough House were, of course, not realised. Within months, Jennie told her mother she had attended so many balls that, in spite of the size of her trousseau, 'I don't know what to wear' – the age old cry – 'as I have already worn all my dresses 2 or 3 times . . . I am in difficulty about my tulles. I have worn and worn them so much that they are about finished and you know how careful I am.'[27]

Randolph, disliking this frenetic socialising himself, tried to curtail the two women who, in spite of their rigorous education, relished such constant froth. Here is breathless Clara again: 'Lord Hartington took me to lunch in a private room with the royalties, the prince himself giving his arm to Jennie . . . Jennie took her Sir William Cumming all to herself, he being the swell of the party and does not let anyone else talk to him . . . Sir Cumming [sic] . . . began très sérieusement à faire la coeur to Jennie last night . . . there was a party for the Prince and Princess of Prussia. We came away about three o'clock escorted by a whole troop of men.'[28]

Clara did not have to be particularly astute to observe the flirtatious behaviour of Sir William Gordon-Cumming. Well known for his overtures to many women, he was always to find Jennie's beauty especially irresistible. 'I wonder if Leonie tried to protect Jennie from Papa, he being so awfully in love with Jennie. Hence Papa being beastly to Leonie,' is the mature view of Gordon-Cumming's youngest daughter.[29] But the man was later disgraced, and made a social outcast, after being accused of cheating. The events took place at Tranby Croft in Yorkshire where the Prince was staying for the race week at Doncaster. Gordon-Cumming sued some of the other players for slander and the Prince, subpoenaed as a witness, was strongly censored by the press for indulging in the lowest type of gambling. Baccarat, much enjoyed by the Prince and his circle, was illegal at this time.

Besides these endless balls, which obliged her to get some of her dresses remodelled, and the risqué behaviour which demanded careful chaperoning, what else was there to occupy Jennie? Life in London was much more carefully regulated than even the Jerome girls had been accustomed to in Paris. She had thought that as a married woman, without her mother's eager eyes on her constantly, she would be able to emancipate herself entirely. She soon learnt, however, that a lady never travelled alone without taking her maid with her in the railway carriage. 'To go by oneself in a hansom was thought very "fast"' – an adjective soon applied in whispers about Jennie. 'As for young girls driving anywhere by themselves, such a thing was unheard of.' As an accomplished horsewoman she could not fail to have been impressed by the midday riding in Rotten Row. But her immediate pregnancy made it unlikely, however much she yearned to partake, that she did much of this herself in 1874. She would have had to make do with being driven, or perhaps walking, slowly up and down each side, always accompanied, admiring the fashionable world which congregated there. For Jennie, seeing other women mounted on thoroughbred hacks in their close-fitting, tight-braided habits, showing off slim figures to their best advantage, would have been like swallowing poison. The strict observance of Sunday in London, a day of deliberate gloom and depression, was another torment for her.

There was horse-racing, a familiar activity for Jennie. At Ascot in 1874, wearing her slightly remodelled white satin wedding dress, with a bonnet of pink roses and the parasol of Alençon lace, she was much commented upon. In those days Parisian fashions made their appearance in London about two years after they were *à la mode* in Paris. And there were the first stirrings of political life. As he walked into the House of Commons Randolph himself heard a less than encouraging shout: 'There's a rum specimen.'[30] The heckler was presumably referring to his dandified appearance, a source of comment even among his friends. Randolph was known for coloured shirts, occasional tan shoes and an excess of jewellery – Jennie had given him a large diamond ring in the shape of a Maltese cross – as well as his slicked-down hair and trimmed moustache.

At all events, on 22 May 1874, Randolph delivered his maiden speech in the House of Commons. His performance did not augur well. He had spoken in angry tones about the possibility of 'roistering soldiers' occupying a military camp outside Oxford. Disraeli, the seventy-year-old Prime

Minister, thought the content was of no consequence. What mattered, as he wrote reassuringly to the Duchess, was that 'he spoke with fire and fluency; and showed energy of thought and character . . .'[31] Others were less convinced. The *Oxford Times* deplored the bad taste and offensiveness of the Member for Woodstock's maiden speech; Sir William Harcourt, Liberal Member for Oxford, pointed out that a Churchill should not condemn soldiery, and Henry Lucy, *Punch* Parliamentary critic, said, 'the young member was so nervous, his voice so badly pitched, his delivery so faulty that there was difficulty in following his argument. But here and there flashed forth a scathing sentence that made it worthwhile to attempt to catch the rest.'[32]

Of greater concern perhaps for his ambitious wife was that Randolph himself appeared less than enchanted by a political career. Jennie described his Parliamentary appearances at the time as 'perfunctory' and began small-scale entertaining herself. She was not about to compete with the lavish receptions at the Marlboroughs' London home in St James's Square, for which her mother-in-law was renowned. At her own dinners there was an interesting mix of literary people and politicians. She invited both Disraeli and the Prince of Wales. They accepted for the quality of conversation rather than the food. The latter was an area in which Jennie, who thought she could leave it all to the chef, had much to learn. At the first dinner party she gave she was shocked to see the meat, intended as the entrée, arrive floating in the soup, while the poached eggs intended for the latter appeared in solitary grandeur alongside. She was a fast learner. But while Randolph could provide political introductions at the highest level, it was Jennie's warmth and vivacity as a hostess which smoothed his rough edges and made their dinners sparkle.

As the summer gave way to autumn she spent more time quietly in the country at Blenheim Palace where her slowly swelling stomach prevented her from doing very much at all. Pregnancy at that time meant withdrawing from society. For Jennie that in turn meant more time with the Duchess. The two women would have been forced to spend many an afternoon in each other's company. Over the years, the older woman's attitude veered between severe criticism and intense motherly concern. It was not simply that Jennie had won the heart of a favourite son, nor that Frances Marlborough, born in 1822, was an old-fashioned Victorian matriarch with entrenched moralistic virtues and a strongly developed sense of duty. While the timing of Jennie's pregnancy was probably never discussed, it is more than likely, having had at least eleven pregnancies herself and as the mother of six daughters, that the Duchess would simply have known how far advanced her new daughter-in-law was in her pregnancy. The belief that her son was marrying a woman whose morals allowed her to have sex before marriage, an opportunistic woman whose talents, accomplishments, clothes and beauty far outshone those of her own daughters, in short, a foreign intruder, would not have endeared her.

But on Monday, 30 November, at 1.30 a.m., Jennie gave birth to her first child, in a room on the ground floor just beyond the Great Hall, which was speedily made ready for her. There are conflicting reports about what exactly brought on the birth. According to some accounts she was dancing in the Palace when the pains started, others that she was out hunting in the park. It makes for a dramatic account to imagine her rushing away from one of her beloved balls while the other guests were still partying and just making it to the ground-floor room hastily prepared for a birth. Winston himself enjoyed the tease of his birth circumstances: 'Although present on that occasion I have no clear recollection of the events leading up to it,' was his standard comment. His mother never clarified the circumstances, although it was clear that her intention was to have the baby in London. It seems that, in spite of her ambivalent attitude to hunting, Jennie had in fact gone out with the guns several days earlier, on Tuesday, 24 November, according to Randolph, when she had had a fall. This was followed by 'a rather imprudent and rough drive in a pony carriage' back to the Palace which 'brought on the pains on Saturday night. We tried to stop them, but it was no use. They went on all Sunday.'[33]

Randolph explained to his mother-in-law in Paris: 'Of course no Oxford physician could come. We telegraphed for the London man, Dr [William] Hope, but he did not arrive till this morning. The country doctor is a clever man and the baby was safely born after about eight hrs labour. She suffered a good deal, poor darling, but was vy plucky and had no chloroform.' The boy was, he said within hours of the birth, 'wonderfully pretty . . . with dark eyes and hair' and 'healthy considering his prematureness'.[34] Today, a framed letter from Randolph to the clever country doctor, Frederick Taylor, thanking him for his services and enclosing a cheque for 25 guineas decorates the wall of this room, once allotted to Marlborough's domestic chaplain, Dean Jones. It is now the first point of call for the thousands of tourists who pay homage to Churchill at Blenheim. Dr Taylor subsequently moved to a successful London practice.

Early the next morning the bells of Woodstock Church rang to announce the arrival of a new Churchill. The baby was at this stage, and for some years to come, heir presumptive to the Marlborough dukedom. And there was the usual announcement in *The Times* of London: 'On the 30th

Nov., at Blenheim Palace, the Lady Randolph Churchill, prematurely, of a son.' The Duchess wasted no time in informing the Jeromes of 'dear Jennie's safe confinement' and of the birth of their first grandson. She assured them that Jennie 'could not be doing better' and told them how the pains began: 'we began to see that all the remedies for warding off the event were useless . . . the doctor only arrived at 9 a.m. this morning to find dear Jennie comfortably settled in bed and the baby washed and cleaned'.[35] Frances assured Clara that her daughter could not have better nursing care than that provided by Lady Camden and Lady Blandford, both mothers themselves, and that she herself would visit her 'by turns'.

The baby was to be called Winston after his Churchill ancestor, father of the first Duke, and Leonard after Jennie's father. From the first, he combined the attributes of both. Leonard was invited to be a godfather but it is not known if he accepted the honour. Randolph was aggrieved, after sending his father-in-law three telegrams of news, that Leonard apparently failed to reply. He cabled Mrs Jerome angrily: 'It is so unsatisfactory when people don't appreciate one's news.'[36] Lady Camden and Lady Blandford were both godmothers.

Clearly the parents were unprepared, but it is not clear just how unprepared. Mrs Jerome had already ordered some baby clothes from Paris, but the basic layette had to be borrowed from the local Woodstock solicitor's wife whose own baby had not yet arrived. A week after the birth Randolph was sent to London to make arrangements for nursery furniture and a cloak or pelisse for the baby. As was normal at the time, there is no account of Winston's birth weight – routine reporting of birth weight was not common until the twentieth century and not required by law until the mid-1950s – but three days later the Duchess described him as a healthy, pretty little child, adjectives rarely used for pre-term babies. Nowadays most premature babies, that is those born before thirty-one weeks' gestation, survive thanks to state-of-the-art, high-tech floodlit incubators or special care in a neonatal ward. None of this was available to Jennie. In the latter half of the nineteenth century a few six-week-premature babies did survive with luck and very careful nurturing. For example, when Alexandra, the Princess of Wales, gave birth to her first child in 1864, premature by some two months, he was described by his grandmother Queen Victoria as 'a poor little boy' who weighed barely four pounds. The baptism ceremony was to be delayed until the baby was 'full size'.[37] But there is no record of any extra support needed to ensure the survival of the new Churchill baby.

By 4 December, the baby was sleeping through the night with no sleeping draught. Jennie was, though, according to the fashion, encouraged not to breastfeed him but to allow her milk to dry up as quickly as possible. Whether she was consulted about this often rather painful process is unrecorded. The baby was passed on to a wet-nurse, of which, wrote the Duchess, there were 'masses . . . I truly think she will get on much faster than if she were in London. She is of such a placid disposition.'[38] Mrs Jerome replied politely that she was certain Jennie could not have been more comfortable in her own home, and that she hoped her daughter's confinement had not given the Duchess too much trouble and inconvenience.

Jennie remained with the Marlboroughs at Blenheim until Christmas. The baby was baptised in Blenheim Chapel on 27 December, then the family returned to their new home in Mayfair. Jennie by this time had engaged the comfortingly plump Mrs Everest, a forty-one-year-old widow (although there is no evidence of a Mr Everest having ever existed), whose heart and home was in Kent, to look after the baby. She became much more than nurse or nanny to Winston. She became his confidante. 'Mrs Everest it was who looked after me and tended all my wants, it was to her I poured out my many troubles both now and in my schooldays,' Winston was to write later.[39] To the day he died, he always had a picture of her hanging in his bedroom and in his youthful novel, *Savrola*, he writes of a nanny thus:

> She had nursed him from his birth up with a devotion and care which knew no break. It is a strange thing, the love of these women. Perhaps it is the only disinterested affection in the world. The mother loves her child; that is maternal nature. The youth loves his sweetheart; that, too, may be explained. The dog loves his master, he feeds him; a man loves his friend, he has stood by him perhaps at doubtful moments. In all these there are reasons; but the love of a foster mother for her charge appears absolutely irrational.

Jennie for the next decade at least, was to remain in the sparkling distance for this baby, a mother who, in a memorable phrase conjured out of glossy recall, 'shone for me like the evening star'. As she flitted in and out of Winston's childhood, either late back from a mud-spattered ride or late off to a perfume-soaked dinner engagement, she 'seemed to me a fairy princess; a radiant being possessed of limitless riches and power'.[40] It is a powerful and persistent image of Jennie. Others saw her differently.

The Jeromes came to visit as soon as they could, Leonard travelling from New York and Clara, separately, from Paris. When Leonard arrived,

Jennie and Randolph took him to the races, a successful outing as Randolph won £200 – always an important consideration to ensure the latter's good mood.

With the birth of this new grandson relations between Jennie and the Duchess improved superficially and Jennie felt accepted. But within a year of Winston's birth Jennie became engulfed in a debilitating family quarrel. It may not have been of her making but she was burnt severely by the scorn of her parents-in-law. Blandford, either trouble-making or flirting or both, had presented her with a beautiful piece of jewellery, a ring which, in apparent innocence, she showed to Frances. Livid, her mother-in-law pronounced that this was not destined for Jennie; it belonged to Albertha, Lady Blandford, whose marriage to her elder son had all but collapsed.

Without adequate outlets for his natural aggression, Randolph was easily embroiled. A furious row between the two brothers erupted. Jennie offered to return the ring, but it was too late. The Duke had by that time written to Randolph accusing him of behaving dishonourably and 'treacherously abusing the confidence which you yourself pretended you shared with your mother about Blandford'.[41] Randolph told his father that as long as such expressions remained in force 'further communications between us are not only in your remark useless but impossible'.[42]

Jennie, caught in the middle, behaved like a loyal wife. She apologised. She also thanked the Duke and Duchess for all their past kindnesses. Nonetheless she had, however unwittingly, been the cause of the row. She took full flak from the Duchess, who felt bitterly that Randolph's previously unquestioned devotion to his parents had been undermined by his devotion to his wife. The Duchess attacked her for daring to refer to the episode as a quarrel. 'It is much too serious for that. It is a bitter sorrow to find both our sons torn against us . . . Randolph has trampled over our affection . . . As for you, dearest Jennie,' she went on, 'time will prove to you that I have treated you as a daughter . . . though at times I may have thought you unwise I have not intended to offend or pass judgment on you. I wished to be more a mother than a mother-in-law and perhaps I was wrong . . .'[43]

Jennie was devastated by such self-justificatory ferocity. Writing to the Duchess she described the letter which Randolph had received from his father as 'such as no man should write to another'.[44] But Randolph, his dignity as a husband deeply offended, was 'quite decided to stand no impudence . . . from any of the family'.[45] At the end of the year Jennie escaped to Paris without Randolph or the baby to see her mother, do some skating and find some peace. Pouring balm, she advised her implacable husband to drop all his arguments. 'Why talk about or occupy yourself with it?'[46] In time, this particular fight was patched over. But relations with the Marlboroughs were never to be calm. There was worse to come.

5

I Quite Forget What It is Like to be
with People Who Love Me

~

IN RETROSPECT, THE dispute over the ring was merely a dress rehearsal for the disastrous argument which soon followed. This second quarrel had much more serious, longer-lasting and wider-ranging ramifications.

In October 1875, the under-employed Prince of Wales set off on a grand tour of India. The Prince took with him a number of personal guests as well as three chefs, a studgroom, a chaplain and the Duke of Sutherland's piper. When he suggested a detachment of Life Guards, his mother the Queen, who disapproved severely of his life of gambling and the turf, drew the line at that. After all, the House of Commons was paying the vast sum of £112,000 and the Indian Government contributing a further £100,000 for this expedition of dubious purpose. Although there would be plenty of state banquets, opportunities for pig-sticking, elephant- and tiger-hunting and present-exchanging, the main advantage of the visit was that it would occupy the thirty-four-year-old heir to the throne for several months.

Among the friends who went with him were Charlie Carrington, the third Baron, then unmarried, Francis Knollys, Randolph Churchill's best man and the Prince's close friend, Lord Aylesford, known as 'Sporting Joe', and Lady Aylesford's brother, Colonel Owen Williams, who returned early as his wife was dying. Lord Aylesford, too, made an unscheduled departure on hearing about the scandal that was rocking London society. His wife Edith was having a barely concealed affair with Jennie's maverick brother-in-law Lord Blandford. As soon as Edith's husband had left for India, Blandford took up residence with his horses at an inn near Packington Hall, the Aylesford house outside Coventry. From there the Marquis visited the hall 'not in an ordinary way, but surreptitiously . . .', according to Charles Russell QC, subsequently explaining matters to a House of Lords Committee of Privileges. Russell said that Blandford had passed many nights with Lady Aylesford and that the servants knew all about this.

Once news of the scandal broke, cables and telegrams awaited the royal party at every port of call. In Nepal, the Prince denounced Blandford as the greatest blackguard alive. Bertha, Lady Blandford, a woman of limited intellect and narrow experience with a penchant for practical jokes, made her feelings known in a different way. When her errant husband came late to breakfast one day, he lifted the lid from his plate to find, instead of a poached egg, a small pink baby doll.

At the beginning of 1876, Blandford and Lady Aylesford eloped. While her lover tried to organise a deed of official separation Lady Aylesford wrote to her mother-in-law, the Dowager Countess of Aylesford, explaining her actions and begging her to look after the children. The Duke of Marlborough was soon dragged in, too, in the vain hope that he might persuade his son to give up Edith Aylesford and avoid the great public scandal which would inevitably ensue if the case reached the divorce courts. What mattered was not that the affair was taking place – there was nothing unusual about that – but that it was publicly talked about and therefore betrayed a whole social class. Everyone had something to lose, some more than others.

Into this venture Randolph was soon inveigled, not entirely unwillingly. There were dark mutterings of a duel between Blandford and Edith's brother, although duelling had been illegal since the 1840s. At the end of February 1876 it seemed Randolph was having some success in calming his brother's passions. Aylesford appeared willing merely to separate from, and not divorce, his wife. She would then be granted an establishment of her own and allowed to retain her children. Had she been divorced she would have been totally ostracised from society.

But at this point Randolph himself took an irrevocable step. He believed that the Prince of Wales had, by inviting Sporting Joe to accompany him, deliberately encouraged this affair in order to draw attention away from his own, earlier liaison with the lovely Edith. Randolph was in possession of some letters written by the Prince to Edith which Edith had foolishly shown to Blandford, who had handed them over to Randolph. These letters indicated an indiscretion, if not a physical affair. Now Randolph intended to use them. He went to Princess Alexandra and threatened to produce them as evidence in court if Lord Aylesford went ahead with his divorce. He let it be known that 'he held the crown of England in his pocket'. This was blackmail. It was an extraordinary way to behave for one who was not a direct participant – indeed the two brothers had, a few months earlier, been fighting with each other. The threat ratcheted up the severity of the scandal by several degrees.

Randolph's involvement cannot simply be explained by his desire to defend the family honour. More likely, the Prince's fondness for Jennie was the reason he was so enraged. Whether or not the Prince had had his own affair with Edith Aylesford was not proven. But the letters were, according to the opinion of the Solicitor General, so damaging that 'if they ever came before the public YRH would never sit on the throne of England'.[1] Randolph's threat cast a particularly dark shadow as it came only months after the shocking Mordaunt divorce case, which had brought opprobrium on the Prince for writing similarly indiscreet letters. It had also resulted in the young wife, Harriet Mordaunt, who confessed that she had had sex 'often and in open day' with the Prince of Wales, being declared insane and put in an asylum. If the Prince were merely to be mentioned publicly in a divorce case it might encourage the perception of him as a philanderer. His sensitivity sharpened, he now demanded an apology or a duel. Randolph could not accept such a challenge from his Prince – a fact of which the latter was well aware. This made it, in Randolph's view, a cowardly suggestion. But he did offer to apologise to Princess Alexandra and appointed Lord Falmouth to stand as his second if the Prince appointed a nominee. 'The only apology which circumstances warrant my offering,' Randolph wrote to Lord Hardwicke, Master of the Buck Hounds, brought in as intermediary by the Prince.[2]

And then, just as the affair looked set to spiral dreadfully out of control, the participants started to back down. Before Aylesford returned from India, Blandford escaped to Holland, and the Queen herself, infuriated by this 'dreadful, disgraceful business', wrote that if the Prince of Wales insisted that the letters were harmless then so they were, whatever the Solicitor General thought about them. Nonetheless, it was of course better that this view was not put to the test in the courts.

With the Prince's return in May, things quietened down. He went very publicly to the opera, Verdi's *Un ballo in maschera*, with Princess Alexandra where he was loudly cheered. 'The whole assembly rose and it seemed as if the demonstrations of welcome would never cease,' according to *The Times*.[3] Aylesford, now understanding the royal ramifications if he sought to divorce Edith, in the end did not do so. Instead he went to live in Texas, took up farming – and drinking – and died at the age of thirty-five in 1885. Edith and Blandford lived together on the continent for some years and had a son, Bertrand, in 1881. But even after Aylesford's death, and Blandford's divorce from Bertha, they did not marry, while relations between Blandford and Randolph were edgy, at best, for the rest of their lives.

The significance of the Aylesford scandal for Victorian England was the way the case portrayed women's sexuality for the first time. For Jennie, the young mother, being plunged into this maelstrom of malice was to test every fibre of her resolve. She was nervous and fearful at the thought of a duel, but then she told Randolph, who had gone to Amsterdam to meet his brother, that she was 'boiling with rage'.

> You ask me what I think of yr father's 2nd epistle. I think it very bad. He is quite willing that you should do all in your power to prevent Blandford from disgracing himself and his family – but is not at all willing to take upon himself any of the responsibility or share any of the désagrément which must arise from being at open war with H.R.H. But my dearest, there are few as generous as you and not many brothers would risk what you are risking for one so worthless as B., tho he be yr only brother.[4]

Her unswerving loyalty to Randolph throughout the crisis was impressive. She well knew the risks involved and that ostracism from the Prince of Wales's circle was the likely result. Yet she insisted that she would not be weeping over exclusion from Marlborough House balls. She minded much more that she did not have Randolph with her. 'My own darling dear Randolph,' she wrote tenderly in April 1876, two years into their marriage, 'I wld give anything to have you here tonight. I feel so wretchedly – if we are to have all these ennuis do for heaven's sake let's go through them together. As long as I have you I don't care what happens.'[5] Insisting that he was starting to get bored by the whole business, Randolph promised that he would get back as quickly as he could. 'I am always thinking of you and the baby and wondering what you are doing . . .'[6]

For Jennie and Randolph, as well as for the principal protagonists, the affair had permanent consequences. The Prince of Wales declared them *personae non gratae*; not only would he not meet the Churchills at any house in London but he let it be known that he would not go to any establishment were they were received. One stalwart who loudly resisted the royal pressure was the Irish adventurer and former lieutenant in the 11th Hussars, John Delacour. Delacour, a debonair friend of Randolph's, who was to play another key role in Jennie's life a decade later, told the Prince: 'Sir, I allow no man to choose my friends.' It was a brave pose but perhaps not surprising for one who was no stranger to the divorce courts himself, having been named as co-respondent, but found not guilty of adultery, in May 1876.[7]

John Delacour was a man surrounded by scandal since his birth in 1841. His mother, a Galway beauty called Josephine Handcock, was mistress of Ulick John de Burgh, fourteenth Earl and first Marquis of Clanricarde, a former ambassador to Russia and a notoriously cruel absentee Irish landlord. Their illegitimate son was passed around among relatives, his name changing from John de Burgh to John Delacour, until, aged eleven, his natural mother died and he inherited a fortune from her estates. But he gambled on cards and horses and by the time he was twenty-one had lost most of it having been forced to relinquish his inheritance for a mere £4,500. By the time he rallied to Randolph's support in 1876 he had sold his commission in the army and devoted himself to London society and clubs.

Another loyal supporter was the American-born Duchess of Manchester, a schoolfriend of Jennie's, who reminded the Prince: 'I hold friendship higher than snobbery.' But there was a sting in the tail for Jennie. She was especially angry that the Prince had resorted to using Charles, Earl of Hardwicke – 'a nasty hateful creature . . . a man of that kind'.[8] Hardwicke, according to Randolph, was a troublemaker who invented things. Worse, he had 'made up to' Jennie, 'and last year', she reported, 'people saw us a great deal together'.[9] Now she was worried that if Randolph pursued a quarrel with him directly it might make people think 'that yr brouille is about anything else but Blandford's affair'. In these circumstances Jennie, who clearly had attracted Hardwicke's eye and had confided as much to Randolph, admitted her fear lest her own name be muddied. When Randolph encountered him by chance in Bond Street he gave Hardwicke 'one of my scowls' – the sort of prolonged look of vitriol that Randolph did so well, hoping for a row. But Hardwicke turned away. 'What a snake.'[10]

Amid such unpleasantness, the Churchills decided to go to America, to take stock. Randolph was, according to his loyal wife, in need of a little solace and distraction. He was also not well. No name is given for his malady yet, but from now on he was often unwell and in need of a rest cure. A heavy smoker in spite of Jennie's constant attempts to make him curtail the habit, he told her he was consulting the family doctor, Oscar Clayton FRCS, at his Harley Street rooms for a variety of ailments including rheumatism. Clayton advised a trip somewhere warm, such as Nice, gave him a sheaf of prescriptions, one of which Jennie took with her by mistake when she went to Paris to say goodbye to her family before the American trip, and said he wanted to see him two or three more times. 'Don't you go and spend too much money,' Randolph wrote to his wife in Paris.

Visiting America and the Jerome relatives was important for Jennie as she barely knew her native land and wished to show off her still new husband. But above all she needed to get away and be among her own people once again. One month she was the very heart of the Marlborough House set, the next she was ostracised entirely. They were accompanied to America by another of Randolph's good friends, W. H. 'Tommy' Trafford. Trafford was to become his most frequent travelling companion. In 1876, the Jerome name ensured that she was of greater interest than her husband, but still they could not escape the prying press eyes. A New York reporter wrote: 'He was then unknown to fame and, as he lounged in the doorway of Mr Jerome's house one summer morning smoking cigarettes, he was the picture of a brainless fop. He was small, nattily attired in lavender trousers, figured waistcoat and blue velvet smoking jacket and his mild eye stared at New York through a single glass . . . but his looks belied him.'[11]

They went first to Canada, 'where we seemed to spend most of the time eating melons and having cold baths so overpowering was the heat'.[12] Then she took Randolph to see her childhood home at Newport and, after that, to visit the Philadelphia Exhibition, where they were accompanied by her father's brother Lawrence Jerome, and then briefly on to New York. Leonard wrote to his daughter, 'I am so glad you and Randolph enjoyed your visit so much. I have never known one take so decidedly in our "new country" as Randolph.'[13] He was less impressed with Randolph's inability to write and thank a Jerome relation for some kindness shown and had to remind Jennie to do so instead.

While they were away a formal apology for the Prince of Wales was eventually drafted by the Lord Chancellor, which Randolph agreed to sign, fittingly, in Saratoga, the site of General Burgoyne's surrender to the Americans in 1777. On their return they learnt that the Duke of Marlborough had been appointed viceroy of Ireland, a position he had previously refused but now found imperative to accept. It was the only way of removing his family from the unpleasant position they now occupied in London society. Randolph was to act as the Duke's unpaid private secretary, unpaid in order that he might retain his seat in the House of Commons. Disraeli, elevated to the earldom of Beaconsfield in the middle of these negotiations, had strongly urged the family to accept, in spite of the huge expenses such a move would incur, as the only way to draw a line under the scandal.

The couple now began three years of exile which were to have dramatic consequences. But the experience gave the socially disgraced Randolph a chance for redemption. Had they remained in London where he had little to do but engage in quarrels, his bitterness against the superficiality of London society, 'which had now ceased to smile upon him',[14] might have prevented his subsequent political career from taking off in the way that it did, a view espoused by his son Winston. His friendship with the brilliant Tory lawyer Gerald FitzGibbon dates from this time. FitzGibbon's letters were to keep Randolph informed about Irish politics until the end of his life. Almost every Christmas, long after they had left Dublin, Randolph returned to FitzGibbon's famous Christmas house parties.

On a bitterly cold day in December 1876, the Duke and his son arrived in Dublin. The rest of the family followed, and early in January 1877 the Marlboroughs made their formal state entry. This was an event of great pomp and circumstance as the Duke, in uniform, rode with a glittering staff around him. The rest of the family, in carriages with postilions and out-riders, drove through the crowded streets to the black and grimy Dublin Castle. In addition to the Duke and Duchess, there was Jennie and Randolph with Master Winston, Sir Ivor and Lady Cornelia Guest and the three unmarried daughters, Lady Rosamond, Lady Georgiana and Lady Sarah Spencer-Churchill. Winston, not yet two when they moved, would retain his earliest memories of Ireland. For the next three years the family lived in the Little Lodge, a low white building with a verandah set in Phoenix Park, about a stone's throw from the magnificent Vice-Regal Lodge.

Here Jennie was once again thrown into intense proximity with her mother-in-law. This relationship – far more complex than the usual mother–daughter-in-law bond – was a source of both anguish and comfort from the start. It was to be tested to the extremities in the next few years as the two women were forced to live under each other's ever watchful eye. The two remarks so often quoted – Jennie's about the Palace trembling at the rustle of her skirts and the Duchess's about not wanting that 'Upstart Winston' to succeed to the title – disguise a much deeper understanding between them. The relationship should not be reduced to this. But on the surface, at least until 1897, lurked a real fear that if Blandford's son the Earl of Sunderland, known as Sunny, did not produce an heir then Winston would be next in line to succeed as duke of Marlborough. (Sunny was three years older than Winston.) The Duchess was deeply conscious of the family position: no other warrior family had survived in such state for so long. No Nelson, no Wellington, not even a Napier. If she was waspish about Winston, it was because she believed that he was, like his mother, lacking in decorum, and that he would exploit rather than preserve the dignity of the dukedom. Later, he would write a very full account of John Marlborough, into which he poured out his admiration and respect for the family, but she was not to know that – although she might have guessed that the initial impulse for it had been to make money.

Frances Marlborough was a woman of compassion and talent with a highly developed sense of *noblesse oblige*. She was one in a line of Marlborough duchesses with a streak of ruthlessness determined to uphold aristocratic values at a time when they were under threat as never before. She had taken into the heart of her family Clementine, the orphan daughter of her father-in-law by his second wife who had died in 1850, having herself suffered the death of a four-year-old son that year. Clementine, who had lived through the death of her elder brother Almeric when he was nine, was brought up as if she were Randolph's sister – she was just a year older – rather than his aunt.

When the Marlboroughs moved to Ireland *The Times* had spoken of it as a land of peace and prosperity. But this situation was to change dramatically while the Churchills were there. Home Rule, the process of allowing Ireland more say in how it was governed, came to dominate British politics from about 1870 onwards. The issue was given powerful impetus with the failure of the potato crop later that year. It was not long before sectarian terrorism, already smouldering, took fiery hold. While the liberal-minded Duke did his best travelling the country to support religious toleration for Catholics in the North by promoting land purchase for small farmers and better educational opportunities, the Duchess also worked hard at transcending the Catholic and Protestant divide, refusing to be influenced by anything other than need. Brimming with 'her usual energy' – as Jennie tactfully described it in her *Reminiscences* – the Duchess started an Irish Relief Fund in December 1879. As famine swept the country it was she with her constant charitable activities who proved effective in countering the image of an uninterested aristocracy. She insisted that her Famine Relief Committee should be non-sectarian, and was helped by the fact that, although avidly Protestant herself, her late sister had married the Earl of Portarlington and converted to Catholicism. She studied the failures of similar relief efforts in earlier famines and, in running the Committee, used the same organisational determination that so terrified the Blenheim servants. Her Fund ultimately brought in a total of £135,000, which was distributed in such a practical and businesslike manner that even the Nationalist press was obliged to praise the vice-regal endeavours. Jennie declared that the scheme added greatly to the popularity of the Duchess and that Queen Victoria awarded her the third class of the Victoria and Albert Order at the end of her time in Ireland.

Jennie travelled around the country on occasion with the Duke and Duchess, which opened her eyes to the 'heart rending poverty of the peasantry who lived in their wretched mud-hovels like animals'. But there is scant evidence that seeing such neglect and misery at first hand inspired her to undertake charitable work alongside the Duchess. Philanthropy in the form of handouts was not her style. Jennie and the Duchess, who was then in her mid-fifties, came from different worlds, united only by their love of Randolph. Frances Marlborough would never have been the sort of woman who could give Jennie the worldly advice she craved. Once Jennie was back in London, Mrs Fanny Ronalds, her father's one-time lover then living in Cadogan Place, was better able to do that. Mrs Ronalds, who never divorced, was the mistress of the composer Arthur Sullivan for some twenty years until his death in 1900. She and Jennie became close friends.

By comparison, it is easy to see how Jennie's pursuits, once they had decamped to Ireland and were under close scrutiny, appeared as pleasure-loving indulgence. The Duchess, Jennie considered, was spiteful. When Jennie found that her letters were being opened before she received them she was furious and complained to Randolph. But what could Randolph do?

It is so often assumed when the marriage of Jennie and Randolph is dis-cussed that money and rank were the principal motivations. But there was intense and passionate love between them in those years, an undercurrent of which never died but was transmuted into concern, duty and loyalty. 'I hope I am not very ill natured but it seems to me a terrible thing to marry a man caring so little for him,'[15] Jennie wrote to Randolph when she heard the news of his sister Rosamond's imminent engagement to Lord Fellowes (later Lord De Ramsey). Randolph considered the match 'an excellent thing for the general tranquillity of the family'.[16] Jennie, ever romantic, considered that the way her sister-in-law talked about her future husband behind his back was too awful. 'However, I daresay it will come all right and she is just the sort of woman to make a good wife once mar-ried.' She added, revealingly, that even if she did not care for him she would pretend to.

Jennie, still intensely in love with Randolph, felt unhappy and isolated in Ireland. Mrs Everest took full charge of the baby. He was brought down to her every day at teatime, as was the aristocratic wont. The rest of the day she spent occupying herself as best she could with singing lessons, playing the piano, drawing and painting. Clara still came for extended stays and, whenever she could, she used her as a model, until her sister got bored. 'I expect to improve myself wonderfully,' she said, trying to sound cheer-ful.[17] She was often alone either because Randolph was travelling with his father around Ireland or because he was in London to see his doctors or his bankers or to attend to Parliamentary business. Even Winston, when he came to write about this time, remarked on how often his parents were apart. 'She and my father hunted continually on their large horses,' he said, 'and sometimes there were great scares because one or other did not come back for many hours after they were expected'.[18]

Her letters strike a pitiful note; she just about 'gets through the day', she tells Randolph. She longs to have him back, misses him dreadfully and says she hates going to bed without him. 'Do you know, darling, this is the longest separation since our marriage and I hope the last.' In fact, she is so homesick without him that 'I don't think I can stand it much longer without you.'[19] She feels dull and blue when she thinks of all the fun going on in England but tries to convince herself that she is happier in Ireland than she would be over there.

She is especially jealous when she thinks of Fanny and Cornelia having tea with him. 'Do you remember the tea you gave me in Paris at the Hôtel de France . . .'[20] She tried unsuccessfully to rekindle the passion of their first year. 'Not once do you say you will be glad to see J again,' she tells him. 'I suppose c'est nous entendu but it is pleasant to be told so.'[21] The sisters understood her anxieties. 'Randolph was incapable of loving or noticing any human being as such. He admired his wife . . . but neither she nor her sons would ever hear the warm words for which they yearned,' is how Jennie's great-niece Anita Leslie described their relationship around this time.[22]

Notwithstanding her unhappiness in Ireland, she had no desire to venture into the London society from which she was now excluded and where 'really we have *so few* friends'.[23] When Rosamond's wedding was being planned she half hoped it would be in London so that she might have 'a tiny peep de cette ville enforcé'.[24] The one pursuit which gave her some independence – a little too much it sometimes seemed – was riding. As the pictures of her in riding habit show, Jennie at twenty-three, with whip in one hand, leather glove in the other, silk top hat and tiny waist, was devastatingly, dramatically good looking. Hunting in Ireland became a 'ruling passion', whether in the woods or open fields. She would beg, borrow or steal any horse she could find. Some of her best days with the Meath and Kildare Hounds she owed, she said, to a little brown mare she had bought in Oxford. She hunted – sometimes with Randolph, sometimes with Colonel Forster, Master of the Horse – with almost every pack of hounds in Ireland and was never to find hunting anywhere else as thrilling. And sometimes, inevitably as Randolph was so often in London, she went riding alone. While this led to conflict with her mother-in-law, her small son soon learnt a new song, 'We Will All

Go Hunting Today'.[25] One evening Jennie went to dine at the Vice-Regal Lodge only to be told by the Duchess 'with seeming great delight' that she had met Lord Rossmore driving through the park.[26] The Duchess first criticised her daughter-in-law for what she described as a silly flirtation, and then, writing to Jennie, concluded in her highly moral tone: 'I will say no more.'[27]

The fifth Lord Rossmore of Rossmore Park, Co. Monaghan, formerly Derrick Westenra, and a former officer in the 9th Lancers, one-time Grand Master of Monaghan Orangemen and a magistrate, owned an estate of nearly 15,000 acres yet he was by the 1880s virtually bankrupt owing to wasteful expenditure. He had no political influence in Ireland and was regarded by most as a semi-comical figure. As the second son, he had not expected to inherit, but his elder brother died suddenly in 1874. Rossmore knew how to ride a horse and was desperately attracted to Jennie.

In 1877, Jennie had to write begging Randolph's forgiveness because Rossmore had called in one day 'and I saw him, quite by mistake. I was annoyed because it was luncheon time and I had ordered lunch today, he did not stay long as I had ordered the carriage at 3. I told him he must not call here any more as living alone I could not excuse and could not make an afternoon for him . . .'[28] But they had quite a conversation before he finally left, some of which she reported to her husband, about deteriorating relations between the Rossmores and Marlboroughs. According to Jennie, the Duke had treated him and his family in such a way that 'nothing would ever induce them to speak to him again . . .'. A few days later she had to tell her husband: 'Poor Rossmore. I'm afraid he is making a fool of himself and it will end badly. I'm so sorry he is so cheery et tu sais mon faible pour lui.'[29]

And there the story might have ended. However, when Rossmore came to write his memoirs in 1912, a frothy book teasingly entitled *Things I Can Tell* (there was clearly much he could not tell), he described the first time he met Jennie, deliberately suggesting that this occurred after Randolph had died and she had remarried. 'I think the loveliest woman I have ever set eyes on . . . was Mrs Cornwallis-West,' he wrote disingenuously. 'The first time I saw her was at Ascot . . . suddenly my attention was arrested by the appearance of a lady who was accompanied by half a dozen men. I thought her the most beautiful creature imaginable, and dressed in white and wearing a big white hat she was perfectly delightful to look at and I cried out . . . "good heavens who's that?" "Why that's Mrs Cornwallis-West . . . nobody her equal."' He simply couldn't take his eyes off her, he admitted, and, determined to meet her, introduced himself, saying 'with true Derry daring: 'Come on, let's have a dance.' 'Well, and I will yer honour,' she replied with the most tremendous brogue.'

He described dancing with Jennie as 'seventh heaven . . . I must say that Mrs Cornwallis-West was enough to make any man forget everybody and everything.'[30] Rossmore's eulogy is probably genuine enough – except that at the time the introduction took place she was Jennie Churchill, the young wife of a politician whom she loved and who was jealous of his wife's admirers, of whom there were many. His alteration of the dates might indicate his need to conceal the storm that he knew he had caused.

In spite of her loneliness, Jennie maintained in public that her life in Ireland was 'very pleasant'.[31] Parts of it were. Sometimes Randolph brought nationalist politicians to dine at the Little Lodge and they laboured amiably to convert Lady Randolph to Home Rule. She was admired by many men in Ireland and in turn responded to the 'geniality and ready wit' of the Irish male. 'During the three years we lived there I cannot remember meeting one really dull man. From the Lord Chief Justice to the familiar carman, all were entertaining.'[32]

There was one who especially admired her at this time: Edgar Vincent, lately commissioned into the Coldstream Guards. Vincent, three years younger than Jennie, was a lowly subaltern, son of a rector, who happened to be stationed in Ireland at the time he first set eyes on her. Later he became well known as Sir Edgar Vincent, Viscount D'Abernon, financier, politician and diplomat, described by Margot Tennant (later Asquith) as among 'the four best looking men I ever saw'.[33] He was not only handsome, but brilliantly intelligent, a linguist, superb horseman, gambler, witty raconteur and, on account of his extramarital affairs, nicknamed 'the Piccadilly stallion'.[34] It is hardly surprising that his description of Jennie in Ireland, although written with the benefit of hindsight, is the one that has passed into mythology; his is the one to which her own son resorted to conjure up not just his mother's image in those days but her effect on men. 'I have the clearest recollection of seeing her for the first time,' the diplomat Lord D'Abernon wrote.

> It was at the Vice-Regal Lodge at Dublin. She stood on one side to the left of the entrance. The Viceroy was on a dais at the farther end of the room, surrounded by a brilliant staff, but eyes were not turned on him or on his consort but on a dark, lithe figure standing somewhat apart and appearing to be of another texture to those around her, radiant, translucent, intense. A diamond star in her hair, her favourite ornament – its lustre dimmed by the flashing glory of her eyes. More of the panther than of the woman in her look, but with a cultivated intelligence unknown to the jungle. Her courage

not less great than that of her husband – fit mother for descendants of the great Duke. With all these attributes of brilliancy, such kindliness and high spirits that she was universally popular. Her desire to please, her delight in life, and the genuine wish that all should share her joyous faith in it, made her the centre of a devoted circle.[35]

The myth is by now well established that Jennie was not a good mother, yet it was surely not by chance that Winston, in his first book of memoirs, chose a description of her that stated precisely her overarching genetic fitness to be a mother for descendants of the great Duke. The passage is an important one because it dramatically reveals her above all as a woman who challenged the dominant sexual morality- a wild woman of the jungle, an animal being who was powerful and threatening, as the Duchess surely recognised. A panther is both ferocious and predatory – what man dares confront such a wild and untameable beast? Yet D'Abernon is careful to add that Jennie is also kind, tries to please and delights in life. The animal imagery can be read in another way: could Jennie be at the same time a caged creature hounded and hunted by the aggressive attention of men?

Some defend Jennie's unmaternal behaviour as typical of aristocratic mothers of her day, leaving all daily care to the nanny. At least she had chosen as primary carer a woman of great sense and stability, who provided Winston with deep love and the constant attention he needed, in stark contrast to what he received from his glamorous mother. She tells Randolph of long walks she takes with Winston at this time – but then has to feel the wrath of the nanny for invading her territory. Proud as any mother, she sends Randolph occasional reports of the way Winston 'chatters 19 to the dozen as usual', about his teething problems, his outings to the circus and his need for new clothes. 'Everest has been bothering me about some clothes for him saying it was quite a disgrace how few things he has and how shabby at that . . .'[36] On another occasion she wrote: 'Winston has just been with me – such a darling he is – "I can't have my mama go – and if she does I will run after the train and jump in," he said to me. I have told Everest to take him out for a drive tomorrow if it is fine . . .'[37]

It was during his time at the Little Lodge that Winston was, in his inimitable phrase, 'first menaced with Education'.

The approach of a sinister figure described as 'the Governess' was announced . . . Mrs Everest produced a book called *Reading Without Tears* . . . I was made aware that before the Governess arrived I must be able to read without tears . . . I did what so many oppressed peoples have done in similar circumstances; I took to the woods. I hid in the extensive shrubberies – forests they seemed – which surrounded 'The Little Lodge'. Hours passed before I was retrieved and handed over to the Governess.[38]

Winston remembered the arrival of this dark figure as a time when a steadily gathering gloom spread over his life, and he had to abandon all the interesting things he wanted to do in the nursery or in the garden. 'My mother took no part in these impositions but she gave me to understand that she approved of them and she sided with the Governess almost always.'[39] It is significant that Winston never sought to blame his mother for unpleasant aspects of his childhood. His anger and resentment were always directed at others. Hence he became, as he said, 'a troublesome boy' or, in his mother's and grandmother's words, 'a most difficult child to manage'. His parents' love, however little they had for him, was sacrosanct. Nothing must be allowed to disturb the image he created of them. In time, this devotion to family was extended and all family ties, even loose ones, were hugged closely; authority was, crucially, to be challenged if not actively resented.

Mrs Everest – whom he took to calling Woom, an abbreviation of a childish attempt to say 'woman' – told him his first stories about the wicked Fenians. One day when he was out riding his donkey she thought she saw a long procession of Fenians approaching. 'We were all very much alarmed, particularly the donkey who expressed his anxiety by kicking. I was thrown off and had concussion of the brain. This was my first introduction to Irish politics!'[40] On another occasion he remembers he was about to go to a pantomime at Dublin's Theatre Royal only for the expedition to be cancelled at the last minute because the theatre had been burnt down.

Jennie's loneliness and desperation are caught in numerous letters to Randolph in these years. Lacking a purpose in her own life, her need for him was touching – 'I count the hours for your return.' Her concern for his ailments, however minor, was more than dutiful – 'I am so distressed at thinking of you with one of your abominable colds'[41] – and her worries about their financial situation unsettled her. Already in Ireland the couple were living beyond their means, not helped by Randolph's ruinously heavy gambling at the races. Jennie often wrote vainly asking him not to gamble. They were constantly looking at ways to raise more income to fund their lifestyle. Typically, he would write to her only about his winnings, which that autumn included one of £500 on a single race. Bets were often £50 a time, Newmarket his favourite course. But the canny Duchess knew better. 'It is very sad to think of your losses,' she chided.[42]

As early as January 1876 Randolph was raising a £5,000 loan, 'the last we can make on our present resources'.[43] When the money from Leonard Jerome's settlements did not always arrive promptly he turned on his wife, accusing her of being unbusinesslike. 'I was very much annoyed at receiving the enclosed from Coutts,' he told her. 'I think it is too bad of your father . . . these kind of irregularities make bankers very suspicious of me.'[44] The financial worries increased and before they left Ireland there was discussion about taking out another loan, or borrowing from the old Duke, neither of which was possible. Randolph even considered selling his horses.

In January 1879 the Marlborough solicitor was able to raise a loan of £2,000 for the Churchills, 'positively the last we shall be able to make', Randolph wrote gloweringly and somewhat repetitively to his wife.[45] The loan reduced their income by about £110 a year, but at least they were now able to settle some outstanding bills. 'I enclose you the list of what I have paid. It is a great thing getting them off one's mind,' he told Jennie. Not surprisingly, perhaps, he added that he had a bad headache.[46]

Leonard Jerome was clearly trying to do his best for them, yet he was no longer in possession of significant sums and was conscious that he had two other unmarried daughters who would need dowries. In an undated letter to Jennie at around this time he wrote, not altogether soothingly, that he wanted to increase her £2,000 allowance and had been working out ways of how he might do this:

> if I could feel that it would do you and Randolph the slightest particle of good or momentary relief. I am not going to preach you a sermon on economy. I leave that to your mother. Whatever I *think* about it I shall *say* nothing. The club house forms your allowance, enough to pay the interest – as a club house it must have a club as tenant but there aren't many of those left. As an apartment house it would always command a good rent, probably 10,000 more than it now brings in. I had not intended to arrange this till the last of next year but as you want the 10,000 I may as well do it now . . .

He promised to see his lawyers as soon as possible and have a paper for her and Randolph to sign within a week. He concluded by asking for news of his grandson. 'How is that "naty" boy Winston? His last photo in knickerbockers is very fine.'[47]

Meanwhile Clara, three years older than Jennie and now approaching the end of her twenties, had by 1879 met the captivating Moreton Frewen. Frewen came from an ancient landowning, political and clerical family, mentioned in the Domesday Book and based in Sussex since the seventeenth century. Born in 1853 and so two years younger than Clara, Moreton was the second of four sons, resplendent with ideas yet barren of his own money or resources. He was a true Victorian adventurer, as charming as he was feckless. There was never a time when he did not have a wild idea on the go that would make his name and his family's fortune. These included plans to bring Siberian timber to England by the Northwest Passage, open only for three weeks in the year, to collect bats' guano from a cave in Texas (an idea which ended when samples killed his friends' gardenias) and an option on trams in Denver which he let slip while on a hunting adventure. The silver-tongued Frewen was constantly proposing some scheme or another but most of these lost money, eventually earning him the nickname 'Mortal Ruin'.[48] Leonard Jerome, who may have thought he recognised a kindred spirit, watched all of this with misgivings, amazement and finally anger.

Mrs Jerome could hardly look with favour on such a match. Nor could Jennie, knowing what she did of Frewen's philandering reputation and in particular of his romance with the beautiful actress then just beginning to make her name, Mrs Lillie Langtry. Moreton suavely tried to dispel such doubts in a letter to 'Dear Lady Randolph'. 'For fear you may think me ungracious enough to bear malice let me write you a few lines to say how right and reasonable you were to oppose Clara's selection. I should have thought you a careless sister indeed had you done otherwise. Still, I am not inclined to admit that she is doing a foolish thing.'[49]

Clara, who had suffered from Jennie's and Randolph's social exclusion in London, was not prepared to let Moreton go. Notwithstanding Jennie's and her mother's concerns she now went back to New York, where she made plans for a wedding. At the time of his proposal to Clara, Moreton was trying to make money through a cattle-rearing scheme in Wyoming. Clara bravely agreed to accompany him but on condition that they would return to London within four years.

Meanwhile Leonie, not yet twenty and thus almost of marriageable age, now came to stay from time to time with Jennie. As early as 1876, Jennie had hoped to take her out a little during the season, convinced that her younger sister would have been 'a complete success'. But the Churchill reputation made this extremely tricky, and in addition Leonie's romances were proving unsatisfactory. Moreton had introduced her to Charlie Fitzwilliam, a younger son of the fifth Earl Fitzwilliam of Wentworth Woodhouse, a magnificent stately home in Yorkshire. The pair wanted desperately to marry. Jennie strongly approved of the match and wrote to her mother, 'Of course, if you ask me not to encourage Fitzwilliam I won't. At the same time I am dreadfully prejudiced in his favour.'[50]

Jennie realised how difficult it was to marry well and tried to explain this to her hopeful mother, whose views had been fixed in 1870s Paris. 'When I look around here it seems to me the chances of *any* girl are very small – there are so few *partis* and when I see a girl like Georgie [Lady Georgiana Churchill, Randolph's sister] with everything that money, dress and position can do for her, hanging on for year after year!'[51] But it was money, or the lack of it, which was again the stumbling block. Charlie had no inheritance and, on learning that Leonie was no heiress, his parents put a stop to the relationship by threatening to cut off his allowance if he persisted in seeing her.

Leonie, earning her epithet among the three sisters as 'the wise' (where Clara was 'the beautiful' and Jennie 'the witty'), well understood that her father had no fortune to bestow on her and that to marry a man cut off from his parents' source of income would doom the relationship from the start. 'Of course', Charlie wrote to her, 'we should never be well off but we should have enough to get along with comfortably . . .'[52] Leonie did not consider this a sensible way to proceed. Her reaction was in stark contrast to Jennie's and Randolph's romantic refusal to be cowed by parental objections and makes plain Jennie's formidable strength of character. But it is also a reflection on the severe depletion of Jerome finances in the intervening years. Both sisters had drawn lessons from watching Jennie's and Randolph's life of constant financial worry and responded in different ways. Clara was to suffer for her roseate romanticism. Leonie, although she married for love, took a more determinedly practical approach to married life.

For six years Winston was secure in the knowledge that however little he saw of his radiant mother, he was her only child. But on 4 February 1880, just before the family left Ireland, she gave birth to a second son, John Strange Spencer-Churchill, also premature. One puzzle for historians is why Jennie, who managed to conceive so easily in 1874, did not have a second pregnancy for another five years. The Princess of Wales, for example, had six pregnancies in very quick succession until, worn out, she was allowed to stop at the age of twenty-six and Bertie sought his pleasure elsewhere.

Contraception was known and used by prudent women, especially those indulging in affairs with men who were not their husbands. Condoms, then referred to as French letters, were available in a few places, but were considered unpleasantly uncomfortable. Men of pleasure did not always consider 'responsibility' to be anything they need be concerned about. It was mostly left to women either to abstain during known fertile periods, to douche thoroughly with a solution of sulphate of zinc or alum, or to use beeswax discs which blocked the entrance to the uterus, or sponges moistened with diluted lemon juice inserted into the vagina or other new, and sometimes painful, devices. But only privileged women had access to these articles. Most females would not have known of their existence, let alone where to buy them.

The most likely reason for Jennie's failure to conceive is that she and Randolph were already living quite separate lives. Randolph was often to be found sailing (or yachting as he called it) in Ireland, catching lobsters, cooking and eating them on the rocks and, of an evening, meeting FitzGibbon and his friends. Sometimes he went yachting for a month at a time, or fishing in Norway, recommended because its cool climate had a beneficial effect on his health. 'Of course you would find Yachting more amusing than being over here where there is nothing on earth for you to do,' Jennie wrote bravely.[53] She had been brought up by her mother never to scold a man, so she didn't: if you scold him he will go elsewhere. But Jennie was a woman who craved intimacy and her loneliness at home was evidently painful.

As early as January 1876 Randolph had remained in London for her twenty-second birthday, sent her many happy returns from the Carlton Club and told her unconvincingly, 'I wish I were there to spend it with you.'[54] Missing birthdays and anniversaries quickly became the norm. On 15 April 1879, he wrote to his mother telling her of the two days he had just spent fishing in the Suir and of how he had 'added another Irish county to my peregrinations in this island'. He wished her many happy returns of her birthday and reminded her, 'as perhaps you may remember', that it was also his wedding anniversary. 'Having been married five years I begin to feel highly respectable.'[55] Respectability may have been paramount for him, but it was never likely to be enough for her.

Or perhaps they were no longer intimate on account of a disease Randolph had contracted which he believed to be syphilis. There is no evidence that Jennie knew at this stage the nature of her husband's chronic indisposition, and it is unlikely that she did. It is today hotly disputed whether he ever had the disease, although in the last years of their marriage the doctors treating him clearly thought he did and, much to his fury, they then discussed his illness with his wife. The facts, however, are that Jennie, having shown how fertile she was in 1874, did not become pregnant again for five years at a time when contraception was notoriously haphazard and when, under normal circumstances, she would have had no need for it. Having a second child as a playmate for Winston and to alleviate her own boredom and inactivity would have been a natural expectation among her social class.

After visits to his London doctor, Randolph wrote to Jennie of a variety of ailments from which he was suffering in the first years of his married life including repeated colds. 'I really do not think anybody ever has as bad colds as I do . . .'[56] A few months later, when he complained of sciatica, Dr Clayton told him he was 'below par' and advised a holiday in Germany. Next, believing that he was suffering from rheumatism, he reported in January 1879: 'Dr Clayton told me I was not at all well and that I must look after myself.'[57] He returned a few weeks later, grumbling that he was no better. In an undated letter around this time he also complained of indigestion and went to Pau and the Pyrenees – without Jennie. These symptoms are by no means proof of the first stage of syphilis but indicate a young man rarely in good health for no particular reason.

According to Frank Harris, an admirer of Randolph and subsequently literary agent for Winston, but a man whose scrupulous regard for the truth is open to doubt when competing against the merits of a good story, Randolph was infected with syphilis while an undergraduate at Oxford. Claiming to have been given the details by Louis Jennings, the American journalist who later worked closely with Randolph, he starts insouciantly enough, 'Here it is, as I heard it from Jennings that evening at Kensington Gore.' According to the Harris version of events, Randolph had just made a speech on his pet idea that the relationship of master and servant in the home of an English gentleman was almost ideal. Warming to his theme the young Churchill apparently went on to explain that the relationship between the aristocratic class and workmen in England should form the basis of Tory Democracy as he conceived it. He was to refine these views as he matured politically.

After much rowdy cheering from the youthful audience, Randolph drank a 'stirrup cup' of champagne with them and 'remembered nothing more'. The following morning he awoke to find himself in a filthy room with a revolting old prostitute sharing his bed. 'She had one long yellow tooth in her top jaw that waggled as she spoke.' He threw some money at her and ran straight to the doctor for an examination. The doctor gave him some strong disinfectant and after three weeks he believed himself cured.

The author Julian Osgood Field in *Uncensored Recollections* published in 1924 gives a not dissimilar account. He too believed that Randolph had contracted the illness during his Oxford days and that although he was always happy to consult specialists he rarely followed the recommended treatment long enough for a cure.

> He would say 'all right' and do nothing. He came with me in Paris, at my earnest entreaty, to see a famous physician; but when we got to the doctor's he wanted to back out, and I had to take him to the Hôtel Chatham bar and refresh him with brandy cocktail before he would go any further. Then, when we got to the great specialist's apartment as the waiting rooms, dining rooms, salons were all crowded as usual I tipped the manservant to let me put Randolph by himself in the kitchen and then leaving him there for a moment . . . obtained immediate access to the great man and arranged with him that he should see my friend at once . . . when I returned triumphant to the kitchen with this good news I found that Randolph had bolted down the *escalier de service*! I rushed after him, dragged him back; the doctor saw him at once; prescribed for him and warned him. But all in vain. Randolph had the prescriptions made up all right but calmly informed me two days later . . . that he had 'chucked the whole damn lot away!'

Such a story rings true if only because morbid fear of syphilis was very real and even had a name – syphilophobia. It was known that, once the disease was suspected, doctors could do little other than prescribe mercury, which especially when taken as chloride of mercury (a compound of mercury and chlorine) often induced a terrifying form of mercury poisoning that was as dangerous as the illness. Few willingly swallowed such a dubious cure.

The descendants of Jennie's sister Leonie, the Leslie family, believed a slightly different version of events: that Randolph's syphilis was contracted from a chambermaid at Blenheim shortly after his marriage to Jennie. This story, equally unprovable, is far kinder to Randolph than one which accuses him of knowingly marrying with such a dangerously communicable disease, even if, as many men did, he hoped he had been cured once the obvious infection had cleared up. And it does, at least, fall within the realms of Randolph's philosophy. Eleven years after Jack's birth he wrote to Jennie in reply to her telling him about friends of theirs, Lord and Lady Gerard, whose marriage had collapsed on account of the husband dallying with the staff: 'Tell Mary from me that she is a fool not to forgive Billy. What does one occasional cook or housemaid matter.'[58]

Doctors by the 1880s were giving clear and emphatic advice that 'with syphilis one must be content to remain a bachelor . . . If already married it is a man's duty to preserve his wife . . . [there is] an absolute obligation to frighten him about the risks for his wife.' In his book *Syphilis and Marriage* published in 1881, a popular volume at the time, the American-born French physician Alfred Fournier wrote: 'It becomes my duty to remind you that you have not the moral right to associate others in your personal risks, i.e. to make your wife and children share the possible consequences of your disease.' Syphilis can take between ten and twenty years for the most serious tertiary manifestations to appear. It can be singularly benign initially and yet end in the most serious symptoms. Smoking always made it worse and doctors were at pains to advise against. Syphilis often appeared to be cured after the initial chancre and fever passed to the extent that some young men looked upon it as an initiation rite of sorts. All they were left with was a penile scar. But in fact they were merely in remission and it was soon recognised that, for most sufferers, syphilis was a lifelong illness even if the symptoms, which were interspersed with lengthy periods of apparent good health, varied widely. These included rheumatism, arthritis, gout, eczema, hypertension, epilepsy, headache, stomach ache, jaundice, mania, depression, dementia, schizophrenia, deafness. Insanity and paralysis often did not occur until decades after the first infection. There were so many potential ravages of the body for which syphilis could be responsible that one doctor concluded: 'with syphilis almost anything may be expected at any time.'[59] In the pre-penicillin era of the mid- to late-nineteenth century, untreated syphilis was a common sight in physicians' waiting rooms.

From this distance in time, all the biographer can do is assemble the clues and seek retrospective medical diagnosis based on archival information, which cannot be conclusive. But, even if Randolph suffered from a number of symptoms well known to be associated with secondary syphilis; even if contemporaries believed that he had been infected either by a prostitute or by a Blenheim chambermaid; even if he was given prescriptions for mercury, arsenic and potassium; even if all those are known factors there is still no proof that Randolph had actually contracted syphilis. And in one sense it does not matter. As will be shown in later chapters, when Randolph suffered increasingly from neurological disorders which might have been epileptic bipolar disorder or a brain tumour just as well as syphilis, Randolph and Jennie behaved in such a way that it is clear he believed he had the disease and, later, both Jennie and Winston did too. Contemporaries whispered about him. He might as well have had syphilis. Their lives were blighted.

And so, if Randolph was not Jack's father, who might have been? The Leslie family believed it was Star Falmouth, a big and broad military man with a thick moustache – the sort of physical characteristics that appealed to Jennie. She told her mother about his amazing moustache when she first described him. Evelyn Boscawen, the seventh Viscount Falmouth, was, like most of his family for generations before him, educated at Eton. They were descended from the Boscawens, an ancient naval family. But, unlike them, he did not pass into the sixth form nor did he follow his father to Oxford. He was sent into the army class and then the Coldstream Guards, where he eventually became a colonel. From an early age, hunting and racing seem to have been his passion. 'Handsome and stupid' is a description Anita Leslie uses, but she adds that he was not too stupid to become assistant military secretary to the Duke of Marlborough in Ireland and to keep Jennie Churchill's affection all through her life. After Dublin, where he saw a lot of the Churchills, he lived partly at Mereworth, a 4,500-acre estate in Kent, as it was closer to London for weekends than the main family estate at Tregothnan in Cornwall.

Winston's cousin Shane Leslie did not hold his military capabilities in high regard. 'As to Star Falmouth,' he wrote, 'he held the title and a military rank for he was chosen to drill and inspect the Ludgrove boys in my time 1896. . . . His great successes were racing for he won Derbies with Fred Archer as his Jockey . . . Jennie put her seduction entirely on him. You can calculate when they first met by when Jack was born.'[60] In fact, they had first met at Ascot races, shortly after Jennie married. Seven years older than Jennie, he was a bachelor at this time and did not marry until he was forty in 1890. Jennie had many visits from the 'Star Man' and his name occurs regularly in the diaries and notes between the Jerome sisters. Jennie refers to one visit, an occasion which for someone else might have been an embarrassing *faux pas*, to be found entertaining a man, alone, to tea, but in the Jerome lexicon was an amusing family joke. 'Such an absurd thing happened yesterday. The Star Man was having tea when a very grand carriage drove up. A powdered footman rang, wigs, silk stockings, and inside a very fat old frump. Who on earth is this old demon? "Why it's my mother, that's Lady Falmouth," the Star answered. Tableau!'[61] Lady Falmouth was calling on friends.

Yet this story, as told here by Jennie to her mother, prompts further questions. Jennie had clearly been taken by surprise. Why did Falmouth's mother choose that moment to arrive for tea at the wrong place? According to one version, Falmouth was so captivated by Jennie that on a visit to her house, when she resisted his advances, 'in his fury and resentment he raped her on the drawing room floor'.[62] It is very possible that something traumatic and potentially compromising happened between Falmouth and Jennie and that Jennie later tried to turn this into an amusing story to hide the truth, even if the latter were not so dramatic as a rape.

Jennie's nephew, Seymour Leslie, tried to help Anita as she was researching her biography of Jennie. But, on the subject of who was 'Jack C's putative father', he recognised that family gossip was not the same as proof. Although the Leslie children were steered towards believing that Falmouth was a friend of their uncle Randolph rather than of their aunt Jennie, Seymour, whose long years of lying immobile made him a good observer, thought differently. He believed that Falmouth was Jack's father. Both families knew each other well and Seymour recalled: 'For some time we occupied a flat immediately opposite the Falmouths' front door in South Audley Street and I repeatedly visited Lady Falmouth [Star's wife] and played with the two elder boys . . . Falmouth [was] then known as "Star" and [was] a general; the eldest boy was called "Twinkle".'[63]

When Anita discussed Jack's birth in her biography she wrote that he was called John Strange after a middle-aged friend of the Duke of Marlborough, Lieutenant Colonel John Strange Jocelyn, later to become the fifth Earl of Roden after the premature death of his nephew in 1880. Roden, a pompous but kindly sportsman thirty years older than Jennie, was invited to be Jack's godfather – an honour he appears not to have taken up. The Rodens were an ancient family whose lineage could be traced to the time of William of Conquer, but they owned their peerage more recently to George III in 1771. They were a family of soldiers and John Strange Jocelyn was apparently 'exceedingly handsome' and daring.[64] Jocelyn may well have admired Jennie enough to invite her to his 9,000-acre estate in Ireland and she, at twenty-five, may well have become enamoured by a man of fifty-five. But although others believed he could have been Jack's father it seems unlikely that, if that had been the case, Jennie, whose discretion was renowned, would have left such a heavy-handed clue as naming her son after him. A few paragraphs later, Anita Leslie in her biography talks of Viscount Falmouth's devotion to Jennie and explains the proprieties which allowed her to entertain gentlemen such as him to afternoon tea without causing a stir.

At all events, Winston always loved Jack, protected him, deliberately sought out his company and considered him his brother. When Jack was dying in 1947 Winston's understandable sadness was not simply because the impending loss forced him to contemplate his own mortality. He unforgettably told his doctor Lord Moran that Jack's approaching death was 'like the lash of a whip across my bare and quivering heart'.[65]

A few weeks after Jack's birth there was a general election in England. Gladstone won, so the Duke's appointment in Ireland came to an end. The Marlboroughs and their entourage had to leave the country at a time of great political turmoil. The small Churchill family of two children, nanny, cook and servants now set up house at 29 St James's Place, a cul-de-sac in the heart of London's clubland. Randolph had been looking for a suitable house for some time but remarked that it was difficult to find one they could afford where the bedrooms had enough space for all Jennie's voluminous dresses. This one was a short walk away from Marlborough House to the south and South Audley Street to the north. Randolph, having retained his seat at Woodstock, albeit by a mere 60 votes, now had fire in his belly and Jennie was keen to begin political entertaining. The 1880s were to be their decade.

Randolph grasped every opportunity to spend time at Blenheim with his family. Shortly after Jack's birth, in the autumn of 1880, Jennie poured out her heart in a letter to her mother from the Palace. It is worth quoting at length because it expresses much of the agony Jennie was experiencing at the time. Quite possibly the Marlboroughs suspected dubious parentage of this child, although Randolph, it should be said, treated both sons in exactly the same way – with indifference. Jennie had been staying for more than a month at Blenheim. The children had charming nurseries there and were well looked after and she, too, had a nice room and sitting room on the ground floor where she could paint and do more or less what she liked. But, as she confided to her mother, she would have been much happier living quite alone in their own little house without seeing a soul.

Her candour is revealing. She was proud and such a letter risked inviting in response either an expression of pity or a rebuke for her hasty marriage, neither of which she would have welcomed. Yet Jennie was clearly distraught and the prospect of Mrs Jerome's visit filled her with such delight that she let go.

> I quite forget what it is like to be with people who love me. I do so long sometimes to have someone to whom I could go and talk to. Of course R is awfully good to me and always takes my part in everything but how can I always be abusing his mother to him when she is devoted to him and will do anything for him. The fact is I *LOATHE* being here – it is *not* on account of its dullness – *that* I don't mind. But it is gall and wormwood to me to accept everything or to be having to argue. I hate it, it is no use disguising it, the duchess hates me – perhaps [because I am] a little prettier and more attractive than her daughters. Everything I do or say or wear is found fault with. We are always studiously polite to each other but it is rather like a [dam] ready to burst at any moment.[66]

Jennie said that since both Clara and Leonie 'know what her ways are like there is no use describing les petites misères that make up the total of one's existence here. But what one can laugh at in the abstract is more bitter when one is living with a person and accepting their hospitality. I know I am very foolish to mind what can't be changed but it is trying.' Finally, she asks her mother if she could possibly send to London for her return to St James's Place a barrel of American eating apples. As if this would make anything better.

6

Rather a Relief to Get Winston off my Hands

~

JENNIE EXPLAINED TO her mother that the reason she and Randolph were so 'dreadfully hard up, in spite of Papa's most generous tips', had nothing to do with her extravagance on clothes. 'You don't know how economical one tries to be. I've not brought back one winter dress [from Paris].'[1] Instead, to economise, she had bought some dark-red, thin flannel material in Woodstock for twenty-five shillings and had it made up by her maid. She insisted that the shortage of cash was entirely due to all the political entertaining she and Randolph were now undertaking. While she was at Blenheim, where she stayed with the boys at the end of 1880 since they could not afford their own country house, Randolph was generating 'political dynamism'. She told her mother proudly of a big political dinner in Woodstock Randolph was organising at which six or seven hundred people were expected:

> The expenses are very great . . . the building alone costs £120 and as we are to make up the balance I suppose it will cost us quite £100 or £140. But this demonstration is of great importance to Randolph and the thing must be done well with Lord Salisbury* and a lot of swells coming. I hope Papa will hand over money punctually and I will say, like the beggars say all the time, all contributions en plus thankfully received![2]

On another occasion she wrote to her mother: 'I haven't been to many balls as I simply cannot afford to get dresses and one can't wear always the same thing. Besides I was not bidden to the one I wanted to go to [because of the Prince] and I did not care about the others. Money is such a hateful subject to me just now . . . don't let us talk about it.'[3]

The exile in Ireland – and especially the political conversations at Howth with FitzGibbon and his friends – had served an invaluable purpose for Randolph. He was one of the few English politicians at the time who actually knew Ireland at first hand. From now on he could (and did)

---

* The third Marquis of Salisbury was Foreign Secretary in Disraeli's Government, and succeeded as leader of the Conservative Party on Disraeli's death in 1881.

exploit Irish issues to make his name at Westminster. Randolph Churchill, hitherto an obscure backbencher with a privileged background, burst into the political limelight. 'A protean adaptability and a political sensitivity had been added to the arrogance and ruthlessness which were his heritage,' is how his biographer Roy Foster put it. It was not only the *Oxford Times* which observed that 'his wonderfully clever speeches surprised even his most ardent admirers'.[4] From now on national newspapers also hung on his every pronouncement. Suddenly it seemed, as his son Winston wrote later, 'his hour had come'.[5] For Jennie, too, the years of social disgrace lived out in Ireland were, in retrospect, an important political apprenticeship as well as a maturing personal experience. She recognised that, since they could not as yet enter the same house as the Prince of Wales, 'much of the vain and foolish excitement of London society was closed to us and politics became our entire and all absorbing interest'. The pain of the Prince's continuing antipathy to her husband was one she bore with stoicism. She had seen another route.

In January 1881 she watched from the cramped and uncomfortable Speaker's Gallery, where she now went as often as she could, as her husband made an impassioned intervention in the Home Rule debate. He believed the Bills under discussion would further embitter Ireland against England and result in 'the undying dislike and distrust of the Irish people'. Perhaps she was especially moved by this speech of her husband's because she had seen the desperation of Irish poverty herself, the sunken cheeks, bare feet and torn rags that passed for clothes. Or, more likely, she had now seen the fire in Randolph's belly which she had always believed to be there. Attacking a government pamphlet on one occasion he had thrown it on the floor and then stamped on it to loud cheers. 'Everyone rushed up to me to such an extent that I felt as tho' I had made it,' she told her sister.[6]

A few months later Disraeli remarked of Randolph: 'When they [the Conservatives] come in they will have to give him anything he chooses to ask for and in a very short time they will have to take anything he chooses to give them.'[7] By the end of the year Gladstone's private secretary was also noting: 'R. Churchill continues to "star" in the provinces and there is no denying that he is making a position for himself . . . It is sickening to think that a man of such unscrupulousness and with such utter want of seriousness should be coming to the front in politics and would on the formation of a Tory government be trusted with governing the country.'[8] For Randolph, a born opportunist, the formation of the Fourth Party, or Randolph's Cabal, was key to his newfound success. In the wake of

Beaconsfield's death in April 1881, the rivalry between Salisbury and Northcote for the position of Tory leader led to an intensely weak opposition facing the revived Liberals. This gave an opening to the loose grouping that was the Fourth Party, which seemed on occasion to pose a real threat. The pretext for launching the party was the Bradlaugh case when the Radical MP Charles Bradlaugh, a man notorious for his free-thinking who vehemently advocated birth control, insisted on his right to affirm rather than swear an oath on his election to the House of Commons. This issue was seized upon by Sir Henry Drummond Wolff, a middle-aged career diplomat and longtime family friend whom Jennie described as 'a godsend if anything went wrong, and a joke from him saved many a situation'. Wolff was actively supported by Churchill and by John Eldon Gorst, a man who appeared stern but who 'could always make himself seem pleasant'.[9] The fourth member was Arthur Balfour, wealthy, brilliant and young. Balfour's loyalty to the small group was never entirely certain, however. It was his admiration for Jennie that linked him in. Her friendship with Balfour and Gorst – the three of them often went to concerts together – was so close that she was sometimes described as a fifth member of the Fourth Party. Jennie referred to them as her 'weird' friends, as opposed to her 'fashionable' friends; 'one solemn with beard and eye glass, the other aesthetic with long hair and huge spats'.[10] All three were music lovers, and, through Balfour, Jennie came close to but was never quite accepted by the Souls, the intellectual and sexually adventurous circle of Edwardian aristocrats whose leader was Balfour himself.

The patrician Balfour, nephew of Lord Salisbury, was, like Jennie, a talented amateur musician and the pair often played piano duets together. He once sent her a note from the House of Commons telling her that he was 'groaning and swearing on this beastly bench. While you are listening to Wagnerian discords I am listening to Irish grumblings. There is a great deal of brass in both of them otherwise there is not much resemblance. I am sitting next – I might be sitting next to you! I am an unhappy victim . . .'[11]

Churchill, in attacking Bradlaugh, not only found his political voice but quite possibly hoped that an attack on the man's republicanism and what had been publicly described as his moral depravity might help his own social rehabilitation. Jennie clearly believed that it did and told her sister that the Prince of Wales seemed 'highly pleased' with Churchill's stance. For Jennie the excitement of the Fourth Party was much more than vicarious. There was a real sense that something might be achieved by an alliance at whose epicentre she stood. She was there partly as a supportive wife, listening at a time when women could do little more in English political life. She provides an amusing description of the other women who crowded into the Speaker's Gallery, cramped in a small dark cage with their knees against the grille, their necks craned forward and their ears painfully on the alert. She knew it was an honour to listen to a debate from the Speaker's Gallery as seats there required an invitation from the Speaker's wife. Seats in the Ladies' Gallery, equally cramped, were granted by ballot. But her account also indicates that the women who listened to politicians were not part of her fashionable world. Jennie, straddling both, did more than merely listen. Politics captivated her and, with her innate theatricality, she was able to help Randolph, who was always nervous and apprehensive, with his delivery. It was an aspect of their lives that kept them close. 'Those years, when the Fourth Party was at its zenith, were full of excitement and interest for me. Our house became the rendezvous of all shades of politicians. Many were the plots and plans which were hatched in my presence . . . how we used to chaff about the "goats" as we called the ultra Tories . . . great was to be their fall and destruction.'[12]

One of Jennie's activities was acting as hostess and arranging dinners. 'Her salon', Winston wrote in his novel *Savrola* of his heroine Lucile, 'was crowded with the most famous men from every country. Statesmen, soldiers, poets and men of science had worshipped at the shrine. She had mixed in matters of state. Suave and courtly ambassadors had thrown out delicate hints and she had replied with unofficial answers. Plenipotentiaries had explained the details of treaties and protocols with remarkable elaboration for her benefit.' *Savrola* was Churchill's only work of fiction. Published in 1900, the allegorical tale features a dictator, President Antonio Molara, who is challenged by Savrola, a man of the people. Savrola leads a democratic effort to restore political liberties and enlists the help of Molara's beautiful wife, Lucile. They fall in love and, after a violent revolution in which Molara is killed, are united in love.

Jennie's actual guests included politicians (Sir Charles Dilke, Sir William Harcourt and Joseph Chamberlain were regulars), artists (Leighton and Millais were her friends) and journalists or writers (including Thomas Escott, editor of the *Fortnightly Review*). Randolph did not shy from asking Escott to place an article in the *Fortnightly* by his brother-in-law, Moreton Frewen. Over the years, Randolph showed many acts of kindness in trying to use his influence to Frewen's advantage, prompted by his wife's concern for her struggling sister. It was Randolph's reputation enhanced by Jennie's magnetism that drew Escott and others so willingly into the charmed Churchill circle. Thanking Escott for a book he had sent her, Jennie wrote with characteristic playfulness, 'I am sure that reading it will be a liberal education. *Of course*, I do not mean in a political sense.'[13] She wrote proudly to her mother about Randolph's performances 'covering himself with glory . . . when this government goes out (which they say will be soon) I fancy R and his boon companion Sir Henry Drummond Wolff must be given something'.[14] Both hoped for this with particular intensity; for 'being given something', read being paid.

There was one other key issue around this time affecting Churchill's meteoric rise – his serious but mysterious illness which sent him out of action from the end of February to October 1882. Leonie, who had come to London hoping for a sparkling season with her elder sisters, found life with Jennie precarious as Randolph lay 'fulminating on a sofa' for several months. Jennie nursed him at home and wrote in her diary for 2 March – a rare entry referring to Randolph – 'up half the night with R'.[15] Afterwards there was a marked change of tempo, an escalation of frenzied activity and, most of the time, a race to achieve. But he was subject to wild mood swings and a few months later he wrote to Wolff: 'They do not know how easy it would be to be rid of me. I am sick of politics which only play the dickens with one's health and are a dreadful tie.'[16] Says Foster, 'It is conceivable that from this date he knew the nature and severity of the illness which eventually, in the form of general paralysis brought on by syphilis, finished his career. When he returned to Parliamentary activity it was "with a new sense of mortality".'[17] Certainly from now on his strategy is identified by a marked impatience and an inability to wait on results. He had vicious public arguments with political colleagues; Lord Hartington, for example, he denounced as 'vile, contumacious and lying'.

What emerges in his Parliamentary behaviour was presumably a reflection, perhaps minimised, of what happened at home. Whereas he may have been indolent or wayward before his illness of 1882, he now became aggressively determined and would brook no opposition. He was a driven man. Jennie's life, already painfully circumscribed by financial stringency and social exclusion, was now mired further by her husband's temper, devilish energy and personal ambition. One letter survives, but there may well have been more in similar vein, reflecting his attitude to his wife. Not only was the Duchess critical of which balls she attended, Randolph, too, reprimanded her for the company she was keeping. Having opened a letter to her from the French aristocrat Boni de Castellane, Randolph himself replied to 'the blackguard . . . but I really do think, my darling, you ought to be more careful in your manner to men who are always ready to take a liberty. I have such confidence in you that I never bother you but these kind of things are very annoying and vexatious.'[18]

In the spring of 1882 Jennie rented Beech Lodge, a roomy country house (since demolished) with peaceful gardens near Wimbledon, where she hoped Randolph could convalesce out of sight of prying London eyes. As soon as he had improved sufficiently they went to America once again, always a place of recovery for Jennie. And it was while in New York that they heard the news of the Phoenix Park murders, the assassination on 6 May of Lord Frederick Cavendish, British Secretary for Ireland, and Thomas Henry Burke, his Under-Secretary, in Phoenix Park. Jennie and Randolph had known Burke well from their time in Dublin and were shocked by the killings. The pair had been stabbed to death by members of the Invincibles, a terrorist splinter group of the Fenians. Two of those arrested turned State's Evidence, five were hanged, and three were sentenced to penal servitude. Charles Stewart Parnell, the rising Irish politician, was alleged to have been personally involved in the plot but was later exonerated.

Just a few months later Jennie was to meet some of the murderers while they were awaiting execution in Kilmainham Gaol. Staying in Dublin for the Punchestown Races, which she loved, she could not refuse an offer to visit the prison. She wrote later of how the youngest of the 'wretched' men, as he was leaving the small room where he had been brought by the prison staff, suddenly turned and asked her to help his wife if he 'had to go'. 'This depressed me dreadfully,' Jennie wrote. She then explained how a surprise visit from the Inspector General meant that, since the proper permits had not been signed for her admission, she would have to hide in the cell herself until he had left. Yet Jennie, with an ear for a good story, tells all of this with a light tone and little political explanation.[19] She knows that terrorism exists in Ireland but describes the escort of constabulary in full uniform as 'comical'. When she eventually took up charitable causes it was charity on her own terms. Relief of the poor and deprived was not her style. Politics and politicians were. Her exhilaration derived from the cut and thrust of personalities, from being involved at the centre of events, not from the intellectual discussion of issues nor from the welfare of the deprived. Canvassing in elections for relatives and organising women's political associations were then almost the only routes available for politically savvy women. To speak in public on any issue was considered an impropriety.

Home Rule for Ireland was the central issue of the day, a topic Jennie and, especially, Randolph understood in a way few other British politicians did. Once the Liberal Party had split over this there was scope for others to express myriad views. But most women used their organisational abilities, if not for charities then for smaller-scale issues – local government and the temperance movement, for example, in the latter of which the radical Rosalind Howard, Countess of Carlisle, became a prominent figure. She was also a keen advocate of women's suffrage, about which Jennie was less than enthusiastic.

From now on, Jennie took to accompanying Randolph to many of his political gatherings in the country. They would often stay with the local magnate, who might be chairing the meetings, and she would learn about local gossip and the importance of swaying a few key votes. Sometimes she went, on her own, to a local school or factory, presented flowers or attended prize-givings. She was, as Randolph knew, an immense political asset. Her later involvement in the Primrose League was to exploit this further.

But 1882 ended badly. Randolph having recovered somewhat, they moved into a new home, at 2 Connaught Place. Although on the less fashionable north side of Hyde Park, it was a bigger house and the move was quite likely made possible only by Leonard Jerome giving them some cash when they had been to America a few months previously. There was a roomy nursery at the top where Mrs Everest soon established herself with her two charges. Their friends called the house 'Tyburnia', a reference partly to the tablet on railings opposite the front windows recalling the 'thousands of poor wretches' who had been hanged there, Tyburn Gate having been the principal place of public execution in London until 1783. But it was also a snobbish reminder that such a house in Chelsea or Kensington was beyond their means. Wilfrid Scawen Blunt described the area (it was Bayswater) as 'the wild west'.[20]

As the address was not everything it might have been, Jennie used her artistic talents and innate good taste to create a sumptuous and unusual interior. She had discovered many beautiful pieces of old furniture in Dublin 'where they had found their way from the dismantled houses of impecunious Irish landlords'. These were Jennie's 'stage properties', as her brother-in-law Blandford teasingly described them. Judging from surviving pictures of the house, she stuffed as many of these in a room as she could. But she also sought out furniture in London. Once, in a dusty old shop in the City, she found some large painted panels for which the owner wanted £300. Jennie considered this a bargain and, 'full of my *trouvaille*, rushed home with a glowing tale in the hopes of persuading Randolph to buy them'. Randolph, deep in political discussion, responded in a word: 'Preposterous.' Jennie concludes: 'I reluctantly gave up the panels which were sold shortly afterwards and turned out to be Morlands, worth today perhaps £7,000 or £8,000.'[21]

Jennie stamped her idiosyncratic style on every room. While Randolph was away she turned her hand to painting a musical scene on her bedroom ceiling and took lessons from a 'little man'. It was, she told Randolph, very tiring painting all morning and having people in in the afternoon. But when the visitors were Arthur Sullivan and she, Sullivan and Lady de Clifford had dinner à trois 'and could talk music to our hearts' content' she was happy.[22]

But Connaught Place was notable chiefly for being the first private house in London to have electric lighting, the source of much comment. It is hard to imagine today quite what a dramatic change was effected through lighting at the push of a switch. The Churchills had a small dynamo placed in a cellar underneath the street, so noisy that it frightened any horses as they approached their door. The light was such an innovation that people used to ask permission to come to the house and inspect it. In the event the installation of electric light, although promised to them free of charge, turned out to be yet another expense they could ill afford. Once Randolph had spoken enthusiastically in the House in favour of an Electric Lighting Bill he felt he could no longer accept the gift of installation. 'Unfortunately, there being no contract, we were charged double or treble the real price.' But, in the midst of all this, suddenly Jennie herself became dangerously ill. For twenty-eight days in December 1882 she had a raging fever, a temperature that rose to 103 degrees and no idea of the cause. She was told neither the nature nor the seriousness of her illness. Yet her two doctors, Laking and Gull, were keeping her husband, who was away trying to improve his own health, fully informed. Randolph knew how ill his wife was for 'I had quite given you up,' he wrote to her in an extraordinarily touching, if solipsistic, letter from France: 'I have been quite unable to write to you or to anyone else since I heard of your illness. I would give anything to see you again. Why, dearest, if anything happened to you my life would be broken . . . the worry and anxiety about you have made me rather seedy.'[23] Such apparent tenderness bears a whiff of the sort of remorse typical of one who expresses himself more lovingly in letters than in person.

He urged Jennie to come out to Nice as soon as she was able to travel. Yet there was never any doubt that his illness was the more severe, nor any serious suggestion that he should come home to London to nurse her. He was listless and lacking in motivation; even politics and Parliament temporarily held little attraction for him. 'I seem to have lost all interest in things political,' he wrote to Wolff from Monte Carlo.[24] Jennie told Randolph she was 'a bag of bones', so weak that she had to spend all day in bed and be fed on slops of soup, milk, medicine and brandy. Yet she repeatedly told him how sorry she was to hear that he was not well.

Once again, he was away on her birthday, her twenty-ninth, in January 1883. She professed not to mind, saying: 'I shall not acknowledge it to the world. 26 is quite enough!'[25] She constantly reassured him that she was being looked after by her mother and Leonie, and, as she slowly started to gain strength, the tone of her letters was apologetic, contrite and full of concern for his health. She even apologised that when he had been ill a few months before, she might have been 'very piggy' to him, for now she understood how one likes 'to have someone quick about one'. But she advised him against trying out a new treatment as she said she could not bear to hear of another new French doctor. 'French air and sun will do more to get you right,'[26] she asserted, advice which she knew he wanted to hear, presumably echoing his own refusal to accept an unpleasant diagnosis.

Only when she was almost well again was she finally told the name of her illness: typhoid. Randolph, wondering how she could possibly have caught such a disease, suspected that there was something wrong with the drains in the new house. Jennie equivocated in response to his repeated requests to her to come to Nice, mostly because she was worried about the expense. Of course, she would much prefer to stay with him there than recuperate at home, she wrote, but she was deeply worried whenever she reflected on their 'money difficulties'. There were outstanding bills for wine and furniture, she reminded him, although she was so anxious to get well that she tried not to worry too much. 'Sometimes these thoughts will press on me. The house books are all paid up to date.' She yearned to be with him, 'but to tell you the honest truth, I don't care wildly about Nice and Cannes. I would much rather (I am only saying what would please me) spend a fortnight in Paris and then come home again . . . a week or two by ourselves would be so much pleasanter . . .'[27]

As she recovered from the first serious illness of her life she spent as much time as she could with her mother and two sisters. They made a brave little band. Leonie, husband-hunting with no money, and Clara, now married and living not far away at Aldford Street, but even more frequently alone than Jennie as her new husband searched the world to make his fortune. The Aldford Street house was rented for them by Leonard after Clara, approaching thirty, had finally agreed to marry Moreton Frewen and travel out west with him. His looks, aristocratic credentials and sweet talk had carried the day. Clara and Moreton were married on 2 June 1881 at Grace Church, New York, the church of choice for New York's elite, many of whom owned pews. But, although it was a grand occasion, there was no dowry for Clara, other than a necklace of thirty diamonds. Nor did Moreton have any money of his own. He just talked as if he did, and continued throughout his life to behave as if a fortune was just about to be made. After the reception, held at the Jerome house on Madison Square, the couple set off for the ranch in Wyoming that was dubbed Frewen Castle by the local cowboys. At first Clara, who took a French maid with her, enjoyed the scenery and the novelty of it all. But within months she miscarried, and the baby, a girl christened Jasmine, was buried at the ranch. Clara, devastated, went immediately to New York to recover and never returned to the west.

Like all women of her class, Jennie found that engaging footmen and cooks and other domestic chores, however unfulfilling, was an essential activity. Her interests lay elsewhere, in entertaining, interior decorating, involving herself in the social and political whirl, in painting and riding. Nonetheless, looking after her children occupied an important, if small, part of her day and, when her boys were at home, there is evidence in a diary for 1882 (apparently the only diary of hers that has survived, now in the possession of descendants of Jack Churchill) that she tried her best to be a good mother, either by reading to them or by going for walks with Winston or even, as she wrote on 17 January that year, by giving him his lessons.

Winston was, like any clever child, increasingly demanding. She told her mother how much she had enjoyed taking him to watch the guard mounting at the Horse Guards for the Queen's birthday. On another occasion she went with him and without Randolph to Calais, where they stayed at one of the worst hotels she had ever experienced. One day she took him to a pantomime which featured a large poodle brought on stage and introduced as Lord Randolph Churchill. 'It ran and barked and squeaked at everyone,' she reported.[28] But her letters at this time cannot hide the difficulties she had in trying to control her much loved but wilful firstborn son. 'I hope Winston won't be too troublesome,' she confided in Randolph just before a visit to Blenheim where his grandmother Frances was somewhat stricter. The word 'troublesome' was one which Winston himself knew was applied to him with increasing frequency. Jennie added: 'Yr mother thinks he is so good and certainly he is wonderfully well behaved in church but he is very naughty at times and it is all I can do to manage him . . .' Another day she confessed: 'Winston was rather naughty this morning but after a lecture and some verses to learn he became more amenable.'

When Mrs Everest, fast becoming indispensable, occasionally had a day off, Jennie managed, but only just. 'Everest and Jack will be back on

Monday . . . rather a relief to get Winston off my hands – tho' he is very good.'[29] Mrs Everest had by now become the fixed and primary focus of Winston's life, even though she had to be shared with Jack, which caused inevitable jealousy. Now there was a new complaint added to the others levelled against Winston – that he was, to say the least, an unhelpful influence on Jack. 'He teases the baby more than ever,' Jennie complained to Randolph.[30] When Sir Henry Drummond Wolff met Jack at Connaught Place and asked the toddler if he was being good, Jack replied: 'Yes, but brother is teaching me to be naughty.'[31] Mrs Everest had a sister who lived at Ventnor, on the Isle of Wight, and, whenever possible, she now started taking the two boys with her there on holiday. Her sister's husband, John Balaam, was chief warden at Parkhurst Prison, having worked there for nearly thirty years. It was he who evidently fired Winston's childish imagination on these holidays, taking him for long walks over the downs. He told the young boy 'many stories of mutinies in the prisons and how he had been attacked and injured on several occasions by the convicts'.[32]

These holidays to Ventnor were crucially important for Winston. Jennie acquiesced, presumably finding it convenient for Winston and Jack to be away. Randolph, when consulted, merely questioned whether Everest's friends were 'respectable people' and told Jennie to ensure that she did not let him play with other children as 'he will catch scarlet fever or something if he does that'.[33]

But, as Randolph's career revived along with better health, Jennie became increasingly involved in political life, and Winston was sent away to school. His later account of having to 'go away from home for many weeks at a stretch in order to do lessons under masters' is one of the most brilliant and poignant pieces of memoir in the language. To what extent he embellished his recollections in the intervening fifty years is a matter for debate. He was not the first English child to suffer the rigours of a harsh boarding-school routine. *My Early Life* was written in 1930, nine years after his mother's death, thirty-five years after his father's, at a time when Winston himself, painfully out of office, needed to create an image that fitted his idea of being saved by destiny for the highest role in the land. It is undeniably a beautiful piece of writing. It is also a clever piece of writing.

'It is said that famous men are usually the product of unhappy childhood,' Churchill himself wrote later. 'The stern compression of circumstances, the twinges of adversity, the spur of slights and taunts in early years are needed to evoke that ruthless fixity of purpose and tenacious mother wit without which great actions are seldom accomplished.'[34] It is

Jennie's mother Clara Jerome showing the strong features that lent weight to stories of Native Indian blood in Jennie

Leonard Jerome, a man whose unconquerable spirit led him up a new financial hill every time he fell down

The magnificent Jerome mansion on Madison Square in New York City built in 1859 when much of Manhattan was undeveloped farmland. It housed a fine private theatre and adjacent three-storey stable

Above left: Jennie, aged ten, dressed as a Vivandière for a costume ball given by August Belmont. She wrote later, 'for days I did not sleep with the excitement of anticipation but on the eventful night I was found in a flood of tears, the explanation being that I did not look at all as I thought I was going to – a situation which, alas! has often repeated itself' *Above right:* One of many studio portraits of the three Jerome sisters, known as the beautiful (Jennie), the witty (Leonie) and the wise (Clara). The sisters remained close throughout their lives

Below: Jerome Park opened on 25 September 1866 and was described by the *New York Tribune* as 'the social event of all time . . . a new era in the horse racing world'. On opening day the Park was filled with almost as many representatives of low life as of high life

Jennie, immaculately groomed in her riding gear and panther-like, as she appeared when she first attracted attention in Ireland

Lord Randolph Churchill, the young Member of Parliament, as he looked when Jennie fell in love with him

The ground-floor room in Blenheim Palace where Winston Churchill was born on 30 November 1874. He joked later in life that he was happily content with the decision he took to be born at Blenheim

Number 48 Charles Street, adjacent to Berkeley Square, was Jennie and Randolph's first London home, which the Duke of Marlborough bought for them. It was intended as Winston's birthplace

Lee Remick as Jennie, walking up the staircase of Blenheim Palace in the 1974 television series *Jennie: Lady Randolph Churchill*. For many, this series created the image of Jennie that has persisted today

Clara Hall Jerome seated in black with her three daughters and seven grandchildren c.1888. Jennie is standing imperiously at the back with Winston next to her

The iconic image of the beautiful Jennie as a young mother with smouldering eyes and flanked by her two young sons, Winston and Jack, c.1889

On the carpet-covered lawn at Cowes: Leonie, the 'devoted Hugh' Warrender, Jack Churchill, Jennie and Winston, pale and convalescent in a wicker chair

Count Charles Kinsky, the man Jennie loved and lost, posing on his horse Zoedone, on which he won the 1883 Grand National. Kinsky bought the chestnut mare and had her trained especially for the National with himself as jockey

Three of Jennie's lovers, Lord Falmouth, Lord Rossmore and Major Caryl Ramsden of the Seaforth Highlanders, who led her a merry dance. According to the words of a popular tune, 'kissing a man without a moustache is like eating an egg without salt'

Jennie, posing for the fashionable Parisian photographer, Gaspard-Félix Tournachon, known as Nadar, c.1885. Nadar photographed hundreds of nineteenth-century Parisian notables over many decades, had a keen eye for the personalities of his sitters and was renowned for his pictures of writers, musicians, poets, critics and political radicals, many of whom were part of 'la vie de Bohème'

possible that Winston's childhood was not quite as painful as he painted it in *My Early Life*. The myth that created Winston Churchill as the greatest Briton who, from an early birth onwards, had to battle against adversity to scale the heights may have been based partly on fact. But it began its life in the pages of this memoir. Jennie was never a cold mother uncomfortable with expressing affection. She and Winston always had an open and warm relationship even when she needed to reprimand him. Many children complain they are not loved enough. Winston was skilled at doing precisely that.

In November 1882, when he was first sent away five weeks after term had commenced to St George's School near Ascot, he was an eight-year-old from a background that was both privileged and deprived. He was excited as well as agitated at the prospect of living in an unfamiliar place: 'The fateful day arrived. My mother took me to the station in a hansom cab. She gave me three half-crowns which I dropped on to the floor of the cab and we had to scramble about in the straw to find them again. We only just caught the train. If we had missed it, it would have been the end of the world. However we didn't, and the world went on.'

Winston goes on to describe with wry humour the lessons to which he was subjected. But there was not much amusing about descriptions of flogging with the birch, which was an important feature of school life. On his own admission, Winston made very little progress and was so frequently in trouble one assumes that he came often to know quite how ghastly that brutal form of punishment was. His parents had chosen one of the most fashionable and expensive preparatory schools for boys in the country, one which prepared boys for Eton, Harrow and Winchester. But the headmaster, the Rev. H. W. Sneyd-Kynnersley, a man of High Church and low morals, was a particularly revolting sadist who not only enjoyed inflicting a cruel flogging on the small boys in his care but then took pleasure afterwards in clearing up the explosions of excreta left on his walls by his terrified victims. Winston wrote later that the floggings exceeded in severity anything that would be tolerated by the Home Office in any government reformatory.

Clearly, the boy was deeply miserable at this school, which declared its snobbish credentials by the shiny new crest erected above the entrance, intended to catch the eye of impressionable parents. He wrote many letters begging for a visit from either his mother or Mrs Everest. But in most of his letters, probably knowing they would be censored, he concealed his extreme unhappiness from his parents. Within weeks of arrival he wrote: 'My dear Mamma, I hope you are quite well. I am very happy at school.'

He added that he had spent a very happy birthday, evidently alone, and concluded: 'Do not forget to come down on the 9th Decer.'[35]

Should Jennie and Randolph have looked harder for warning signs? If his teachers recognised that he was at once backward and precocious, 'reading books beyond my years and yet at the bottom of my Form', why did not his parents? Why did they have to wait until he was in such a low state of health and so seriously ill that the family doctor, the celebrated Robson Roose, who then practised mainly in Brighton, advised removing him?

Lady Soames, Winston's youngest daughter, speaks with a degree of objectivity derived not merely from her biographical skills but also from never having known Jennie. She insists that she never heard her father say one disparaging remark about his mother. But she cannot wholly absolve her grandmother from blame. 'I have rather a negative spin [on Jennie's mothering skills] derived from my mother who didn't like her and thought she only discovered Papa when he became famous.'[36] Mary Soames herself, having often wondered if that was an entirely fair comment, says she did once ask a very old cousin who had known Jennie 'whether Lord and Lady Randolph were really such awful parents'. She explained that this cousin, Sylvia Henley, a woman of impeccable honesty and truthfulness inculcated in an earlier age, took a minute or two to compose her answer, but her reply was unequivocal. 'I think that even by the standards of their generation . . . they were pretty awful.'[37]

Yet the dangers, in these days of plentiful educational psychologists, of applying hindsight, of assuming that nineteenth-century parents understood their children or even considered it their duty to try, are all too apparent. It seems hardly fair to conclude that because Winston's childhood is mentioned only twice in Jennie's *Reminiscences* she was not interested. After all, she scarcely mentioned lovers either. That tough schools produced worthy men was an *a priori* assumption. If the occasional flogging was the way it was achieved, then it was best not to inquire too closely, many believed. 'Taking it on the chin' was a Jerome family motto which Jennie, with occasional lapses, applied as sternly to herself as to her sons. 'All three sisters were hard on their children when they were young,' explains Jennifer Leslie, Leonie's granddaughter. 'Don't be a bore, grow up or go away, were the usual response to an unhappy incident . . . That's how it was.'[38]

But Mrs Everest did not subscribe to this view. When she noticed the horrific scars and birch marks on her young charge, who had soon turned pale and weak and susceptible to a variety of illnesses, she immediately told his mother. Anita Leslie remembers discussing the school with Winston, her father's cousin, at a time when she herself was the mother of an eight-year-old. He told her: 'If my mother hadn't listened to Mrs Everest and taken me away I would have broken down completely. Can you imagine a child being *broken down?* . . . I can never forget that school. It was *horrible.*'[39]

Jennie, one might point out in her defence, was young – twenty-eight – when Winston first went away – and knew nothing of English boarding schools. This one had only recently opened its doors, so there was little reputation to garner. She was, in the autumn of 1882, still worried about her husband's health, in great emotional turmoil and, by December of that year, seriously ill herself. On such random facts are myths established. But, had she not fallen so dangerously ill that winter, might she have visited him more and discovered his suffering for herself?

A particularly painful letter survives. Jennie wrote to Randolph in Monte Carlo on 26 December about Winston's first school report. Kynnersley also sent her a bill for the next term: 'I must own I think rather a strong order to have to pay £52 for one month,' was Jennie's response. 'As to Winston's improvement I am sorry to say I see none. Perhaps there has not been time enough. He can read very well but that is all, and the first two days he came home he was terribly slangy and loud. Altogether I am disappointed. But Everest was told down there that next term they meant to be more strict with him . . . when I get well I shall take him in hand. It appears that he is afraid of me.'[40]

But a brief perusal of her 1882 diary gives a clue to her lifestyle before she fell ill: she painted, rode horses, shopped, went for drives with friends and occasionally engaged in charity work with the Duchess – 'drove to Stonesfield to give away blankets etc.'. From this evidence, it is impossible to conclude that hers was anything other than a life of leisure, typical of married women in her social milieu, with the various activities fitted in largely in order to pass a long day. She was often alone, without Randolph, and would entertain gentlemen friends to luncheon – chiefly, but not exclusively, the Star.

One of her most frequent guests at this time was the beautiful and wayward Blanche Hozier, mother of Clementine, who would later marry Winston. The former Blanche Ogilvy was young, passionate, promiscuous and unhappily married to a much older man, Henry Hozier. Although she did not separate from her husband for another eight or so years, her scandalous lifestyle and marital disharmony were well known and gossiped about at the time. In 1891 Wilfrid Scawen Blunt wrote in his 'Secret Memoirs' that she had had at least nine lovers.[41] That Jennie was so openly friendly with such a woman – they sometimes met at least twice a week – might indicate a certain brazenness on Jennie's part. Blanche, whose first child Kitty was born in 1883, was then living with her husband at Queen Anne's Gate in deep infidelity. One of her most intimate friends was Bay Middleton, believed by some to be the father of Clementine (who was born in 1885), and a man whom Jennie had got to know while in Dublin.

William George Middleton, nicknamed 'Bay' possibly on account of his reddish-brown hair, was a brilliant rider to hounds and steeplechaser with an expert knowledge of horsemanship gained since his earliest childhood. On his father's side he came from a prominent Scottish sporting family with large estates in Ayrshire. His ebullient personality and enormous, often irresistible charm was offset by a strain of melancholy and a deep interest in the theatre. He was the sort of gentleman whose idea of a thoroughly good practical joke was to challenge a woman to discover his hiding place in her bedroom when he had crawled into the bolster on her bed. In 1876, aged thirty, he was asked to 'pilot' the thirty-eight-year-old Empress Elisabeth of Austria, a woman of exceptional beauty and talent at steeplechasing. For five seasons – two of them in Ireland – Bay Middleton guided and directed the Empress Elisabeth on her horse. It was at this time that Bay met Jennie, as her life in Ireland also revolved around hunting. In 1877 he was engaged to be married to the heiress Charlotte Baird but was far too busy hunting and partying with the Empress. Gossip about his activities – although he was not romantically linked to Jennie – was rife.

The friendship between Jennie and Bay continued once they were back in London, and his name is often mentioned as one of her party. In his 'Secret Memoirs', Wilfrid Scawen Blunt, one of Blanche's former lovers, wrote on 22 June 1892: 'lunched with Blanche Hozier. She tells me that . . . Bay Middleton was the two elder children's father. He broke his neck at a Steeplechase in the spring.' If Blanche discussed such matters with Blunt, it seems likely that Jennie, too, would have been the recipient of her innermost thoughts at a time when Bay was a regular part of their circle. The Empress had just left England in February 1882 and, in the autumn of that year, Bay married his patient fiancée Charlotte.

Such was Jennie's life. What of Randolph, himself bullied and miserable as a schoolchild? Is it reasonable to expect him to have resisted repeating the pattern of parents doing precisely what was done to them? Randolph, when well, was preoccupied with politics, with changing the Commons leadership as well as with cultivating new areas of Conservative support.

His activities as leader of the Fourth Party, and his popularity with the masses thanks to his powerful demagoguery rather than any concern for their welfare, meant that he was suddenly being mentioned as a potential leader. It is precisely because the chance of Randolph leading the Tory Party appeared so real at this time that Gladstone was driven to abuse all Churchills, from John of Marlborough down, adding emphatically: 'God forbid that any great English party should be led by a Churchill!'[42]

But political success is not an excuse for neglecting one's children. There is no evidence that Randolph knew anything about the Sneyd-Kynnersley establishment before sending Winston there. Certainly some fathers at this time made it their business to find out about their children's welfare. For example, Joseph Chamberlain took serious pains to ensure that his children should be properly looked after at school. When it was proposed that the young Austen Chamberlain should be beaten for some trifling offence, his father sent a curt telegram to the headmaster warning that, if anything of the kind occurred, Austen would be removed from the school instantly.[43] Both Winston's parents, by contrast, tolerated a system in which he was beaten mercilessly and sadistically.

Winston was not alone in suffering at St George's. Roger Fry, the art-historian friend of Virginia Woolf, was head boy before Winston arrived. In this role he was obliged to assist Sneyd-Kynnersley in his cruel floggings. He described how 'in the middle of the room was a large box draped in black cloth and in austere tones the culprit was told to take down his trousers and kneel before the block over which I and the other boy held him down. The swishing was given with the Master's full strength and it took only two or three strokes for drops of blood to form everywhere. [The headmaster] took an intense sadistic pleasure in these floggings.'

And yet – a telling indication that Jennie was not alone in putting up with what she probably knew was happening – Fry's parents had been assured in advance this was a school *where there were no punishments*. How did his parents reconcile their consciences, the adult Fry asked, for 'I cannot doubt that they knew or else they would have expressed more surprise than they did when later on I revealed the horrid fact to them'?[44] The writer Maurice Baring, who was born the same year as Winston but attended the school just after he had left, similarly had little positive to write about it. By the time he was there 'dreadful legends' were told about Winston. 'He had been flogged for taking sugar from the pantry and so far from being penitent he had taken the Headmaster's sacred straw hat from where it hung over the door and kicked it to pieces.'[45]

For two years Winston was, not surprisingly, miserable at school while his parents were apparently oblivious. The argument might be made that other children 'survived' such treatment. But Winston, small for his age, newly displaced by a younger brother, the son of a prominent and controversial politician and described by another pupil as 'displaying exhibitionism and a quarrelsome attitude', was, it is now evident, particularly vulnerable. At the very least, Winston clearly perceived that his parents were visiting him less than other parents. Some of the letters from St George's make for almost tragic reading. At least one has a pencilled dinner-invitation list on the back – 'Cadogans, Gladys, Sir R Peel, Duke of Portland' – Jennie perhaps carried this about her for days wondering when or what to reply, her concerns over organising the dinner, in the end, taking priority. The enforced separation, in addition to that of any upper-class family where the nanny was the primary carer, did not make the relationship any easier between mother and son. 'I shall be glad when Winston goes back to school he is so idle and of course that is conducive to naughtiness and, à la longue, one can't manage him,' Jennie complained.[46]

By 1883 Jennie's life entered a new and more demanding phase. In the autumn Churchill, Gorst, Wolff and their friend Algernon Borthwick of the *Morning Post* refined a brilliant initiative to capitalise on all the untapped female goodwill which they recognised could be used so effectively to galvanise the middle classes, or rather to cut across classes. They invented a support group to be called the Primrose League – a mark of respect to Disraeli, whose favourite flower it was – as a means of spreading Conservative principles among as wide a swathe of the population as they could reach.

Lady Dorothy Nevill, a close friend of Randolph's mother, liked to claim that the League had originated at her Sunday luncheon table where many leading lights of the more militant section of the Conservative Party, especially Randolph, regularly met. Here she said was first conceived the idea of 'moulding into a compact body the more active and energetic partisans of the newer and more democratic school of Conservatism . . . a club of young and enterprising Conservatives'.[47] Officially, the League was formed by four members of the Carlton Club in its card room on 17 November 1883. For Churchill, the inspiration was always Tory Democracy, or his own brand of political opportunism, which brought together the upper class and their natural followers in the working class, enshrined in his motto 'Trust the people and they will trust you.' Shrewdly, he understood the importance of carrying with him an increasingly literate working class.* This transformed the Conservative Party, traditionally the party of the squirearchy, and membership of the League soon grew to nearly two million.

The League, loosely inspired by the Orange Lodges and with Masonic undertones, was organised around local clubs, called Habitations. Male members were poetically known as Knights, women as Dames, and badges and decorations based on the Primrose were encouraged in order to reinforce the message. Initially, there was little support for allowing women to be members. But Randolph believed that, though without a vote themselves, they could and often did influence their husbands' vote. And so his mother, the Duchess of Marlborough, was made president of the Ladies' Grand Council and Jennie became dame president of many of the habitations. As she frankly admitted in an interview with the *Pall Mall Gazette*, she used the League as a means of electioneering, made so much more difficult by the 1883 Corrupt Practices Act, which prohibited the payment of election agents.[48] Almost all of Churchill's relatives were involved in the League in some way, and were given numbered diplomas upon enrolment. Jennie was number eleven. It swiftly became a formidable canvassing weapon and provided a 'raucous but effective vehicle of propaganda for Churchill as much as for Toryism'.[49]

Jennie, never interested in the finer points of intellectual political argument, travelled the country doing what she did best – organising concerts, recitals and garden parties to spread the message. She was astute enough to see how ridiculous the paraphernalia was. 'We laughed immoderately over the grandiloquent names – the "Knights Harbingers" (or "Night refugees" as we dubbed them) . . . We criticized freely the Brummagen gaudy badges and "ye ancient" diplomas printed on vellum,' she says in her *Reminiscences*.[50] But she understood full well the significance of the League and, however quaint the ceremonies, however comical the songs and recitations, however boring the meetings, was determined to do all she could to further its aims, which in effect were the promotion of her own husband.

She worked strenuously on behalf of the Primrose League for many years. She could not have been more supportive of Randolph's personal political cause. But although she developed genuine political interests, women at this time were unable to do much more than support from a distance with feminine decorum. As the *St Stephen's Review* commented:

* In a speech given in Birmingham in April 1884 Randolph defined his core belief as promoting popular support for the monarchy, the House of Lords and the Church of England – the traditional bulwarks of Toryism. In fact he was fundamentally an opportunist.

'Each Dame may drive in her luxurious carriage to the rendezvous and, with sweet persuasive words, we can imagine the undecided voter induced to step in . . . how the scale may be turned by the influence of the Dames of the Primrose League.'[51] Perhaps Jennie's neglect of her young son in the 1880s owed less to her growing involvement in politics and more to the fact that she had met the man who was to become the core of her emotional life. By 1883 a new name is creeping into the letters between Jennie and Randolph – that of Count Charles Kinsky. That year the handsome Austrian won the Grand National at Aintree on Zoedone, a short-legged chestnut mare he had bought the previous year from a stable at Oakham. Kinsky had him trained for the National with himself as jockey. Jennie already knew Kinsky by then as he gave her a beautiful side-saddle with high pommels after the race as a 'thank-you' gift for her encouragement. Suddenly, the brave Austrian Count was the talk of fashionable London. Every hostess wanted him at her table – or more. One of the first to invite him was Lady Castlereagh. Arriving late at her dinner party, he explained that because his cab driver was drunk and his own English so poor (it rapidly improved) he had gone to the wrong house. One of the other guests said: 'I suppose you were very angry with your cabman?' 'Oh yes,' said Charles Kinsky. 'I did give him one hell of a rowing. He drove me all over London,' and, waving his arms to express himself, he knocked the plate of soup which was being handed to him right into the lap of the beautiful Lady Castlereagh.[52] Kinsky often told this story, insisting that his hostess took the unfortunate accident not only with perfect good humour but continued her conversation with him as if nothing had happened.

Cosmopolitan in his every fibre, he was immensely popular and at ease in the upper echelons of society in a variety of European capitals. But he especially loved England. Charles Andreas Kinsky, born in Vienna in November 1858, eldest son of Prince Ferdinand Kinsky von Wichnitz und Tettau and Princess Marie zu Lichtenstein, was the man Jennie loved best all her life. He was everything she desired in a lover: linguist, pianist, brilliant sportsman and champion jockey, devastatingly good-looking heir to the fabulous Palais Kinsky in Vienna as well as to the Kinsky legend.

According to the romantic Kinsky myth, a hunting party in medieval Bohemia, led by a princess, was attacked by wolves. The entourage immediately scattered, but one man stood by the Princess and drove off the wolves, killing three. In gratitude, the King knighted the brave young man and a coat of arms featuring three wolves' teeth was chosen to record his gallant act. Throughout the middle ages the fame, and power, of the

House of Kinsky spread. Soon the family was well known throughout Europe for its breeding of top-quality, gold-coloured horses, known for their courage and stamina, especially in cavalry charges.

After a brief spell in the army – Charles joined the Dragoon Regiment Number One in 1877 – he then began to study law but, following his father's advice, gave this up to pursue a diplomatic career. Appointed honorary attaché at the Austro-Hungarian Embassy in London in 1880, he spent thirteen years there altogether, becoming a full attaché in September 1886. Few diplomats knew more about England and the British people than he. These years were interrupted by short stays in Berlin, Dresden and Vienna itself, and later he was sent to other Austrian embassies in Brussels, Dresden, Rome and St Petersburg. But the thirteen years in London correspond to the years of his greatest relationship with Jennie Churchill. She was profoundly in love with him. She was not alone in her admiration of the man. Within the Churchill family Randolph himself, in spite of his wife's much talked-about intimacy with him, also delighted in his company. Moreton Frewen called Kinsky 'the best Austrian that ever was', and Leonie was to invite him to stand godfather to her second son.

According to a 400-page personal file on him in the Austrian Staatsarchiv there is an indication that his twenty-three years of diplomatic service were not altogether smooth.[53] He sometimes complains about having been slighted for preferment, and that his potential was not fully recognised by his superiors. In one letter he says explicitly that while in England at the Austrian Embassy he had negotiated for himself a certain amount of free time which was at his disposal to allow him to pursue his own interests. Perhaps this is what led to his superiors' failure to consider him seriously enough. But it was this 'free time' that enabled him to see as much as he did of Jennie. Even when he was sent on short postings abroad he retained his London flat as well as his string of hunters in Leicestershire.

Jennie's sisters soon considered the relationship with Kinsky a *fait accompli*. Writing to her mother, Clara Frewen reported: 'Randolph is going to Ireland to stop with Lord Dunraven for the Easter Holidays. Kinsky is here for a week and Jennie comes every day to see me.'[54] Thus were the proprieties observed – more or less. In one of his schoolboy letters to his young brother, Winston wrote that after he returned to London for the weekend: 'I went, as Mamma had told me, to Aldford Street, where I found Mamma and Count Kinsky breakfasting.'[55] Leonie, too, carefully fed her mother tidbits about the relationship. Describing a visit to the House of Lords in June 1884 she noted: 'Jennie, with Kinsky, came in after . . .'[56]

No intimate letters between Jennie and Kinsky have survived. Scattered in the Churchill Archives are a few anodyne notes – mostly from 1900 onwards – referring to arrangements or condolence letters. There are a few letters from Kinsky to Jennie's sisters written in his big round handwriting from his home address, Wien Freiung 4, with a blue coronet on the left-hand side preserved in other archives. They are distinctive, easy to spot. One can imagine how Jennie's heart lurched when she received one. Kinsky descendants believe that Charles, 'a very tactful and extremely discreet person', a diplomat *par excellence*, destroyed his from Jennie. Yet piecing together the accounts of family members on both sides reveals how deep was the feeling each had for the other.

'Stories concerning Charles K and Lady R were often told to me by my grandmother, Sophie Kinsky née Mensdorff Pouilly . . . a clever and very well informed old lady, free of prejudice,' is all Kinsky's nephew Prince Clary could tell biographer Anita Leslie in 1967. Jennie was, according to this man, 'the only woman he really loved.' Some cousins and I used to have a sort of hero worship for this uncle and we often discussed what would have been if they could have got married.' Prince Clary went on: 'Charles Kinsky was my mother's cousin and a great friend of hers, so I remember knowing him very well from my earliest childhood until his death. He was quite fearless, racing or hunting, but also in a different way, whenever he had to stand up for his opinions or beliefs.'[57]

He was also a man of extravagant tastes dependent on his intensely conservative family who could never have entertained the prospect of a marriage with this American woman – even had she been free to marry – other than with horror. Like the Churchills, he was a regular gambler and often in serious financial difficulties when he lost a lot of money in one night. Usually, he borrowed the money from the great saviour of gamblers, Sam Lewis, until his father in Austria made good. But, after one loss too many, his father made him promise never to borrow money again from Jews such as Lewis. In this, and in one other matter of great consequence, he did not stand up to his father.[58]

It is impossible to say precisely when Winston first become aware of his mother having lovers. According to William Manchester in *The Last Lion*: 'All we can say with certainty is that Winston knew about Jennie's affairs. The question is when?' Manchester then tells a story of how the young boy's suspicions were aroused by spotting a flaw in his mother's stockings. 'In the late 1870s fashionable women in London wore red hose. Red was his favourite colour. As she left home one noon, according to this account, he noticed a blemish in her left stocking just above her shoe and when she returned several hours later he saw the imperfection had moved from her left ankle to her right.'[59] Whether such an account can be believed, or whether Winston himself believed as a schoolboy that his mother had lovers, is a moot point. Kinsky, like most of his mother's male admirers, certainly became a warm friend and father figure to Winston.

But it would not be long before others gossiped about her private life, gossip that the young Winston refused to countenance openly but which found its expression in his novel *Savrola*. 'As she stood there in the clear light of the autumn evening, she looked divinely beautiful,' the twenty-five-year-old Winston wrote of his heroine, five years after his father's death. It is a book he could never have contemplated writing during his father's lifetime.

> She had arrived at that age of life when, to the attractions of a maiden's beauty, are added those of a woman's wit. Her perfect features were the mirror of her mind, and displayed with every emotion and every mood that vivacity of expression which is the greatest of woman's charms. Her tall figure was instinct with grace, and the almost classic dress she wore enhanced her beauty and harmonised with her surroundings. Something in her face suggested a wistful aspiration.

By the end of the novel, Winston's beautiful heroine Lucile has found that to which she wistfully aspired. Once she expresses her love for Savrola 'life was more real and strongly coloured than in the cold days at the palace amid splendour, power and admiration. She had found what she had lacked, and so had he.'

Savrola should not be read as a thinly disguised account of his parents' relationship. But the portrait of the lovers, Lucile and Savrola, bears more than a passing resemblance to the way the son viewed his mother's suffering at this time. However much Kinsky replenished her inner life and shored up her battered emotions, her private life with Randolph, who was away as much as he was home, fishing, walking, climbing mountains or searching for a healthier climate, was as turbulent as ever. As Winston observed, and re-created in his novel: Lucile and her husband saw each other 'less frequently and in those short intervals talked more and more of business and politics.'[60]

In reality, money and the difficulty of paying bills was the root of many of Jennie's and Randolph's problems. But 1883 was difficult for Randolph in a different way. In July his father died, very suddenly, aged sixty-one. The night before, he had dined with Randolph and seemed in fighting form. He, too, had started his political career as MP for Woodstock and, although not responsible for any significant piece of legislation, had gone on to hold a prominent position in more than one Conservative cabinet and was generally considered to have acquitted himself well in Dublin as viceroy. He was a stabilising influence on both his surviving sons, but Randolph in particular had a genuine admiration and affection for his father. It was said that when they worked in Dublin together the son would often put his arm around the father and kiss his cheek.

The Duke's death released some money but not enough for Randolph's brother, George, now the eighth Duke, for whom it was largely entailed. According to the terms of the Duke's will, after various bequests mostly to his children, the residue of the personal estate was to be held in trust for the Duchess until her death. Then it was all to come to Lord Randolph Churchill. Not surprisingly, Leonard Jerome, who seems to have been told the news rather quickly, breathed an all too audible sigh of relief: 'The Duke's action in regard to Randolph must make his brother furious and they were anything but friends before. I am so glad to hear of R's good fortune. In course of time you ought to be very comfortable,' he wrote to his daughter.[61]

The new Duke, furious at the distribution, speedily embarked on a sale of some of the family's great art treasures to raise cash. When Randolph objected, describing the pictures as a trust, the Duke countered sarcastically: 'I look to your conservative teaching, my Dear R, to open to me a vista of careful undertakings and an area of cultivated thought.'[62] The family arguments erupted violently and publicly in the summer of 1883 as Randolph, having striven to defend his brother's tattered reputation in the press, was now engaged in a virulent private feud over family heirlooms. His desperate mother, depending increasingly on the favoured younger son to stop the actions of the elder, succeeded only in raising the temperature. In this heated atmosphere Churchill decided he would give up the Woodstock seat. His mother implored him to think again.

After the old Duke's funeral Randolph went away first to Pontresina in Switzerland and then with Jennie and the boys on holiday to the Austrian spa resort of Bad Gastein for the rest of the summer. Meeting his friend Wilfrid Scawen Blunt, who found the place desperately dull, Randolph reprimanded him in lugubrious tones for not understanding that he must do nothing, 'since it was a *sine qua non* of the baths that you do nothing'.[63] Hardly a holiday chosen with the needs of his young boys uppermost.

On their return they moved into Blenheim, always the place of safest refuge for Randolph, even with the new Duke, for the winter. The brothers found some sort of accommodation. Since much of the day was spent hunting, Jennie at least managed to keep herself occupied in a way she enjoyed. But she was feeling desperately low, impoverished and worried about her own father's health. As she told Randolph, her mother had responded by asking for her favourite piece of jewellery:

> I have got something very sad to tell you . . . Mama has taken away the diamond star and how poor I am. I have got *nothing*. Of course I could not refuse to let it go and she wants to sell it to put the money in Moreton's ranch as she says if anything were to happen to Papa she might have very little to live on. Luckily for me my heart is not set on jewels but I do feel sorry to have it go as it was so becoming and the only thing I ever wore.[64]

In course of time, Leonard had written consolingly, Jennie and Randolph ought to inherit more money. But time was the commodity they never had and the money a mere dangle in the future awaiting the Duchess's death. Randolph was able in February 1884 to raise a loan of £31,000 from the Scottish Widows Life Insurance Office on the strength of his mother's fortune.[65] But the decline in his own health hardly made him a creditworthy risk able to raise further loans other than among his friends, putting him increasingly on his mettle to make some himself.

7

Lord Randolph Churchill will Probably Always Retain a Great Power of Mischief

~

JENNIE WAS THIRTY years of age in 1884 and at the height of her beauty. She fizzed with energy and unfulfilled dreams. But the man she had married now turned his back on her. The parties she wished to attend were still barred to her.

That year her patience, along with Randolph's dazzling political success, persuaded the Prince of Wales that it was at last time to rekindle the friendship with the Churchills. He agreed to meet Randolph at a dinner on 9 March hosted by the Attorney General, Sir Henry James. James, a bachelor with a string of illegitimate children, was one of Randolph's closest cronies. The men shared holidays and James had been manoeuvring for months to bring about peace between Marlborough House and Connaught Place. It was to take another two years before the Prince dined At Home with the Churchills, on 16 May 1886. When he did so Jennie's beauty and charm were said to work wonders and the evening was a great success. But the initial reconciliation – so important that the Prime Minister, Gladstone, a man who loathed Randolph but always behaved charmingly to Jennie, was invited as witness – marked their rehabilitation into London society after nearly a decade. In her memoirs Jennie conflated the two events, but her comment that this time the reconciliation was a lasting one was correct. The Prince however, commented tartly to his brother Prince George that he 'thought it best to be on speaking terms though we can never be the same friends again'.[1]

Eighteen-eighty-four was a turning point for the Churchills in many ways. Randolph had now shown his ability to speak so compellingly that one American journalist described him as 'the political sensation of England'.[2] Exile had focused him: Ireland had given him an identity. His dramatic rise can be dated to a speech he made early that year, known as the 'chips' speech. Randolph maintained that chips were all that Mr Gladstone had given to those who supported him in 1880. 'Chips to the faithful allies in Afghanistan, chips to the trusting native races of South Africa, chips to the Egyptian fellah, chips to the British farmer, chips to the manufacturer and the artisan, chips to the agricultural labourer, chips to the House of Commons itself.'[3]

A few days after this speech, aware that under the provisions of the Redistribution Bill the family borough of Woodstock which he had represented for almost ten years would be swept away, he boldly agreed that at the next general election he would fight the Central Division of Birmingham, fast overtaking Manchester as the great industrial centre of the country. Although he did not abandon Woodstock immediately, taking his fight for Tory Democracy into the stronghold of radicalism in this way was a direct challenge to Chamberlain and John Bright, two of the three MPs who represented the Midlands city. On a good day there was a touch of genius about Randolph and many of his decidedly non-Victorian notions caught the mood of the moment.

But, while he seemed to be winning the hearts of Tory working men, the press, with a few exceptions, attacked him viciously. Jennie kept thousands of Romeikes (press cuttings supplied by the clipping agency of that name), even the unpleasant ones, sending many of them to her father in New York, who never gave up hope of Randolph's eventual triumph. Yet Jennie wrote of how even George Buckle, editor of *The Times*,

> who was by way of being a friend of ours, often, if not invariably, wrote slating articles on him. One night I met him at the Speaker's after a particularly poisonous leader had appeared in the morning *Times*. Coming up, he half chaffingly asked me if I intended to speak to him or if I was too angry.
>
> 'Angry? Not a bit,' I replied. 'I have ten volumes of press cuttings about Randolph all abusive. This will only be added to them.'[4]

Jennie's robust attitude was important. She recognised an essential truth that publicity had to be weathered. 'Great abuse of a public man only seems to help him to office,' she wrote. But the remark also indicates her understanding that the turbulence in their private relationship also had to be weathered. She had long ago decided that managing this was what mattered. Discretion – appearing calm and supportive in public – was going to require all her strength. Emotional toughness came at a price.

During the first six months of 1884, Randolph was also fighting for control of the National Union of Conservative Associations – today's Conservative Central Office. This was crucial as a power base. It was the body that decided policy, and Randolph wished to increase his power inside the party. He succeeded not only in boosting the powers of the National Union, but in getting himself elected chairman of the strengthened organisation. And so the summer of 1884 raced by in frenetic activity and travel. Randolph, believing that above all he must keep himself in the public eye in every way possible, issued a number of public letters. He came out openly for Fair Trade, a type of protectionism which appealed to working-class voters and which gave Tory Democracy its economic bite. His friend Lord Dunraven was President of the Fair Trade League. He tried to position himself as the voice of compromise on the controversial Franchise Bill, which was to enlarge the electorate by two million people, and spoke out strongly on matters of foreign policy. His rapprochement with his party leaders, or, more precisely, the deal he is believed to have struck with Lord Salisbury (that he had been promised the Indian secretaryship in return for toeing the line), gave him a new strength and made him appear indispensable to the Conservatives. Talk of Randolph not simply as a rising minister or future leading statesman but as a possible leader of the Tories, a thrilling prospect for Jennie, was on many important lips and in many echoing corridors.

Aware of her usefulness, Jennie accompanied her husband when she could. In April they were in Birmingham together, visiting some of the 'principal manufactures' and then laying the foundation stone of a new school in an area of growing prosperity. But sometimes Jennie went alone, as on the occasion when she distributed certificates to members of the local St John Ambulance Brigade. Such carefully crafted activities may be commonplace for an MP's wife today but were daringly new in the 1880s.

In May, the *Pall Mall Gazette*, normally supportive, made a shrewd assessment of Randolph's artful exploitation of his political and personal position.

> Lord Randolph Churchill looks at the sea of upturned faces as if he really liked and was interested in every one of them. He has himself one of those striking faces which inspire interest and he has an eminently sympathetic manner and voice . . . In a word, Lord Randolph Churchill has, or seems to have, soul . . . Added to this our political Ishmael artfully fosters the idea that every man's hand is against him, that he is in disgrace at court, that his leaders won't speak to him, though in fact he dines with them frequently, and that he has nothing to trust to but the people's favour. When therefore he appears bareheaded before the populace, accompanied by his young and pretty wife, we have the perfect historical type of the aristocratic demagogue 'qui a bien étudié sa bête'.[5]

Randolph's manoeuvrings within the party, as well as his feverish travel around the country, built up as summer went on. In August he was in Manchester, for most of September he was in Scotland, either seeing his sister Anne and brother-in-law, the Duke and Duchess of Roxburghe at their magnificent baronial home, Floors Castle, or staying with politicians such as W. H. Smith and Sir Stafford Northcote off the coast of Ross. But in a newspaper interview he maintained perversely that he preferred going either to Paris and living a boulevard life, or to Brighton and lying twenty out of twenty-four hours in bed.[6] At all events, he was spending so little time at home with his family that Joseph Chamberlain felt free to comment on the state of his marriage in the House: 'I do not know what the domestic habits of the noble lord are but I confess I am inclined to augur badly of him if he thinks it a matter of suspicion for a gentleman to stop at home with his family.'[7] His remarks were met with cries of 'Oh!'

With all this political activity it was not only Jennie's needs that were overlooked. Winston's letters in 1883–4 make pitiful reading as he begged for visits from his mother, from Everest and Jack or indeed from anyone – and counted the days until he could come home. 'You must send somebody to see me,' he wailed in February 1884.[8] A few months later he reprimanded his mother: 'It is very unkind of you not to write to me before this, I have had one letter from you this term.'[9] His letters were short, probably censored, revealing little of his childhood traumas. But surely his school reports sounded a warning bell? His first report said he must treat his work more seriously, his second that he 'does not understand the meaning of hard work . . . Spelling about as bad as it well can be.' The report following his third term described him as 'very naughty' and 'troublesome'. His fourth declared that he was 'rather greedy at meals'.

But it was his fifth, covering the period from 1 March to 9 April, which was almost tragic in its admission of failure to teach. In it he was described as 'very bad – is a constant trouble to everybody and is always in some scrape or other. He cannot be trusted to behave himself anywhere. He has very good abilities.' His penultimate report from St George's declared that the boy 'has no ambition' and was 'still troublesome'.[10] What seems so blindingly obvious today – that a boy with such marked abilities who was failing to achieve must be suffering through a fault of the school, not his own – was not so evident to Victorian parents. Nonetheless, Jennie's blindness to her son's needs at this time cannot be excused. She freely admitted that without Everest she could not manage the boy, and sometimes 'I'm afraid even she can't do it.'[11]

Finally, the decision was made to remove Winston from St George's after less than two years. Most likely, Mrs Everest's testimony had been the deciding factor. Randolph's absences may have given Jennie increased independence in certain spheres, but he was unquestionably consulted on this matter. It was decided in September to send the boy, not quite ten yet, to a much gentler school run by two elderly spinsters, Kate and Charlotte Thompson, at 29 and 30 Brunswick Road, Brighton. It was thought the sea air would do him good. Also, it was near the family doctor, Robson Roose, who was based in Brighton and could therefore keep an eye on him. St George's was in future avoided by all the family. Jack Churchill, when the time came, went to a preparatory school at Elstree and the Leslie and Frewen children to Ludgrove and Speldhurst Lodge, Tunbridge Wells.

An outsider who met Winston at this time was enormously impressed not merely by the boy himself but by his mother's confidence in his abilities. George Smalley, the American newspaperman, was staying with the Churchills at one of their rented summer homes, Great Forsters, a fine old Elizabethan mansion near Egham in Surrey. He recalled how Winston wanted to go boating one morning on the river and invited his mother, younger brother and the American guest to accompany him.

> He took command of the party, first on land and then on the water. Nobody thought of disputing his claim, including his mother. I had lived enough in boats to see that Winston, though with no great skills in watermanship, knew what he was about and though he ran some needless risks, it was never necessary to interfere. The critical moments were never dangerous and we landed as we had embarked, quite safely.[12]

Yet, almost as soon as Winston settled in at his new school, Jennie and Randolph dashed off for two months to New York. The holiday was partly to attend the wedding of Jennie's youngest sister, the twenty-five-year-old Leonie, to Jack Leslie, an Anglo-Irish Grenadier Guardsman and talented artist she had met years before in Dublin. Once again, neither set of parents was happy about the match. Once again, Leonard Jerome had to endure insults from the groom's parents, horrified that their son was marrying the daughter of a speculator – a gambler who, it was believed, made money at someone else's expense.

'My son', wrote Sir John Leslie to Leonard, 'is acting entirely in opposition to my desire and without my approval . . . I think you ought to know that I am in absolute possession of my estates,' he added as a stinging rebuke.[13] These estates, scattered around Ireland, amounted to approximately 50,000 acres of land generating revenues of over £21,000.[14] But although these revenues were declining, the Leslies' aspirations to distinction were not. Sir John, who had been created baronet after serving as MP for Monaghan, and his wife Constance viewed a marriage between their only son and Leonie Jerome, sister of the well-known socialite Jennie Churchill, as a *mésalliance*. They had other daughters to consider and worried that this was a mismatch which could spoil the girls' chances.

Nonetheless, in October, Leonie, the last of Leonard and Clara Jerome's daughters to marry, wearing a dress of white satin and brocade draped with lace, and her mother's veil of point d'Alençon lace, took her vows at the fashionable Grace Church in Manhattan as her sister Clara had before her. The reception afterwards at the Jerome house, 25 Madison Square, East 26th Street, was for intimate friends and family only. The New York papers reported that she had married a man with an income of £30,000 a year – as she no doubt wished she had. Leonie, like her two sisters, had married for love rather than money. As she told her mother, the reality was that, like her sisters, she was 'awfully hard up'. Jack Leslie was going to ask his father for another £200 a year, other-wise 'one can't manage on £1,200 if one takes a house by the year and is in the Guards. I don't worry because the Leslies are sure to see us through and we have no debts to speak of.'[15] The Leslies did 'see them through', just, and the connection gave Leonie status, a castle (of sorts) and, eventually, a title. She recognised, as Jennie had warned her mother, how hard it was to marry well even for those who had money, which the Jeromes by this time did not.

Over the years, Sir John and Lady Leslie came to admire this American daughter-in-law. But in December 1884 they made it clear that she was unwelcome at their impressive London home, Stratford House. This mansion, built by Edward Stratford, later the second Earl of Aldborough, between 1770 and 1776, boasted a magnificent Angelica Kauffmann ceiling; Disraeli and many others had been royally entertained there. Instead, the young couple moved in at first with Jennie and Randolph at Connaught Place, an arrangement which thrilled Mrs Jerome, aware of the frequent loneliness at the core of Jennie's life but feeling powerless to help her proud daughter. 'What a delightful surprise,' she wrote to Jennie. 'Such a nice house and such a lot of jolly little people living together . . . Try to be good and enjoy yourselves.' But although the Jeromes rejoiced vicariously in 'Dear Randolph's success – I think he well deserved it and I hope he will come back well and strong to enjoy life for many long years' – there is also evidence of a mother's pain in this letter, ostensibly written to wish her daughter a happy new year. Clara Jerome admitted:

'I seldom write to you, my dear child. I don't know why unless it is, I hear all about you so often that I almost imagine that I hear from you. We read about Randolph's departure in the newspapers . . .'[16]

The departure this time was for India on 30 December. Jennie took both sons to wave their father off. Randolph would not return until April. According to Winston, advising his own son in 1953, this fact-finding trip was proof that a deal had been struck between Lord Randolph and Lord Salisbury promising him office as soon as possible. At the time Randolph maintained it was undertaken on grounds of health, not politics, and it seems there was an element of truth in that. At all events, Randolph now gleaned the same first-hand knowledge of India – unusual in British politics then – that he had earlier acquired of Ireland.

He wrote regularly to Jennie during his travels, although not always as fully as he wrote to his mother. Jennie insisted she shared all his letters to her with her mother-in-law but complained that she did not receive the same courtesy in return. If the Duchess had an interesting letter from Randolph she passed it on before Jennie had a chance to see it. Yet Randolph's letters to Jennie, from which she carefully quoted in her memoirs, 'made me greatly regret that I had not been able to accompany him'. But why had she not? 'I cannot tell you how much I wish you were with me,' he told her on 1 January 1885.[17] Perhaps the expense had weighed greatly, or perhaps she had decided she should be on hand for Winston and Jack?

Winston, even at the new school, continued to wrench at his mother's heart strings. 'You must be happy without me, no screams for Jack or complaints. It must be heaven on earth,' he wrote chillingly on 21 January.[18] Most likely, Randolph and Jennie needed to be away from each other. Whatever the reasons, when they were apart they showed in their letters a tenderness to each other and a lack of the rancour that increasingly characterised their day-to-day relationship.

The newspapers covered Lord Randolph's activities in detail. The political year of 1885 began brutally with the beheading of General Gordon by Islamic fundamentalists at Khartoum on 26 January, an event which dealt a heavy blow to Gladstone's faltering government. Queen Victoria herself was unhappy with Gladstone's ineptitude over the killing and the Government's failure to send out a relief mission in time. Randolph, at thirty-six a young thruster whose bellowing rudeness so irritated and flummoxed Gladstone, was abroad and therefore not in the House for the main debate. His presence was missed by his party. Yet his fury at the dilly-dallying failure to rescue Gordon was well known. 'The way Randy talked to

Gladstone was really no imitation of any way any man had ever spoken to another in our senate chamber,' was a common view.[19] From abroad, Randolph wrote to *The Times* accusing Lord Granville of being probably the worst foreign secretary England had ever had.

Leonard Jerome read all the press reports thoroughly. Randolph's rise genuinely delighted him, suggesting that perhaps he was not yet as aware as his wife of the state of his daughter's marriage. Or perhaps he believed that success might transform the relationship. 'Over and over he has been smashed, pulverised, so [?] ruthlessly squelched that he was considered done for ever. And yet a little after, up he comes, smiling as though he had never been hit at all,' Leonard wrote, echoing the way he, too, had determinedly struggled back from the brink of financial disaster. 'I confess I am amazed, so young! So reckless, inexperienced and impulsive! That he should have fought his way up through the fiery elements without, as the trotters say, a "skip or break" is indeed wonderful.'[20] Winston also from now on took great pride in his father's career and repeatedly asked for Randolph's autographs to distribute among his schoolfriends. This was not simply touching – he sold them to make money.

But, although he seemed to flourish at his new school, Winston still begged for more letters and visits from his mother. He even wrote to 'Woom' not simply asking her to come but complaining that he was going to 'give Mamma a lecture' for not writing to him. However, on 12 February, when the school put on a play followed by a grand party, Jennie did indeed travel to Brunswick Road, a visit which meant a lot to Winston, who was, she told Randolph, 'wildly excited'. But she also reported that she thought he looked rather pale and delicate and far from strong. 'What a care that boy is,' she added. 'But he acted quite wonderfully and looked so pretty.'[21]

There is no record of Lord Randolph ever visiting Winston at the Brunswick Road school other than in a crisis. Even when he was in Brighton for other reasons he could not find the time, much to his young son's deep disappointment. 'I cannot think why you did not come to see me . . . but I suppose you were too busy to come,' the boy chided.[22] Almost as soon as Randolph returned from India he went away again – to France with Sir Henry James – and was not back again until June. That month the Gladstone Government finally fell, replaced by that of the arch Tory, Lord Salisbury. And Jennie, after four months, at last got round to sending Winston his 'long promised' hamper of food.

Churchill was now appointed to high political office for the first time. In June 1885 he was made secretary of state for India in Lord Salisbury's new cabinet, a post which required him to fight another by-election in Woodstock shortly before the borough was swept away. This was the seat Randolph had held for ten years and on which his marriage to Jennie had depended. But this time he chose not to defend it personally. His decision was partly motivated by ongoing quarrels with his brother, now Duke of Marlborough, although still referred to in the family as Blandford. The eccentric eighth Duke spent most of his time conducting scientific experiments in a laboratory he had had built on the top floor of the Palace. Randolph was therefore relieved that his wife, aided by his sister Lady Georgiana Curzon, was prepared to undertake all the electioneering on his behalf. Although the Duke grudgingly allowed Lady Randolph to stay at Blenheim, she was forced to set up her committee rooms at the nearby Bear Hotel.

The women's activities were not groundbreaking in feminist terms. But Jennie attracted considerable press attention as she drove around the borough in a horse-drawn tandem sporting the chocolate and pink colours of Lord Randolph's racing stable. The two women visited all the outlying areas in this way asking for support. Although the other candidate, Corrie Grant, a radical, also called upon women to canvass for him, his helpers were of a decidedly more earnest, less glamorous type. It was generally agreed that Jennie's personal appeal to the voters in her gorgeous rustling gowns and enormous hats made all the difference. She herself wrote that, of the nine elections in which she was involved, Woodstock in 1885 was the one which left the pleasantest memories.

Randolph won by 532 votes to 405. He was not there himself to savour the victory. In the course of the evening of 4 July, he sent his wife a grateful telegram: 'Brilliant success almost entirely due to you and Georgie.' After the result was announced Lady Randolph herself took the floor. She asked for silence. But the loud cheering went on. Finally the noise abated and she said clearly if somewhat demurely: 'I cannot make you a speech but I thank you from the bottom of my heart for having returned Lord Randolph Churchill for the third time.' At this, loud cheering took over yet again followed by a spontaneous rendering of 'Rule Britannia' and 'For He's a Jolly Good Fellow'.

Henry James, the Attorney General, wrote to congratulate her: 'My gratification is slightly impaired by feeling I must introduce a new Corrupt Practices Act. Tandems must be put down and certainly some alteration . . . must be made in the means of ascent and descent therefrom; then arch looks will have to be scheduled . . . the graceful wave of a pocket handkerchief will have to be dealt with in committee.'[23] But not everyone approved of women openly involving themselves in politics even in this secondary fashion. A postcard to Lady Randolph, signed 'A Working Man', commented on the 'humiliating and unmanly position' of Lord Randolph Churchill in having to send his wife to struggle for his seat at the Woodstock by-election.[24] Jennie, however, was exhilarated. 'We were most important and felt that the eyes of the world were upon us,' is how she described it in her memoirs. 'I felt like a general holding a council of war with his staff in the heat of a battle.'[25] She went on: 'I surpassed the fondest hopes of the suffragettes and thought I was duly elected and I certainly experienced all the pleasure and gratification of being a successful candidate.'[26] For, as she boasted a few months later at a Primrose League event in Birmingham, there was not the slightest doubt that ladies could have great influence in politics if only they chose to exert it.

Randolph's new job, as he frankly admitted to his close friends, had long been a 'financial necessity . . . as they are very hard up', according to Lewis 'Loulou' Harcourt, private secretary to his father, Sir William Harcourt, the former Home Secretary.[27] But for Randolph, quite new to the strains of official life, being a member of the cabinet in what was known as the Caretaker Government – it was intended to hold office only until a general election could take place – was exhausting. He took his job extremely seriously, a severe task for a man in his state of chronic poor health, and he was not used to all the calls upon his time. Wilfrid Scawen Blunt, who met him at the India Office soon after his job commenced, remarked at first: 'I found Randolph very cheerful. "They will never make an official of me," he said with a funny smile.'[28] But a couple of weeks later, on 22 July, he wrote how Randolph 'looked fagged and ill and complained of the stairs, though in truth it was only one flight and not a steep one. He seemed quite exhausted.'

Sometimes these bouts of ill health lasted but a day and Randolph returned to his 'usual quickness'. On 7 August for example he made a statement in the House on the Indian Budget which Blunt described as 'a very masterly speech'. But the next week he was 'very dull and tired'. A few days later, when Blunt called on him at Connaught Place, he was ill with congestion of the lungs. At the end of 1886 his friend was shocked to find that Randolph had aged so much he seemed 'like a man who has had a stroke'.[29]

As Randolph himself wrote in August to Sir Mountstuart Elphinstone Grant Duff, the Governor of Madras, apologising for not having been able to reply sooner, he had been taken ill and 'the work of the session has been hard and left several of us in a rather dilapidated condition and the stumping, which party managers consider essential in view of the coming elections, most depressing . . . extra parliamentary life is making modern parliamentary life impossible'.[30] Again in October and November he was sending Grant Duff notes apologising for his lack of regularity in reports. He confided to his friend the Viceroy, Lord Dufferin, with whom he was on excellent terms, that platform speaking entailed extreme strain and illness while 'the constant necessity of trying to say something new makes one a drivelling idiot'.[31]

Understanding the intensity and uncertainty of Randolph's ill health – veering from headaches and a sharp cold one day to congestion of the lungs the next – and recognising his inability to discuss his unnamed illness publicly help explain the desperate plight in which Jennie found herself every day, never sure whether he would even be able to get up and function for a full day. Similarly with his personality: he could be charming and witty one moment, abusive and rude beyond imagination the next. Some commentators had already drawn their own conclusions. The *Spectator* talked about his 'political insanity', adding that 'Lord Randolph Churchill will probably always retain a great power of mischief,'[32] while Lord Derby wrote in his diary three days later that he was 'probably more or less mad'.[33] His legendary rudeness made many enemies, one of whom was Florence Nightingale. 'Lord Randolph – the boy with the drum – is doing untold harm – literally untold because the India office is a "secret society",' she wrote waspishly, implying that he made a lot of noise without understanding the consequences.[34]

The rudeness, as the *Pall Mall Gazette* had noticed, was especially potent when laced with aristocratic demagoguery. It was mostly controlled when harnessed to the House of Commons, where he established his reputation from a corner seat below the gangway, often with a fistful of notes. On a good day he seemed full of courage with a healthy contempt for authority which endeared him to his colleagues. But, as contemporary critics noticed increasingly, it came naturally to him to bark at those he considered his inferiors. Women fell into this category. But gentlemen, too, were at first astonished then dumbfounded and frightened. 'He yapped and barked at those people at whom he was told to bark and yap because it was as the breath of his very nostrils to yap and bark.'[35] His sneering attack on the MP George Sclater-Booth, who was trying to introduce a small constitutional measure, was typical. He set the House roaring when he mused out loud: 'Strange . . . strange how often we find mediocrity dowered with a double-barrelled name!'[36]

By comparison with his brother, described in the press as 'a foul-lived fellow, a ruffianly wife-beater',[37] Randolph was a peaceable fellow. However much he may have abused Jennie verbally there is no evidence of physical attack. But colleagues could not fail to notice their troubled relationship. As Henry Labouchère, the Radical MP and editor of *Truth*, a magazine devoted to the exposure of social fraud, wrote to Chamberlain at the end of 1885: 'Though he gets on pretty well with his wife when they are together he is always glad to be away from her.'[38] Frank Harris vividly describes a domestic scene between Randolph and Jennie at this time. Harris was having a political discussion with Randolph about Irish Home Rule when the door opened and his wife appeared.

> Naturally I got up as she called out, 'Randolph,' but he sat still.
>
> In spite of his ominous silence, she came across to him, 'Randolph I want to talk to you!'
>
> 'Don't you see', he retorted, 'that I've come here to be undisturbed?'
>
> 'But I want you,' she repeated tactlessly.
>
> He sprang to his feet. 'Can't I have a moment's peace from you anywhere?' he barked. 'Get out and leave me alone!'
>
> At once she turned and walked out of the room.[39]

However unreliable Harris may be in matters of sexual boasting, it seems likely that he had witnessed such a scene. *Punch* carried a similar vignette under the heading: 'Grandolph's Teachings':

> When you rush in to dress at five minutes to eight and you are to dine two miles off at eight sharp, when your shoe strings break, your studs roll on the floor, your links refuse to catch and you suddenly discover an iron mould in the centre of your shirt-front, then when a sweet patient voice from the other room says, 'Oh, my dear! Don't use such awful language!' Then bethink you of Grandolph and explain that your fervent utterances were only 'blessings in disguise'.[40]

By the late summer of 1885 Randolph recognised that his health and nerves, as it was euphemistically put, were giving way too often. Blunt was not alone in fearing for his friend's survival; Henry James, Sir Charles Dilke, Chamberlain and Labouchère all gossiped among themselves about his increasing debility. 'R Churchill is in a very bad way,' Labouchère wrote to Rosebery. 'The action of his heart has given way and he takes a lot of digitalis. He says that he must knock up if he has to sit up in the House of Commons as he cannot sleep after 6 in the mornings and breaks down if he does not go to bed early. This he says he does not want to do . . .'[41]

In addition to poor health, money was as great a cause for concern as ever. There were discussions about the possibility of moving in with the widowed Duchess at 50 Grosvenor Square – a move Jennie fought against but which they were eventually forced to make in 1892 – or selling the lease on Connaught Place. But economising did not come easily to either of them. Randolph, encountering difficulties in taking out further loans, drew closer now to his friends in finance, especially the Rothschilds and Lionel Cohen. Many of these were Jews and even the Semitic origins of his political associate in the Fourth Party, Wolff, did not escape the notice of some commentators such as Harris. But his friendship with Jews was not simply a question of access to cash. When his friend the highly respected art dealer Asher Wertheimer, son of an immigrant, who lived a few doors away at 8 Connaught Place was blackballed from the St Stephen's Club, Randolph himself resigned in protest.

In this crisis, as he faced the important November general election, he depended more than ever on Jennie. He had never seriously expected to win at Birmingham, no matter how beautiful his wife nor how effectively she campaigned, and he lost by a margin of 773 votes. However, an admirer who had won South Paddington agreed to stand down immediately in Lord Randolph's favour so that on the following day he was duly elected to the new Parliament for a London constituency for the first time.

There was one small excitement for Jennie, too; in November she was invited to Windsor because Queen Victoria wished personally to confer the Insignia of the Order of the Crown of India on her. Jennie adored this sort of recognition. On the appointed day she travelled to Windsor and was received by the Queen in a small room; the decoration comprised a pearl and turquoise cipher, attached to a pale-blue ribbon edged with white, which the Queen pinned on Jennie's left shoulder. 'I remember that my black velvet dress was thickly embroidered with jet so much so that the pin could find no hold and, unwittingly, the Queen stuck it straight into me.'[42] Jennie received a note the following day from a lady in waiting telling her that the Queen had found her 'so handsome'. On such small morsels Jennie survived.

The politics of the next few months were complicated and gladiatorial. The House was dominated by Gladstone's determination to give Ireland Home Rule and everyone was viciously manoeuvring, gambling on the outcome. Parliament reassembled on 21 January 1886 and Lord Salisbury's administration fell five days later. Randolph was now out of office again but not out of the news. He went to Belfast on 22 February and, having decided that 'the Orange card' was the one to play spoke rousingly at an anti-Home Rule rally of 'the lamp of liberty and its flame, the undying and unquenchable fire of freedom'. Ulster will fight and Ulster will be right, the phrase that became his calling card, was coined later in a public letter written by Randolph in May. But he had inescapably declared his colours. Winston was to describe this speech as 'one of the most memorable triumphs of his life',[43] and even Leonard Jerome was cautiously impressed: 'I hate religion in politics but I have no doubt in the present instance it is justifiable.'[44]

For the next six months Randolph was without salary. But the spending did not stop. Lady Randolph Churchill was by now one of M. Worth's most valued customers. She brought him considerable publicity. On 6 March she attended a Drawing Room, a ceremony where young girls were presented to the monarch by a female relation who had previously been presented. This would mark, symbolically, their entrance into the adult world and was generally held at Buckingham Palace. On this occasion 200 girls were presented, so the afternoon must have dragged on interminably. It was hardly a newsworthy event. But the story for most of the newspapers, both in London and New York, which reported on it was Lady Randolph Churchill's dress. She achieved a 'startling and successful toilette',[45] according to *Vanity Fair*, which had a week earlier released the extraordinary news that she would be dressed 'from head to foot in orange'.[46] 'Diamonds flashed in her ears, on her throat and arms, and her dress glistened like a glass of golden wine held to the sunlight. It was the most remarkable in the room and many are awaiting its reappearance . . .'[47] wrote an American journalist.

The dress, more accurately described in a long story in the *New York Times* as amber bronze, was made by Worth but from Jennie's own design. She had sent the couturier a watercolour drawing 'executed by her own fair hand and showing plainly each tint, fold and plaiting. The dress is really a marvel of skill and artistic beauty.' The report continued:

> The skirt had a train of palest yellow satin brocade with long panels of brown velvet at the side, almost smothered in a cascade of fine old Venetian point lace and piped with cordings of cream, pale blue and venus pink, the new flesh tint. The front is of the pink in a heavy brocade and over this falls a gauze of palest yellow caught by tiny blue birds' wings at the sides. The bodice consists of a laced bertha of bronze brown velvet with a fullness of yellow gauze over the bust and the short sleeves of cream blue and pink ribbons made into a narrow band and veiled in gauze.

The excited reporter went on to describe 'a 2 yard long train falling in plaits from the waist and about the edge is a vandyked flouncing of lace in which is hidden tiny bows of the three ribbons, the tints peeping out like a rainbow through the clouds'. According to this reporter: 'The delicate beauty of the dress and the harmony of the colours are indescribable. Yellow is one of Lady Churchill's most becoming colours but, like many beautiful women, she looks well in any tint.'[48] Another similarly gushing article around this time, describing further gowns made by Worth for Jennie, insisted that 'her dresses, the way she wears her hair, her very tones are imitated'.

But not all articles in the American press were so uncritical and even this one remarked that the specially commissioned drawing of Jennie in the newspaper revealed 'the pathetic beauty of her dark eyes'.[49] The *Brooklyn Daily Eagle* some months previously had carried a snide story about:

'Dear Lady Randolph', as Mr Leonard Jerome's daughter is usually called on this side of the Atlantic. One would imagine that every woman and girl in or out of New York society had been a close and intimate acquaintance of Lady Randolph's when she was on this side of water. Her plucky and brilliant political fight for her husband has received liberal advertising in the American press and it is usually looked upon as a Yankee innovation . . . a man who sells photographs near the Fifth Avenue Hotel has had such a run on Lady Randolph Churchill's portraits that he has got out a lot of unusually big and striking ones and they retail to 'Dear Lady Randolph's' bosom friends on this side of the water rapidly at from $1.25–$2 a piece. Lady Randolph Churchill is in reality less known among women of her own age in New York than almost any other belle . . . when she has visited America since her marriage, she and her husband have been extremely exclusive and their stay in town invariably short. Lord Randolph Churchill impressed men here as being an overdressed, foppish and pretentious little man.[50]

But on 13 March 1886 Randolph and Jennie faced a different and hugely dramatic crisis. Winston, at eleven, still a delicate child not yet fully recovered from his treatment at St George's, nearly died of pneumonia. Luckily, Dr Roose, now a family friend, was close at hand. As long as the temperature was nudging 105 he barely left the boy's side. On this occasion, both parents rushed to Brighton to be with him. But Dr Roose advised that Mrs Everest should not be allowed in the sick room yet as 'the excitement of seeing her might do harm'.[51] Another implicit criticism came in a note from Jennie's brother-in-law Moreton Frewen, who wrote that he was sure 'you will make the more of him after being given back to you from the very threshold of the unknown'.[52] Although he soon recovered from this illness, Winston's health continued to give cause for concern. Dr Roose took him that year to see Dr Edward Woakes, the eminent aural surgeon, perhaps on account of a longstanding problem with his ears and balance. His speech defect continued to bother him for years, making it hard for him to pronounce a clear S. But although he consulted a doctor about this and was told, quite literally, that he was tongue tied, he learnt to manage the problem himself.

Just as Winston recovered, politicking began again in earnest. Gladstone's government was brought down again in June on the Home Rule Bill, requiring yet another election in July. Jennie, 'ably assisted by Mr Balfour MP', campaigned for Randolph in Manchester, where she opened a branch of the Primrose League. But although Randolph spoke only twice during the election – he was exhausted and had gone salmon fishing to relax when the results were announced – he was repaid handsomely for his undeniable contribution to the Conservative victory. Salisbury knew what he had to do.

As Queen Victoria wrote in her journal on 25 July: 'Lord Salisbury came to me again at four and we talked over everything . . . he feared Lord Randolph Churchill must be Chancellor of the Exchequer and Leader, which I did not like. He is so mad and odd and has also bad health.'[53] Nonetheless on 3 August 1886 Lord Randolph Churchill, at thirty-seven the youngest to hold this position since William Pitt, accompanied Lord Salisbury and the cabinet to Osborne to kiss hands formally and accept the seals of office. On this occasion, it was noticed how much he was smoking – incessantly – and how nervous he seemed. One of his first reactions to the prospect of high office was that 'we want the £5,000 a year badly . . . I cannot understand how we get through so much money'.[54] His poverty, gambling and indebtedness was, by now, as well known as his ill health and the ever more precarious state of his marriage. There had even been a whip-round in his constituency to pay his election expenses. But, as he scaled new political heights, his private life was again plumbing the depths.

Letters between Jennie and the Dowager Duchess in 1886 indicate that serious quarrels between Randolph and his wife had all but ruptured the marriage by this time. Whether Jennie yet knew that Randolph's doctors believed he had syphilis is not certain. Rather, it seems, she believed his coldness toward her was because his affections had been won by another woman. She was thirty-two and utterly miserable. She still loved him and was not ready to give him up. Her sisters knew her deepest fears, although from now on she found a greater understanding with Leonie than with Clara. An undated letter from her younger sister at around this time tried to offer comfort. She told Jennie 'not to worry about any other woman's influence – he will always be alright when you are with him'.[55]

Throughout that summer Jennie appealed to her mother-in-law for advice. The two women had never had an easy relationship but now formed an alliance of sorts. Frances Marlborough wrote Jennie a series of 'stiff upper lip' letters offering few crumbs of comfort in her desire to help. The Duchess tried to avoid censuring her beloved son who, she insisted, 'has a good heart' and would give Jennie 'credit' for not making a fuss. She advised her daughter-in-law to absorb herself in domestic duties, such as looking after the children and the new cook, and to avoid excitement and the society of those friends who, after pandering to your words, 'would gladly see you vexed or humbled as they are jealous of your success in society'.[56] She also advised keeping her troubles to herself 'for you have a tell tale face' but added that she understood how hard that would be. Only her sisters were to be trusted. The Duchess then suggested that, if Jennie did not accompany Randolph on his planned trip to Serbia she might like to come and 'vegetate' with the Marlboroughs and 'we will try and make you as happy as possible'.[57] The Duchess admitted frankly that Jennie was enduring what she called a 'great crise'. But she then insisted that whether or not she passed through it depended on her. She had some advice:

> though it is a humdrum task, try to make yourself so essential to him that he must recognise it. He hates bother and yet he likes things to be nice and well managed . . . I am sure you say it is easy to preach but the question is, is it not worth it to you when you are clever and young and attractive?
>
> You must now sacrifice yourself and your pleasure to give yourself up to the task perhaps for many a day. I have no doubt of your success for I know in his heart he is truly fond of you and I think I ought to know.[58]

Jennie's sense of confusion, fear and disappointment are palpable. She shot back three letters to the Duchess within the space of two days, all of which made the Duchess's heart ache. This time she was flummoxed: unable to advise anything beyond further persistence and discretion, the latter not simply to save her son's reputation and to maintain appearances, although she did fear that 'mischief might easily be made' if Jennie discussed things with anyone. She also knew that blowing the affair into the open would scupper the marriage, which Jennie wanted to preserve. It is this abiding tenderness on Jennie's part that shines through the correspondence and seems so remarkable. Whatever Randolph did or said, however difficult he was to live with, in twenty years her desire to support and comfort him never completely deserted her. The Duchess saw it clearly, and while insisting it was only affection which motivated her, exploited Jennie's love and cruelly blamed her for the current crisis. She called on Jennie 'before it is too late . . . to give up that fast lot you live with . . . flirting and gossiping'.[59] And she urged her, 'although you will have your children to cheer you', to see if Mrs Jerome might come over to visit. 'For I dread you being left alone in London.'[60]

Jennie was not entirely alone in London and one of the friends with whom she established a close relationship was Marie, the Russian-born Duchess of Edinburgh, who married Victoria's second son Alfred in January 1874, just at the time that she and Randolph were engaged. Quite how much Marie knew of the troubled marriage is not clear. Mostly the two women played piano duets and went to concerts together. In April 1886 Marie gave Jennie a beautiful bracelet as a memento of playing eight hands at your 'hospitable house'.[61] But there is a distinctly conspiratorial, gossipy tone to the correspondence. Marie complained to Jennie of a dinner she gave which was 'very proper, most respectable and consequently dull'.[62] On another occasion, after commenting on how monotonous and unanimated she found British society, she advised Jennie: 'I hope you will not let Lord Randolph go to Paris without you. It is most dangerous!!!'[63] Jennie still maintained her piano-practising routine in these difficult days and, in spite of feeling horribly nervous, even performed at concerts with audiences of 600 people.

The Jeromes must have known of Jennie's desperation by now, but the correspondence reveals little as they were circumspect and she was proud. However, Leonard had written at the beginning of the year that he and Clara had been talking it over and had concluded that 'a little trip to Monte Carlo just now would do you both good'.[64] A few weeks later he wrote to say how sorry he was that 'you could not come here. You must look out or you will break down.'[65] But Jennie had her own circle and she tried to carry on a normal social life as best she could, lunching, walking or – her favourite activity – ice-skating at the elite Prince's Club.

Frances suggested also that Jennie herself write to Randolph, begging him 'not to break your heart'. Even if he did not answer at least he would have read it and understood her feelings. She undertook to meet with Randolph herself, have a long conversation with him and afterwards to report to Jennie. 'I cannot understand his being so hard if he realises all you suffer. Perhaps he is full of other things. I *cannot* believe there is another woman.'[66]

But there was another woman: Lady de Grey. Her name had been scribbled on the back of one of Winston's letters as someone to be invited for dinner. She and her second husband were at the heart of the

Marlborough House Set. The Countess de Grey was one of the most stunningly beautiful women of her generation, with dark hair and a long, swan-like neck. Oscar Wilde, immensely struck by her beauty, dedicated his play, *A Woman of No Importance*, to her. Born Constance Gwladys Herbert in 1859, a sister of the Earl of Pembroke, she had first married in 1878 the fourth Earl of Lonsdale, who died suddenly four years later, leaving her with a baby daughter. Lord Lonsdale was an eccentric and when he died in mysterious circumstances at a house he used for entertaining actresses, his widow, who was in Monte Carlo at the time, does not seem to have mourned for long. In May 1885 she married Earl de Grey, son of the first Marquis of Ripon, Viceroy of India and heir to Studley Royal in North Yorkshire, the estate which comprised the imposing ivy-clad ruins of the twelfth-century Cistercian Fountains Abbey. The Abbey is today considered one of the most spectacular heritage sites in Europe. They had a quiet London wedding, in contrast to the grandeur of the beautiful family home.

Gladys de Grey (she preferred the simpler spelling of her name) was a noblewoman of passionate and jealous temperament. She took an active interest in a variety of artistic ventures; her musical soirées were well known for her practice of inviting either the wife or the husband of a couple, not both, whichever she considered the more interesting. Her name was rarely out of the Court Circular announcements as she often accompanied the Prince of Wales – sometimes with her husband, sometimes alone. When she fell in love with Harry Cust, a bachelor celebrated for his amorous adventures, and discovered that he was already conducting a liaison with Theresa, Lady Londonderry, she wreaked vicious revenge. She found compromising letters from which she read aloud excerpts to her friends, among whom was Leonie Leslie. She then sent the whole package to Lord Londonderry with disastrous consequences. The Leslies (and others) ever after referred to her as 'the letter thief'.

Leonie and Clara tried to persuade Jennie that Randolph, however much he might have admired Gladys de Grey, was not indulging in an affair with her. 'I think she is very silly about R,' Leonie wrote to Clara, 'although I never like to say so to her as she takes it to heart. But he is not the least devoted to Gladys de Grey . . . only as she has no flirtation on hand she suddenly notices his coldness. It has been like that for years . . .' Leonie had sharply observed Jennie's deteriorating marriage and, as she told her elder sister:

After thirteen years married life, both living in London and going chacun de leur côté she ought not to expect more. There is no reasoning with her but I really don't see what more she can expect and if Jack and I lived as separately for ten years and then were on as good terms I should be thankful. She worries when he goes to Brighton for a Sunday! Why he has always done that and, as for Gladys, she has as much to do with it as I have – even Kinsky says Jennie imagines it all.[67]

They were probably correct in their assessment of Gladys and Randolph. Randolph was rather smitten, but, Leonie insisted, 'all the royalties were tremendously down on her and the Prince said if she tries any of her pranks je taperai dessus . . . However, I do not encourage Jennie abusing her as I think it is better not to stir up R. I don't think Gladys is really so much to blame as I think R has <u>other</u> loves. Only Jennie had better not know this so don't you or Mama mention it.'[68]

Quite what Leonie meant by '<u>other</u>' is impossible to know. His name was occasionally linked to the actress Ellen Terry, a friend of Labouchère and a guest at weekend parties Randolph was known to attend. But it is also true that Churchill relaxed in the company of men: Natty Rothschild, Tommy Trafford, Henry James, Harry Tyrwhitt, Windham Thomas, the fourth Earl of Dunraven and even Charles Kinsky were his companions of choice on holiday. Men who entertained him, made few demands on him and may even have paid his way as well as their own. Men who had their own reasons for travelling abroad, away from wives. Men who were fond of his wife in some cases. But in this gossip-soaked atmosphere his increasing visits to Paris were whispered about as opportunities for heterosexual adultery, rather than homosexual liaisons, although some gossiped about that possibility, too. There is little evidence of this, other than one curious occasion related in Trelawney Backhouse's unpublished recollection, 'The Dead Past', now in the Bodleian Library. Backhouse described his first meeting with Lord Rosebery, with whom he claimed to have had sex,

at a small soirée in his magnificent Berkeley Square mansion . . . among the guests were the Oxford Scientist, the genial and very eccentric Prof Roy Lankester FRS, John Addington Symonds, who wrote of Michael Angelo's male love and of Greek Pederasty, homosexual to the finger tips, Lord Randolph Churchill and Arthur Humphries, the genial Piccadilly publisher, George Alexander the great actor . . . Lord Drumlanrig then known as Viscount Douglas of Hawick, Bozie Douglas's elder brother . . .

This was a very Uranian soirée. As well as himself, Rosebery, Lankester,

Addington Symonds and Drumlanrig were all Uranians (one of the contemporary terms for homosexuals), according to Backhouse.[69]

Probably, like the short continental holiday Randolph took in early October 1886 'secretly and silently'[70] – travelling as 'Mr Spencer' he still attracted a posse of reporters – these Parisian trips were opportunities to see doctors or to escape from political pressures. According to his biographer Roy Foster, he and Trafford shared a flat in Paris and he once said to a sister-in-law that he only liked 'rough women who dance and sing and drink – the rougher the better – great ladies bore me'.[71] Jennie, after ten years, had started to bore him.

As the year moved on, it became well known in their circle that the Churchills were effectively living separate lives. Even when not travelling, Randolph, deeply immersed in his political life, would stay at the Carlton Club rather than Connaught Place, further fuelling the rumours. And all the while Winston's bold demands on his mother did not lessen. He asked if he could learn the violoncello, a request which did not find favour. In mid-December 1886 he begged her to come to Brighton to watch a play instead of conducting a dinner party at Connaught Place. 'Now you know I was always your darling and you can't find it in your heart to give me a denial. I want you to put off your dinner party and take rooms in Brighton and go back on Monday morning . . . and perhaps take me with you.' He included a programme for the evening, recognising that 'mice are not caught without cheese'.[72]

Winston's demands were overtaken by events. On 23 December *The Times* announced Randolph's resignation from the Government. The stated grounds were his objections to what he deemed excessive estimates for the army and navy as well as his opposition to the form of the new Local Government Bill, which he did not consider sufficiently liberal in its scope. The announcement caused fury in several quarters. The Queen was angered by such a display of impertinence, Jennie distraught to have been ignored. Many of Randolph's friends and associates subsequently wrote accounts of what had happened in an attempt to understand and explain. Although not all were wholly surprised by such a rash action, many had not realised the extent of his sickness. The label 'mental instability' was now to stick ever more firmly.

Jennie, in her own account later, admitted that her husband had decided not to share this important confidence with her in advance. 'I was at that moment occupied with the details of a reception we were going to give at the Foreign Office.' The night before the resignation, she, Randolph and Sir Henry Wolff had been to the Strand Theatre to see a performance of

Sheridan's *The School for Scandal*. 'Questioning Randolph as to the list of guests for the party, I remember being puzzled at his saying, "Oh, I shouldn't worry about it if I were you: it probably will never take place."'[73] She could extract nothing further from him.

Shortly after the first act he left the theatre, ostensibly to go to his club but in fact to go to the office of *The Times* and meet the editor, Buckle. Randolph assumed that Buckle would be grateful to have advance copies of his resignation letter, which he had written three nights before while staying at Windsor Castle and on Windsor Castle notepaper: a serious impropriety, which the press made much of. At this stage Randolph probably still believed his resignation was merely a threat – not the first time he had used such tactics. He expected that the editor of *The Times*, a man Jennie and he had entertained, would, in return for the scoop, write a supporting leader, backing Randolph's view of the extravagance. This might have persuaded Salisbury not to let Randolph go. But, although there are various accounts of this late-night interview, it seems clear that Buckle refused to do this. Randolph raged at such ingratitude and Buckle then told him that *The Times* was not to be bribed. Randolph nonetheless gave Buckle permission to publish the letter next morning, which he duly did.

Salisbury stood his ground and reacted with his legendary sang-froid. He had read and ignored Randolph's letter when it had arrived the previous night in the middle of a ball he was hosting at Hatfield House at which the Duchess of Marlborough was a guest. She left the following morning without seeing either the host or hostess, although, according to one spectator, upon seeing *The Times* she let out a shriek followed by a fit of hysterics and then tears. 'Oh Sarah,' she said to her daughter, 'why are my sons so unlike other people's sons?'[74] Salisbury had decided to take on Churchill at his own game. He was prepared to admit that, by resigning just before Christmas, 'Randolph's ways are inconvenient.'[75]

Jennie, albeit writing years later, recounted her own reaction as one of dignified distress. Anguish and bitterness (or gall and wormwood, a favourite expression) are more likely. She recognised that the letter signed his political death-warrant.

> When I came down to breakfast, the fatal paper in my hand, I found him calm and smiling.
>
> 'Quite a surprise for you,' he said.
>
> He went into no explanation and I felt too utterly crushed and miserable to ask for any, or even to remonstrate. Mr Moore [the Permanent Under-Secretary at the Treasury] rushed in, pale and anxious, and with a faltering

voice said to me: 'He has thrown himself from the top of the ladder and will never reach it again!' Alas! He proved too true a prophet.[76]

It is one of the few sections of the book which brilliantly recreates not only what living with Randolph must have been like but the atmosphere in which Winston grew up. Parental approval is a common enough need. The son's unwavering determination to avenge his father's ill treatment stems surely from these months.

Salisbury telegraphed the Queen with the news. But she too had already read about it in *The Times* and was furious not only that a mere journalist had been informed before she had but at Randolph's audacity in using Windsor Castle notepaper, behaviour which other politicians considered 'most monstrous and discreditable and grossly disrespectful'.[77] Only weeks beforehand, impressed by Randolph's meticulousness and regularity in providing her with a full account of business in the House, she had been revising her opinion of his abilities. On the night he was there she had been 'rather sympathetic about his health and asked if he thought he would be able to stand the strain of a long session as leader'.[78] This goodwill was now set at naught.

Christmas *chez* Churchill that year must have been icy indeed. Reginald Brett, Lord Esher, one of the few who remained in close personal communication, went to Connaught Place on 25 December. He found Randolph, who normally spent Christmas at Howth with his friend FitzGibbon, 'lying on the sofa in his large grey library smoking cigarettes and completely prostrated by the excitement of the last two days. He said he was shunned like a pest and no one had been near him, not even those who owed everything to him.'[79] His mother begged a meeting of Salisbury at her London home and pleaded with him 'as a father' to forgive her son. But there was nothing Salisbury could or would do.[80] 'Did you ever hear of a man who, having got rid of a boil on the back of his neck, ever wants it back again?' he is reported to have said. Randolph was broken.

Within days matters between Jennie and Randolph deteriorated to such a degree that divorce was seriously under discussion. Even in 1886 it was hard to keep the private life of such a prominent politician out of the press, and the tone of some stories in the immediate aftermath of this débâcle was especially cruel. Some of the scandal sheets now began hinting what society had known for at least a year: that all was not well with his marriage.

On 6 January 1887 John Morley, the Liberal MP and former editor of the *Pall Mall Gazette*, told the well-informed Lewis ('Loulou') Harcourt of a detailed report 'which he has from a press man, that proceedings are going to be entered at once in the divorce court by Lady Randolph Churchill against Lord Randolph Churchill and Lady de Grey and by Lord Randolph Churchill against Lady Randolph Churchill and John Delacour'. Harcourt in his diary said he could hardly believe it as 'Lord Randolph would not be fool enough to commence proceedings and I don't think Lady R could make out a case against Lord R and Lady de Grey. They have been very intimate for some time but I believe it has been purely intellectual and not physical. Lady de Grey always appears to me to be absolutely passionless.'[81]

Passionless she was not. And John Delacour's involvement in this story is not necessarily what it appears, that he was another of Jennie's lovers, although they were undoubtedly close. It is possible that, by allowing himself to be cited as co-respondent, he was doing Randolph a favour. Delacour was a loyal if occasional friend who strikes an increasingly pathetic figure, short of funds, mentioned, if at all, in the correspondence for his poor health and financial difficulties. In 1890 Delacour eventually married a north-country heiress, Theresa Harriet Mary Towneley. Since his address was listed as 76 Eaton Place he cannot have been as poor as all that. Earl Dunraven describes him as 'a type of the idle rich (though he was not rich) that does not, I think, any longer exist'.[82] But he had stood by Randolph once before in his argument with the Prince of Wales. Perhaps he was obliged to stand a favour again so that the name of Lady Randolph's real lover – a man who would have raged at Randolph for stooping so low – was not mentioned. However, within hours, London was full of gossip and on the diplomatic circuit it was learnt, via Henry White of the American Legation, 'that Count Kinsky (Lady RC's supposed lover) has been hurriedly recalled to Vienna!'.[83]

A few days later Jennie was personally accosted by at least one journalist demanding to know if there was any truth in such rumours. Arthur Brisbane, London correspondent of the *New York Sun*, sent her a letter referring to 'details of a separation which the writer alleges to be pending between yourself and Lord Randolph'.[84] Brisbane wanted to make an appointment with Jennie and told her that he had also tried to question her father in New York as 'rumours are current there of the story'.[85] Randolph threatened legal action for libel if Brisbane dared repeat such rumours. He did not dare. But the rumours did not terminate. Lord Derby, in his diary for 19 January wrote: 'Letter from Lady S who tells me among other matters that R Churchill is taking steps to get rid of his wife whom he accuses of playing tricks with four men. A pleasant disclosure of manners in that set.'[86]

By the end of the month Randolph and Jennie appeared to have patched things up. Their public engagements were carefully watched. On Sunday, 23 January they appeared together, in public, presumably hoping it would scotch further rumours. They attended a première of *Ruddigore* at the Savoy and, in the fashion of the times, 'received quite an ovation'. Harcourt wrote in his journal: 'I hear that the danger of divorce proceedings between them has blown over.'[87]

Patching things up was what most Victorian couples in such situations did. Following the Matrimonial Causes Act of 1858 divorce was possible but expensive and difficult, especially for women. It was a subject for the theatre and the gossip columns. Jennie told Randolph shortly after they were married that she had been to see a play where the man said, 'nothing was so fashionable as a divorce and that in fact no well regulated family ought to be without one'.[88] But her comment was made at a time when she could still joke about the subject as something that happened to other people.

In the 1880s divorce was still shameful and Queen Victoria's attitude to divorced women reinforced this. Adultery by the wife was grounds for divorce, but adultery by the man had to be allied to some other matrimonial offence if the woman was to obtain a decree. The number of couples divorced in the UK climbed steadily until it reached 708 in 1886, but, if one compares that with more than 25,000 divorces in the same year in the US, which had then approximately twice the population of Great Britain, one has an indication of how many couples were acting with restraint. Jennie would have had to think long and hard about the ramifications for herself as well as for her family had she accused Randolph of both adultery and cruelty. She well knew the insatiable appetite of all the newspapers for every crumb about their private life. It is not hard, therefore, to see why she held off.

The future looked bleak for both Jennie and Randolph at the beginning of 1887. Although Randolph remained convinced for a long time that his departure from government was temporary, others were less sanguine or made sport of their difficulties. As Harcourt recorded in his journal on 16 February, 'the favourite question and answer in society at present is: 'Why did Lord Randolph leave the Government? Because he did not approve of the Austrian alliance.'[89]*

---

* There is an ironic postscript; Randolph fell because he wanted to control spending on armaments, which he believed the country could not afford. In this he was supporting the views of the deposed Gladstone, whose desire not to spend money on defence was blamed for the death of Gordon. Yet thirteen years later the ships which both had opposed were used at the battle of Omdurman, where Winston made his name and Kitchener sought to avenge the death of Gordon by destroying the tomb of the Mahdi. Jennie received the news of this with a great and proud heart.

8

All that You are to Me

~

THE DREAM HAD shattered. Just as Jennie glimpsed a reward for her love and loyalty it was snatched away. As her mother-in-law had reminded her a few months previously, she did at least have the comfort of her two sons. But there was little else to cheer her. Bitterness was what she recalled feeling as the toadies and sycophants fell away and vanished. In her memoirs written two decades after the events she is describing, Jennie is frank about this bleak period of her life without revealing the real reason for her gloom.

> When I look back at the preceding months, which seemed so triumphant and full of promise, the *débâcle* appeared all the greater. I had made sure that Randolph would enjoy the 'fruits' of office for years to come and, apart from the honour and glory, I regretted those same 'fruits' . . .
>
> How dark those days seemed! In vain I tried to console myself with the thought that happiness does not depend so much on circumstances as on one's inner self. But I have always found in practice that theories are of little comfort.[1]

By the time she wrote this, life had thrown her yet more vicissitudes. Yet she had found, in her inner self, more steely resolve than she knew she had. Jennie was not prepared to be one of life's victims. She had her own circle of friends – as well as her sisters – and Randolph, while sometimes believing that he was without a friend in the world, had his. One indication of the traumas of these days is that there are scarcely any letters preserved in the Churchill Archives between Randolph and Jennie during the years 1887 to 1890. A picture emerges through the letters and memoirs of others.

The Earl of Dunraven proved Randolph's most dependable ally. Five years older and considerably richer, he thought Randolph 'quite the most courageous man I have ever met'.[2] He constantly urged Randolph to fight back. But, as Randolph pathetically made clear to his closest friends, even though he hoped to be recalled, he lacked the strength or stamina to fight back himself. He deeply resented the humiliation, when he was ill and struggling to get words out, of people assuming he was 'tipsy'.

Other friends who stood by included the Prince of Wales. It is no coincidence that Jennie turned from her 'depressing reflections' in the *Reminiscences* to the memory of a charming visit to Sandringham to celebrate the Prince of Wales's birthday. It is a good indication of her ability to grasp the best that life offered. She describes in great detail the long leisurely breakfasts – 'None of the royalties appeared before noon' – the prolonged luncheons, then tea, dinners, card games and of course 'sport'. Jennie had never liked shooting and was deeply offended when occasionally women had a go, crawling on all fours to stalk their prey until 'Crash! Bang! And the glorious animal became a maimed and tortured thing . . . if these things must be done, how can a woman bring herself to do them?'³

Much of the surviving correspondence between the three sisters is taken up with frothy discussions of clothes, especially those worn by Jennie at Sandringham when several changes a day were *de rigueur*. Should it be the black tulle with a black veil and black gloves and or white tulle and veil? At the same time Leonie, in Paris, asked Jennie whether she should wear her Roman dress with green sash, her blue with yellow sash or her blue velvet dress 'with a blue velvet tail added'. The latter was a clear message to the other sisters of how economical she was being – adding to an existing gown rather than buying something new. But the apparent superficiality masks the deadly seriousness of such matters.

What Jennie wore was what people remarked upon. One of John Singer Sargent's most memorable paintings is the full-length portrait of Ellen Terry as Lady Macbeth wearing an exquisite gown covered in glowing green beetles' wings. Terry herself maintained that the costume was inspired by the 'beautiful' Jennie, 'who wore a dress at supper one evening which gave me the idea . . . the bodice was trimmed all over with green beetles' wings'.⁴

It would be easy to assume that the Prince's interest in rehabilitating the Churchills was because of his fondness for Jennie. From the start he was so closely involved in the intricacies of their marriage he even made Randolph promise that Jennie could get a new gown for the Sandringham ball, which she did – a black tulle from Mme Valentino. But his sensitive defence of the man to his mother, who was deeply aggrieved at what she considered Randolph's duplicity – being prepared to discuss important matters of state with her when he was on the verge of resignation – indicates there was more to it than that. As long as Churchill was a political figure, so was his wife.

He accused his mother of being,

if you will allow me to say so, rather hard on Lord R. Churchill. I do not enter into the question whether he was right or wrong in resigning on the point at issue between him and his colleagues but he has at any rate the courage of his opinions . . .

Lord Randolph is a poor man and a very ambitious one, but he gave up £5,000 a year in ceasing to be Chancellor of the Exchequer. Now that he has left office I am not likely to see much of him as he goes but little in society. Though I certainly do not agree in all his public views (and I have often told him so) still, I cannot help admiring many of his great qualities. Should his life be spared (and he has not a good life) he is bound to play sooner or later a prominent part in the politics and destinies of the country.[5]

The rapprochement in the mid mid-1880s between Jennie and the Prince was important. It is often rumoured that Jennie, aged thirty-two, and the portly forty-five-year-old Prince now indulged in a physical relationship. And maybe they did. But there is no proof. Each valued the friendship of the other, which lasted until the Prince's death in 1910, and there are dozens of surviving notes from the Prince to Jennie, mostly undated, the bulk of which were sent from about 1886 until 1890. Jennie's letters to him, which are probably too discreet to yield any clues, are locked in the Royal Archives at Windsor. When Anita Leslie wrote in 1969 inquiring about the relationship she was told by the librarian at Windsor, Robin Mackworth-Young, that 'the engagement diary . . . of Albert Edward, Prince of Wales, shows that he met the Churchills on three occasions only between January and October 1875 inclusive. There is no suggestion of any kind of affair.'[6] He made no comment about the later years. In 2003 such material as there may be at Windsor remained closed to Jennie's latest biographer.

There is no doubt that the Prince admired Jennie and had done since he first met her at Cowes, even to the exent of encouraging the marriage to Randolph. In the first year of her marriage he sent her a small bracelet. And there is no doubt that Jennie would have flirted with him, since that was how she behaved to men in general and princes in particular. Had he made overtures, she would have considered rejection the height of bad manners. Nor would she have written about the relationship, so schooled was she in the arts of discretion. There is undisputed evidence that after 1886 the Prince called many times to visit Lady Randolph at Connaught Place (and later at Great Cumberland Place) and that she received him there alone. Given that the Prince was well known not to feel a need to linger with a woman after indulging in sex, these brief visits could have been love-making trysts. But the tone of the (largely undated) notes, although very close, gives little away.

Addressed mostly to 'Ma Chère Amie', there are invitations to the theatre (with others), there is an exchange of photographs and there are some notes more suggestive than others, often giving her less than twenty-four hours' notice of an impending visit. On one occasion when she had not been free to attend the theatre with him, he wrote: 'In revenge, I will arrive at your hospitable mansion at 2 sharp.'[7] Another time he asked: 'Would it be very indiscreet if I proposed myself to luncheon?' Or 'Unless you are engaged may I propose myself for luncheon?' Or 'I have to sit on a Royal Commission from 12–4 tomorrow but if I can get away by 3 I will call with pleasure on the chance of seeing you?'[8] And what does it all amount to? Scholars of Edwardian sexual habits might say that a man who visits a lady at lunchtime has no expectation of sex because there are too many servants about, but that he who calls in the afternoon, when the servants have been dismissed and there is just enough time for the complicated undoing of corsets, does have such an expectation. So, is the note where the Prince tells Jennie he will be calling at 3.45 p.m. code for an illicit rendezvous? Most likely Jennie was clever enough to amuse and comfort the Prince with her conversation and laughter in the way that she had been trained to do since childhood and their friendship, however close it may once have been was a platonic, slightly teasing one.

In 1887 Jennie hired as her chef the woman who was to become a legendary figure in Edwardian London: Rosa Lewis. Lewis was only twenty when she joined the Churchill household. She worked at Connaught Place for a short time during this deeply troubled period in her employers' lives. She warmed to Jennie and felt sorry for her. While there she cooked many meals for the Prince of Wales and knew exactly what he liked.

> Whatever it was it had to be very plainly cooked. If he had a pear it would be a perfectly plain pear – no colouring; and the only flavouring he liked with his fruit was kirsch. He also liked very plain boiled bacon and flat Kidney beans; and he was especially fond of plain boiled truffles. He didn't like anything coloured, or anything sloppy or anything that would spill down his shirt-front; just simple plain cooking and truffles I used to do specially for him. If a dinner party was being given in his honour, this dish used to be there every time, just served in a white serviette.[9]

One of the reasons the Prince enjoyed dinners with Jennie was because she catered for his whims without toadying. She also had a sense of humour but never went too far. Rosa remembered the trick she played of pretending she was wearing a jubilee bustle which played 'God Save the

Queen' every time she sat down. In fact she had a small servant underneath her chair with a musical box. The Prince, involved in numerous staid celebrations to mark his mother's fifty-year reign, was reduced almost to hysterics by this performance, which she often repeated that Jubilee Year.

At all events, after 1889 the Prince's love life was taken care of for some years by Daisy, Lady Warwick, friend and admirer of Jennie, who ensured she was included in their group. 'Lady Randolph was like a marvellous diamond – a host of facets seemed to sparkle at once,' she wrote of her.[10]

Within weeks of his resignation and rumoured divorce, Randolph was in Paris with Harry Tyrrwhitt. He then moved on to sunnier Algiers, where he told Jennie there were hordes of English but he was managing to avoid them. Unconvincingly, he said he had not given a thought to politics since he left. The correspondence between the couple for the next three months as he travelled around North Africa and then southern Italy is mostly full of Jennie's detailed reports of the political scene. Even Randolph complimented her on being such a good correspondent and chastised her only occasionally for forgetting to send *The Times* leader each day or for attending any Salisbury parties – 'you wld make yrself much too cheap'.[11] Had she asked him earlier he would have advised her not to attend, he said. But his reprimand came too late.

She defended herself by telling Randolph that Natty Rothschild thought her action 'perfectly right'.[12] 'Dearest, I do hope you will not disapprove . . . if it does no good it can do no harm and I am sure it will stop some of the carping.'[13] How hard Jennie tried to buttress his bruised ego, telling him how other politicians were in awe of him or were jealous of his criticisms and admired him! And if, as his friends now believed, Randolph was severely ill and mentally unstable, it is revealing that he should have preserved any letters at all from his wife. But he did. Evidently he carried them around on his travels and brought them back home.

Jennie was not merely keeping the Churchill torch flickering. Her letters, as well as those from his mother and George Curzon, then a young Conservative politician and close friend of Randolph, helped him to try and understand the turbulent political situation he had left in his wake and which he persisted in considering was not unsatisfactory for him personally. 'What a fool Lord S. was to let me go so lightly. This is a very conceited thing to say but yet I feel it is true,' he confided in his wife. Randolph told Jennie he thought W. H. Smith made a poor Leader of the House, 'and no amount of newspaper or society puffing will make bad parliamentary action good. The poor old goat [Sir Stafford Northcote] was a genius compared to this worthy bookseller. Arthur Balfour will fail as

Chief Secretary [for Ireland] . . . as you will see, his want of physical and moral strength, his utter and hopeless ignorance of Ireland will be fatal to him.'[14]

In the most difficult of circumstances Jennie was extraordinarily loyal and unselfish, pleased that he was enjoying himself somewhere warm, as the cold that winter of 1887 in London was 'perfectly odious'. Presumably she did not know precisely what her husband and his cronies had said about her or her loyalty might not have stretched so far. But she must have been aware of some of the gossip besmirching her reputation; the American scandal sheet *Town Topics* commented: 'Society has invented a new name for Lady R. Her fondness for the exciting sport of husband hunting and fiancé fishing has earned her the title "Lady Jane Snatcher".'[15] Because she was often seen out accompanied by different men while Randolph was abroad, mostly salmon fishing in Norway, she attracted much of the flak whenever the state of their marriage was discussed. She escaped out of London when she could, travelling to Dublin or Rutland, where Kinsky kept a racing stud and where she gave another concert but, she assured Randolph, did not hunt.

'I can't tell you how my blood boils', she comforted him, 'when I hear of the abuse and ingratitude of the party. But it will all come right and the same people will be fawning on you in a short time.'[16] She genuinely believed he could make a comeback. In the meantime it was best that he was away from the unpleasantness. But Winston was not spared the attacks. Taken to a pantomime that winter, where the audience hissed during a sketch about his father, he 'burst into tears and turned furiously on a man who was hissing and said "stop that row, you snub-nosed radical"'.[17]

Jennie's days during the months when Randolph escaped abroad – often staying with his friend Tommy Trafford – were full, so full that she did not allow herself the luxury of 'taking stock', she just occupied herself. She gave piano recitals, including a major fundraising performance at Wimborne in Dorset – her sister-in-law Cornelia's 'habitation' – in aid of the Primrose League. Jennie always preferred playing the more rumbustious Beethoven to the romantic, controlled Chopin, at which Leonie excelled, and the many hours of serious practising were also a form of therapy. There were political meetings at Connaught Place too because, much to her disgust, some South Paddington worthies had asked her to organise a Women's Jubilee event and she felt unable to refuse. She went occasionally to visit Winston at Brighton. And she was painting, well enough to send at least one of her works to an exhibition of the Irish Fine Art Society in Dublin.

Her tone towards Randolph in these troubled days was loving and warm, far from that of a woman ready to end her marriage. She begs him to look after himself 'and don't forget me'.[18] In another, one of the most touching letters that has been preserved in the entire correspondence between them, she tells her ailing husband, at the nadir of his career and health: 'It is a blessing to think that you are well and happy. It helps reconcile me to much that is disagreeable here where people are venomous and ill natured . . . You are good to me and I trust you utterly and don't care tuppence what they say. Enjoy yourself as much as you can and come back well, ready to fight the whole lot . . .' She then reminded him of 'how much I think of you and all that you are to me'.[19] As she explained to Leonie in Ireland, although she felt very sick at heart at all that Randolph had thrown away, she believed 'his head was turned at that moment and he thought he could do anything. However, "it is an ill wind that blows NO good' and R has been so much easier and nicer since that I ought not to regret the crisis."[20]

Leonard and Clara were wintering in Monte Carlo in the weeks after Randolph's resignation. The Prince of Wales was also there at this time, and Jennie, learning of an encounter from her father, was able to tell Randolph that the Prince had been 'most kind, and came and talked at breakfast and said nice things of you and also said he hoped they had not minded the ridiculous and ill-natured things which had appeared in the papers abroad as he knew how perfectly untrue they were'.[21] Back in London, it was difficult, Jennie told Randolph, to know who was, or was not, a friend. After Monte Carlo the Jeromes came to England, partly to see their grandchildren. Leonard continued to offer whatever financial help he could. But by 1887 there wasn't much spare cash. He hated to refuse his girls anything on the grounds of lack of finance and was constantly thinking up new schemes, deals and arrangements to raise money, as well as being deeply engrossed still in racing matters.

Leonard's own entrepreneurial temperament helped him understand and sympathise with his newest son-in-law. But only to a certain extent. As he told his wife in July 1887, he did not have faith in Moreton's cattle schemes 'or in anything else that he had on the stocks . . . I wish he would settle down and begin all new again.'[22] Leonard explained to her that after paying Jennie an annual allowance of $10,000, funded through rent from Madison Square, now a club house, and Leonie $2,000 (Clara received nothing, largely on account of Moreton's pride, an inequality the sisters silently accepted), she had $4,000 to do with as she pleased. If she wanted to make an investment in a scheme of Moreton's, that was her business. Moreton was so convincing that almost everyone he approached was taken in by his confident assurances that he was on the brink of making his own and everyone else's fortune.

Randolph, similarly desperate for cash, especially now that he was out of office, was to remain a reliable supporter. He may have felt partly responsible for Moreton's situation since the latter had resigned as secretary to George Goschen when Randolph resigned and Goschen was promoted to Chancellor of the Exchequer. It is often claimed that Randolph 'forgot' Goschen in his calculations. But telling others that he had forgotten Goschen was Randolph's way of insulting the German-born economist, the implication being that he did not consider him adequate to the task. Winston, in his adulatory biography of his father, maintained that to have Goschen in the Government was not fatal to his father's schemes, 'for there were no schemes' – an accurate account of Randolph's instability at this time.

In 1887 Randolph wrote to Sir Salar Jung, the exiled Indian nobleman and former Prime Minister of Hyderabad, recommending his brother-in-law 'who possesses considerable literary experience and is very energetic and intelligent and well acquainted with many persons of position and consequence here', as his factotum.[23] Leonard had his doubts. And that was without knowing Moreton's unquenchable habit of 'borrowing' money from his close family members – wife, sister-in-law and even children. 'He rode roughshod over all the family and [Clara] was mercilessly exploited to her dying day by her husband,' wrote their elder son Hugh Frewen.[24] Now that all three sisters were married, their fortunes (or lack of them) became increasingly intertwined as they tried to help each other. Writing to his 'sweet little woman' – other terms of patronising endearment included 'dear old thing', 'sweet thing' and 'goosey wifino' – Moreton told Clara in November 1887: 'I find I am obliged to take a hundred of that £250, [though] it leaves you only a hundred – if you are really pressed perhaps Jennie can lend you a hundred if it is only for a few weeks. What a curse poverty is.'[25]

In other notes dating from this time Moreton continually sends Clara his love but no money. He unashamedly told her to ask if Randolph could give any further help with letters, or else to ask Jennie to write to Sir Salar Jung – for whom Moreton now worked – apologising that she was not able to see him to say goodbye and to express her regret that she and Randolph were out of town and therefore saw nothing of him when he was in England. Sir Salar had been exiled by the Nizam, the Muslim ruler of Hyderabad, but Frewen was trying to win back the Nizam's approval on the ground that this would be financially advantageous to all.

Moreton's current scheme was to organise the building of a railway for which Salar Jung would provide the capital, 'but we shall share the profit openings in all directions'. He added: 'If I make a million in railroads I will send Jane [his name for Jennie] "a bit".'[26] Of course, Moreton – 'the insufferable Moreton' as Anita Leslie called him – never did make a million.

Throughout, the family supported each other in spite of the various cross-currents. The fierce defence of relatives against critical comment from outsiders which animated Winston was learnt at his mother's and aunts' knees. The Leslies despised Moreton and Jennie pitied Clara for the dance her husband led her. Randolph found Moreton amusing and John Leslie dull. But the women all pulled together in the late summer of Jubilee Year when Moreton told Clara to rent a large country house for Goodwood Races and to organise a magnificent house party in honour of the Nawab, Sir Salar. Leonie and Jennie lent their staff only to have Moreton insist they wear Frewen livery. In the event he settled for having the buttons changed to those with a Frewen crest. Kinsky, who was part of the house party, enlivened the long weekend by bringing his private Hungarian band, which had a full repertoire of Strauss waltzes played *con brio*. The light-footed Jerome girls were in their element. But the party did nothing to replenish the already drained Frewen finances. Moreton now told Clara she must sell the furniture by auction at once before any trouble arose. He knew that Jennie and Randolph were also hard up but was not shy about suggesting that his wife should approach her younger sister for a short-term loan, just a few weeks, or about agreeing to Jennie's offer to buy Clara's diamond stars, which held such symbolic power for the sisters, for £500, adding, 'and when times are good you can have them back again'.[27]

Leonard tried to help Moreton and, dining with his friend the newspaper proprietor Joseph Pulitzer, asked if he might find some work for him. Pulitzer, not surprisingly, wanted to know what experience the young man had had in journalism. But then in March Leonard had to talk to Pulitzer about a more urgent matter.

According to a small article in the *World* of 27 March, Lord Randolph Churchill had now resigned from his own domestic cabinet. This time Leonard was furious. 'Your London man called several times to see Lord Randolph but was not admitted,' Leonard complained.

He then wrote, stating certain reports he had heard concerning Lord Randolph and his wife, and might he have an authentic statement from his Lordship to cable to the *World* in New York.

[Lord Randolph] did then and there write to the man denying the truth of the stories *in toto* and authorizing him to cable the same to the *World*. But, as my dutiful daughter told me, [the reporter] added some comments on the small doings that were far from complimentary. Hence instead of cabling the *World* exclusively the only word that ever did or ever will come from Randolph on the subject, he substitutes his own in order to be revenged.[28]

Pulitzer replied to his old friend insisting that he personally had not been in the office when the despatch arrived. Of course, he would not have allowed publication of anything that alluded to Leonard Jerome's daughter in this way. He offered 'anything you may wish in the way of correction' and sent one of his most capable reporters for the job.

Leonard was not satisfied. He wanted scalps, especially that of 'this London fellow'. In his view 'it is simply one of those cases of a kicked out interviewer who takes his revenge in fabricating the vilest slander. Imagine', he asked his friend, 'a perfect stranger calling on you half a dozen times and, finally getting in, states his business to be to ascertain how you were getting on with Mrs Pulitzer. That's your London correspondent. I should like to ask Mrs P what she thinks of him.' In his rage Leonard demanded: 'If you say 2 or 3 times in the proper place that you have reason to believe that there is no proper foundation whatever for the statement last Saturday of a disagreement between Lord and Lady Randolph Churchill, that will do for me.'[29] In the event, the newspaper carried a small correction, buried on page four, on Sunday, 3 April. It referred to an alleged disagreement which, upon inquiry, was found to be entirely unfounded. 'The relations between Lord Randolph and Lady Churchill are of the most happy character . . .'

But, as everyone close to them knew, and many who weren't, this was far from being the case. Other journals – English and American – continued to carry bitingly sarcastic comments, and poems even, about the erratic behaviour of 'Randy Churchill'. Such constant battering took its toll. Each of the sisters had turns feeling dull, or low, or – the most they would allow themselves – feeling rather in the dumps. And from this time on they each tried to buoy the other up and get through until the next crisis caused by husbandly neglect, lack of cash, the disappointment of a lover or a child. None of the three found it easy to live cosily with reality. Paris and shopping were the time-honoured Jerome remedies, long before the expression 'retail therapy' was invented. When Clara felt 'blue' because she had no money, Moreton generously suggested that a month in Monte Carlo might help. But Clara was more than blue; she was desolate about the prospect of losing her house. With Moreton away so much, the house was all she could cling to in her loneliness. Now she felt the destruction was complete. All her personal things had gone, excepting some jewels which she kept at the bank. She forgave Moreton but increasingly sought comfort elsewhere. 'Mother's tragedy', wrote Hugh Frewen, 'was that all her life she needed and yearned for affection, but never learnt how to command it.'[30] 'Good,' wrote Shane Leslie alongside this comment.

For Jennie in 1887, the problem was not simply that that they had no money and that Randolph was in the political wilderness. It was that Charles Kinsky, a diplomat after all, travelled a lot. When he was away she had the blues, as she admitted to her sisters. One way of stirring Kinsky was to make him jealous. When Leonie hinted to him that Jennie had another admirer, the debonair sportsman Peter Flower, Kinsky demanded an immediate explanation.[31] Flower, the younger brother of Lord Battersea, was a brilliant rider, a great gambler thoroughly unconcerned about money and, according to Margot Tennant who fell deeply in love with him at this time, not only a man whose 'vitality revived and restored everyone he came into contact with', but also 'the best dressed man I had ever seen'.[32] This was precisely Jennie's type. Jennie described Margot at this time as a pushy young lady who 'sallied forth on a prancing steed'.[33] In Margot's autobiography, where she devotes nearly a chapter to her love affair with Flower, which ended shortly before her marriage to H. H. Asquith in 1894, she describes how she decided one day to pay a visit to her unnamed rival for Peter Flower's affections. This was a beautiful dark-haired lady with wonderful wild eyes who played the piano. Black Jane was the name which the Souls, many of whom Margot was close to, had bestowed on Jennie for her raven hair.

Jennie tried to lose herself in the many public functions that summer held to celebrate the Queen's Golden Jubilee to which Randolph, as an ex-cabinet minister, and Jennie were invited. It was safer for Jennie to write colourfully about these activities in her *Reminiscences* than to reveal the true texture of her married life. Winston implored her to request permission from the school for him to come up to London and see 'Buffalow [sic] Bill' as well as Jack, Everest, his mother and home.

As the traumatic year drew to a close there was good and bad news. Moreton, in dire financial straits, was now insisting that Clara must sell the house. If she couldn't do that, she should 'register a bill of sale of furniture . . . then if you see your way to let it, go ahead . . .' But, casting around for others to blame for his lack of success, his finger fell on Jennie, 'who I do believe has never written Sir Salar even a line to thank him for those pots and pans'.[34] A couple of months later he said of his wife's sister: 'Jane is a dear . . . but she has not got Leo's depth of character.'[35]

Jennie and Randolph had further worries of their own in the autumn of 1887. Randolph had been toying with the idea of forming a new Centre Party in alliance with the now disaffected Liberal Joseph Chamberlain and Lord Hartington. Jennie, still nurturing hopes for Randolph's return, did her best by organising interesting parties. But the plans foundered, partly because of the lack of enthusiasm of Hartington, partly because of the refusal of Randolph's close friend Lord Rosebery to join them and partly because Randolph's volatility made him politically untrustworthy. Jennie, in what today seems a fairly harmless jest, asked Lord Hartington at this time if he intended responding to Randolph's invitation. He told her he had not yet decided and feared being called either a man or a mouse depending on his response. 'Or a rat,' added Jennie, pleased with what she considered her bon-mot. 'I repeated it to Randolph, who, to my discomfiture, gave me a severe lecture on the iniquity of ill timed jests.'[36]

This was Randolph's last serious attempt to regain political power and influence. Soon after this he announced he was sick of politics and was going to turn his attention to racing. He began buying yearlings, which he had trained by Bob Sherwood, thinking this might really make him some money. When a friend told him he was not nearly rich enough to race on such a large scale and that he would soon be broke, he replied: 'Nearly all you people who go racing are fools and no really clever man has ever taken it up seriously. But now that I have done so I shall succeed.'[37] Randolph put his heart into racing in a way he had never done with politics. Together with Dunraven, he soon built up a good stud of horses with one out-standing mare – L'Abbesse de Jouarre. The name came from a new book by the French historian Ernest Renan, which Jennie was reading. Randolph's friend the Hon. George Lambton recalled his huge love for all his horses, but especially L'Abbesse. Whenever he went round stables his pockets were always bulging with apples and sugar. On one occasion they were talking together when suddenly they heard a tremendous kicking, squealing and neighing in a box a little further down the yard. As they opened the door of the box 'the old Abbesse came rushing at Randolph like a dog, trying to put her nose into his pocket for sugar and apples; he had not forgotten them and, being a most emotional man, tears rolled down his cheeks'.[38] Love of horses was something that Jennie and Randolph, as well as Kinsky and Dunraven, always shared. It was at this time that they took a lease on Banstead Manor, a handsome, ivy-clad house on the Chieveley estate, just outside Newmarket, 'where I passed many a pleasant week. We would ride out in the early morning from six to seven to see the horses do their gallops,' wrote Jennie. 'It was a most healthy and invigorating life.'[39]

Once again, however, both parents were too preoccupied to visit Winston for his thirteenth birthday in November. Nor would they be with him for much of the forthcoming holidays. They had decided that he was to go to Harrow, not Eton, in spite of the latter having been home to six previous generations of Marlboroughs, a decision based partly on Randolph's memories of his own unhappiness at Eton. The headmaster of Harrow, the Rev. J. E. C. Welldon, promised to find a room for the boy 'somewhere'. Winston fell in with these plans but, rather pathetically, had to ask his father where *he* had been to school – Eton or Harrow? As he grew older, the letters still begging for visits take on a greater poignancy. 'I wish you could come to the distribution of prizes at the end of this term but I suppose it's impossible,' he wrote to his father in the autumn of 1887.[40] Almost worse are his requests at least for Jennie to be at home when he was going to be there. 'My darling Mummy, I do wish you were at home it would be so nice.'[41] To his requests for parental visits were now added requests for money and food.

The reason they were not at home that Christmas was because they went to Russia on a six-week semi-official visit. Precisely why they went accompanied by two of Randolph's friends, Tommy Trafford and the Marquis de Breteuil, a strange *ménage à quatre*, was never explained. Perhaps they were relying on the diplomatic skills of Henri Charles Joseph Le Tonnelier, eighth Marquis de Breteuil, who was, as Jennie reminded readers in the *Reminiscences*, descended from a family whose ancestor had been ambassador to the Court of the Great Catherine. The Breteuil family were ardent monarchists, having served the kings of France – Louis XIV, Louis XV and Louis XVI – mostly in diplomatic roles, throughout the seventeenth and eighteenth centuries. The Château de Breteuil near Tarbes, south-west France, was a gift from the Austrian Empress Maria Theresa, the mother of Marie Antoinette. This Marquis, six years older than Jennie, was, like all her admirers, a dashing horseman. He was also a much decorated soldier during the Franco-Prussian War and, later, a politician and outspoken member of the Chamber of Deputies.

But Randolph never travelled unaccompanied and Breteuil was a friend to both. Several of Jennie's lovers were also friends of Randolph's. Only Trafford and Tyrwhitt do not appear in the guest lists of those invited to dinner at the Churchill home. Not surprisingly, this journey caused some anxiety in both Court and cabinet circles. Russian expansion in Central

Asia was being watched with great concern by the British Government, as were Russian interests in the Balkans, which clashed with those of Austria-Hungary. The Queen informed Lord Salisbury that she considered it of great importance that the Russians should know that Lord Randolph was going on a private journey, in no way charged with any message or mission from her Government. The Prime Minister assured her that the Chargé d'Affaires at St Petersburg had been instructed to let it be known that Lord Randolph Churchill did not represent the opinions of either the British Government or the British people.

Anyone with royal connections was right to be wary of Russia in 1887. Earlier that year there had been an attempt on the life of Tsar Alexander III. It was not the first time the Tsar had been a target, but this assassination attempt was serious and Alexander Ulianov, brother of Lenin, had been executed in May that year for his connection with the plot. So the fear of what could happen in St Petersburg was real enough. Victoria may not have liked the unpredictable Randolph. But 1887 was her Golden Jubilee Year and she didn't want it spoiled by unpleasantness. *The Times* asked whether his trip was in fact 'a secret mission to the heads of the Panslavists; or is bear hunting his object . . . for anything and all things are possible with this young and eccentric English Lord'.[42]

Jennie had been hesitant about accompanying her husband on this trip right up until a few weeks beforehand. Randolph, holed up at the Hôtel Bristol in Paris, assured her he would be delighted if she wanted to come as she would find it interesting and amusing. 'On the other hand, there is the expense to be considered and the boys' holidays,' he reminded her.[43] Perhaps, in addition to her natural spirit of adventure, the knowledge that they would pass through Berlin, where Charles Kinsky was currently posted, on their way out and on their return, was what finally swayed her. Although Jennie made arrangements for Winston and Jack to be looked after by their Jerome aunts, things did not go entirely according to plan and Winston's painful letters to his mother cannot have made her feel easy. It was, he kept telling his mother, so dull without her at home. To make matters worse his aunt Clara fell ill. Then, by New Year's Day, Mrs Everest was seriously ill with diphtheria, at which point the ever faithful Dr Roose moved the boys to his own house. Winston wrote: 'it's very hard to bear . . . we feel so destitute'.[44]

Part of the trouble was the old Duchess. Winston was adamant: he did not want to go and stay with her at Blenheim, and so his aunt Leonie tried to keep him away. But Frances Marlborough was not to be trifled with and wrote to Leonie telling her so:

I had made every arrangement to take great care of him knowing he is susceptible to colds and I do not think there could have been as much danger as there is in going to Pantomimes in London. Besides, I feel it's all an excuse of that horrid old Everest to prevent my having him . . . I feel that Randolph and Jennie would not have objected to me seeing a little of him as really I hardly ever see him and must say I am very much vexed.[45]

In the end, when Winston did go and stay with her at Blenheim, she admitted she found him a handful, especially compared with Jack, who was 'not a bit of trouble'. Winston on the other hand, as she complained to Randolph, 'thinks me very strict but I really think he goes out too much and I do object to late parties for him. He is so excitable.[46] The Duchess further whinged that, although she had heard nothing from Randolph and Jennie, the newspapers were full of their doings in Russia.

Jennie was lionised during this trip. Several Russian princes were struck by her unusual black hair and smouldering eyes and, just as the Souls called her Black Jane, so the Russian aristocracy dubbed her 'Dark Jennie . . . no other woman could so deliberately impose her beauty. When she entered a ballroom there was always a moment's hush.'[47] Her outfits were discussed in great detail. What she wore was of greater interest than what her husband said. In her *Reminiscences* she devotes more than thirty pages to these six weeks. It's a slightly frivolous account. 'The people were charming and hospitable and full of *bonhomie*, and we saw no signs of that grinding despotism and tyranny which is supposed to be synonymous with Russian life.'[48]

Of course they didn't. Instead of hearing about the repressed peasantry, persecuted religious minorities or tightened censorship they were taken on visits to the opera, ballet and theatre. They were indulged with lavish entertaining and lots of sleighing and skating, at which she excelled. The Russians, she was disappointed to note, did not dance on ice, so she reigned supreme. She was reminded of her childhood, skating on frozen ponds and being driven in a coach and four by her father. It was an exhilarating time which enabled her to regain her vitality. As she wrote to her mother, they were treated like royalty – a dangerous pleasure. An introductory letter from the Princess of Wales to her sister the Tsarina helped. Randolph used the letter to give the impression that he had royal backing for this visit. And he did send long informative letters to the Prince reporting on what he had seen. A week before they left there was a vast ball given at the British Embassy for which 800 invitations were sent out. It was, according to *The Times*, simply a variation of Lady Morier's usual 'Thursday Evenings At Home' in honour of the distinguished English guests. 'The *élite* of St. Petersburg society . . . crowded into the State apartments of the Embassy, where Lord and Lady Randolph Churchill formed the centre of attraction.'[49]

This was not Randolph's entertainment of choice, but he could not fail to be aware of Jennie's powers of attraction. She was in high spirits when they arrived in Berlin on 23 January 1888 as guests of the Ambassador and his wife, Sir Edward and Lady Malet. Jennie spent as much time as she could riding or going for drives with Kinsky. Randolph had some political meetings but, wielding no power, he could hardly have been surprised that Prince Otto von Bismarck, the German Chancellor, was out of town. He did however have conversations with his son, Count Herbert Bismarck, an enormous man with an equally large reputation for womanising. Herbert Bismarck had just emerged from a very public divorce scandal involving a well-known singer. He and Jennie were immediately attracted and their names romantically linked for some years. 'A kindly man', is how Jennie tactfully recalls him in her *Reminiscences*. 'Although to English ideas he may perhaps have seemed a little rough and uncouth . . . he left many friends to deplore his premature death.'[50]

The visit to Russia unleashed a new creative talent in Jennie: she started to write. It was a way of earning a small amount of much needed money. It also opened doors to the artistic and intellectual world to which she aspired. Randolph, who now talked scathingly of the 'beastly House of Commons with all its intrigues and stupidity', spent increasing amounts of time travelling around the country. A week at Newmarket, where he gambled, would be followed by a week abroad for his health, where he complained of being bored. They rented another house for the summer, in Egham this time, but he wrote to Jennie warning her not to spend money she did not have. In particular, he hoped, she was not contemplating buying a new brougham. 'If you have no bills to pay, which I greatly doubt, keep your money till next year,' he instructed. 'You seem rather like Winston about money.'[51] The article she wrote, about society in Russia, for the *New Review* was quite possibly the first for which she was paid. She sent a draft to the journalist George Smalley for his comments. He replied over nine pages apologising for his frankness and brutalities but treating her as a professional embarking on a new career. After all, as he pointed out, she had no shortage of people ready to offer her compliments. He suggested she begin with 'whatever is most vivid in your memory and make it just as vivid on paper. Not only impressions but what caused your impressions.' He advised her to make the article much longer 'as there must be a great deal of material which you haven't used – if you care to give it thought and time you might make something very memorable indeed'. He told her to include details, with all the colour she could put in them, as well as anecdotes, disguising the names and places if necessary.

Smalley was one of a number of journalists she knew and liked. But she was not above learning a new craft and did not assume that just because she was Lady Randolph Churchill whatever she wrote would be of interest. Smalley encouraged her to steer clear of anything which smacked of a guidebook style. 'All you want is a frame in which to hang your picture.' He then sent her a copy of Madame de Sévigny's letters, suggesting that if Jennie took them to pieces and put them together the process would perhaps help her enormously as 'they are written without any thought of the public – even if you have read them, do so over again.'[52]

She took his advice – and her writing – seriously. Other commissions were to follow in the wake of this, although the interest of some editors was piqued simply because of her name. Lloyd Brice, editor of the *North American Review*, on the strength of reading her 'very interesting' article on society in Russia, approached her to write an article about women in English politics, 'looking especially at the position of women in high places having power'.[53] Her journalism had a spark, as her nephew the writer Shane Leslie pointed out. She succeeded in making her articles both 'piquant and in good taste'.[54]

But the occasional article, however much it amused Jennie, was not enough to make a dent in their outgoings. The spending went on, as did the peripatetic lifestyle, which was seen by the sisters as economising. A few weeks in London were followed by short stays at Blenheim, Sandringham, Wimborne, Norwich or Newmarket. Never anywhere for less than a day, of course, and mostly always by the trains, which were improving all the time. There was Paris, too, where the Jeromes felt at home, and at the end of 1888 the Leslies took an apartment in the Rue Tilsitt, close to the Arc de Triomphe. John Leslie had resigned from the Guards in order that he could study art at the prestigious Julien's Academy. For Leonie the days dragged and she wanted her sisters to gossip with. 'I long to be in London,' she wrote to 'Dearest Clarinette', 'as I can never sleep in Paris and that makes me seedy and one thinks of all one's bothers at night partly with the Rothschilds . . . I never saw so many Jews as in Paris.'[55] Three days later she insisted she had been 'a great goose' to have written such a blue letter. The trouble was apparently that 'Mme Gustave Rothschild glares at me because R insulted her daughter when she was in London last month . . .'[56]

Fin de siècle Paris was the Jerome girls' adventure playground. It was glittering, amusing, seductive and full of artists. Paris was always the European city which conjured up the potent mixture of culture and bohemianism to which so many American expatriates responded. Although there was not enough room in the Leslie apartment for all three sisters to be there together, they saw it as a place where they could return to their carefree girlhood days. Now married women, mothers, each with serious worries that they relished the opportunity to share, Paris offered them a sanctuary, a place of giddy escape where in 1889 they could recreate something of their snatched youth. They knew how to enjoy themselves and between them there was never any shortage of scandal and tittle-tattle.

Leonard, who so often put $100 bills, or cheques, into envelopes for his girls, wanted to do more. He suggested to his wife, staying at Connaught Place with Jennie, that they should go to Paris and 'establish ourselves alongside of Leonie and Jack. I will pay all the extra expenses – whatever more it may cost you to live three months in Paris instead of St Leonard's, I will pay . . . For Christmas week, Jennie and Randolph might come over and visit us. The scheme strikes me as very sensible.'[57]

In fact the Churchills split: Randolph going to Monte Carlo, where he gambled and lost, while Jennie went to Paris. The invitations for her and Leonie flooded in long before her arrival in January – one of the reasons why Leonie liked it best when Jennie came to stay. Leonie warned her that the Marquis de Breteuil wanted her to dine 'quietly' on the day she arrived, while Maimie Bischoffsheim, the American wife of Ferdinand Bischoffsheim, wealthy art collector and member of the Chamber of Deputies, was 'clamouring' for her to dine. Mrs Moore had invited her to the opera and 'opera boxes are scarce', while Charles-Marie Vidor, the composer, teacher and for sixty-four years organist at Saint-Sulpice, which housed one of the finest organs in France, was also keen to meet her. Vidor remained a friend for years. The clear if unspoken assumption among all three sisters was that it was acceptable to be surrounded by male admirers – 'gentleman callers' as they were euphemistically entitled. In one undated letter of Leonie's to Clara from Paris at this time she reported that she 'enjoyed Kinsky's little visit, he spent all Wednesday with me . . . we dined with Breteuil . . . Robert is very devoted . . . de Courcy called today but I was at my music lesson . . . tell Jennie Breteuil wants her to dine Thursday 24th and 26th, thank Esterhazy for his letter . . . Soveral never writes so I suppose he has forgotten all about me.'[58] In another she tells her sister that she is sorry Henry Higgins 'went back yesterday as he is so pleasant . . . Sir Henry Hoare sent me some lovely flowers from Cannes!!! My admirers are rather old!!'[59]

These men may not all have harboured illicit intentions. Certainly the Marquis de Soveral – the Portuguese Ambassador rudely referred to as the blue monkey because of his dark five-o'clock shadow – had a well-deserved reputation as a useful cover for others while cultivating a Don Juan image for himself. Luiz Soveral, reputedly the illegitimate son of King Carlos of Portugal, well known for his quick wit and sparkle, never married and remained one of Jennie's close friends throughout her life. There was probably no one in her overlapping circles who knew as many details of who was sleeping with whom as the Marquis de Soveral. In 1889, he was more interested in Leonie than in Jennie. Leonie clearly found him both useful and entertaining – the Café Anglais was their favourite place to dine when they were not at the opera or theatre – and remarked about seeing him again: 'Cela ne me fait ni froid ni chaud, so he can please himself.'[60]

And there was a certain safety (if exhaustion) in numbers. But there were clearly double standards. When Moreton, en route to America, cabled Clara to allay her concern that Lillie Langtry was on board ship, a woman he had known before his marriage, he wrote only half in jest: 'I don't see any nice women out here and I fear I am getting . . . beyond that little game. But if it were otherwise and some nice creature took care of me while I am five thousand miles away you ought to be rather pleased . . . On the other hand if someone looks after you when I am that distance off well that is quite another pair of shoes.'[61]*

That January, Clara, desperately trying to make ends meet in England, was fed by Leonie with all the Paris gossip, for which she had an insatiable appetite. Jennie, complaining that she was always hustled and late for everything, had no time to write. Leonie's excitement at having Jennie to stay fizzed through her letters. There was an audible buzz when Jennie was around, so 'I dread when she will go,' she admitted.[62] On a typical day they would have a late breakfast together at 11.30; at noon Jennie went off for clothes – not just to the couture houses but also to small shops she knew where, for example, she could buy guipure lace at bargain prices. In the afternoon, between 1 and 4, she sat for her portrait 'by a funny little artist', according to Leonie who, she said, Kinsky knew all about. She was home at six to change and then went out for dinner or to a play.

Leonie shared in Jennie's life but had some adventures of her own. She accepted an invitation to the theatre one night with a woman she thought

---

* Moreton introduced Lillie Langtry to Freddie Gebhardt, one of Leonie's former suitors, and then wrote rather coarsely that lilies were 'dreadfully boring when not planted in a bed' (quoted in Anita Leslie, *The Fabulous Leonard Jerome*, p. 284).

'rather fast and common', but who was so kind it would have been churl-ish to refuse. When Jennie went out for a walk Leonie entertained a man who, she told her sister, 'begins to bore me . . . We dined at the Alphonse Rothschilds, then to the opera. Kinsky turned up and is off to London today. Lunch with Soveral.' But Jennie, with her almost unquenchable vitality, was the magnet. One night the women stayed up until 4 a.m. danc-ing. 'Jennie looked very nice and was much admired.' The only cloud on their horizon was the arrival of Gladys de Grey. This, Leonie knew, wor-ried and unnerved Jennie. Her suspicion of Gladys de Grey never went away entirely. Perhaps what irked her most was that this woman, who was to become a key supporter of Covent Garden Opera and the principal pro-moter of the Ballets Russes of Diaghilev, knew so little about music. Gladys loved the drama and the spectacle and the way promoting it ensured that she was at the centre of that drama, thus enriching an otherwise meaning-less life. And of course she had the money to indulge such aspirations.

Another night they dined at Maimie Bischoffsheim's, but were rather appalled that the other guests were six divorced women 'invited to meet us!!'. Mrs Bischoffsheim was a celebrated literary hostess, both clever and beautiful, who ran a salon to which Jennie was subsequently invited more than once. Parisian salons during this gilded age offered a stylish hothouse environment where wealthy hostesses encouraged fusion between aristo-cratic French society and the exuberant artists and writers of the Belle Epoque. Proust, nurtured in such salons, would bring the atmosphere vividly to life in *À la recherche du temps perdu*. Jennie, still happily fluent in French, flourished on these occasions not merely because of the stimulat-ing intellectual conversation but because they were places to meet artists and writers, which she now craved. It was here that she met the French novelist Paul Bourget, with whom she formed an immediate romantic attachment. It has always been assumed that the pair became lovers.

She insists in her *Reminiscences* that when she first met Bourget 'and began a friendship which has lasted unimpaired to this day' he was 'then unmarried'. Two years older than Jennie, Bourget was a journalist and poet who had spent several months living in England and had a broad literary education. He wrote on many subjects but was best known for his novels, which explored human motivation and the intricate emotions of women – often, but not always, wronged women. He had just had published a con-troversial novel called *Mensonges* (Lies) which, while not universally admired, added greatly to his reputation as a novelist. He was the man of the literary moment. As Jennie noted, many women, today's feminists, were irate at his description of a *mondaine*, his heroine. She recalled his being attacked once and being asked why he did not create a real woman of the world in his books. He angrily replied that he thought he had done so. 'But, unlike most Frenchman, he could stand chaff.'[63]

Bourget was also a long-time friend and disciple of Henry James. But the two men had a problematical relationship for a number of reasons. In the first place James, although not entirely free of anti-Semitism himself, disliked the more extreme anti-Semitic views of Paul Bourget. James also disliked what he termed Bourget's 'out-and-out eroticism . . . as well as this exposition of dirty linens and dirty towels. In a word, all this is far from being life as I feel it, as I see it, as I know it, as I wish to know it.'[64] Leonie's letters were similarly revealing. She moaned: 'I have not got a penny and am so overdrawn at the bank that I can't draw more. I have not bought one thing except a play bonnet and a sortie de bal . . .' Then she added an additional, but possibly not unrelated, complaint: Paris was too full of Jews for her liking. 'Saturday we dined with Ephraim . . . I sat between him and some Rothschilds. I was nearly sick. Those Jews kill me. Nothing but Sassoons, Lamberts, Ephraims.'[65]

The women were experiencing Paris at a time of great intellectual and political ferment. Although it was to be another five years before the country was split by the Dreyfus affair, anti-Jewish rumblings had already started to disturb French aristocratic society. Edouard Drumont's book, *La France juive*, caused an immense stir in 1886 and there were continuous social attacks on Jewish officers in the French army. Jennie and Leonie could not fail to be aware of these cross-currents as they flitted to and from a variety of drawing rooms. One of their visitors was the devious, shadowy and extremely handsome young Captain Ferdinand Esterhazy, who later served as a second to a Jewish officer, Captain Crémieu-Foa, wounded in a duel occasioned by offensive anti-Semitic remarks. From men like Bourget, friend of the extreme nationalist writer Maurice Barrès, they would have heard a strong anti-republican, pro-military, anti-Semitic and later anti-Dreyfusard line. But Jennie, largely thanks to Randolph and his close friendship with the Rothschilds and their Jewish circle in London, did not share Leonie's prejudices. And even Leonie could be impressed by Jews: 'They have SUCH Rembrandts and things,' she told Clara of the Gustave Rothschilds.[66]

The Jeromes also knew the anti-republican and deeply reactionary French politician General Georges Boulanger who, for a brief moment in January 1889, looked set to stage a coup. Jennie maintained that she had never believed in Boulanger, but others thought differently. After all, the Jeromes, especially Clara, had a strong residual affection for the French monarchy. The Prince of Wales, writing to Jennie in Paris to arrange a meeting with her and her sister, said that 'he hears we are tremendous Boulangistes'.[67]

Jennie's principal escort in those weeks of 1889 was the charming, suave and worldly Breteuil. Proust, who came to know Breteuil later and often stayed at his château, also found him captivating and transformed him, under the transparent pseudonym of the Marquis de Bréauté, in *À la recherche du temps perdu*. Proust portrayed him as a man whose monocle 'bore, glued to its other side, like a specimen prepared on the slide of a microscope, an infinitesimal gaze that swarmed with affability'. In Proust's novel he wore pearl-grey gloves, a crush hat and white tie and was a 'would-be connoisseur of art who loved to give advice with an air of expert knowledge on things he knew nothing whatever about . . .'. Once Jennie returned to England Leonie passed on news of Breteuil, 'who says you treat him badly and never write'.[68] Jennie was amused by him, flattered even. But there is no indication that her heart was engaged. They continued to meet and correspond throughout her life, and sometimes Randolph went without her to stay with him.

Jennie met one other large character in those weeks who was destined to play a role in the Jerome sisters' lives: the exiled King Milan of Serbia. When she first met Milan he had just abdicated in favour of his son after a fierce quarrel with and divorce from his wife Natalie. Jennie did not warm to Milan, finding him uncouth and extravagant. She described him in her memoirs as 'one of the most uncivilised beings I have ever encountered. A short, thick set man with inky black hair and moustache and of little or no education save what his natural intelligence helped him to pick up, he was, notwithstanding, an agreeable personality.'[69]

The two pages Jennie devoted to Milan in her *Reminiscences* were to cause her sister Clara much pain. Perhaps she knew that Jennie, who was sometimes required to 'cover' for her, thought the pair 'ridiculous creatures'.[70] Milan came to London and, although he never succeeded in penetrating high society, became completely devoted to Clara. He showered her with amazing bouquets of gardenias and romantic declarations of love, as well as lavishing her children with gifts and toys. He threw an enormous party in her honour at the Amphitryon, a highly fashionable restaurant of the day at a time when restaurants were a rarity. Jennie found it amusing that ignorant people called it the Hermaphrodite. Emile, the gourmet patron, spared nothing in his attention to detail, and on this occasion the walls of the private room were entirely covered in orchids. The bill was no less spectacular than the food 'for Milan had absolutely no sense of the value of money', observed Jennie, another arch-spender. Within a short time he even begged Clara to divorce Moreton and marry him. Clara did not then know that Milan had a mistress who had borne him two sons. What Clara loved was the romance of being loved and the excitement of being spoiled – of being noticed even. She declined his offer – but not for the reason her daughter Clare Sheridan said she gave to her children: because of them. She said no because Moreton continued to convince everyone who knew him that one day, *one day*, the family fortunes would be made thanks to him.

Eighteen-ninety was a dreary and hateful year for Jennie. In January she was laid low with some unnamed malady from which she took a long time to recover. Kinsky, who was not devoting himself to her exclusively, nonetheless worked himself into a fury about Randolph's abuse of her. He believed she had been forced to travel before she was well. 'I dare say it's R's fault,' he wrote to Clara. 'He is such a selfish and brutal fellow. I dare say he wouldn't wait any longer. Anyway he ought to have been the one to see that she didn't travel too soon. What does it matter for one day or two? But not he! I am told he dragged her to hear one of his speeches when she was already very ill. He is a heartless, selfish brute and if it wasn't his fault he ought to have made her stay at home and let her off her journey for a few days.'[71]

Randolph was constantly abroad for his own health that autumn, travelling for three months to Monte Carlo en route to Egypt and then to the Riviera. But Jennie was seriously unwell herself and her letters are peppered with asides such as 'not in my usual form', or 'I get tired very easily', or 'I really haven't felt well'. She wrote how she envied him being away as she found London awfully depressing, but 'I don't seem to have the heart to go out anywhere.' She told Randolph how very pleased she would be to see him again as 'we are both getting too old and life is too short to be so much apart'.[72] Five years on, recovering from the brink of rupture, Jennie's resilience had triumphed and her deep-seated devotion to and sympathy for Randolph permeate the remaining time they had together.

She went to see her mother-in-law every day and, in November, had an interview with Welldon about Winston's progress at school. A few weeks later she told Randolph that Winston, who was now sixteen, had passed his preliminary examinations in all subjects and was in a special class preparing for the Royal Military Academy, Sandhurst, the British Army's officer-training centre. She thought Randolph should reward his son for this achievement by buying him a gun, for which he yearned. 'He ought to have a little encouragement,' she told her husband.[73]

But her time and emotional energy were largely taken up with her ailing father. Leonard Jerome never gave up hope that his sons-in-law would somehow make good and continued writing letters of encouragement in the year before he died. 'I hope I live to see the day when [Randolph] will be the great leader in that richest of all rich fields, Free Trade,' he wrote to his wife in May 1890 on his return from London, where he had been that spring.[74] He then moved into a frugal suite of rooms in a Manhattan hotel for his last months in the city.

To the end, Leonard Jerome worried about racing fixtures at the Coney Island Jockey Club and Sheepshead Bay as much as he worried about his children and shoring up their precarious marriages. At the time of Jennie's and Randolph's most serious rupture he tried to act as honest broker, meeting Randolph alone in London to talk things through with him. But to Leonie he admitted failure. 'Randolph is going out of town as he will not meet Jennie at present.'[75] He was equally preoccupied with a proposal to lease Jerome Park for ten years in the hope that he could turn it into the Auteuil of New York. But in the autumn of 1890 Leonard was exhausted, suffering from rheumatism, gout and general ill health. In October, so weak and 'hard stricken', as Shane later put it, he agreed to leave the Brunswick Hotel in New York where he had a room and come to England. He went first to the Frewen house at 18 Aldford Street, where Jennie had tea with him most days and the grandchildren were brought in to say their goodbyes. 'The beautifully panelled dining room on the ground floor was given over to the invalid. There he sat in a big backed red velvet chair while timid grandchildren peeped at him. They were told he had "galloping consumption". It was merciful', Shane wrote in some notes about his grandfather, 'that it galloped.'[76]

But soon the London fogs necessitated a move to Brighton, where it was hoped the sea air might improve his lungs. He was taken to Lion Mansions, a large apartment house facing the old pier long since washed away. Jennie, visiting him there, told Randolph that his mind was as rigorous and clear as ever. 'He was unselfish and cannot bear anyone to make the slightest sacrifices for his sake.'[77] Jennie watched him sink, profoundly depressed to see the man who had never wavered in his belief in her suffer from a hacking cough and spitting blood. She almost could not bear it. He was so patient and never complained. He had tried so hard for his daughters. Now it was all over.

On 3 March 1891 Leonard Jerome died in Brighton, 'a broken but uncomplaining man'.[78] He was seventy-three. His wife and daughters were by his bedside. His body was embalmed and then interred temporarily in

Kensal Green Cemetery until it could be returned to his native land to be placed in the family vault. A few months later Moreton Frewen, who was travelling to America on the SS *Majestic*, offered to escort the body. There was, as ever, an argument, this time over whether Clara should go with him, Moreton maintaining that he saw 'no adequate reason for taking Clara over the water with me'. In any case, he believed that Leonard's body should remain in England 'where his children and grandchildren are all settled . . . The mausoleum was prepared before any of his daughters were married.' But he agreed eventually, 'now that the last sad ceremonies and rites have been performed' and 'if such is your wish', to ensure that the remains of Leonard Jerome were returned to America.[79]

In September 1891 the body was finally laid to rest in Greenwood Cemetery, alongside Jennie's younger sister Camille, without further funeral rites, and this, too, caused an argument. Jerome's old friends were deeply disappointed to be denied an opportunity to show their respect for such a man, in one broker's words, in the country 'where he was best known and where his good qualities were appreciated . . . It really seems too bad that such a man should not be buried here at home with all of the ceremony and deference to which his standing in the community entitled him. Everybody who knew Mr Jerome can recall one or more instances of his generosity and consideration for his fellow creatures.'[80] Certainly his daughters could. Yet this man, who had once been worth millions of dollars, died leaving outstanding debts. Clara Jerome devoted her final years to ensuring that these were settled before her own death in the hope that nobody should ever know.

9

Dying by Inches in Public

~

JUST BEFORE LEONARD died, Moreton came up with his most amazing scheme yet – the Gold-Crusher. This machine, Moreton assured friends summoned to his house to hear the wondrous news, could extract gold from refuse-ore in derelict mines. By this means he intended not merely to make the fortunes of all who invested with him but to increase the world's gold supply. Both his brothers-in-law were persuaded to invest in the project, as were several of their friends. Randolph even brought the Prince of Wales to have a look. The Prince promised to mention 'your little coffee-grinder' to his financial adviser, Sir Ernest Cassel – who was, however, sceptical.

Hard-pressed Clara was now persuaded to host dinner parties for potential investors, one of whom was Baron Moritz de Hirsch, the Paris-based Jewish philanthropist who was also close to the Prince of Wales. Jennie had known the Baron and his wife Clara for some time, but it was not until the 1890s that his name appears regularly in the correspondence. De Hirsch is one of those 'known' to have been one of Jennie's lovers, according to William Manchester in *The Last Lion*. The evidence is flimsy but the idea is not impossible. She devoted a page to him in her *Reminiscences* as a man of enormous generosity who 'had the real "*joie de vivre*" and delighted in seeing people amusing themselves'. The Baron, a genial character whose illegitimate sons were adopted by his wife, had a vast estate at St Johann in Hungary where Jennie stayed for magnificent shooting parties. But de Hirsch also spent time with Randolph, who often found him, not surprisingly, 'much taken up with discussions of the Jewish question'.[1]

Born in Germany in 1831, de Hirsch made his fortune from setting up the funding to build the Oriental Railway linking Constantinople to Europe. Following the death of his son Lucien in 1877, he established a charitable foundation to assist immigrants trying to settle in the United States and another to help mass emigration of Jews from Russia to agricultural colonies in Latin America. He was one of the most generous and well-connected men of his era. Anita Leslie wrote that the de Hirschs had been 'delighted' to accept an invitation to one of Jennie's dinner parties for the Prince of Wales, where the guests included the Roseberys and the Russian Ambassador. Yet de Hirsch, descended from a distinguished family of Jewish court bankers who had mixed with European nobility for generations, already had access to these people. Obligingly, he now invested a small amount in the ill-fated Gold-Crusher.

By 1891, as Randolph's bitterness increasingly took hold, he lost the will for political action. He desperately needed to make some money and believed that South Africa and gold, but not the Gold-Crusher, might offer him one final chance. He spent most of that year travelling in Africa. However, his precarious health made it difficult for him to undertake such an arduous trip searching for gold without a personal doctor in attendance and much expensive kit. He decided therefore, reverting to first principles of 'Tory Democracy', to present his travels to his constituents as a mission to search out suitable areas for emigration for the depressed British working man. In fact, he was part of a syndicate with a total capital involvement of £15,994 held at Rothschilds. He had persuaded his sisters, mother and friends including Breteuil, Colonel North (the 'Nitrate King') and Algernon Borthwick to put up a stake in his venture. But he did not want Moreton to be part of this expedition. Nor did he like the way Moreton had ploughed ahead and engaged a personal doctor for him. If he took a doctor at all he wanted to find his own, or pick one up out there. But, as he wrote frankly to his brother-in-law:

> I cannot go on with the Gold-Crusher. All my available resources are taken up with my journey to Mashuonoland and I am not able to take up the shares offered to me. On reflection, I am of the opinion that you and I had better not go to South Africa together. We shall not agree on business matters as we take such a totally different view of things and we might quarrel or separate out – a result to be avoided. Therefore let us agree to treat our plans as if they had never been made. I shall not retain the small Gold-Crusher to take with me.[2]

The ever optimistic Moreton appears not to have taken offence, although he did suggest that Randolph might at least offer to buy a special camera which the doctor had already purchased for him. Randolph, who had by then spent £1,750 on his own personal equipment, was not of a mind to pay for photographic apparatus which he insisted the good doctor had no authority of any kind to buy.

In the event, Randolph and Cassel were proved right. The amazing Gold-Crusher never did make the mountains of gold out of the old mines bought for it to munch. Kinsky, a fellow investor in the machine, wrote to Moreton more tactfully 'as a good friend' warning him to do things 'in as strict a way as possible and not to be carried away by your spirits and enthusiasm . . . as it's such a pity people don't feel the confidence in you they might, though much is brilliant in your character'.[3] Quietly, the invention was dropped, and Moreton immediately came up with another idea: electrified sea water or electrozones, which might have had some use as a disinfectant had the irrepressible man not tried to market the revolting liquid as a fish sauce.

Randolph's trip attracted enormous publicity. His legendary rudeness was often out of control and his frequent and vitriolic attacks on the Boers embarrassed Cecil Rhodes, the British-born financier and Prime Minister of the Cape Colony who established De Beers Consolidated Mines, which by 1891 owned 90 per cent of the world's diamond mines. Randolph's behaviour lent weight to Boer accusations of British high-handedness. *Punch* was one of several magazines back home which lampooned 'Grandolph' and his search for gold. The *Clarion* caricatured him as a wasp or other insect, declaring that 'next to the influenza bacillus Lord RC is perhaps the most heroic personage of the week'.[4] By leaving England Randolph may have kept himself in the public eye, but the comments were rarely kind and usually deeply sarcastic, especially where his marriage was concerned. The *Clarion* could not resist mentioning 'the significant fact that the shield to the key hole of the main door of Lord Randolph's London house is much scratched'.[5] Jennie bore all of this intrusion into her disintegrating private life stoically.

During the nine months of his travels Randolph and Jennie exchanged regular letters full of news about the boys, racing and properties. There was, mostly, now an underlying fondness and concern for each other's health. But the intimacy had evaporated – she is sometimes 'Dear Jennie' – and he could rarely resist any opportunity for reprimanding her. In April, he admitted he had been 'very cross over what I thought was the extreme heedlessness of your actions and you know that when I am cross I say a great deal more than I really mean'.[6]

However, the trip was proving a moderate financial success, which helped. The American engineer representing Rothschilds had found gold-bearing reefs and determined the direction and depth necessary for a shaft to reach them. On the strength of this Randolph sent Jennie some fine diamonds, one of which weighed about 7 carats before it went to Amsterdam to be cut. After receiving one of these diamonds she told Randolph what a beauty it was, adding that she had had it made into a pin, with a screw at the bottom for safety. 'How *Dear of you* to send it to me.'[7] The syndicate became a limited company with capital of £30,000 and, though Churchill was later forced to sell some of his shares to pay off debts, the residue of his investment realised £70,000 after his death.[8]

But, for the present, the Churchills had no money – the Frewens even less – and so Connaught Place was finally given up. At first, while Randolph was still travelling and Clara was in Paris with Leonie, Jennie and Moreton moved in together to Aldford Street. 'We make a very good ménage,' Jennie told her elder sister, 'though I see little of him as I lunch and dine out.'[9] Moreton confirmed the picture. 'Jane is here – at least I suppose she is – but she is on the fly and I see nothing of her.'[10] The arrangement suited because Charles Kinsky was back in town, staying mostly at the Turf Club in Piccadilly. But, as ever, Jennie did not have his undivided attention. He was going to 'squeeze himself elsewhere', she told 'dearest Clarinette'. The Churchills might not have enough money for a house, but Jennie begged her sister to choose her a chic little black hat for Newmarket, 'something in the sailor line, all black or white and black'.[11]

Jennie escaped from London whenever she could and made one groundbreaking trip to Bayreuth with Leonie. The two sisters were enamoured with Wagner, an acquired taste in 1891. Jennie had, some months before, engaged a German musician to give a series of lectures in London about Wagner's music. But at Bayreuth Jennie was hit by raging toothache, which might have marred the pleasure slightly, had not some cocaine, offered by a woman seated behind her, eased the pain and enabled her to attend all the performances. There was another dampener on the trip, though, which cocaine could not help and that was the continuing froideur in her relations with Gladys de Grey.* Even the Prince of Wales, who, according to Wilfrid Scawen Blunt, was 'generally better informed on matters of this kind than other people',[12] heard about the encounter but joked later that 'there does not seem to have been any danger of you and Lady de Grey eating each other up as both of you had your protectors'.[13] Jennie's blind spot over Gladys de Grey was uncharacteristic.

Randolph's return to London at the end of the year marked a dramatic

---

* Wilfrid Scawen Blunt wrote of Gladys in his 'Secret Memoirs' that 'she is still making a fool of herself about Jean de Reske, the singer, who she says is the only man who moves her to physical passion . . . though he says he loves another woman and divides himself between them to her great anger. But she has accepted the position . . . she is a clever woman, [Lord] Lytton says, but not a wise one.' (Wilfrid Scawen Blunt, 'Secret Memoirs', 14 July 1890, Fitzwilliam Museum, Cambridge, vol. XIII, ms 30-1975, p. 298.)

decline in his appearance. Many of those who saw him at this stage remarked on how dreadfully changed he was, partly because of the full beard he had grown which he may have hoped camouflaged his gaunt look but which in fact aged him. Jack told Winston it was horrid, and Jennie described it as 'a terror'. She promised Winston she would bribe Randolph to shave it off, but if she did she failed, and it remained. It seems likely, if his affliction was syphilis, that any remission was over and he had now entered the grim tertiary stage.

Tertiary syphilis was the term loosely used, often by laymen, to encompass a variety of symptoms when it was believed they resulted from the initial infection. Tabes Dorsalis, one of the symptoms of which is numbness in the hands or feet, was another name given to this stage. Nineteenth-century doctors had their own shorthand for the final stage, calling it General Paralysis of the Insane (GPI), and GPI was the diagnosis they gave Randolph. Without the evidence from a neurological examination, record of blood pressure or brain scan, it is impossible at this date to establish whether Lord Randolph Churchill had contracted syphilis. The spirochete responsible for syphilis was not discovered until 1905 and the definitive blood test, the Wasserman Reaction, was not available until a couple of years later. There are those today who believe that 'Churchill's main symptoms are much more consistent with a less titillating neurological diagnosis.'[14] As Dr John Mather, medical historian to the International Churchill Society, points out, there is no proof of when or how he might have been first infected and the accounts that do exist are conflicting. In addition there was in the late nineteenth century a clear predisposition toward syphilis as a diagnosis. There is no evidence that Jennie or either son was infected with syphilis and, since contemporary advice (incorrect as it later proved) was that all intimacy between husband and wife in cases of suspected syphilis must immediately cease, the assumption must be that if he believed himself afflicted they lived apart from an early date in their marriage. This probably had happened by 1885 or 1886. But there is no evidence that suspected syphilis was the sole reason for their marital difficulties at that time.

In his search for diagnoses other than syphilis to explain the changes in personality, the problems with speech and the evidence of neurological and other deterioration, John Mather quotes Robson Roose himself, who wrote two years after his patient's death that 'excessive smoking, too much alcohol, tea and coffee often resorted to by overworked persons are frequent causes of sleeplessness'. According to Mather, 'much of Randolph's behaviour during his last five years seems to be no more than an accentuation of his prior personality'. Randolph had, to Jennie's chagrin, always been a heavy smoker. Forty a day was not unusual. Mather believes that chain-smoking provides a likely explanation for his longstanding problem with circulation. 'Spasms in the arteries reduce circulation which causes numbness and pain due to lack of oxygen in the tissues.' Mather advances the possibility that Randolph developed a left-side brain tumour for which no surgery was available. 'This would also be consistent with the circulation problems in his hands which in turn would be related to his intermittent heart failure and arterial spasms from nicotine in cigarettes.'[15]

However, according to a neurological specialist who has evaluated the evidence for this biography, the idea that a brain tumour caused Lord Randolph's symptoms is also problematic. 'The intermittent nature of some of his symptoms coming and going would be much against a brain tumour [while] the course of the disease over several years would be unusual unless we were dealing with a benign type of brain tumour . . . these would tend to cause slowly progressive problems in one part of the brain, perhaps with additional epilepsy.' This doctor, while emphasising that no certain diagnosis is possible, concludes that 'syphilis cannot be ruled out, especially if it was present in its meningovascular form, which can cause stroke-like episodes'.[16]

At all events, Lord Randolph himself seems to have believed, from about 1886 onwards, that he had a severe degenerative neurological condition which was possibly syphilis. It was Dr Roose who sent him as early as October 1885[17] for a specialist opinion from Dr Thomas Buzzard, an expert in managing neurosyphilis, or late syphilis of the brain, and consulting physician to the National Hospital for the Paralysed and Epileptic in London. By 1890 Randolph was seriously ill with palpitations for which Roose prescribed belladonna, laudanum and digitalis – the latter to alleviate cardiac weakness deemed to result from the syphilis. Mercury was the standard cure for syphilis and although there is no surviving note proving that he ever took this, in June 1894 his doctors told him that they wanted to see the effect of a new treatment, which is thought to have been mercury, as comments were made about a noticeable darkening of his complexion.[18] Randolph was away in South Africa for most of 1891 and spent much of 1892 trying to recuperate at spas in Austria and Germany, which did little to stop the deterioration.

A handful of those who did not know the cause or name of Randolph's affliction continued to urge him to return to politics. The *Punch* journalist Henry Lucy, who saw him at the end of 1892, told him that now was the moment 'when your people are in opposition and you can again take a leading part.' Randolph replied: 'Oh no, I am quite out of politics now and besides, I shall see far less to oppose in the measures of the present government than I did those of the last.'[19] He made several more speeches in early 1893, virulently anti-Home Rule and excruciatingly memorable for all present as his articulation was slurred and his tongue tremulous. After one such speech in February 1893, Moreton told Clara that 'he was very nervous, almost inaudible, but when he found his voice it was, I hear, admirable'. By the end of the year his speeches were hardly reported. 'There is nothing more graphic in Churchill's decline', wrote his biographer Roy Foster, 'than the way in which he simply fades out of the newspaper columns which had done so much to make him what he once was.'[20] Randolph tried to convince his family that accounts of his shaky voice and hand were 'awfully exaggerated and some of the press lie dreadfully'.[21] He maintained to his mother, wife and doctors that he had never felt the slightest bad effect from a speech, and was furious at gossip about his condition or with Jennie if she overdid concern for his health. His insistence that he was always on the verge of recovery, while remaining obsessed with a cure for the symptoms, was of a piece with the euphoria which characterised his manic state.

Not only was he deeply disillusioned with politics but the tone of his letters indicates that at one level he knew, from about 1891 onwards, he had not long to live. 'So Arthur Balfour is really leader and Tory democracy, the genuine article, is at an end,' he wrote to Jennie just before his return from South Africa.

> Well I have had quite enough of it all. It confirms me in my decision to have done with politics and make a little money for the boys and ourselves. I hope you don't intend to worry me on this matter and dispute with me and contradict me. More than two thirds in all probability of my life is over and I will not spend the remainder of my years beating my head against a stone wall. I have many things and many friends to make me happy without that horrid House of Commons . . . I have had a good time but now reproach myself for having left you and Mama and the boys for so long.[22]

Before the year was out, he made one final and humiliating pitch for a job, hoping that Balfour, then Leader of the House of Commons, would use his influence with his uncle Lord Salisbury to secure his appointment as ambassador to Paris. But Balfour snubbed him and in December he learnt that the first Lord Dufferin and Ava had been given the posting. Jennie was deeply aggrieved on his behalf: 'The idea is too galling that the only thing you ever asked for should be refused!' she wrote supportively.[23]

But that winter she was fighting another battle, this time with Winston, now seventeen and objecting vehemently to his mother's plans to send him to a French family in order to learn the language. It was initially proposed by his headmaster, the Rev. J. E. C. Welldon. Yet Jennie's attempt to send her son to France appears as yet another painful episode in the mother–son correspondence. At the end of 1891 Welldon strongly urged that Winston should go to France to improve his conversational French as this would strengthen his chances of passing the entrance examination to Sandhurst. Yet again the boy bombarded his mother with reasons why he should not go, cursing his fate and everyone who connived in the trip. 'I can't tell you what trouble I have had with Winston this last fortnight,' Jennie told Randolph, recognising her son's disappointment at not being at home with his family for Christmas to welcome his father back. 'He makes as much fuss as tho' he were going to Australia for 2 years.'[24] But though Winston came up with every argument he could think of, including telling Welldon that Baron de Hirsch's sons, with whom he hoped to ride, spoke English fluently, on this she remained firm. 'You can be quite certain my darling that I will decide what is best, but I can tell you frankly that I am going to decide and not you.'[25]

Winston had one more shot at making his mother feel badly, telling her how 'utterly miserable' he had been made by her treatment of him. 'Never would I have believed that you would have been so unkind . . . I am so unhappy but if you don't read this letter it will be the last you'll have the trouble to send back.'[26] But there is another way to interpret this episode. Winston was pushing his mother to the limit, but he did not persuade her to give in nor did the argument damage their relationship. That Winston clearly understood he could treat his mother in this way and retain her unconditional love demonstrates the iron strength of their bond. Far from being manipulative, he was simply strong. With his mother he learnt how far he could push and still carry those who loved and supported him, basic leadership skills. He also understood the growing shift in parental responsibilities and that, after Randolph's absence of nearly nine months away, his mother was now the primary influence. Lady Warwick commented on the unusual mother–son relationship at this time. She believed that Jennie encouraged him to debate with her. 'True to her American training, she did not check Winston when he asked questions or argued with her.'[27]

Winston did eventually go to France and, in an attempt to make the trip palatable, Jennie persuaded Breteuil, Trafford and de Hirsch to entertain him. Although he complained on Christmas Eve that he had not heard a word from all those 'friends' that she had spoken of, and complained further that 'with you "out of sight is out of mind"',[28] in the end he seems to have enjoyed the trip. De Hirsch, ingeniously, took him on an interesting visit to the Paris morgue, and Breteuil and Trafford also provided diversions. But he never mastered confident French, as his mother had hoped.*

Shortly afterwards Breteuil announced that he was marrying an American heiress, Lita Garner, whose sister Florence had recently married the charming but unlucky Sir William Gordon-Cumming. Writing to Jennie on his return from the United States Breteuil told her, 'I am happier every day and will never forget that you had pushed me . . . what I miss is not seeing you any more . . . believe me, again, of my attachment.' Jennie, jealous no doubt, was less than complimentary about the match and told Randolph that she hoped Breteuil's new wife would 'keep sane'.[29]

Any mellowness Jennie might have detected immediately following Randolph's return from gold-prospecting did not last. The letters between the pair throughout 1892 were cool, with Randolph often reprimanding Jennie for spending too much money or seeing men of whom he disproved, or both. He reproved his elder son for profligacy too and warned him that the Bankruptcy Court was not far off unless he changed his habits. Mrs Jerome, as well as Leonie and Clara, were now aware of Randolph's frantic worries about money and of the brutal way he treated his family as a result.

His forty-third birthday came and went in February 1892. But this time it was Jennie who forgot 'that unpleasant fact'.[30] She was in France. A month later he was not so forgiving and told her he was very cross to read in the newspaper that she had had her pocket picked at Monte Carlo in the casino. 'Very disreputable. I do hope you are not gambling.'[31] Three days later he was angrier and this time wired advising her not to go to Naples as 'two lone women cannot go off yachting with a strange man without exciting comment probably of a very ill-natured character'.[32] Since the family had now left Connaught Street and moved into 50 Grosvenor Square with the Dowager Duchess it is hardly surprising that Jennie wanted to get away – to Naples or anywhere. She was once again distraught.

'Quite between ourselves, I don't think yr Mother cares about my staying here if she goes away and she has postponed her departure indefinitely. I am not going to bother you with it all and I shall try and do the best I can

---

* Years later, meeting President Charles de Gaulle, he expected his private secretary Anthony Montague Browne, who was fluent in French, to translate.

for myself and the boys – but I feel rather "mis" over it all – I know "beg-gars cannot be choosers" but I feel *very* old for this sort of thing,' Jennie wrote gently.[33] She told him she had already been to Hudson's, the house-hold furniture remover and depository, and settled what was to be sold. Some pieces were to go to Grosvenor Square but not all; there was room only for very little. 'Yr mother does not want to part with any of her things and rather discourages us moving upstairs but really it does not matter if you have what you want and I have my rooms all right – the boys can very soon manage with yr mother's furniture. Things will all settle themselves.'[34]

It was not only selling up and moving that depressed Jennie. In June, Winston made an unsuccessful first attempt to enter Sandhurst. Randolph was furious and although Winston was to try again in November warned that if he failed again he would think about putting him into business. As ever, it fell to Jennie to fight Winston's corner and to point out to her hus-band all the abilities which she believed he had and which would ultimately lead to distinction. A few months later there was a further painful loss as the Churchills also had to give up the lease on Banstead Manor. This had been a refuge for them all in different ways, but especially for Winston and Jack. Holidays there had provided both boys with some of the happiest days of their childhood. While Randolph was away, in the summer of 1891, Kinsky proved an exciting surrogate father for them, setting up a target for shooting practice in the grounds and building a secret den in the acres of uncultivated undergrowth, as well as taking Winston on exciting outings in London.

A letter Winston wrote to his younger brother about one of these trips with Count Kinsky points sadly to what might have been. Winston was breathless with excitement, describing an outing to the Crystal Palace in Kinsky's company on the occasion of the German Emperor visiting London. They not only watched fireworks and drove in the Count's phaeton but drank lots of champagne and were involved in a fracas with a 'cad'. Jennie recognised that Winston needed a gun of his own as he was learning to shoot. It was Kinsky who organised this. She also felt that at almost seventeen 'he is getting a bit too old for a woman to manage . . . he really requires to be with a man'.[35] Equally significant and demanding action was her understanding of the differences between her two sons. Jack she knew would only flourish out of Winston's orbit. Tactfully, she told Randolph it was the difference in their ages 'beginning to tell and poor Jack is quite worn out rushing about after Winston'.[36] She did her best in the circumstances.

Shane Leslie said in later years what a wonderful stepfather the Count would have made. The fact that he caught childhood illnesses such as measles from Winston seems not to have bothered him unduly. That summer was probably the high spot of the relationship between Jennie and Kinsky. So enamoured was Jack of this exotic sportsman that when he too went to Harrow he hung a picture of Kinsky in his room. Winston, covetous, tried to buy this off him. Yet Jennie was, as ever, discreet. Telling Randolph about a house party she had hosted, she was careful to point out: 'Kinsky slept at the farm opposite as there was no room for him and he did not mind – Everest has been ill with pleurisy – poor old thing and of course I would not turn her out.'[37] For appearances' sake, Mrs Jerome and Leonie were frequently guests at Banstead, too.

Although Jennie and Kinsky were often at the same weekend house parties, Kinsky was constantly on the move. Perhaps it was the knowledge that he was not, in today's parlance, 'able to commit' or that his family was putting pressure on him to marry well that forced Jennie to look elsewhere for male companionship. By the summer of 1892 she had formed a new attachment, one of which Randolph did not approve. He admitted the relationship in private conversations with Natty Rothschild: 'I suppose you know she is living with Freddy Wolverton,' he told his friend.[38] Natty immediately shared the news with Loulou Harcourt. Randolph asked Jennie not to go to a party which Wolverton was giving that July, preferring her to see Claude Lowther, an eccentric art collector whom he considered safer.

Frederick, Lord Wolverton was a nephew of Gladstone's friend and supporter, the late second Lord Wolverton, a man of great wealth and generosity who had been Postmaster General for a brief period in 1886. The family had made their fortune as merchant bankers in London and had large estates at Iwerne in Dorset. The second Baron Wolverton, who was head of the bank, was a flamboyant personality who determined to turn Iwerne into a first-class sporting estate where he could indulge his love of hunting and shooting. He built a stud farm on the edge of the village where he bred racehorses and hunters and allowed large areas of woodland to develop into coverts for game birds. The Prince of Wales was a frequent visitor. Lord Wolverton died suddenly in November 1887 aged sixty-three, leaving an immense personal fortune, but as he and Lady Wolverton had no children the estate and title passed to his nephew Henry. Henry died unmarried the following year and in 1889 his twenty-four-year-old brother Frederic inherited. When Jennie became friendly with Freddy he was in his late twenties, titled and an immensely rich landowner. Jennie may never have felt the same profound love for Freddy as she did for

Charles Kinsky. But, as Randolph's health declined, the prospect of a new life with Wolverton must have seemed thrilling.

Randolph meanwhile was often to be found at the Carlton Club, where he fumed about life in general and his wife in particular. Concerns about money and health, his twin anxieties throughout his life, both now reached a dizzyingly worrying climax. It is noticeable from his letters how shaky his handwriting had become and, although he told Jennie that his doctors, the ever faithful Roose as well as the neurosyphilis specialist Thomas Buzzard, were reassuring, that was not the case. He told her that they had given him some medicine to help prevent his 'giddiness', but there was in truth little else they could do. He felt aimless and depressed. In this mood, his temper could flare up over anything and money was a frequent trigger. In the summer he was furious with Jennie for not keeping control over cheques she was paying for bills in which there might be mistakes. 'Something in your letter made me mad,' he told her demanding that she meet him at Grosvenor Square to go through the accounts[39] − an indication that, as he had told Natty, she was not actually living there. But then he begged her: 'Let us be friends again.'[40]

Ever since her sister Clara had stayed with Jennie in the early days of their marriage she had been witness to Randolph's erratic temper. Now his explosions were more frequent and Jennie's mother and sisters could have had no illusions about what she had to endure on a daily basis. Clara had obviously recounted one particularly painful episode to Moreton. He replied:

> I am so sorry for dear Jane; very sorry; but good times are at hand and when they come in full measure we shall be able to make things much more comfortable for her also. She is a great dear and, with all her faults, I am devoted to her . . . poor dear, kind Jennie, I shall so long to know things are tolerable with her again. She of all people must be fretting under such circumstances. He is a hateful creature in many ways . . . Dear sweet Jenny [sic] I am so sorry for her worries, worries too not like ours to be got over. He is an impossible man that; a bad-natured man essentially but the sense of the mistakes he has made would embitter a much better disposition than he has.[41]

Moreton's remarks point to an interesting comparison; Moreton and Clara also lived in a constant state of financial crisis with fewer sources of credit. His letters in the early 1890s, typed in purple ink, are bursting with references to their shortage of cash, to being 'very dry' and to the need to borrow or to keep going, as well as with such laments as how hard 'grubbing' is or 'I have not got a bob and I don't know where to turn.' But Moreton buoys up his wife not merely with his talk of love for her but through his constant optimism. In March 1893 he admits: 'I cannot even find a tenner . . . the cupboard is so very, very bare at this moment. What a hard world it is in these days but please God it will right itself. I hate to think of you over there without me, with nothing to amuse you . . . we shall get our deserts ere long.'[42]

However, in October Jennie herself fell dangerously ill. She had been suffering from unnamed pains in her pelvic region for some time, was easily exhausted and wondered if the pains were a sign of depression. 'I used to think the pains were in my mind,' she told Randolph. 'But they were really *the thing* [italics added] beginning. I've got lots of pain.'[43] She was worried about Winston having been 'ploughed' in his first army examination for Sandhurst and was deeply sad about giving up their London home and now Banstead too. Wandering around the empty country house she remembered that they had forgotten to be photographed there as she had wanted.

Randolph wrote to her: 'What you tell me about yourself shows that you ought not to delay much before getting put thoroughly to rights.'[44] Five days later he told her he was anxious to know 'what the doctors decided to advise you. I should be doubtful of the wisdom of going to a party so soon after any operation.' Then he added matter-of-factly: 'I expect although you will be fairly well after ten days you will have to keep quiet for some time . . .'[45] But the next day he suggested Jennie should catch a train and come up for a week to Floors Castle, his sister Annie's home at Kelso on the Scottish borders and one of his favourite hideaways as he could live there quietly and enjoy the fishing. This time he was there to comfort his sister, mourning the sudden death of her husband, to whom he had been greatly attached. He said Jennie could spend a week there without getting bored and in any case told her 'not to worry so much about yourself'.[46]

However, Jennie was in no fit state to travel. She consulted Roose who, after examining her under ether, sent her immediately to Dr Thomas Keith, a prominent surgeon well known for his pioneering use of electricity in treating uterine tumours. Keith was the author of several books on the subject including *Contributions to Surgical Treatment of Tumours in the Abdomen*. He believed she was suffering from a swelling near her uterus as well as pelvic peritonitis and cellulitis. He ordered complete rest if Jennie wished to avoid the risk of an acute attack and an emergency operation. She told Randolph she felt 'somewhat bruised' by the doctors. They had found a growth in the rectal area, 'the size of a hen's egg . . . which was either an enlarged ovary or tube or boil or both'.[47] They hoped this might shrink of its own accord which, with total rest, was often what happened.

'We have to face many months of terrible anxiety and to underrate the importance of the illness would be of absolute harm to the patient as there is no margin for mistake or carelessness,' Roose wrote to Randolph on 22 October.[48] But by the end of the month, notified by Roose that Jennie's condition had deteriorated, Randolph finally returned to London. He admitted to his mother, 'I don't think I should have ventured to leave her. There is a fate against me fishing this year and it is no use struggling.'[49] Loulou Harcourt understood the severity of Jennie's illness and wrote in his diary on 27 October the news that she 'had been desperately ill with pelvic peritonitis for some days and was *in extremis* on Sunday but is now recovering' – a state of affairs he had presumably learnt of from Randolph. Four days later Harcourt's father 'spent a pleasant Sunday with Rhodes and R Churchill. The latter reports his wife better though I hear she is not out of danger yet . . .'[50] On 1 November Harcourt went to Lady Jeune's, where he again met Churchill and after much talk of bimetallism and politics, Randolph 'was inclined to abuse his wife – though her life is still said to be in danger'. What was he abusing her over this time?

Randolph must have been aware that Jennie's life was in the balance when he returned from Scotland and wrote to Winston and Jack on 25 October that although their mother had been extremely ill the day before 'and we were rather alarmed . . . Thank God today there is an improvement and the doctors are vy hopeful.'[51] But at the end of the month he too was ill 'with a sharp outbreak of what vulgar people call "shingles" and what doctors call "herpes". I have it all over the chest, shoulders and right arm,'[52] which necessitated the employment of two nurses at Grosvenor Square. In this situation he suggested that his mother should stay away until Jennie was 'really convalescent'.

Whatever the cause of Jennie's pains, it is clear that in the autumn of 1892 she nearly died. If she was suffering from an inflamed appendix, which ruptured, she would not have survived the poison entering her system. Surgery was not then recommended. The first well-known case of the appendix being removed was ten years later when King Edward VII was the patient. Had it been an ovarian cyst, caused by peritonitis, Keith would probably have operated, albeit unwillingly. Most likely it was a uterine fibroid – again removing this surgically was an operation he did not like to perform as it carried a mortality rate of 8 per cent. But Jennie was lucky – her swelling seems to have gone away of its own accord. She avoided an operation and, helped no doubt by her robust constitution, she recovered her natural strength within about three months. Her vitality took longer to re-emerge.

There was worse to come. Eighteen-ninety-three began disastrously with the nineteen-year-old Winston falling from a high tree and sustaining severe concussion. He had been indulging in characteristic daredevilry while staying, with his mother and brother, at the home of Randolph's sister Lady Wimborne, near Bournemouth. Jennie was at his side with 'energetic aid and inopportune brandy'[53] within minutes. Randolph for this crisis came from Dublin as soon as he could. Winston suffered from deep shock and a ruptured kidney and was unable to work for a couple of weeks. His recovery was made more painful by the knowledge that he had, at the second attempt, failed the entrance examination to Sandhurst. This time he was sent to a crammer in London to help him in a third and final effort. Now living at home once again he witnessed his father's deteriorating health at close quarters. But in the Easter holidays he went to recuperate with his uncle Blandford's American widow, Duchess Lily, the former Mrs Lillian Hammersley, whom he had married in 1888. Blandford, the eighth Duke, had died suddenly in November 1892, which meant that until Sunny produced an heir five years later Winston was heir presumptive after his own father. The whole family, having once made snide personal remarks about Lily, descending to criticism of her weight and facial hair, now revised their opinion, recognising her goodness and kindness of disposition. She and Winston formed an especially close rapport: she understood him and spoiled him.*

Randolph and Jennie, once Winston was well again, resumed their pattern of separate travels – he to Monte Carlo, she to Paris – punctuated by letters concerning the usual health and money problems, now exacerbated by Winston's exam prospects. They had little to say to each other beyond his pleas to her not to spend too much money. But in August they were both at a spa in Germany when Winston, on a walking tour of Switzerland with Jack and their tutor Mr Little, wrote with the good news that he had finally been accepted into Sandhurst. Randolph still did not think it such good news as Winston had passed 'by the skin of his teeth' and had missed the infantry by eighteen marks. The cavalry, requiring a more expensive lifestyle, was easier to get into.

* The eighth Duke's first wife, Lady Blandford, did not remarry and lived until 1932.

Jennie wrote warning Winston that 'Papa is not as pleased over yr exploits as you seem to be!'[54] Two days later came the blistering response from his father, reprimanding him for 'the extremely discreditable' performance and declaring that his 'failure demonstrated beyond refutation your slovenly happy go lucky harum scarum style of work for which you have always been distinguished at your different schools'. It was a long and particularly cruel letter. Randolph also reminded Winston of all the advantages he had had and complained that despite 'all the efforts that have been made to make your life easy and agreeable and your work neither oppressive nor distasteful, this is the grand result that you come up among the second or third rate who are only good for commissions in a cavalry regiment'.[55] Finally he warned him that if his conduct and action at Sandhurst resembled past performance then his responsibility towards him was over. At the end of the summer Winston was awarded an infantry cadetship after all, and this improved matters somewhat.

Meanwhile, Winston continued to write to his mother begging her to intervene and organise an allowance with his father. She was a go-between whom Winston felt able to address in a much more open way about his plans for the future. To her he was able to admit how unhappy he was that his father did not approve of his letters which, he insisted, he took great pains over. 'If I write a descriptive account of my life . . . I receive a hint from you that my style is too sententious and stilted. If on the other hand I write a plain and excessively simple letter it is put down as slovenly.' His father, he felt, would go on treating him as a child until he was about fifty years of age. By contrast, 'It is a great pleasure for me to write to you unreservedly instead of having to pick and choose my words and information.'[56] To his mother he also now felt able to moan about his health and skin problems. And to her he was able to admit that he wished he was joining the 4th Hussars, the regiment of the dashing Colonel Brabazon, rather than the 60th Rifles where Lord Randolph had pulled strings with the Commander in Chief, the Duke of Cambridge, to get him accepted.

There was another matter, too, which indicated the more adult relationship he was now reaching out for with his mother and that was the family treatment of Elizabeth Everest. When Jennie had been too preoccupied or too busy to visit Winston at Harrow his devoted nanny had made the journey. And though other boys jeered at him Winston had still not been ashamed to embrace his old nurse in public. Now Winston was equally courageous in voicing his criticism to Jennie of the way in which the Duchess wanted to 'pack her off' as she was no longer needed. He could not, in all decency, allow her 'to be cut adrift without protest in the manner which is proposed . . . I should be v sorry not to have her at Grosvenor Square because she is, in my mind, associated more than anything else with HOME. She is', he bravely reminded his mother, 'an old woman who has been your devoted servant for 20 years. She is more fond of Jack and I than of any other people in the world'.[57] In a fifteen-page letter Winston was painfully honest about his fondness for Everest and his understanding that it was not his mother's doing to let her go before she had properly made up her mind where to go or what to do. He conceded that the Duchess had 'every right' to discharge a servant for whom she had no further use, but it must be done with fairness and generosity, 'and it is in your power to explain to the Duchess that she cannot be sent away until she has got a good place'. He begged his mother not to be angry with him for writing in this way. But, in spite of Winston's noble intentions, Everest was not required at Grosvenor Square. She continued to correspond with both Jack and Winston, who sent her small amounts of cash.

Money remained a major problem for Jennie and Randolph. 'You can imagine, dearest,' Randolph wrote to Jennie, 'but I have no money at the present moment. I am overdrawn . . . selling at deep levels . . . I must not sell more than £500 . . . I will try and send you £105 to the Hôtel Scribe in Paris.'[58] They spent more time apart than together but Randolph maintained his right to advise her as to those he considered suitable for her to dine with. At the end of November, they paid a rare visit together to Sandringham. This was deemed worthy of newspaper comment 'in view of the fact that Lord and Lady Churchill seldom visit the same house together'.[59]

To Jennie, and anyone else who asked, Randolph continued to insist that Buzzard and Roose were so satisfied with his own condition 'they didn't even consult'. It was a tragic period of public decline and private delusion. By this time Jennie had been to see Randolph's doctors herself. She had to understand her husband's condition. When Randolph discovered that they had informed her of what they considered to be the truth, there was a furious row – his anger all the more understandable if he had something to hide.

He raged at Buzzard over 'a group of interfering people by no means all friends who are scattering the most absurd rumours about my bad and worse health. I was much upset and somewhat indignant at hearing that Lady Randolph had been to see you and Roose but I have had an explanation . . . from which I find that what she said to you, though in my opinion needless, was of a different character than what I had been led to believe.'[60] Randolph's fury on learning that his doctors had discussed his illness with Jennie is all too easy to imagine. Confronted by his rage Jennie tried, presumably, to obfuscate. Randolph asked Buzzard to give him a frank and urgent opinion of how he should deal with his wife and his mother since 'the only thing which has really troubled me and really might have made me ill is all this stupid gossip and fuss about my health'.[61]

Almost every letter between the unhappy pair now complained of a cold, or a cough, or tiredness at the very least. Often it was more serious and then he had to send for a foreign doctor, one of whom 'found my lung very congested but in a healing stage. He has made me wear cotton wool on my chest and given me some medicine. I have no fever.'[62] Jennie was tender in response but desperately worried about the future. She gratefully accepted the occasional small cheques her husband sent. One came with a pitiful note which said he was destitute of news 'but really the cheque is the thing'.[63] His knowledge that his memory was failing was particularly painful for them both. 'By the way when is Jack's birthday and I forget whether I sent Winston his February cheque?'[64] Jennie responded in the way she always had, aware that they had only a few months left together, by going to Paris.

And it was there, alone, that she spent their twentieth wedding anniversary, contemplating the hopes that she had embraced with such confidence in 1874. Randolph scrawled a note: 'delighted to hear you have had a good time. Love to Breteuil' – it was all he could manage. But then he begged her to come back as it was 'so lonely at Grosvenor Square, breakfasting and dining alone . . . I shall be glad when you return'.[65] And it was while she was in Paris that Randolph had yet another searing exchange of letters with Winston – with Jennie in the middle – as Randolph discovered that a valuable watch he had given his son had suffered two accidents and had had to be repaired. Jennie – 'the best and sweetest Mamma in all the world' – again tried to soothe matters between father and son.

She warned Winston that he was spending too much money. He really could not go on like this. She tried to comfort him by enclosing £2 'with my blessing and love' so that he could buy himself a cheap watch. She sent him other cheques which, she warned, would make his father very cross if he knew, as well as a clown costume that he needed for a Sandhurst fancy-dress parade. Jennie and Winston now formed a tight bond. She continued to support the failing Randolph, who, she insisted, 'gives you a very fair allowance and you ought to make do'.[66] And as she prepared to invest as much of her emotional energy as she could in her elder son she did not shirk from reprimanding him for being so careless and childish. She worried that his extravagance, which mirrored her own, could spoil his chances in life, telling him he was a 'perfect sieve'[67] as far as money was concerned. In the last months before Randolph's death it is clear that mother and son retained the capacity to wound each other more than any other person. At the same time no one gave the same pleasure that they could to each other. The roles were in a state of flux and several of their letters took on the tones of a lover. He wrote to her as 'His own Darling, Dearest Mama' and on occasions signed off with 'I think of you always and long to kiss you again.' She ended almost all her letters with a plea to Winston to take care of Jack, now for a brief time his roommate at Harrow.

Jennie, having finally been taken into the confidence of his doctors, knew that her ailing and unpredictable husband must, in his final weeks or months, be protected from himself, but above all for her sons' sake. Even so, as Jennie's nephew Shane and others recognised all too clearly, 'he slowly died in public by inches'.[68] 'There was no retirement, no conceal-ment,' as Randolph's childhood friend Lord Rosebery observed, adding that he was 'the chief mourner at his own protracted funeral, a public pageant of gloomy years'.[69]

In desperation they made extravagant plans for a world tour which would keep them out of society for almost a year. The doctors, while understanding the need to 'get the patient away',[70] were not happy with this grandiose scheme and proposed instead a short journey somewhere near at hand accompanied by a medical man to see what effect the change of climate would have. Randolph, who had always made the decisions, was implacable. He insisted that he had already discussed his plans with them and, having gained their approval, had now made arrangements which could not possibly be altered. He raged: 'I have taken my passage . . . made arrangements for letters of recommendation, ordered my outfit and done everything that was necessary and now you tell me to go to Norway.'[71] What, he asked them, should he do in Norway? – though it was a place where he had been content to go in the past. He told them he now had an opportunity of going round the world and that he would certainly avail himself of it. When Buzzard pointed out that New York in July could be uncomfortably hot, Randolph shot back that from his experience July in New York was temperate. 'But in any case I cannot change my plans and on 29th June Lady Randolph and myself sail in the white star SS Majestic' – coincidentally the same ship that had, two years earlier, con-veyed Leonard Jerome's body back home – 'and I hope you will get me an agreeable and clever doctor.'[72]

The day before the departure Dr Buzzard wrote to Jennie plainly stating his anxiety for the future and earnestly counselling her 'to insist upon an immediate return to England in case Lord Randolph should shew any fresh symptom pointing possibly to disturbance of the mental faculties'.[73] In some of Dr Buzzard's notes, now deposited at London's Royal College of Physicians, he described his patient as 'altogether . . . well into the 2nd stage of GP'. And so the tragic pair sailed away from Liverpool on 27 June 1894, arriving in New York six days later. They were accompanied by Dr George Elphinstone Keith, the young son of Jennie's peritonitis doctor, whose weekly reports made plain quite how stoic Jennie was to have undertaken this extraordinary trip with its planned itinerary intended to take them from New York to Boston, Montreal, Vancouver, San Francisco, Yokohama, Shanghai, Hong Kong, Macao, Singapore, Rangoon, Mandalay, Calcutta, Bombay and Cairo, then up the Nile, finishing up in Randolph's beloved Monte Carlo in June 1895. No wonder Drs Roose and Buzzard were concerned. Randolph was not expected to return alive. As a precaution the Churchills also travelled with a lead-lined coffin.

'*I HATE IT*,' Jennie screamed silently to her elder sister from the Bay of Bengal. 'I shall return without a friend in the world and too old to make any new ones.'[74] It was a desperate time for her. As she reached the mid-point of her life she saw staring at her a blacker and deeper abyss than anything she had hitherto known, or prepared herself for. Like Wagner's Flying Dutchman, she felt herself forced to sail around the world for an eternity until she could grasp the romantic love constantly eluding her. Although she was still in touch with Charles Kinsky, he was away travelling with the Archduke Franz Ferdinand and she feared, rightly, that she had lost him. Her pitiful letters, soaked in emotion, to her sisters made a solemn counterpoint to the dry factual reports sent by George Keith. In August as they arrived in Banff, Randolph suffered his first serious attack of numbness, leaving him very irritable and excited but manageable. By September the symptoms had changed so that Keith was forced to send an extra report – 'in my own defence in case anything happens'[75] – admitting that 'for the time being I have lost all control over your patient. He intends to take a journey tomorrow that I distinctly disapprove of and all I have said has been of no avail. He has absolutely refused to allow me to go with him as he says he does not want people to know he is an invalid.'

They remained in Yokohama for three weeks, where Randolph coped with a haemorrhage and continuing loss of power in his left hand, as Jennie and young Dr Keith tried to manage him and argued about whether he could go on to Burma and India. One hour he might be quiet and good tempered, the next aggressive and cross. He took a violent dislike to his valet, and Keith, terrified that he was on the point of assaulting the man, managed to intervene just in time to prevent a brutal physical attack. The valet was sent home. Keith, deeply unnerved by the episode, told Buzzard back in London that he was at his wits' end 'as he takes my advice when it suits him not otherwise'.[76] Jennie and the doctor lost their battle over Burma and the trio moved on at the end of October to Hong Kong and then Malacca. The patient was now rapidly getting worse, with more mood swings, greater difficulty with speech, 'but no fixed delusions yet . . . one or two fleeting ones a day'.[77]

By the time they reached Singapore, where they were to stay at Government House, both Jennie and Keith were despairing. The latter reported:

> This has been the worst week since leaving home by a great deal, Lord R
> has been violent and apathetic by turns since coming here. He is not sleep-
> ing well, he is losing flesh and I notice a peculiar condition of the lower part
> of his face at times. The lower lip and chin seem to be paralysed and to move
> only with the jaw . . . his gait is staggering and uncertain. Altogether he is
> in a very bad way and although in little things he is becoming very easy to
> manage, in the big and important affairs he is worse than ever.[78]

Randolph meanwhile spun a different tale for his mother, who 'pined beyond words for him'. He concluded a long and rambling letter, in an almost illegibly shaky hand, describing his new treatment for numbness in his hands and feet – keeping them in the hottest water possible for an hour or more – by telling her: 'I was never better in my life . . . never more con-fident of returning to England in June of next year well.'[79] Another time he sent her a lengthy private letter about his health inserted inside the 'official' letter, which his mother assured him 'I have kept quite secret.'[80]

Jennie was now plunged into sorrow and grief for a different reason. At Rangoon she had received a wire from Charles telling her of his engage-ment to another woman. His family, realising the possibility that the American woman with whom he had formed such a strong attachment in London might finally be free and able to marry him, had insisted on his marrying the eminently suitable Catholic Countess Elizabeth Wolff Metternich zur Gracht.

Jennie was appalled and shocked by the news – and had never felt so alone. The mail was spasmodic, to be collected and sent only when they docked, and it took at least eight days for a letter to arrive home. In addition, the itinerary was constantly being modified. From Rangoon they had intended to go to Mandalay at Randolph's insistence, but a cholera outbreak forced them to go first to Madras. After leaving Japan they had three days in China, seeing Hong Kong and Canton, then five days in Singapore. For Jennie this was the nadir of the entire trip, if not of her life. In this sea of uncertainty she had no one on whom to lean. 'I'd give anything to be with you all now,' she wrote. She was, as she told Leonie, quite unprepared for Charles Kinsky's news. 'From his last letter I was not expecting it. Oh Leonie, darling, do you think it is *too late* to stop it? Nothing is impossible you know. Can't you help me? For heaven's sake, write to him.'

Jennie had suffered a double blow. At Hong Kong she had received a cable from Freddy Wolverton which left her 'absolutely crushed . . . I was not prepared for the blow although I suppose he thought that by not writing I should be, I do not blame him. I only blame myself for having been such a fool. I wanted the impossible. These last miserable months, I have thought incessantly of him and somehow it has kept me going. But there! It is best for me not to write about it all.'[81] Her raw heartache in this letter, stranded as she was thousands of miles away, makes for anguished reading. Wolverton's cable has not been preserved, but its cruel contents are clear enough. Their romance was over. She was living on the edge of life with Randolph, staring at a dark ocean and an even blacker future, with nothing else for company but her own thoughts. 'I can't tell you how I long for a little society . . . and yet the worst of it is I dread the chance of seeing people for Randolph's sake. He is quite unfit for society . . . one never knows what he may do.'[82]

The opportunity to be anything that she wanted to be seemed to have vanished with the tide. She told her sister not to be surprised by this letter,

> but I am frightened by the future all alone and Charles is the only person on earth that I could start life afresh with and, if I have lost him, I have indeed paid out for my treatment of him. The only thing I reproach FW for is telling me to give Charles up knowing that he himself did not intend to stick to me. And Leonie darling use all your cleverness and all your strength and urge him to put off his marriage anyhow until I have seen him. He cared for me until recently and if I am only given the chance I will redeem all the past, the world would forgive him and if he still cares for me the girl, I am sure, would be willing to give him up.[83]

Jennie was flaying herself alive. 'Leonie my darling,' she wrote. 'I am ashamed of myself at my age not to be able to bear a blow with more strength of character. I feel absolutely weak some times it hurts me so.'[84]

That she sincerely believed Leonie could persuade Charles to break off his engagement suggests not only her desperation but how out of touch with reality she had become. The intense strain under which she was living had disturbed her own mind. Divorcing Randolph had ceased to be an alternative several years back. But if she could neither divorce him nor live with him as his wife and share his life, what choices did she have in the 1890s? She was incurably romantic, craved physical passion and thought she had found it in Charles Kinsky. She may have been unfaithful to Randolph, but she had remained deeply loyal, a distinction those in her circle would have well understood. Charles Kinsky was the only other man who won her unreserved loyalty, hence her determination never to blame him for the way he let her down. Whenever she had faced trouble it was always Charles to whom she turned. Why had she given him up for Freddy Wolverton, why had she treated him so badly that in the end he abandoned her?

In the close-knit society in which she moved – part Marlborough House, part Souls – where the Prince of Wales was chief puppet-master and Soveral, de Grey, Lytton and Balfour all moved according to his manipulation of the strings, whom Jennie was seeing, with whom she was flirting and to whom she bared her innermost anguish were all known about and gossiped about, even if not written about. If it was believed that Randolph had syphilis – and the Prince of Wales had now been led to that view – was she viewed as damaged goods? Or was her reputation, damaged by her own behaviour, made worse by Randolph's 'abuse' of her in his gentlemen's clubs? Never before nor again was Jennie to plumb these depths, to strip herself of all pride and most of her remaining self-respect. She was on her knees to Leonie over the loss of Kinsky, begging her 'rightly or wrongly to work for this. Tell him that I am so suited to him, that my troubles have sobered me and that I could be all he desired. Besides, I could help him in his career. The future looks too black and lonely without him. Oh, why have things gone so wrong? Perhaps you can put it right. Don't let him marry until he has seen me. It is only a month to wait.'[85] In a November letter to Leonie she concluded: 'Write to Winston sometimes. *Don't let anyone pity me.* I foresaw the consequences of my coming away but would not do otherwise.'[86]

Jennie was more restrained in her letters to her elder sister, although she insisted that letters to Leonie were also intended for Clara and Mama. She addressed them to Leonie simply because she was the only one with a fixed address. From the Bay of Bengal in November she tried to explain to Clara what a dreadful time she was having but refrained from putting all the gruesome details of Randolph's illness in a letter. She knew it was vital to get Randolph home and was dreading having to go trundling around India with him, staying with people all the time and Randolph unaware that 'there is anything the matter with him as he feels well physically. You cannot imagine anything more distracting and desperate than . . . to see him as he is and to think of him as he was. You will not be surprised that I haven't the heart to write to you about places and things . . . when I write to you I cannot get away from my troubles.' But then she remembered Clara's difficulties and that her life was hardly 'couleur de rose' either. 'It's so easy to tell people to be philozophical (I can't spell any more). How can one be?'[87]

By November, Buzzard and Roose were at a loss. They believed Randolph's death was imminent and that they must get him home immediately. But how? In December, having just received a letter from Jennie from Madras, the Prince of Wales asked his private surgeon, Sir Richard Quain, staying with him at Sandringham, to discover the latest information about Randolph's condition. Buzzard replied to Quain, 'very improperly' according to Jack's son Peregrine, who always maintained that his grandfather did not have syphilis and saw this exchange as a gross breach of medical ethics.[88] 'As you are aware,' Buzzard wrote to Quain, 'Lord Randolph is affected with "General Paralysis", the early symptoms of which tremor of the tongue and slurring articulation were present two years ago. You will understand, with the uncertainty as regards the occurrence of mental symptoms, how important it was to get the patient away . . .' He could predict neither when the end would come nor how.

Also that month Winston persuaded Roose to take him into his confidence as well. 'He told me everything and showed me the medical report,' Winston told his mother.[89] Declaring that he had until then never realised how seriously ill his father was, he promised never to tell anyone and asked her not to be cross with Roose. He begged his 'Darling Mama' to 'keep your pluck and strength up.'[90] The information, whether or not it was correct, was to have a profound effect on how Winston lived the rest of his life and was yet another factor in his changing and deepening relationship with his mother. Years later he confided in his private secretary, Anthony Montague Browne, 'You know my father died of locomotorataxia, the child of syphilis.'[91] Of course this was not necessarily proof that that was his father's illness, but it was evidence that that was what his family believed to be the case.

By December, Randolph had moments when he was very quiet and more easily managed, his will very feeble. But at Colombo he had to be restrained by a straitjacket. On the 10th, with home in sight, Jennie wrote from the Red Sea to tell Leonie that they still had to go to Cairo for eight days, there to wait for a boat to take them to Alexandria and then Marseilles. After that they would re-acclimatise in Monte Carlo, 'as Randolph had set his heart on going there instead of Cannes',[92] from where they would finally return to England. She had by then regained her own equilibrium enough to remind her sister not to breathe a word to anyone about what she had written in relation to Charles. She would never think ill of the man, she told her disapproving sister, though 'I know you didn't like him much but I loved him and don't think anyone half good enough for him. It is only right and fair that he should have a nice wife – young without a past – who will give him children and make him happy. I suppose the world will pity me . . . they can all think what they like. From henceforth he is *dead* to me. I want to know *nothing*. He has deserted me in my hardest time and in my hour of need. I want to forget him though I wish him every joy and luck and happiness. Voilà n'en parlons plus.'[93]

And then she recovered and started to make plans. She thought that the Duchess might want to come to France to see Randolph and that Winston might be able to bring her out. Her elder son was planning to go to Germany for a holiday but that could always be postponed. But then she remembered Jack, now aged fourteen and staying at Deepdene with his aunt by marriage, Duchess Lily. Leonie could always look after him if necessary, Jennie presumed, but then concluded that the Duchess would probably have made arrangements for him.

At all events by Christmas the Churchills had limped home to 50 Grosvenor Square, the Duchess's house, where she could take charge. Jennie's devotion to Randolph in these last months had redeemed her somewhat in the eyes of her mother-in-law. Although she still believed that Jennie's fraternising with the fast and gossipy set had caused the ruin of the marriage, she now admitted frankly 'how plucky and merry a travelling companion'[94] she had been. But even she could not bear to see her beloved son in such a pitiful decline and 'wishes now that he had died the other day'.[95] On Christmas Day Jennie wrote to the Prince of Wales, a 'dreadfully sad letter' in which she poured out her anxieties. 'I cannot describe how much I feel for you,' the Prince replied, recognising what 'a fearful time of it' she had endured. 'But you have done your duty by him and I am sure you acted for the best.'[96]

'Oh, why have things gone so wrong?' Jennie wailed to Leonie. And why had they? As she perched in a house that was not her own, with a cold

that made her 'feel like mud', doing what little she could for her dying husband, she had plenty of time to reflect on the past and contemplate the
future. She felt that her life was 'dreadful . . . disorganised, uncomfortable,
no place to sit and everything in confusion'. In the last few months she had
lost Breteuil, Kinsky and now Freddy Wolverton to other women. In
January 1895, Wolverton married Lady Edith Ward, the only daughter of
the Earl of Dudley. Jennie's sons, aged twenty and almost fifteen, were not
yet old enough to earn a living and support her. And a few months before,
Jerome Park, the racecourse into which her father had poured his heart,
had finally been sold off and turned into a reservoir. But agonising over the
past was not her nature; mostly she resisted turbid thought and tried to
envisage a bright future.

Shortly after her return she weakened and had lunch one more time
with Charles Kinsky and assured her worried sisters that 'he and I have
parted the best of friends in a truly fin de siècle manner. So darling, don't
worry about me on that score. I am not *quite* the dark creature I may seem
to you.' She told Leonie there was no need to come over from Ireland quite
yet – unless it suited her: 'no one can do me *any* good . . . and I am really
in a much better frame of mind than you can possibly imagine'.[97] She
maintained bravely that any bitterness she had felt towards Kinsky had
now 'absolutely left . . . He has not behaved particularly well. I can't find
much to admire in him but I care for him.' It was a need she compared to
opium or drink. And what if she had married Kinsky? In her quest to make
up for lost time she might well have lost sight of her sons' needs. In the
throes of a passionate marriage to Charles Kinsky it is highly unlikely that
she would have found the time or the need to devote herself to Winston
in the way that she did. But these were not thoughts she could weigh in the
balance as she nursed her invalid husband. As Randolph, semi-comatose,
lingered, what worried Jennie most was her precarious future. 'What are
we to do if he gets better . . . the general public and society does not know
the real truth and after *all* my sacrifices and the misery of these six months
it would be hard if it got out. It would do incalculable harm to his political reputation and be a dreadful thing for all of us.'[98]

In his last month of life Randolph could talk only with difficulty, slept
fitfully, rallied briefly and then suffered further attacks. He was given occasional sips of coffee but could barely swallow. It was agonising to watch his
pain, for which increasingly heavy doses of morphine brought some relief.
One by one, the family filed into his room. When he saw Winston he
asked him when and how he had passed into Sandhurst. He smiled at Jack
when it was his turn to go in. Jennie scarcely left his side, worried that he

might never wake again and wondering, if he did, what state he would be in. Suffering from exhaustion and neuralgia, when her sister-in-law Georgiana made her take a brief walk outside for fifteen minutes, the first fresh air she had enjoyed in days, it was so bitterly cold that she returned in a worse state. 'I knew the collapse would come for she hasn't eaten or slept since we arrived and would scarcely come out of his room till today,' wrote Clara. 'Nothing more to tell, Darling Leonie, everything here is LUGUBRE.'[99]

Randolph died very quietly on the morning of 24 January 1895 at 6.15. His lungs had begun to fill up very quickly the previous day and this was the immediate cause of death. Shane Leslie always remembered his mother entering his nursery and, in her quiet dramatic way, announcing that Lord Randolph had died. 'The tragedy fell upon our household like the toll of a mighty bell,' he wrote. The Leslies hurried over to Grosvenor Square, where Winston was already reading telegrams. Taken to Jennie's bedside he recalled 'as she lay there with her black, unbrushed hair and the pallor of death reflected in her own face, with those eyes needing no jewels, I realized for the first time that a woman could be very beautiful.'[100] Clara helped Jennie, utterly dazed when the end finally came, with all the arrangements, answering letters and telegrams, as a stream of Randolph's old friends – including John Delacour, the man who had been so much involved with all the troubles of the marriage – came to view the corpse.

On the day of the funeral it snowed. It was a particularly cruel winter when even the Thames froze over. As Jennie looked into the belly of Westminster Abbey she saw all the society and political figures of the day jostling for seats. She heard Dean Farrar intone the service and the slow movement of the Dead March in *Saul*. The two great national figures of the era – Gladstone and the Queen – did not attend, but Lord Salisbury was there. Shortly afterwards he received 'one of the finest hate missives ever written in English',[101] the agonising letter written by Randolph's distraught mother, furious with him for daring to offer his sympathy after all he had done to ensure her son's political failure. Frances Marlborough, who outlived all her sons, wrote of how 'the iron entered his soul . . . For Days and Days and Months and Years even it told on him and he sat in Connaught Place brooding and eating his heart out.'[102] Jennie too, loyal to the end, maintained that Lord Salisbury had much to answer for, 'for there was a time a few years ago when a generous hand stretched out would have saved everything . . . but Lord S and the others were too jealous of him. I feel all this deeply and hope one of these days it will be known.'[103] After the funeral the small family party took a train from Paddington with the coffin and Lord Randolph Churchill was finally laid to rest in the small church-yard at Bladon, just outside Blenheim.

The Prince of Wales had been particularly solicitous in these final months. Now he wrote to Jennie: 'There was a cloud in our friendship but I am glad to think that it has long been forgotten by both of us.'[104] Almost all the condolence letters emphasised how courageous she had been. 'You have done what was right throughout and that deserves the highest title a woman can have . . . to be called a good woman,' wrote Murray Guthrie, husband of Jack Leslie's sister Olive.[105] George Curzon told her: 'Everyone says how tenderly and heroically you behaved throughout . . . you did all that lay in your power.'[106]

10

All my Ambitions are Centred in You

~

'GOODBYE, DEAR LORD Justice – don't forget me *quite* – if you ever had time to write me a letter I should be proud,' Jennie wrote in February 1895 to Randolph's closest friend, Gerald FitzGibbon.[1] She was sending him Randolph's backgammon board, as her late husband had wished, and apologised that she had not had time to write before but was rather exhausted as she was leaving the next day for Paris – the eternal magnet – where she intended staying some months. 'The Hôtel Imperial, Rue Christophe Colomb, will find me for the present,' she told FitzGibbon. After a month in mourning at the Duchess's house in Grosvenor Square she desperately needed to move on. It was a time when widows, following Queen Victoria's own example, were expected to observe strict mourning rituals for at least a year, if not two.

According to Randolph's will, made in July 1883, he left £500 and his effects to his wife, with the income from the rest of his estate to go to his sons. As he had predeceased his mother, any money that Jennie and Randolph might have assumed would eventually come to them could now skip a generation; there was no reason for Jennie to expect the Duchess to leave her anything. The capital held for the two boys came to £75,971 gross, thanks to Randolph's South African investments, but was practically all swallowed by debts. He owed £66,000 to the Rothschild Bank, having become increasingly dependent on it in the last decade of his life. During his brief period as Chancellor he had promoted the Bank's interests in Persia, India and Burma. The Rothschilds, principally Natty, had seen his position as one of great usefulness, not expecting his influence to be so short lived, and in return for general information, if not actual cabinet secrets, had helped him with loans.

Natty Rothschild had been Randolph's friend, but Jennie continued the connection through Alfred Rothschild, the artistic, unmarried son of Lionel, and often stayed with him at his country house, Halton. But this was an arrangement based on friendship, not finance, and Jennie could be in no doubt that from now on she must find a way of living within a very restricted income, mostly comprised of the $10,000 a year which her father had arranged from the rental of her family's home on Madison Square in New York City. If her expenditure exceeded that, she would have to find a way of making money herself. Much of the next twenty-five years was taken up with more or less hopeless schemes to do just that.

But, for the moment, she was in her beloved Paris, not so impoverished that she had to leave behind either her faithful maid, Gentry, or Randolph's butler, Walden. And in Paris this forty-one-year-old, still beautiful widow was, as ever, the centre of her circle, this time of expatriate Americans. She did not stay in the hotel long – by an appalling coincidence Kinsky was there on an extended honeymoon. As she wrote to Jack: 'We had a capital crossing, great crowds, but we accomplished it alright. We have found an apartment at 34, Avenue Kléber.'[2] Soon her sister Leonie arrived, along with her young son Seymour. The poor child was encased in a body suit of plaster of Paris which, it was hoped, would cure his tubercular hip disease. Jennie grew close to Seymour, 'little Chou Chou' as she called him, who had to spend most of his day lying on a sofa, watching the grown-ups. He described the two sisters – 'so different, so complementary' – and well remembered the elegant little salon in which his mother and aunt quietly entertained le tout Paris. Not only was there the Prince of Wales, Vidor and Paderewski, but, according to Seymour, 'it is not too fanciful to imagine that perhaps the young Marcel Proust sat there also'.[3] But the visitor who made the greatest impression on Seymour was the 'friendly Irish ogre', Shane's future brother-in-law, the US congressman William Bourke Cockran.

Born in County Sligo the same year as Jennie, Bourke Cockran was one of the most remarkable and outstanding Americans of his generation. A devout Catholic, he came from a large family of some means and, after an education from the Christian Brothers first in Ireland then, from the age of nine, in France, had been destined for a life in the Church. He was a man of unrivalled eloquence and enormous charm. With his leonine head, large frame and even larger personality he was a man who could not be ignored. As an orator he was outstanding, with a musical voice, clear diction, wide knowledge and the trained mind of an experienced lawyer and politician. So impressive was he that, according to one contemporary, 'listening to him . . . was like being transported to the Roman Senate in its best days'.[4] Others compared him to Edmund Burke, the great eighteenth-century English orator, or Charles James Fox. With his grey hair, deep-set blue eyes and big powerful nose, he also resembled Fox physically.

Cockran came to America in 1871 aged seventeen, with £150 in his pocket, and stayed. While supporting himself as a teacher of French, Latin and Greek, he studied for the bar and soon became prominent in politics as an important member of the Democratic Party and of the House of Representatives. When he met Jennie in 1895, thanks to an introduction from Moreton Frewen, he, like she, was recently widowed following the death of his second wife. He was by then a successful lawyer with a flourishing practice, a man who had experienced life. When his first wife had died in childbirth one year after the marriage Bourke had, briefly, become a heavy drinker. But then he stopped. He never drank alcohol again for the rest of his life and 'in that minute mastered the impulses of his own passionate nature – a nature outraged by misfortune, angry against the world'.[5]

There is no doubt that this principled, brave and spell-binding rabble-rouser would have fired Jennie's dampened spirits in 1895. And there is no doubt that both were passionate and sensitive adults, recovering from personal tragedies and free from other commitments and prying eyes. They would have had much to talk about, ranging from Ireland – he was always fervently in favour of Home Rule – to world politics and even Jerome Park, her father's racecourse, which he knew.

What was to stop them becoming lovers that spring in Paris? Of all the men Jennie knew and flirted with and who fell in love with her, Bourke Cockran seems the most likely, the most necessary and the most irresistible. Yet part of Jennie's most tantalising charm was her enduring air of mystique. Discretion was too boring for what Jennie offered a man. It is, simply, assumed that Jennie and Bourke indulged in an affair in Paris in 1895. They probably did. But there is no evidence. Anita Leslie, Bourke's niece by marriage,* and therefore well informed, talks of 'an amusing friendship' which sprang up between two 'hot blooded individuals'. Her comments are enigmatic, protective; she realised that her grandmother Leonie also fell in love with Bourke, just as she had with Kinsky, but that she left him to 'poor darling Jennie, who wanted to drive around in his open landau and do all those expensive things which Mr Cockran was well able to afford. After all Jennie was unhappily unmarried.' But Anita also recognised that Jennie and Bourke were two beings of violently tempestuous nature who both complained about their 'romance' to Leonie. 'Bourke said that Jennie wore him out – she was so overcharged with energy, and Jennie said it was exhausting to be alone with Bourke. They

---

* In 1906 he married, for the third time, Anne Ide, sister of Anita's mother Marjorie and the recipient of Robert Louis Stevenson's own birthdate, a present to compensate for her own falling on Christmas Day. RLS met the Ides in Samoa where Henry Ide, the girl's father, was Chief Justice (1893–7).

quarrelled unless she had a table of guests where he could show off.'[6] At all events, the couple left Paris at the end of the summer when Bourke returned to America. 'None too soon,' according to Anita. 'Their duet was that of two pairs of cymbals.' Jennie had been revived. She was once again in touch with life. The surviving letters give no clue to the possible intensity of their relationship.[7] A few years later she was writing: 'Dear Mr Cockran' and signing herself: 'Yours sincerely, Jennie Churchill'. Before they parted – although not for ever – Cockran suggested that if Winston was passing through New York he would be happy to meet him and talk politics, perhaps pass on a few tips.

Winston sent his mother news from home while she was away. The Duchess, he told her, looked very pale and worn. Although she 'carped a little at your apartement in the gayest part of the Champs Elysées, she was otherwise very amiable or rather not particularly malevolent'.[8] Winston, meanwhile, 'cow towed and did the civil'. Of greater concern was Clara Jerome's health. The mother who had launched her three daughters on to Europe's stage with such high hopes in the 1870s had herself lived frugally in Tunbridge Wells since her husband's death in 1891. But, at the end of March, when she suddenly fell ill, Leonie and Jennie returned, just in time to be with her before she died on 2 April. There was a funeral service three days later in London. Jennie wrote to Jack at Harrow reminding him that he must be punctual – 11 a.m. at Charing Cross – and he must have some black gloves. She ordered a wreath for him. Among those who attended the service was Fanny Ronalds, admired and adored by Leonard in New York all those years before. Clara Jerome's body was to be returned to the family vault at Greenwood Cemetery in Brooklyn later that summer. Jennie, never emotionally stirred by her mother the way that she was by her father, allowed her sisters Clara and Leonie to escort the coffin home to America while she returned to Paris and then on to Aix-les-Bains before confronting social life in England once again.

There was one more death that summer: in July, Mrs Everest, Winston's and Jack's beloved nanny, died suddenly of peritonitis, the same complaint that had afflicted Jennie only a few years earlier. Winston did all that he could and engaged a nurse, but she arrived too late. He was shocked by Everest's death, and comforted himself with the belief that she did not suffer much pain. 'I shall never know such a friend again,'[9] he wrote, heartbroken, to his mother. He made the arrangements for the funeral – his third significant loss that year – but then had to return to his new life and new regiment, while Jack accompanied his mother for a short holiday in Switzerland.

Lacking Everest, his father and the structure of school, Winston, still only twenty, turned increasingly to his mother for emotional and intellectual support. Occasionally he wrote to her in intense terms: 'How I wish I could secrete myself in the corner of the envelope and embrace you as soon as you tear it open'[10] – an overtly Oedipal admission. But chiefly there were more practical matters to resolve. Within a week of his father's funeral he had asked her to telegraph Colonel John Brabazon, a family acquaintance, about transferring from the 60th Rifles and joining Brabazon's regiment instead, the 4th Hussars, based at Aldershot. He had already broached this difficult topic with her in the final months of Randolph's life when he pointed out how well he was doing at Sandhurst with riding, a skill which would be useless in the infantry, and reminding his mother how much quicker promotions were in the cavalry. But by then his father was in no state to form a reasoned opinion. It was therefore Jennie who, following Brabazon's instructions to her, responded to her son's stirring ambitions and wrote the letter which Randolph neither would nor could write himself to the Duke of Cambridge asking for Winston to be released. The Duke replied on 6 February congratulating her on her son passing out of Sandhurst so well and advising her how best to carry out his wishes.

Winston's letters were mostly about money. His aunt by marriage, Lily, who had married Lord Beresford that summer, had generously bought him a horse for £200. But even so he could not meet his day-to-day expenses. He begged Jennie, while she was in Paris, for a little money and informed her that his mess bill was due in a few days 'and MUST be paid somehow'.[11] The trouble was that money was very tight for Jennie too. She had just bought a large new house at 35A Great Cumberland Place in the favourite Jerome location around Marble Arch. It needed considerable work doing – she wanted it painted from top to bottom, and all mod cons such as electric light and hot water installed – and it would not be ready until November. While it was being renovated and furnished, Jennie went up to Scotland or stayed in smart hotels. As she told her sister Clara, 'the boys are so delighted at the thought of ringing their own front door they can think of nothing else'.[12] For the last year they had had no permanent home and had camped between Leonie's London home, Aunt Lily's at Deepdene, Blenheim and with friends who would lend them a bed.

'You poor dear puss,' Jennie wrote to Clara who, as ever, had less money than any of them. It was an extraordinarily revealing letter. 'You must not get low and blue,' she told her sister, after all, if your health and spirits are good, c'est tout qu'il faut. Remember the saying that 3 things alone are necessary for happiness if you choose to count them. Health, Peace and Competency. I really think you can aspire to all 3 – as for the bonheur du foyer who has it? I haven't for years as you know – but if I had to lead my own life over again with dear R just as it was I would – in preference to anyone else – and so wd you with Moreton – so it is no use repining – cheer up, you have lots of people who love you.[13]

She was fond of dispensing such homilies – her letters to her sons are peppered with examples of such 'shoulder to the wheel' advice. To her enormous credit, she tried to live by these standards herself.

And then, within weeks of Jennie's return from Paris, Winston was off, going with a friend from the regiment, Reginald Barnes, to New York and then the West Indies and Havana. They were to join Spanish troops in the field to help crush a revolt. He had been asked to collect military information and had already made an arrangement with the *Daily Graphic* to publish his war letters, signed with his initials WSC. This gave Jennie, who paid his fare, some mild embarrassment – what was a junior British lieutenant doing with the staff of General Suárez Valdés, the Spanish commander? But it also gave her the chance to introduce him sooner than she had expected to Bourke Cockran. And she was well primed. When interviewed by an American newspaper she insisted that her son was not taking an active part in the campaign and that he was merely on a nine-week leave of absence. She also revealed, but refrained from saying that she had arranged them, that he had letters of introduction from the British War Office and Foreign Office to the Spanish authorities, which enabled him to go to the front and watch the operations.[14]

Winston, deeply impressionable, was bowled over and forever indebted to Cockran. Cockran, in turn, went out of his way to help this unknown young Englishman, meeting him at the port, offering him hospitality at his 763 Fifth Avenue apartment and stimulating him every minute with his talk. Winston wrote to his mother that Mr Cockran was one of the most charming hosts and one of the most interesting men he had ever met. He told her about their deep and wide-ranging discussions together on every conceivable subject from economics to yacht racing. Winston recognised that Cockran was not only a clever man, but one from whose conversation much was to be learned. Winston listened to Bourke in his library, reading favourite speeches aloud, telling his protégé of the importance of timing and drama and sincerity; of giving people the simple truth with clarity and grandeur; above all instilling in him forever the need to defend individual liberty. They ate oysters and hominy together and afterwards the older man sent Winston some speeches for his comments and was 'profoundly impressed' with his responses. Of course, the meeting with Cockran was fortuitous. But it was Jennie's foresight which turned it to her elder son's advantage. Without a son himself, Cockran treated Winston as his own, moulded him, encouraged him and recognised his potential. He became a lifelong inspiration, mentor and father figure.

Winston returned to England not merely with coffee, cigars and guava jelly intended to stock the cellars of 35A. He had gained experience of fighting and had had his first taste of America, in particular New York, the city which had given his mother and her family so much. And his youthful impressions were not all positive. He wrote to his brother that the 'essence of American journalism is vulgarity divested of truth. Their best papers write for a class of snotty housemaids and footmen and even the nicest people here have so much vitiated their taste as to appreciate their style.' He went on: 'Picture to yourself the American people as a great lusty youth who treads on all your sensibilities, perpetrates every possible horror of ill manners – whom neither age nor just tradition inspire with reverence – but who moves about his affairs with a good hearted freshness which may well be the envy of older nations of the earth.'[15]

In February the *Saturday Review* published an article of Winston's on Cuba. He proudly sent Cockran a copy and Jennie forwarded one to Joseph Chamberlain, who praised it as 'the best short account I have seen of the problems which the Spaniards have to deal [with]'.[16] But, convinced that he had to make the running now or opportunities would never reappear, the trip only whetted his appetite for more. He was, in spite of his youth, consumed by an urgent need to be at the centre of events. He might, after all, die young like his father and his uncles. His mother understood how desperately he did not want to go to India, where his own regiment was posted for possibly seven years and where he feared he would have neither 'the pleasures of peace [nor] the chances of war'. A few months in South Africa, the country on everybody's lips, on the other hand, would earn him the South Africa Medal and the British South Africa Company's Star. With two decorations gained in a year he could then look to a career in politics, as he explained to her.

The pervasive image of Winston and Jennie for the next three years is of two characters hurrying like figures in a silent movie. As he races around the globe, testing his personal courage and expanding his knowledge to the ultimate, so she is tearing around England, using every contact she can muster to push opportunities for and awareness of her son. Alongside this double reflection, she is there lambasting him for the same extravagance and want of sound financial management of which he accuses her. Their past, personalities, fates and future are inextricably linked. Winston's transformation from demanding and petulant schoolboy to demanding and confident young adult seems to have happened overnight. His success in life seems almost to have required that his father be removed from the scene. Now Winston Churchill can devote himself to building up his late father's memory. But he needs his mother's support and active participation at every stage. Without Randolph demanding her care and support Jennie of course has more time. More significantly, a restraint is lifted, enabling her to blossom. Just as Leonard had favoured Jennie as the daughter who would achieve great things, so she always knew that Winston would be her great achievement. Warmed by her love and pride, Winston flourished, aware that he had been born to fulfil his mother's aspirations for him. 'The man who has been the indisputable favourite of his mother', wrote Sigmund Freud, 'keeps for life the feeling of a conqueror, that confidence of success that frequently induces real success.'

The forceful letter Winston wrote to his mother at this time, little more than a year after Randolph's death, was reminiscent of those from his schooldays but with more bite; he was emphatic that if she wanted to help him she could. 'I cannot believe', he told her, 'that with all the influential friends you possess and all those who would do something for me for my father's sake – that I could not be allowed to go [to South Africa] – were those influences properly exerted . . . I put it down here . . . that you really ought to leave no stone unturned to help me at such a period . . . it is a little thing for you to ask and a smaller thing for those in authority to grant – but it means so much to me.'[17] She was doing all she could without attracting counterproductive opprobrium for too much pushing. In July 1896 she had raised the idea with Lord Lansdowne, the Secretary of State for War, that Winston might be given leave to get a post in South Africa helping to suppress the uprising in Matabeleland. She wrote also to Field Marshal Lord Wolseley, Commander in Chief of the British Army, about the same possibility. But there were now those who cautioned her that in view of her son's involvement in a recent scandal his motives for leaving the country might be misconstrued.

Alan Bruce, a young Sandhurst contemporary, had wanted to join the 4th Hussars. A group of young officers, including Winston, had made it clear that he was not wanted and told him his father's allowance of £500 a year would be inadequate. Matters deteriorated after he refused to take the hint and was eventually asked to resign from the army. His father, A. C. Bruce-Pryce, mounted a press campaign in his son's defence led by *Truth*, the weekly review owned by Labouchère, Randolph's friend. One of the charges was that Winston Churchill had been guilty of 'acts of gross immorality of the Oscar Wilde type'. It is not hard to imagine how Jennie must have suffered to read of her son having anything to do with this unpleasant affair, dangerously close to some of the lewdest rumours concerning Randolph. Her deepest fear was that all her hopes in her son might be dashed before they had a chance to surface because of a failure of judgement or maverick temperament like his father's. In the event, a scandal was averted, largely thanks to Sir George Lewis, probably the most famous solicitor of the nineteenth century. Within a month Winston had been paid £500 damages, an apology and a complete withdrawal of the allegations. But Jennie's influence, it seemed, was not proving adequate to get him to Egypt under Kitchener or to South Africa, nor in persuading him to calm his headstrong rush through life. Unwillingly, he sailed with his regiment for India on 11 September 1895 – 'a useless and unprofitable exile'. He hoped he would not have to stay there long, however 'agreeable' it was. But, as he warned his grandmother, it was a hard place from which to get leave.

Jennie paused, concerned at the damage he might do to his prospects, but did not give up her attempts even once he had departed. That autumn she continued with her typical Edwardian peripatetic lifestyle which included a stay at Minto House, Hawick – 'Lord Minto told me to send you his love. Capital fellow, Winston'[18] – moving on to Floors Castle, the Roxburghe home, Gosford (Lord Wemyss's place), then back to London, where she met up with Leonie, before travelling to Blenheim on 14 October to play in a concert, and finally to Newmarket for the Cesarewitch. Wherever she went she made an enormous effort to sing Winston's praises, show his letters, promote him and grasp every opportunity. She had transferred all her emotional energy and pride into doing whatever she could for her elder son, recognising his unusual qualities and nurturing them. 'I am looking forward to the time when we shall be together again and all my political ambitions shall be centred in yours,' she told him reassuringly.[19] Jennie's ability to use positively the disappointment of her marriage to Randolph by helping create a myth of destiny for her firstborn and favourite son was a rare gift that she may not even have been fully aware of herself. At the same time Winston's sense of responsibility towards his mother was to become so well defined from 1895 onwards that occasionally it seemed as if the two of them were united against the world.

If she had had money, she would have sent him that. From Panshanger in Hertfordshire, home of Lady Cowper, a renowned hostess who pioneered the Saturday-to-Monday visit, she sent him instead that autumn all the political news, wished she could give him a kiss and did manage to stump up £50, which was sure would be acceptable as 'I know you are hard up but so am I and I pray you to consider that it means a great deal to me and you must make it go as far as possible.'[20] She was trying hard to persuade General Sir Horatio Herbert Kitchener, the British Commander in Chief organising an expedition up the Nile, to find Winston a job. Yet Kitchener, Sirdar of the Egyptian Army, five years younger than Jennie, was a hard man who was never going to fall under her personal sway, however persuasive she could be. The advance into the Sudan was being prepared by thorough administrative work on his part, not by taking young men with pushy mothers.

Nonetheless, she told Winston exactly what he must do: apply immediately to the War Office because the chances of being taken on were extremely remote and the competition tremendous. The War Office would ignore his application but, once he had applied, she could then write to Kitchener herself. She knew there was only a slim 'outside chance of Kitchener's personal influence being brought to bear and I am going to try it for you', she promised. But she warned him that, should the plan succeed, he would have to sign a commitment agreeing to serve in the Egyptian Army for two years 'and there would be no getting out of it if you don't like it. On the other hand, should this fail you must not let it nettle you and make you take a dislike of your work in India. Life is not always what one wants it to be but to make the best of it as it is the only way of being happy.' She also told him frankly that, in her heart of hearts, she did not think Egypt was the best place for him to be. 'But fate will decide.' She concluded by saying that the reason she was telling him of all the trouble she had been to, and the people whose help she had sought simply to get this far, was to try and ensure that, if it did not come off, he would not be too disappointed.[21] 'My darling, peer into that bible sometimes and love me very much,' she wrote to him in India.[22]

She was also concerned about Jack – 'a good old soul' – now due to leave Harrow. She opposed his going into the army like Winston, partly because there was not enough money to find him a cavalry regiment, 'and in anything else he would be lost and unhappy. I think he might do [well] at the bar.' Jack's qualities, she felt, were that 'he has plenty of ability and common sense and good presence and, with perseverance and influence, he ought to get on. The City he hates.'[23] But it was not simply a question of lack of cash. She failed to see the same qualities of leadership or drive in her younger son. Occasionally, she let him know that and urged him to be more like his elder brother – as when he went off to France. 'Darling Child, remember this year is the only one of your life you can give up entirely to French. Make the most of it. Do, like Winston, talk incessantly.'[24] There had not been enough cash for either son to acquire the polish that Oxford or Cambridge would have given, a serious regret for Winston. Leonie once reprimanded her son Shane with the comment: 'Jack and Winston have helped their mother in every way, even by not going to the University in order to work, and both absolutely adore her. I have done everything and given my boys everything but they don't seem to care for me at all.'[25] There was, Shane admitted, more than enough truth in this to leave him with remorse. 'Jack and Winston halved their coming of age fortunes to pay for their mother's debts very nobly,' he wrote.[26] In addition, when there was some discussion about Jack going to university, his elder brother generously encouraged the idea and wrote that 'if money prevents I could borrow a further £500, which he might repay when he comes of age. I think he had set his heart on it.'[27]

So, with his mother's help, Winston determinedly set about educating himself, making books his university. He started with Henry Fawcett's *Manual of Political Economy*. Next on his list was Gibbon's *Decline and Fall of the Roman Empire*, followed by Lecky's *European Morals*. As soon as he was in India she sent him, among other works, twelve volumes of Macaulay – eight of history and four of essays – Plato's *Republic*, Aristotle's *Politics*, Darwin's *On the Origin of Species*, and as many letters as she could write to keep up his interest. He read widely and voraciously from now on – although not the Hindustani grammar which Jennie urged on him – including articles, letters and speeches from Cockran, which he could study at his leisure and even imitate. He also read and reread his father's speeches until he knew many of them by heart. In addition to the books, he asked his mother to send him his bicycle, a dozen shirts and various items for butterflying, such as a net, a box of pins and a 'killing tin'. His six months in India may have given him plenty of time to read but he wanted his mother to know that 'life out here is stupid, dull and uninteresting'.[28] Calcutta, too, where he went for Christmas, was 'full of supremely uninteresting people'. What relieved the tedium of life in India was that by this time he had met Miss Pamela Plowden, 'the most beautiful girl I have ever seen', as he told Jennie. Winston was to remain smitten with Pamela, daughter of the Resident at Hyderabad, for several years.

Jennie went to Blenheim for Christmas that year. She still loathed the Dowager Duchess, who, she told Winston, 'was not making herself pleasant to me and we have not exchanged a word'.[29] But she was determined to maintain the Blenheim connection for her sons, and that year she enjoyed the company of another American, the former Miss Consuelo Vanderbilt, who had a few months previously married Winston's cousin Sunny, ninth Duke of Marlborough. The old Duchess's deepest feelings of resentment towards Jennie can be clearly glimpsed in the way she urged her new granddaughter-in-law to become pregnant quickly. Almost as soon as she was introduced to her she said: 'Your first duty is to have a child and it must be a son because it would be intolerable to have that upstart Winston become Duke. Are you in the family way?'[30]

Jennie was not optimistic of Winston finding a role in Egypt 'as I am told Kitchener is not taking anyone under 27', but she never crushed his hopes. And so, in his intervals from polo, she encouraged him to find time for reading. She realised that his desperate desire for action was only a pre-amble to political life and, once he was engaged in politics, she understood from experience that he would keenly feel his want of knowledge. She was doing all she could and more to keep him in India and to help him stay solvent. She was even in occasional correspondence with a superior officer in Winston's regiment, Captain Kincaid Smith – another of those whom William Manchester characterises as one of her lovers, yet without apparent evidence – who made it clear that for the young Lieutenant to leave India after only six months would unsettle him and would not look good to his superiors.

It is all too easy to see Jennie's actions on behalf of her restless son as those of a shameless lobbyist. But in a twelve-page letter loaded with intense love, anger and fear she tried to convey to him some sense of long-term strategic planning. 'It is with very unusual feelings that I sit down to write to you,' she began on 26 February 1897.[31] Letters, she told him, were usually a pleasure. But this time it was the reverse. The specific problem was that after a visit to Cox's Bank that morning she had discovered that he had spent not only the whole of his quarter's allowance due that month but an additional £45 knowing that this would leave him overdrawn, the bank manager having already warned him this would be the case.

I must say I think it is too bad of you, indeed it is hardly honourable, knowing as you do that you are dependent on me and that I give you the biggest allowances I possibly can and more than I can afford. I am very hard up and this has come at a very poor moment and puts me to much inconvenience. I found £100 for you when you started for India in order that you should not lose by the speculation and I sent you £50 for your birthday, all of which I could ill afford. I have paid off your debts but I have told them at Cox's not to apply to me in future as you must manage your own affairs and you will have to lose the 4th Hussars.

I cannot increase your allowance. As for your wild scheme of coming home for a month – it is absolutely out of the question not only on account of money but for the sake of your reputation. They will say you can't stick to anything . . .

I confess I am quite disheartened about you. You seem to have no real purpose in life. For a man life means work if he means to succeed . . . many men at your age have to work for a living and support their mother. It is useless my saying more. One has been over this ground before and it is not a pleasant one. I will only repeat that I *cannot* help you any more and if you have any grist in you . . . you will try and live within your income and cut down your expenses in order to do it. You cannot but feel ashamed of yourself under the present circumstances. I haven't the heart to write more, your Mother.[32]

And what of Jennie's own life at this time? Was it anything more than a reflection of her son's, centred on an endless social whirl? Why was she so cash-strapped? A month later, chiding Winston again, she admitted that money was the only subject on which they fell out. She knew she should not get so angry with him but 'unless something extraordinary turns up, I see ruin staring me in the face'. She explained that 'out of £2,700 a year, £800 goes to you two boys, £410 for house and stables, which leaves me about £1,500 for everything. I now have to pay interest on money borrowed. I really fear for the future. I am telling you this, Darling, in order that you may see how impossible it is for me to help you and how you must in future depend upon yourself.'[33] To help her out, Winston sent her his horse Firefly, in the hope that she would be able to sell him. A week later she was diverted by sorting through Randolph's political papers, a task officially entrusted to Ernest Becket and George Curzon, the documents' custodians. Jennie found the pair conscientious but slow, 'and it will not be an easy thing to write a good biography'.[34] She knew the task would require a big man. In her concern to urge Winston to stay put in India she told him that sticking at it was what his father would have wanted. She added that it was also what the Prince of Wales, with whom she had dined, had suggested.

Jennie's relationship with the Prince took on a new intensity in the years following Randolph's death. Although it seems unlikely that they became lovers now, they might have picked up on an older pattern of slightly risqué flirtation. He was jealous, teasing, possessive and avuncular towards her all at once. Jennie was no longer in awe of him and no longer feared the ostracism that had been so painful twenty years earlier. While she may have listened to his cautionary words, she no longer felt obliged to follow his advice. Perhaps her wilfully independent streak added to her attractions for him. They were in close and regular touch after 1895 and met either in France or at Cowes, where she continued to stay at Rosetta Cottage – an emotional attachment she could not discard – or at Sandringham, where she was a regular visitor in spite of gossip to the effect that the Princess of Wales did not approve of the presence of Lady Randolph Churchill.[35] But he now came frequently to see her at her new London home, often at very short notice, usually at about 5 p.m., signed his letters more intimately 'Toutes à Vous, AE'. He liked her to appear in her Japanese dress. Or else he simply asked for a Japanese tea, a geisha tea or a tea à la geisha. The fashion for Japanese culture was not new. *The Mikado*, by Gilbert and Sullivan, had been a huge hit since its opening night on 14 March 1885. But, as increasing numbers of the wealthy travelled to the Far East, the vogue for Japanese flowing silks and what passed as Japanese culture became more widespread.

These revealing notes, mostly undated and sent to Great Cumberland Place, are unquestionably suggestive. It was brave of Jennie to appear in front of a man who was not her husband in a Japanese gown, without a corset. She had had an entire Japanese costume made by a smart tailor in Kyoto when she had visited the Far East as part of the world tour the previous year. The tailor had also given her lessons on assembling the outfit, necessary because the costume comprised many parts including an under-dress, over-dress, collar, sash, cushion for a belt and the belt itself. The erotic potential in taking these pieces on and off is not hard to imagine.

Such behaviour marked her out as a New Woman, as a bohemian rather than an aristocrat. But there was always an element of bravado in her relationship with the Prince; it was the tone of lovers who have once been intimate but are no longer so. Now more than ever she was not afraid to speak her mind to him, and the correspondence – one-sided as it is while the Windsor Archives remain closed – contain an occasional hint of minor arguments between them. 'I am glad to know that you had no intention of being rude', the Prince wrote, 'in the letter I received from you yesterday . . . as regards the olive branch to which you allude . . . I thought there was no quarrel between us.'[36]

Already by September 1895, the year of Randolph's death, he was teasing her about rumours that she had been seen frequently in the company of Hugh Warrender, a handsome twenty-seven-year-old officer in the Grenadier Guards. Gossip-hungry as ever, he asked her for more details of her new victim. Winston, too, made reference to the young soldier he could see had fallen in love with his mother and, when begging her for more letters, even suggested that she 'turn on the devoted Warrender'. The devoted Warrender was to remain an adoring fixture for the rest of Jennie's life. The pile of letters that survive indicate a deep but distant love, possibly never more than a romantic enchantment. Today a romance, even a love affair, without a sexual dimension is plainly uncommon, but it was less so in the 1890s, and Hugh Valdave Warrender – Eton, Sandhurst, the Guards; recreations fishing, gardening and shooting – was a model of correctness and English reticence. He never married and died in 1926, aged fifty-seven.

Jennie's attraction both for and to much younger men who were physically fit and classically handsome became obvious now that she was a widow. Inevitably, gossip was rife in the closed circles in which she moved. It is impossible at this distance to analyse the chemistry but, in the company of a virile young man, flames were lit, torches carried. This does not mean that she had an affair with every captain who fell victim to her charms. But the aura was undeniable and the enduring myth created. Her nephew Shane was fond of telling how, walking on the moors with her one day when he was still an adolescent, Jennie fell and broke her ankle and the pair tried to crawl back. 'In the end, with all my strength, I half carried her home. I could feel for the first time why men loved her. She was exquisitely grateful.'[37]

Two years after her husband's death Jennie's life was still focused on promoting Winston, and she used her visits to various country houses to this end. But none amused her as much as they should have thanks to her constant anxieties about money. She promised Winston that once the visits were over at the end of the year she would remain in London and try to economise. But that was never going to be easy in 1897, the Diamond Jubilee Year marking Queen Victoria's six decades on the throne, when everything conspired against her regaining some financial equilibrium. It was not simply a year of bell ringing and hymn singing – Jennie's friend Sir Arthur Sullivan composed an especially rousing Jubilee Hymn – there were constant celebrations ranging from street parties to banquets, impossible to ignore.

The high spot of the year was unquestionably the Devonshire House Ball on 2 July. No wonder Jennie was having trouble economising. 'Of all the private entertainments for which the Jubilee has provided the occasion none is comparable with the magnificent fancy dress ball given last night at Devonshire House by the Duke and Duchess of Devonshire' is how *The*

Times described it the following day. Jennie herself wrote that 'rarely had the London social world been so stirred . . . for weeks not to say months beforehand it seemed the principal topic of conversation . . . what characters were our friends and ourselves to represent?'[38] Jennie herself appeared as the sixth-century Byzantine Empress Theodora, a woman apparently as powerful as she was beautiful, a former courtesan who became the wife of the Emperor Justinian I. It was a role that suited Jennie's kind of flaming beauty. Shane commented somewhat cruelly that she would have resembled Theodora even without fancy dress. Queen Marie of Romania, whose mother played duets with Jennie, was struck by her 'flashing beauty' at this time. 'She might almost be taken for an Italian or a Spaniard. Her eyes were large and dark, her mouth mobile with delicious, almost mischievous curves, her hair blue-black and glossy, she had something of a Creole about her. She was very animated and laughed a lot, showing beautiful white teeth, and always looked happy and amused.'[39]

Her magnificent costume was made by M. Worth in Paris, inspired by a mosaic of Theodora at San Vitale, Ravenna. It comprised an under-dress of eastern fabric, with a long, heavily embroidered, jewelled and appliquéd cream tunic over it, worked in squares of green and gold. She carried a Madonna lily and an orb based on the 1661 Sovereign's Orb and Queen Mary's 1689 orb, and wore a heavy crown and a jewel-encrusted, three-tiered headband. A photograph of her as 'the wicked Theodora' was despatched to Winston, at his request, in India. Another went to Captain Kincaid Smith, also at his request.

But it was not simply the endless parties that were a drain on her finances; she also lost money in a serious fraud. A swindler by the name of James Cruikshank had persuaded Jennie, a gambler by nature but now at her most vulnerable, to invest in a scheme that would make her a fortune. Of course it did nothing of the kind. It lost her some £4,000, and Sir George Lewis once again had to sort out the disaster. 'My own affairs are in a dreadful state,' she told Winston. 'I had hoped to put them right but how it is to be done heaven knows . . .' She hated having to write to him about 'disagreeable things' – reminding him to deal with bills and dishonoured cheques. 'My darling boy, you can't think how all this worries me. I have so many money troubles of my own.' She so wanted to help, to give him money and to have him home. But if he came back on leave 'think of the expense. Every creditor you possess in England will be down upon you.'[40] She missed him hugely – 'Darling, how I wish that we were together' – wanted him on hand as her number-one adviser, someone she could discuss things with. She often lay awake at night worrying about him. He, too, needed her to listen; he was lonely in India, where he was considered something of a bookish outsider. There was no one else to whom he poured out his heart and his hopes as he did to her at this time. The mail boat arrived but once a week. Her letters were thus the climax of his week.

But keeping him on track was the priority. So she tried to cajole him to stay in India, reminding him of the wonderful experience he was gaining. And then she praised him too. 'I am so proud of all your great and endearing qualities,' she wrote from Brooksby in Leicestershire, en route to Paris. 'I feel sure that if you live you will make a name for yourself but I know to do it you have to be made of stern stuff and not mind sacrifice and self denial. I feel I am reading you a lecture,' she added, 'and you will vote my letter a bore but you know that I do not mean it in that way.'[41]

She sent him more books and advised him to go through another course of reading. But he, meanwhile, had sailed from Bombay on his way to Italy hoping that if he went to report on the sudden flare-up of hostilities between Greece and Turkey his mother could find a newspaper that wanted his reports, whichever side he found himself on. 'Lord Rothschild would be the person to arrange this for me,' he instructed her.[42] But he arrived after it was all over, came home to England briefly in June 1897, in time for the Jubilee Ball, and then returned to Bangalore.

Still aged only twenty-two, he was also writing a novel, a political satire drawing upon an image of his mother, in his spare time. He wanted Jennie to read it in draft. But he put this to one side when he heard that Sir Bindon Blood was advising him to come up to the North West Frontier at Malakand as press correspondent. He set off in August, telling his mother once again to see about getting his letters published and paid for and to use her own discretion in editing them, too. She failed to persuade Buckle, editor of *The Times*, to publish them but by November 1897 five had appeared in the *Daily Telegraph* – albeit for only half of what her son had hoped to be paid. Nonetheless, she was having discussions with the *Telegraph* editor to 'try and shame the old devil to pay you properly'. At the same time she advised against too much 'haggling' since the letters had served their purpose in enabling him to reach the front and getting him noticed. 'You will get plenty of kudos (can't spell it). I will see that you do, darling boy.'[43]

She followed this up with more encouragement. 'By the time you receive this you will have had a wire from me telling you to write an account of the fighting you saw and I think it important to be first in the field. You might make quite a pretty thing of it . . . you will, of course, have to be discreet and, if you sign it, to leave as much personal out of it as possible.'[44] Then all she wanted was to see him safely back in Bangalore, where she hoped he would settle down and do some reading. She still had not given up her barrage of letters to Kitchener, but held out little hope of this working out for him. In the meantime, constantly reminded by him how 'damned poor' they were, she worked tirelessly to sell his literary efforts. When he sent her one of his articles, he told her, 'you should not get less than £20 for it as it is a very good story – in my opinion – so don't sell it without a good offer'.[45] Throughout the time Winston was away, Jennie nurtured his burning sense of destiny. 'I have faith in my star – that is that I am intended to do something in the world,' he told her.[46] She responded that she believed in both their lucky stars: his and her own.

Winston was engaged in highly dangerous exploits which saw several of his brother officers killed in action. Before the year was out he was mentioned in despatches for his 'courage and resolution'. But during these months of frenetic activity, as he tested his personal courage to the utmost, she did not flinch nor try to dissuade him from the task he had set himself. She could have been in no doubt about the constant danger her son was in; he wrote her detailed accounts of riding his grey pony along the skirmish line and of bullets narrowly missing him. On the contrary, she set about fulfilling myriad practical tasks, and above all, wherever she went, making sure that everyone of note whom she knew, from Arthur Balfour to George Curzon and the Prince – 'people who can be helpful to you later on' – read his letters. Following an introduction from Balfour, she went to see about getting him a publisher. These were activities he could not possibly have undertaken himself. She could hardly have done more.

By January 1898 Jennie had secured terms from Longmans for *The Malakand Field Force*. 'It's a great thing that your first book should be published by such a good firm as Longmans and also that it should be done at their expense,' not always the case for a first book at the time, as she pointed out to her son.[47] She was quite shameless, too, in her efforts to get the book noticed, writing to Frank Harris among others asking for favourable reviews. But she failed dismally in her choice of proofreader; she gave her brother-in-law Moreton the dubious honour and he was a disaster. Winston could barely believe the 'gross and fearful' blunders which had got into the finished copies. He sent his mother pages and pages of examples of:

emendations made by Moreton which have the effect of making the passage as bald as if written by a Harrow boy . . . Altogether there are about 200 misprints, blunders & mistakes, though some of these, perhaps 100, will only be apparent to me. With great courage, Moreton has in places altered what I wrote & made it appear nice and plain and simple so that an idiot in an almshouse could make no mistake . . .

God forbid that I should blame you my dearest Mamma. I blame myself – and myself alone for this act of folly & laziness which has made me ridiculous to all whose good opinion I would have hoped for.[48]

He told his mother he now understood why Moreton's life had been such a failure.

However, Jennie wrote to Winston that, barring the odd repetition of a phrase and clumsy punctuation, 'I think it's capital, most interesting and well written and does you great credit.' She then promised to spread it around 'judiciously'.[49] In fact, the reviews were generally excellent, but it was, Winston had told her, 'your applause that I covet more than any other'.[50] Even when they had disagreements – caused only by how they managed their money or lack of it – he told her: 'It is no exaggeration for me to state that I care more for you at this present time than for any single human being.'[51] He was gracious in his gratitude to his mother: 'I owe you a great deal for all the trouble you have taken and I feel MOST grateful for the spur which your interest and your applause give to my ambitions . . .' He had written *The Story of the Malakand Field Force* in five weeks. He promised to take three years next time.

But there was still Jack's future to be considered. This Jennie discussed freely with Winston. Mostly it depended on how much money there was. She had at first hoped that her younger son would enter the Foreign Office, 'if only he could pass the exams, but I fear he is not clever enough'. Winston suggested the army. 'But you know he would never pass the medical examination with his eye and besides, how could I give him an adequate allowance?' So the next plan was for Jack to go to Germany for a year to learn bookkeeping and 'one of these days make a fortune. He is quite reconciled to it.'[52] Just because Jack was less demanding than his elder brother did not mean he was as easily reconciled as Jennie wished to believe. Indeed he had told her quite frankly that he did not believe the frequent changes of plan had been his fault. He had wanted the army 'but you asked me to give it up because it was expensive and not lucrative, because it might leave you alone and because it was 'no career''.' Now she wanted him to work in the City; 'the life of a cavalry officer appeals to me more but I will do it if it is necessary and if you want me to . . . My only wish is to please you and to do whatever you wish.'[53] Jennie replied gently that it was not too late. If he really wanted an army career he could have one as long as he did not mind living on a small allowance. And she did promise that, as he had by then joined the Oxford Yeomanry and was to have a month's drill at Aldershot, she would at least get him a nice uniform for all the regimental shows, although 'how I am to pay for it I do not know'.[54]

The relationship between Jennie and Winston was now operating on many levels. She was acting as his agent, friend and adviser; but at the same time he was her confidant and she was still, of course, his mother. By January 1898, he had not given up urging her to use all her influence to get him to Egypt – 'it's a pushing age and we must shove with the rest . . . you must make a tremendous effort to get me to Egypt,' he told her. 'Do stir up all your influence . . . don't be afraid of trying every line of attack. So far *I* have done it all myself – you have so much power . . .'[55] The next day he wrote, 'I beg you have no scruples but worry right and left and take no refusal.'[56]

Jennie was telling him repeatedly of a friend of hers in the Seaforth Highlanders, Major Caryl John Ramsden, who was involved in the advance on Khartoum. Ramsden, fourteen years younger than her, was so handsome that he was known as 'Beauty' Ramsden. His letters to Jennie, which she often refers to in her own to Winston, have not been preserved, but they gave her an idea of what was going on. Ramsden flattered her by telling her that Winston was one of the most promising young men in the army. So she assured her son she would try and get to Cairo herself and 'If I do, perhaps I can work the Sirdar with more chance of success.'[57] Winston told her he was very grateful indeed to her for going to Egypt – 'an action which, if ever I have a biographer, will certainly be admired by others. I hope you may be successful. I feel almost certain you will. Your wit and tact and beauty should overcome all obstacles.'[58]

The trip – an opportunity to see her 'Highlander friend' as much as the Sirdar – was, however, full of obstacles. Staying with Ramsden in a Cairo hotel, she continued to bombard Kitchener with notes about her son. Satisfied that she had done all she could, she took a trip up the Nile with Ramsden, stopping to admire the ruined island of Philae, and when Ramsden was ordered to rejoin his unit at Wadi Halfa, Jennie returned to Port Said intending to embark for London. Told that her ship would be delayed for a few days, she hurried back to Cairo in the hope that she might have more time with Ramsden. As she rushed joyously into his hotel room, without knocking, she found him in the arms of another woman: Lady Maxwell, wife of the Army Commander.

The family often recounted this story at Jennie's expense. Even the Prince of Wales, when he got to hear about it, poked fun. Jennie drafted a reply that she was grateful for his sympathy 'as your Royal Highness knows exactly how it feels after being jilted by Lady Dudley'. Leonie claimed that she offered to post this potentially explosive letter but never did. All that seems to have remained of the Ramsden romance was a bracelet and some memories. It is doubtful if Jennie ever considered the cost of such a trip – either financially or to her reputation. It did not advance her son's career any more than her own.

The hotel-bedroom scene, farcical as it may appear today, is strong evidence of Jennie's need for physical sex. Although not all of her attachments were necessarily consummated, it is likely that several were – both during her marriage to Randolph and immediately afterwards. The evidence is partly in the way men and women wrote about her and partly in the sort of men who were attracted to her. Not all women who indulged in liaisons at this time went the whole way, instead merely indulging in the late-Victorian habit of teasing flirtation. Jennie was viewed differently. As Adolphus Liddell wrote in a long letter to Constance, Lady Wenlock, there were a multitude of possible relationships ranging from Lovers, Fondlers and Friends to Lotharios, Carriers-on, Philanderers, Amis caressantes and Platonics. But he concluded that 'few men are capable of being Platonics. They are of two kinds: the man of strong and passionate nature who controls himself for the sake of the beloved and the man of cold and refined temperament who prefers the more delicate conditions of the Platonic.'[59]

As the mirrored relationship between mother and son subtly shifted, Winston now began to berate his mother for her extravagance in clothes, furniture, travelling and entertaining. In order to clear some pressing debts, she had asked her solicitors to instruct Winston to guarantee premiums on life insurance policies she had been forced to take out amounting to £700 a year. He was not pleased. 'Speaking quite frankly on the subject, there is no doubt we are both – you and I – equally thoughtless – spendthrift and extravagant. We both know what is good and we both like to have it. Arrangements for paying are left to the future.'[60] He reminded her that in the three years since Randolph's death she had spent a quarter of their entire fortune in the world. Admitting that he too had been extravagant, he considered nonetheless that his own extravagances were 'a very small matter' besides hers.

I take no credit to myself in this matter as you have kept up the house and have had to maintain a position in London at the same time – we shall very soon come to the end of our tether unless a considerable change comes over our fortunes and dispositions . . . I sympathise with all your extravagances even more than you do with mine – it seems just as suicidal to me when you spend £200 on a ball dress as it does to you when I purchase a new polo pony for £100 and yet I feel that you ought to have the dress and I the polo pony. The pinch of the whole matter is that we are damned poor.[61]

Throughout 1898 Churchill was earning a steady income from his literary outpourings, continuing when he could with his satirical novel and flattered by offers from publishers, who now descended on him, to write major books. It was no doubt with income in mind that he encouraged his mother to think of writing and promised to discuss this with her on his return. But he was so worried about what he saw as her cavalier attitude to money that he started a legal action to prevent her passing on his portion of his inheritance to a second husband should she remarry. It was only his confidence in his 'ability to keep himself from squalor by journalism that persuaded him to withdraw the action'. As he wrote to his aunt Leonie: 'I felt a horrid, sordid beast to do what I did, but I had to contemplate the possibility of Mamma marrying perhaps a poor man that I disliked, some wanderer. But I have withdrawn the conditions now.'[62] Winston's concern is easily understood and his actions are a clear indication that his mother was the source of constant gossip. Every man she was seen with was whispered of, or shouted about, as a potential marriage partner. Some, such as the millionaire William Waldorf Astor, might have solved her financial problems. According to a story in the *American Journal* in 1895, datelined London, 'it is difficult to estimate the power Lady Randolph Churchill would have in preventing a conflict between England and America. Her engagement just announced to William Waldorf Astor would cement the American bond. She is allied to both with bonds of steel [that is to England and America, not to Astor].'[63] Others exacerbated her problems. She faced down as many as she could. To Daisy Warwick, rival, gossip and friend, she wrote from Cowes: 'Dearest Daisy, I am NOT going to marry anyone. If a perfect darling with at least £40,000 a year wants me *very much* I might consider it.'[64]

Winston returned to England again in July 1898 having given his mother instructions this time to arrange two or three political meetings for him as a preamble to his being elected an MP. He told her he wanted one really big meeting of at least 2,000. 'Compel them to come in,' he wrote to her, 'I am sure I can hold them.' And he did. In July he addressed a vast meeting at Bradford which Jennie had organised. He was wise to take on the mantle of his father so quickly before Randolph's contemporaries had forgotten the unfulfilled promise of the man. Jennie received a shoal of congratulatory letters including one from R. B. Haldane, the Liberal statesman and philosopher, complimenting her on her son: 'for there is in his voice something of the strong quality of one that is – alas – still – to the loss of all of us, & of you most of all.'[65] But he also used his leave to make a final bid to get himself attached to Kitchener's army in Egypt, which was advancing up the Nile to reconquer Sudan, Jennie having done all she could here and not succeeded.

Kitchener had politely told her, and everyone else roped in to push, that there was no room for Winston Churchill on his staff. Churchill now exploited his family's connection with Lord Salisbury, who agreed to meet him. Through his private secretary, Salisbury was prevailed upon to send a telegram to Kitchener proposing young Churchill. Again Kitchener replied that he had no vacancies for officers and, even if he had, there were plenty of people he would choose before Churchill. At this point Winston turned to Lady Jeune, an old family friend who had a close relationship with Sir Evelyn Wood, the Army Adjutant General. She told Winston that she had heard Wood at a dinner expressing dissatisfaction at the way Kitchener had passed over officers recommended by the War Office, rejecting a large number. Wood objected to this autocratic behaviour. So Churchill asked Lady Jeune if she would tell Wood that Kitchener had even turned down one of Lord Salisbury's recommendations. She did. Thus it was that after more than two years of trying, Lieutenant Churchill now found himself, finally, attached to the 21st Lancers. He immediately got himself a further commission as a reporter for the *Morning Post*. As he made clear in *My Early Life*, he was well aware that Jennie's persistent badgering had earned him enemies as well as opportunities and that he was a controversial figure, disliked in many quarters for his transparent ambition, his medal hunting and his belief in his own destiny. As he travelled along the Nile it was to Jennie that he wrote full accounts of the dangers he faced and the reality of death for a soldier. He never spared her gruesome details other mothers might wish not to know. In recognising her strength, he was treating her as a sister. He insisted that he did not think he would be killed but added that, if he were severely wounded, 'you would do well to come out and help me back'.[66] Later he wrote, 'I thought about you a great deal, my dearest Mamma, before the action. I fear it must have been with a beating heart that you read the telegrams and looked down the casualty list.'[67]

The Battle of Omdurman, which was intended to achieve the reconquest of the Sudan, and which the twenty-three-year-old Churchill had struggled so hard to be a witness to, proved his first cavalry charge in action. It was also the last full scale cavalry charge of modern warfare. He sent his mother a telegram as soon as he could to let her know that he was unscathed, followed by a letter two days later. His survival amid such bloody and wild carnage – 'the most dangerous 2 minutes I shall live to see' – was, he believed, a matter of fate. He believed it was a sign that 'Fortune was in the giving mood . . . one must back one's luck.' But, as he told his mother, 'and you only . . . my soul becomes very high in such moments'. Churchill, who 'never felt the slightest nervousness', was even urging a second charge until the sight of such horrific mutilation and slaughter prompted greater caution.[68]

He felt certain, having witnessed the deaths of so many fellow officers he had known, that he had been picked to survive. Omdurman may have been a brilliant campaign in which young Lieutenant Churchill and many others distinguished themselves. But what lingered in the mind after so much terrible and bloody fighting were the scenes of death, destruction, vengeance and inhumanity; these were always to haunt him, not least the piles of Dervishes left groaning and unattended on the field of battle. 'The victory at Omdurman', he maintained later, 'was disgraced by the inhuman slaughter of the wounded. Kitchener was responsible.'[69] As soon as it was over he told his mother to arrange some good political meetings the following month in Bradford and Birmingham.

In March 1899 he went to stay in Calcutta with Jennie's longstanding friend Lord Curzon, the newly appointed Viceroy, and was tempted by the possibility of being taken on to Curzon's staff – '£300 a year and no expenses of any sort', as he reported. But even Jennie's influence could not help him with this. Immediately on his return, Winston was beset with financial problems on his mother's behalf. With unintended irony, Moreton Frewen offered to help. Winston, explaining that payment from the *Morning Post* had eased matters temporarily, tactfully declined, but admitted that he was filled with apprehension about the future, both on his mother's account and on his own. He suggested postponing a meeting with his uncle until his mother returned to London, as he wished to ask her first on what days she required his company.

Earlier in the year Winston had written to his mother that, although he hated the idea of her remarrying, 'that of course would be a solution'. It was one that she, too, four years after Randolph's death, now looked to increasingly as a way out of her financial problems. Another guest at the Devonshire House Ball was the Hon. George Frederick Myddleton Cornwallis-West, heavily disguised that night as a simple black slave in the entourage of the Queen of Sheba, a role taken by his sister Daisy, Princess of Pless. George was exquisitely handsome and exquisitely young at the time, a mere two weeks older than Winston. He was also charming, good at shooting and reputed to be the best dancer in London. A soldier in the Scots Guards, George was a weak and unassertive character, like his father William Cornwallis-West, who was a talented painter at the mercy of strong-willed women – first his mother then his wife Mary, who was known as Patsy. George hated his mother, was frightened of her and even considered her 'a wicked woman'.[70] It is not known when the two first became friendly – Jennie would have known the family for years as Patsy was, like her, a Professional Beauty (PB), postcards of whom were greatly in demand, and an intimate friend of the Prince of Wales. The Cornwallis-West family, descended from the swashbuckling admiral friend of Nelson's, were landowners who, hit like many others by the agricultural recession of the 1870s, were in deep financial trouble. They owned 5,000 acres in North Wales at Ruthin and a further 2,000 around Newlands Manor, near Lymington in Hampshire, but falling incomes meant they had difficulty maintaining both. Because the properties were entailed they could never sell more than a small parcel of land at one time and so constantly ran up massive loans which they were never quite able to pay off. They lived way beyond their means, but most onlookers would have had no idea quite how indebted they were as they were skilled at concealing the amount of debt. But in 1887 they were forced to sell their London house in Eaton Place.

Patsy arranged sparkling marriages for both daughters, which it was hoped would bail out the family. In 1891 Daisy married Hans Heinrich, Prince of Pless, scion of an ancient Prussian family. But, although she was given an allowance from her husband, he lived far too extravagantly to permit their fortune to be used on behalf of his in-laws. Patsy's other daughter, Constance Edwina, always known as Shelagh, married Hugh Grosvenor, the Duke of Westminster, himself always known as Bend'or, in 1901. But that marriage, to one of the richest landowners in England, was not happy in the long term and failed to reverse the decline. In that situation all hopes were pinned on the handsome baby of the family, George, to marry an extremely wealthy woman and thus restore the family fortunes. Jennie was not she.

In October 1896 the Prince of Wales wrote one of his jocular letters to Jennie in which he talked of his surprise at receiving a letter from her at Newlands. 'You are evidently up to your old game again,' he told her reprovingly. 'I don't suppose that you took Winston with you. No he would have been de trop.'[71] Less than two years later, again commenting on her relationship with George, the Prince wrote more seriously: 'it is a pity that you have got yourself so talked about – & remember you are not 25!'[72]

George maintained that he first met Jennie at Warwick Castle some time in 1897. Frances, Lady Warwick, one-time adored favourite of the Prince of Wales, was at the 'zenith of her beauty and the castle one of the loveliest places in England', he wrote in his memoirs. Jennie 'was then a woman of forty three; still beautiful, she did not look a day more than thirty and her charm and vivacity were on a par with her youthful appearance. I confess', George added, 'that I was flattered that so attractive a person should have paid any attention to me, but she did and we became friends almost immediately.' According to his account he went on the river with Jennie, who talked to him about Winston, 'already notorious as the young man who had addressed the audience from a box at the Empire on the iniquity of the proposal for shutting up the promenade at that well known music hall; and who had played polo for his regiment when it had won the Army cup in India. His mother had great faith in, and ambition for him, and even at that time believed he would rise to great things.'[73]

At all events in August 1897, just after the ball, Jennie was again staying at Newlands, a regular rendezvous for the Prince of Wales and his circle. Her presence at the annual Milton and Hordle Cottage garden show, held at Newlands, was noted in the *Lady* of 18 August. Her relationship with George must have taken off very soon after that because by the following January he was writing to her in highly colourful and romantic terms. She had become his 'Darling little Missus', or 'Dear Angel'. He put a heart at the top of the letter and scribbled 'Semper Fidelis'. They were soon writing to each other twice a day. He told her, 'when one loves a person very dearly one misses that person more than ever'.[74] And he asked her not to wear Caryl Ramsden's bracelet.

For a brief second, his family seemed to welcome Jennie in the hope that their non-intellectual son might acquire a dusting of culture. Daisy described his relationship with Jennie as 'the best thing that could happen to George – a nice, clever woman will only influence him for the good – Patsy will invite Jennie to Newlands to a little party'.[75] But once they realised the seriousness of the physical attraction they were appalled. The thought of their only son marrying Jennie Churchill, a woman who was clearly never going to provide them with an heir and whose reputation for financial extravagance and sexually charged affairs preceded her, could only fill them with horror. It was a particularly horrifying prospect for Patsy, twenty-one years younger than her husband, since George was heir to the whole estate. If Jennie were to be married to George, Patsy might even find herself homeless. The Cornwallis-Wests made it as difficult as possible for the pair to meet and tried to do everything to encourage a match with Muriel Wilson, or better still, the American heiress May Goelet. In July, when George fell ill, Jennie sent him some roses, which in turn threw his mother into a furious rage. 'She required a lot of pacifying and then only by assuring her that you were anxious for me to marry MG . . .'[76]

But Jennie and George, resorting to a variety of lovers' subterfuges, continued to meet. If she visited him she was to ask the servants first who else was in and leave with just a note if others were at home. When she posted a letter he gave her special instructions to ensure that her letters were not identified. Theirs was a scandalous relationship and both knew it. By November George was desperately in love, reduced to kissing her photograph, and promising to give up everything for her. He sent her passionate letters, told her how clever she was and that he wanted her with him for always. Not surprisingly Jennie was assailed with doubts. 'Of course, the glamour won't last forever,' she conceded to her friend the composer Ethel Smyth, 'but why not take what you can, and not make yourself or anyone else unhappy when the next stage arrives?'[77]

Perhaps her suggestion to her friend Lord Curzon asking if he might have a vacancy on his vice-regal staff for George, was a way of removing him from temptation. But Curzon declined, 'as I can only take one English officer from here and I have fifty applications'.[78] But her vanity, so recently bruised by Ramsden, was soothed and boosted by George's declarations of passion. What they had in common was their love of spending. Occasionally she tried to make George see the folly of it all. 'There is no folly in being devoted to you, my sweet, even if we can't get married . . . I feel more and more like a creeper clinging to and growing on you. It is my prayer that this creeper may be evergreen.'[79] Quite clearly she loved the boy. He was said to be one of the best-looking men of his generation, if a bit short on brain. That he stood to inherit two large estates, or so she thought, cannot have cooled her ardour.

11

The Versatility of Lady Randolph
is Quite Unusual

~

JENNIE UNDERSTOOD THAT marrying George was never going to win the approval of her friends. Many people, whether jealous, shocked or genuinely concerned, involved themselves in trying to separate the couple. Meanwhile she turned to other ways of making a living. In the last couple of years Winston had proved he could live by his pen and he now encouraged his mother to try her hand at something literary. She conceived the idea of producing an international quarterly magazine. This, like everything Jennie wanted, was to be a product of high style and fine quality. The 1890s was the decade of the New Woman, several of whom were working as journalists or editors. Jennie epitomised so many of the characteristics: she was bold, enterprising, highly educated and unconventional, but with one great advantage – she was enormously well connected. How could she capitalise on this?

Jennie maintained that the seed for the idea came from a dinner conversation with Lord Curzon. 'In a despondent mood I bemoaned the empty life I was leading at the moment. Lord Curzon tried to console me by saying that a woman alone was a godsend in society and that I might look forward to a long vista of country house parties, dinners and balls. Thinking over our conversation later I found myself wondering if indeed that was all that the remainder of my life held for me. I determined to do something and cogitating for some time over what it should be decided finally to start a review.'[1] She discussed her idea in great detail with Winston. After all, she knew nothing about printing, publishing, finance or editing. But she knew where to get advice and had the guts to ask. It was now that their roles slowly began to reverse and they settled into what both recognised as a brother-and-sister relationship. From now on they were a team and although the relationship had its rhythms, moments when it worked better than others, they clearly enjoyed the intimacy which could be easily revived when needed and the recognition of how each could help the other. Previously, she had negotiated terms for him. But it was Winston who had the first detailed meeting with John Lane of the Bodley Head before returning to India at the end of 1898. Lane, former railroad clerk then publisher of the notorious quarterly the *Yellow Book*, was the man of the moment. But the *Yellow Book*, identified so closely with Oscar Wilde (even though he did not write for it), Aubrey Beardsley, decadence and scandal, survived a scant two years, from 1895 to 1897 and nearly killed Lane. He was full of good ideas and looking for safer writers to publish.

Winston encouraged his mother with the patronising love perhaps only a twenty-four-year-old can muster: 'You will have an occupation and an interest in life which will make up for all the silly social amusements you will cease to shine in as time goes on and which will give you, at the latter part of your life, as fine a position in the world of taste and thought as formerly and now in that of elegance and beauty. It is wise philosophy, it may also be profitable. If you could make £1,000 a year out of it I think that would be a little lift in the dark clouds . . .'[2] As ever, Winston saw the inchoate venture in terms of what it could do for them both, financially as well as socially.

After Winston's meeting with Lane on his mother's behalf, he wrote her a long letter promising that nothing had been agreed but outlining suggested terms. 'You would have to guarantee say £1,000, the chance of loss on four numbers. £350 of this would be paid towards the first number. This will be your whole liability in the matter, and should the magazine show a balance profit, this would of course not be wanted and you would not lose anything . . . Lane will produce the magazine on an agreed scale – paying the writers, printing, publishing, advertising etc – on a scale previously fixed.' Winston was optimistic that if she could make even £800 a year profit, to be divided with Lane, it would be enough to enable her to continue living in the new house. It would also give her 'the pleasure of influencing thought and opinion and becoming generally known as literary and artistic'.[3]

She discussed the project with several of her friends including Algernon Bourke, 'a literary man and very enthusiastic on the subject'.[4] He advised her that if possible she should make enough from the first number to pay for the whole year and that, for her own safety, she should get up a small syndicate of investors to back her whom she could repay eventually. But the man whose advice she craved was Bourke Cockran, 'to pick your brains a little more'. In London that winter, he had been a 'tower of strength' to her. Now she asked him: could he find a really clever piece for her 'American notes' as she hoped to get 'lots of American talent to write for her. And oh! Do find me a name for my magazine.'[5]

In spite of the formal tone of this letter, it is clear that Jennie and Cockran had continued to see each other during 1896 and 1897. Decorum in the Prince of Wales's circle demanded that even longstanding lovers referred to each other in public by their title. Yet, revealingly, Jennie mentioned 'Bourke' by his first name three times in three months in letters to Jack, on one occasion telling her son: 'I am very much afraid that it will be impossible for me to go to Paris with Bourke next week – as I had hoped – but I am really too hard up – and Winston has been overdrawing his account and I had to make a cheque for £50.'[6] According to Cockran's latest biographer it was probably timing that prevented Jennie and Bourke marrying. 'Cockran was in the political wilderness without a seat in Congress from 1896 to 1904. If the Liberals and the Irish Party had offered him a seat in Parliament during the period from 1895 to 1898, when he and Jennie were still seeing each other, maybe they would have married. But Jennie was never going to leave England and Cockran loved being in Congress . . . By the time the Liberals did offer him a seat in 1903, it was too late. Jennie had remarried and Cockran knew he was going back to Congress in 1904.'[7]

She agonised over the name of her magazine as 'it seemed as difficult to find an unappropriated title as though I were naming a race horse'.[8] As late as February 1899, Winston was still dismissing suggestions such as 'The Arena' or 'The International Quarterly'. 'I beg of you not to be in a hurry. A bad name will damn any magazine,' he told her. He advised her to search for a title that would be 'exquisite, rich, stately . . . something classical and opulent'. He was appalled at his mother's suggestion of incorporating a Jerome family motto – 'Blood is Thicker than Water' – as a subtitle, saying it should be 'relegated to the pothouse Music Hall, that it only needs the Union Jack and the Star-Spangled Banner to be suited to one of Harmsworth's cheap Imperialist productions . . . I confess I shivered when I read your letter.'[9]

The term 'Anglo-Saxon' was proposed by Jennie's long-time admirer Sir Edgar Vincent. 'Review' was added to avoid a copyright issue. These words certainly conveyed more subtly the idea that her son was to spend much of his later adult life trying to bring to fruition: that the interests of the United States were inextricably linked with those of Britain. That the English-speaking peoples of the old and the new worlds had much more than history and a language in common was undeniable. However much horror Winston as a young subaltern professed at the phrase 'Blood is Thicker than Water' being used to sell a classy periodical – in 1898 the cliché had become something of an imperialist slogan – he understood its meaning only too clearly. He had yet to embark on his political career but, much later, he was to exploit the idea in his own way and to his own advantage. For the moment, *Anglo-Saxon Review* served better.

Jennie never tried to conceal her intention of running a profitable periodical. In an introductory essay to the first number, composed in collaboration with Winston, she wrote: 'The first object of every publication is commercial. "No one but a blockhead," says Dr Johnson, "ever wrote except for money."' This was a favourite quotation of Winston's. But she also had higher ideals. She wanted to do something more than simply produce another pamphlet, satire, lampoon. Recognising that the daily production of printed words was incalculably vast and that articles 'full of solid thought and acute criticism, of wit and learning, are born for a purely ephemeral existence to be read one day and cast into the waste-paper basket the next!', she hoped to produce something more lasting which therefore must appear 'in a guise which fits it for a better fate . . . After a brief, though not perchance unhonoured, stay on the writing-table, it may be taken up into that Valhalla of printed things – the library.'[10] She believed that if she charged enough, a guinea a number, her quarterly miscellany would be properly valued. Although it was Lane who first came up with the idea that the magazine should look like 'a famous old book' with expensive paper, gilding on the edges and beautiful leather bindings, she made it clear to him on successive occasions that she was in charge. She not only wanted complete editorial authority, she insisted that the subscription payments go directly to her bank and not to his, as he had initially suggested.

She called upon a number of experts to help her with the actual production. For the bindings, with a facsimile of a traditional pattern, there was Cyril Davenport of the British Museum. He wrote a short essay on each cover at the beginning of the volume. The first, in dark-green leather with a hand-finished gold-blocked abstract design, was a facsimile of Thevet's *Vies des hommes illustres,* executed in about 1604 for James I. Although the covers were not the most expensive type of calfskin leather, but a cheaper sheepskin, they were the highest-possible quality and finish for a commercial venture. Similarly, the designs were made using one block for the front and back, rather than with individual tools, but the work was all hand finished to a high standard with some gold leaf applied by hand.

Arthur Strong, librarian of the House of Lords, was her historical adviser. Lionel Cust, director of the National Portrait Gallery, wrote erudite articles about the illustrations – mostly reproductions of famous paintings – and she corralled a distinguished range of authors, politicians and society friends to contribute original pieces. But, however beautiful the individual volumes, the *Review* was a typical product of its time and its contents uneven in quality. Yet it is doubtful if anyone else could have drawn upon such a wide and disparate range of contributors, let alone had the energy and vision to see the project through.

'It was at once both exclusive and inclusive . . . the progeny of a morganatic and somewhat transitory alliance between Literature and Society (both with a capital). It might be described as the Yellow Book in court dress and bedroom slippers,' is how one critic described it.[11] The first issue, which appeared in June 1899, included a short story by Henry James, an article on wireless telegraphy by Professor Oliver Lodge FRS and a selection of letters from Georgiana, Duchess of Devonshire, edited by the then Duchess. There were as many American as there were English contributors, thus justifying the title. She paid a range of fees from £15 to Algernon Swinburne for a poem, £40 to Mrs Craigie for a play, £40 to Henry James for a story and 30 guineas to C. Robbins for a twenty-eight-page article on 'a modern woman'. E. V. Lucas wrote a jocular poem inquiring:

> Have you heard of the wonderful magazine
> Lady Randolph's to edit with help from the queen
> It's a guinea a number, too little by half
> For the crowned heads of Europe are all on the staff.

Winston told his mother that he hoped she would keep the position of sub-editor open for him on his return home. He was keen to assist 'in any way I can and I do not doubt the affair can be made a success'. As he told her, he could help her in ways 'scarcely anyone else can and nobody else will'.[12] He was right in this and the venture proved a true literary collaboration.

But the friend whose support throughout the ten issues was most critical was Pearl Craigie. Writing under the pen name John Oliver Hobbes, Mrs Craigie, also American, was twelve years younger than Jennie and, although always immaculately dressed, was not nearly as glamorous – she was sometimes described as an American bluestocking. Nonetheless the two women had much in common. Both had been brought to Europe by wealthy parents and both loved music. Both women had married at nineteen, but Pearl had divorced in 1895. She had one child, a son called John, who was a talented writer and a sparkling conversationalist. Jennie believed that without Mrs Craigie – 'a woman of great sympathies, her unselfishness has been realised by all who ever came in contact with her and her valuable time was always at the disposal of anyone she could help'[13] – the magazine would never have got off the ground. It was Pearl Craigie who found her the brilliant and experienced editor whose nose for talent and ability to advise on ideas gave the *Review* its professionalism: Sidney Low.

Low, born in London of Hungarian Jewish parents, the grandson of a rabbi, was one of eleven children and a most prescient choice. He started his career as a university lecturer but was forced into journalism to earn money. His father, like Jennie's, made a fortune and then lost it. He would have identified with her insofar as both needed to make their way in the world according to their wits and their energy. He found Jennie irresistible and was one of her warmest admirers. Low kept a diary, and his account of one of the dinner parties Jennie invited him to at the time she was setting up the *Review* gives a good indication of her appeal:

> Dined with Lady Randolph Churchill. Present the Prince of Wales, Duke and Duchess of Devonshire, Cecil Rhodes, Countess of Warwick, Lady Gerard, Miss Plowden, Lord Hardwicke, Sir Henry Burdett, Winston Churchill and his brother and Mr Ernest Cassel . . . talked with Rhodes on South Africa. The Prince of Wales talked to me after dinner, deplored imperfect knowledge of foreign languages by Englishmen, spoke of Dreyfus case and its scandals and the state of France . . . he also spoke of our hostess's venture, the *Anglo-Saxon Review*.[14]

The first issue was generally well received, although some carped about the price and others, including friends, were all too eager to lampoon Jennie. Daisy Warwick, invited to be a contributor as well as a subscriber, said: 'It was at one time one of Lady Randolph's amusing foibles to be regarded as literary . . . she canvassed all her friends to become subscribers . . . the most important feature of this review was its gorgeous binding. This may have accounted for its short life. Nobody, even the most literary, could have lived up to such a grand binding in a mere review!'[15] An additional weakness was the lack of an overall theme. So keen was Jennie to bring in everyone she knew of note that the quarterly lacked focus. Most commentators remarked on how enterprising the new widow was, one of them declaring that 'the versatility of Lady Randolph is quite unusual'.[16] But this versatility, a desire to make the *Review* all things to all men, also led her into trouble. Among her most valued contributors was Lord Rosebery, Randolph's friend, who wrote her a pithy essay on Sir Robert Peel for the first issue. But in a subsequent volume the article was scathingly criticised,* and Jennie's social life, or what she called 'the exigencies of time and space', meant that she had not realised the offending article was going to appear. She wrote to Rosebery apologising profusely and regretting 'that anything even approaching criticism of him should have appeared in my *Review*'. He replied loftily, insisting he was not bothered, because 'Frankly, I ceased to be a subscriber after the previous number in which I perceived the cloven hoof of politics. Frankly, also, I think the introduction of politics into "the Anglo-Saxon" a great mistake.[17]

George, in the background, was nervous and constantly felt inferior when reminded of Jennie's protean abilities. While he wished he could be of more help in her enterprise, 'I fear my talents (if I have any) are certainly not literary.'[18] From the hundreds of his surviving letters it is clear that his interests at this time did not extend far beyond horses, shooting and point-to-point races. Frosty weather preventing the hounds picking up a good smell was of greater concern to him than what subjects by which authors should appear in Jennie's *Review*. But he did discuss the magazine with his mother, who offered to find someone to write a small article on gardening. And he warned Jennie that she should not have granted John Lane such a large percentage of the gross profits. 'If you only sell sufficient copies to pay the magazine expenses you will still lose as you will have to pay Lane. You ought to have had it nett profits.'[19]

Jennie, however great her concerns, did little to hold back the romance with George as she plunged ahead with her magazine. 'I suppose you think I'm very foolish,' she wrote to one friend. 'But I don't care. I'm having such fun.'[20] By May, George was calling her his 'embryo wife' and by August, if they were not already, they became lovers in Paris. As George reminded her, after this escapade she could no longer accuse him of being a baby. 'I did so enjoy my two days and nights!! in Paris, my love, and trust they were only a foretaste of what is to come . . . no matter how great the folly may be I feel I cannot live without you but want to be with you and take care of you always . . . dearest little Missie, you are right. I do love you as no one has ever loved you, with my whole heart and soul.'[21]

At the same time Jennie was still trying, although not very hard, to cool his ardour for marriage. So was the Prince of Wales, who at Cowes that August commanded the twenty-five-year-old Lieutenant aboard the *Britannia* and explained to him clearly why he should not marry this merry

* See 'Liberalism' by W. Earl Hodgson, *Anglo-Saxon Review*, September 1901.

widow. George, recounting the conversation, told her that the Prince believed that marriage to an older woman was not a good idea in general. He also reminded George of the looming war in South Africa. After several years of negotiations, conferences, letters and raids, war was now imminent as the Boer Republics resisted annexation by the British. No one could possibly predict what might happen within the next three months. The Prince begged George to do nothing in a hurry, reminding him of his duty: if there was a war he was sure to be sent out. There would be time enough to consider marriage when (or, as he did not add, if) he came back.

As summer darkened into autumn, George grew increasingly desolate. 'You said in any case what happens we will stick to each other but, precious, you don't mean by that we should not marry do you? When I am away from you I feel all the more determined.'[22] But news of the scandalous romance had now burst on to the public stage. As well as rumours, there were now newspaper articles announcing the engagement as a *fait accompli* and making snide comments on the difference in their ages. His mother and sister were, he complained, behaving like two hysterical old maids. Winston had to issue a public denial, but even George's adjutant demanded an explanation. 'I told him . . . I would marry you tomorrow if you would but that you were not willing . . .' Then Sir Arthur Paget, George's commanding officer, also wanted 'to have a go at me'. At this point George threatened to leave his regiment if he was pressed to go abroad. 'You won't desert me, Missie, will you? I couldn't bear it. It would break my heart.'[23] Without her, George insisted, his life would be empty and hollow. He could never love anyone else as much. He was, he told her, living through a hideously unpleasant situation with sarcastic remarks about him being made the whole time. 'But I don't mind one little bit, Dearest One, and am only telling you this to show you that you are in no way held up to ridicule.'[24]

But of course she was. And, in a strong moment, after much vacillation and changing of mind, Jennie did call it off. She was worldly enough to realise that they were damaging each other as well as those in a wider circle, which included Winston. Winston had himself written to George, who reported: 'I cannot tell you what he said as he refused me the right to disclose a word and his arguments were very strong . . . in as many words he suggested that matters remain as they are.'[25]

Winston had been approached by George's father, Colonel West, who tried to enlist his support in ending the relationship. But, however uncomfortable he was made by it, his loyalty to his mother was unswerving. He told her, 'whatever you may do or wish to do, I shall support you in every way'.[26] When he received a second letter from Colonel West he told his mother nobly: 'There is not much in it and I did not think it necessary to answer. It is for George to settle with his family: for you to consult your own happiness.'[27] He believed that family pressure would eventually crush George and that the marriage would not go ahead. Nonetheless, he asked his mother to send him a telegram when she had received this letter 'to say that you love me and will write the same sentiment at a greater length'.[28] On 11 October 1899 war at last broke out between the Boers and the British. Grief-stricken, George bowed to the inevitable and a few days later, still professing enormous love for Jennie Churchill, sailed with his regiment to South Africa. Winston had already left as the highly paid representative of the *Morning Post*. Jennie was bereft and confused. To Mrs Craigie she confided that she suddenly 'felt too old to marry, she has no money and is afraid to give up her liberty. Men are so difficult – even the best of them! I quote.'[29]

But, as the century drew to a close, Jennie was busier than ever. There was the merry-go-round of her social life, impossible to cast aside, which involved continual travel around the country. And there was still her music, which required regular practice. She gave a major concert that summer at the Queen's Hall with the Royal College of Music Orchestra, persuading Mlle Janotha and Mrs Craigie to join her in playing the Bach Concerto in D minor for three pianos. Marie Janotha had been court pianist to the German Emperor and was a great favourite of Queen Victoria. Jennie wrote afterwards of this concert that it was the only time she remembered enjoying playing in public.

But the major focus of her attention was trying to make a fist of being an active and professional editor of the *Anglo-Saxon Review*. Fortunately, in addition to her battery of helpers and advisers, she had an efficient secretary, Miss Marshall. But it was Jennie herself who penned invitations to the great and good asking them to become contributors, making sure the copy arrived on time and that they were paid. She it was who constantly lobbied her friends and acquaintances for articles as well as subscriptions. Her dazzling energy and style is clearly seen in the correspondence she had with the American novelist Stephen Crane, whose *Red Badge of Courage* her son had admired and had recommended to Bourke Cockran. She appears breathlessly scatterbrained, absent minded, not serious. But it was all part of the charm, vitality and passion for life that marked her out from the rest. In July she invited Crane to write her an article of between seven and ten thousand words, perhaps about Crete or Cuba, promising him: 'The

Review pays as well if not better than other periodicals.' A week later she urged him 'to consider perhaps a military story, or if you do not care for reminiscences of war, a short essay on any congenial subject', but advised him that she was just off to the Grand Hôtel at Aix-les-Bains. Four days later she wired him from Dover Pier having changed her mind about his writing on 'any subject'. She now said: 'hope you will begin article at once. Would suggest war reminiscences Crete or Cuba.' The following day from Paris, where she was presumably gallivanting with George, she had to apologise. 'I wrote you a long letter but by mistake it was posted without a proper address.' She still wanted the article for her September issue but now offered him a little extra time.

On 10 October she wrote once again in apologetic tones having just returned from Scotland to find 'to my chagrin that it will be impossible to include your article in this number of the review'. She had over-commissioned. 'I hope it will be the same to you its appearing in the December issue, which I am trying to make exceptionally good.' On the 25th she paid him the rather large sum of 50 guineas and the article appeared under the heading 'War Memories'. Crane died the following year, aged twenty-eight, of tuberculosis.[30] But by then there was another, more urgent activity requiring her attention – one that might reunite her with George. She had been asked to preside over a committee of prominent American women in London to organise as quickly as possible the refurbishment of a hospital ship, the *Maine*, bound for Cape Town. Other members included the well-known society hostess Mrs Adair, the two Duchesses of Marlborough, Lily and Consuelo, and her father's old friend Mrs Ronalds, the long-term mistress and muse of the composer Sir Arthur Sullivan and still a close friend of Jennie. But Jennie was to be the chairman and guiding light. The committee first met at Great Cumberland Place on 25 October and that was followed by almost daily meetings for the next two months. A programme of concerts and other entertainments was swiftly organised and a chalk drawing of Jennie by John Singer Sargent commissioned for the programme cover. With her upswept hair and strong jaw set off by a high ruff, she looks beautiful still and more determined than ever. Wealthy individuals were approached for money, and the committee raised almost £45,000. Jennie said afterwards that those weeks were 'perhaps the most absorbing of my life'.[31] Although she was not initially required to accompany the ship she realised that if she did so she would be able to see George and possibly Winston there. She told a different story when she made an appeal for funds through the *New York Times*. Her presence was necessary, she insisted, 'not because my son is there, for he will be a thousand miles away . . . but because I think I may prevent any kind of friction between the American nurses, whom Mrs Whitelaw Reid is sending out, and the British officials in case such friction should arise'.[32] In the event there was friction aplenty and her presence may on occasion have increased rather than lowered the temperature.

But outside events were moving fast and on 16 November Jennie learnt that Winston had been captured by the Boers after the armoured train in which he was travelling had been sabotaged. Jack thoughtfully telegraphed his mother that his brother was not wounded and that his bravery had been splendid. George wrote from Orange River Camp: 'I am so grieved to see by today's paper that Winston has been taken prisoner. I do hope he will be released soon as a non combatant and that nothing will happen to him – how anxious you will be, my poor darling. How I wish I could help you.'[33]

Of course, Jennie agonised over the next few weeks. In her *Reminiscences* she admitted to 'some terribly anxious moments . . . Had it not been for the absorbing occupation of the *Maine*, I cannot think how I could have got through that time of suspense.'[34] But there is also a sense that her courage, which found its match in his own, led her to embrace her son's danger as a challenge.

Ambulance trains and hospital ships were a new feature of this war as Victorian technology was harnessed to military might, and the most famous of the latter was the *Maine*. To have a group of influential American women in charge of a British military hospital ship in wartime was extraordinary. Although the ship and its crew were offered free to the British Government by Bernard Baker of the Atlantic Transport Company, the task of converting this former Atlantic cattle trader into a spick-and-span hospital ship with all the latest medical and scientific equipment fell to the American Ladies' Committee. They had less than two months to raise enough money to fund the refit. The ship was contracted to the Royal Navy for fitting out in November 1899. At vast cost, two new decks were built, allowing for an operating theatre with X-ray apparatus, five wards comprising 218 beds to be painted white and to be made 'cheerful looking', electric light to be installed throughout the ship, together with electric fans to keep the wards fresh and cool, electric refrigerators and disinfectant sprays, and India-rubber flooring, to deaden sound and prevent slipping, was laid in the spaces between the cots.

On 16 December 1899 the Duke of Connaught visited the *Maine*, presented a Union Jack in the name of the Queen and commented that never before had a ship sailed under the combined flags of the Union Jack and the Stars and Stripes. This, too, was thanks to Jennie. America was largely pro-Boer and anti-British in this conflict, and when President McKinley declined to send an official Stars and Stripes Jennie obtained one herself and added the Red Cross as well. On the eve of departure the Duke's brother the Prince of Wales wrote to Jennie to wish her a safe return. 'I admire your courage,' he told her, 'but you were always the most plucky as you were one of the most charming of women.'[35] On 24 December, in heavy fog, the *Maine* pulled away from the English coast, Christmas at Blenheim a distant memory that year. Jennie, in her starched white nurse's uniform with lace frills on the blouse and a red cross on the arm, an outfit which she had designed, looked the part. As her great-niece commented: 'Fancy dress always became her. Byzantine empress or nursing sister – she had a sincerity which enabled her to assume the appropriate stance.'[36] Writing to Leonie on the special *Maine* notepaper with the three flags, American, British and Red Cross, she complained how cold and wet it was on board, adding that they had had to leave before everything was ready. Workmen were still trying to complete their labours before they entered rough water. Jennie did not even have her own writing table and had to make do with a bridge table, nor did she have a proper chair or hooks. The one cheery factor was that she had engaged as her secretary Miss Eleanor Warrender, sister of the devoted Hugh.

Days before her departure, Jennie learnt that Winston had made a daring escape from Boer captivity. But then silence followed. He was wanted, according to the posters, dead or alive. How easy now, with the benefit of hindsight, to be sure that he would survive. Yet how much courage must she have needed to continue with her hospital project while desperately worried for her son's life. The day before she set sail she heard of Winston's safe arrival at Durban and the spontaneous ovation he had received from the crowd as he made a stirring address from the steps of the Town Hall. Winston's beloved, Pamela Plowden, sent Jennie a telegram: 'Thank God – Pamela'. Elated, Churchill took a train that afternoon to Pietermaritzburg, where he spent the night as the guest of the Governor of Natal, Sir Walter Hely-Hutchinson, an old family friend, who now became an admirer of Winston.

Jennie, who should have been as joyful as Pamela, was in fact miserable as she had also received a cable from George telling her that he was being invalided home just as she was setting off. He had collapsed with severe sunstroke, which threatened his heart. 'You must promise to see him and write to me all that he says,' she begged Leonie. 'I am so *devoted* to him that it would be a terrible thing for me if I knew he blamed me for going. Heaven knows, this is no pleasure. I had to go,' she insisted.[37] She said she would do her duty by the ship but left with a heavy heart, desperate to be back as soon as she could.

There were dark mutterings on board almost immediately and a handful of male nurses disembarked before the boat set off. There was criticism about the amount of space given over to the comfort of Lady Randolph Churchill, 'whose cabin is decorated in a manner suggestive of a lady's boudoir, rich in the luxuries of silken hangings and cushions'. Some of the nurses complained that the luxurious cabins fitted out for 'one or two persons' took up so much space that there was no room for a deck promenade.[38] 'Lady Churchill had a large reception room, a bath room and a bedroom on the promenade deck and played the great lady philanthropist with much fuss and feather,' was how one of the disaffected nurses put it.[39] Serious problems arose when the skilled nurses were asked to scrub the decks and undertake tasks which they considered the job of seamen. But there was so much dirt, filth and chaos at the beginning of the voyage that everyone had to do their bit, Jennie explained. Her 'bit' was arranging concerts.

Several South African newspapers were critical of this American Lady Bountiful who, in a typical act of irreverence, on 4 January 1900 'had every scrap of religious literature – tracts, bibles, periodicals, leaflets etc – brought up on deck and the whole pitched overboard for the moral instruction of the fishes'. To compensate, she had the ship ransacked for caramels, which she knew had been stowed somewhere. When they were found, she distributed fifty boxes among the orderlies and nurses, in the belief that sweets were more likely than bibles to create a happy atmosphere on board.

A few days later Lady Randolph celebrated her birthday as the *Maine* crossed the Equator. This event was marked by the ritual shaving of men who had never crossed the line before, 'while Lady C, and her companion Miss Warrender, stood on the bridge with Kodaks getting snapshots of the event'.[40] Jennie found the time dragged and hated the monotony of staring at the sea. She was fortunate to have the company of Eleanor Warrender – 'a capital girl. She and I understand each other perfectly. She is very intelligent and a lady and the whole ship swears by her. She does a lot – acts as librarian, no sinecure with 8,000 volumes on board, typewrites and does a thousand things.'[41]

But the real problems arose through the hostility of the staff to each other. Jennie had asked Mrs Whitelaw Reid, wife of the publisher of the

New York Herald Tribune and a friend,* to select the American male nurses, most of whom came from the Mills Training School. Mrs Reid was, as the member of the Board of Managers of the Nurses' Training School at Bellevue Hospital, eminently qualified to do this. But Jennie found them tiresome. 'You know that stupid American "don't care" and "don't want to",' she wrote to Clara. 'I can't explain but there is no camaraderie or jolliness about them. Most of them are soft prigs standing on their dignity. The fact is I realise . . . they are like priggish medical students.'[42]

Jennie had constant political problems with the staff, some of whom did not like being subject to military drill and discipline, while others either flirted or refused to talk to those they considered beneath them. In overall charge was Colonel Hensman, a retired British military surgeon, whose presence enabled the *Maine* to be officially designated a British military hospital ship. But the real difficulties were with Miss Eugenie Hibbard, the superintending sister on board and a highly experienced military nurse whose great-grandfather had been a chaplain in the Revolutionary Army. Hibbard felt her authority was being constantly undermined by Lady Randolph allowing complaints to come directly to her. In general, Jennie was adept at compromising and sorting out most of the internal dissension, much of which was caused by having women in a position of authority over men. But Miss Hibbard had never had her authority questioned before and did not like it.

The *Maine* arrived at Cape Town on 22 January. 'A round of wild gaiety then began as Sir Alfred Milner, British High Commissioner, and other potentates came on board and there was a big reception on shore.'[43] But then she was instructed to sail immediately to Durban, fill up with patients and return to England. Jennie was furious. She was not about to allow the *Maine* to be used, as she put it, 'merely as a transport for convalescents' after all the international support and advance publicity they had worked for.[44]

As she explained, the ship had been expensively equipped with an operating room as well as X-ray equipment and had qualified medical staff on board to use them. She did not shrink now from exercising her social position and personal appeal to get her way. One of those she spoke to was Sir Walter Hely-Hutchinson, who had so recently looked after Winston and had known the Churchill family for years. His kind invitation to Jennie to stay a few nights at Government House in Pietermaritzburg was

---

* Whitelaw Reid had been a contributor to the first issue of the *Anglo-Saxon Review*. His article was entitled 'Come Consequences of the Last Treaty of Paris'.

impossible to turn down. She spent a precious twenty-four hours there with her sons, both of whom were in the Cape. Pulling rank in this way may not have endeared her to the military. But, while she disliked the thought of staying away from George a day longer than necessary, she had not gone to all that effort merely to run a transport ship. 'I had the pleasure of successfully frustrating three attempts to send us home,' she wrote later. In any case she wanted to see Winston and Jack. On 3 February she wrote to Leonie that she had been up to Pietermaritzburg and seen both sons off to the front. 'It was rather hard,' she admitted to her sister. There was no one else in the world she really cared about. 'But I returned here and as usual have no time to brood. Will you have a look around 35A and tell me if all is well? My new green chair I should like covered. I hope you will give me news of George. I am hearing so little of him I fear his family or people making mischief between us.'[45]

Two days later, the first group of sick and wounded were taken aboard the *Maine*. A train with sixty-seven injured soldiers came alongside the ship: twelve were carried on board on stretchers and the rest were able to walk with some assistance. Many of the casualties were those who had survived the dreadful decimation of the Battle of Spion Kop, a defeat which Winston had reported. According to an account put out by the Central News of Durban, 'Lady Randolph superintended their reception, personally directed berthing and flitted among the injured as an 'angel of mercy'.[46] On 13 February Jack Churchill himself came on board as a patient, wounded in the leg. Winston, having helped to get Jack his commission in the South African Light Horse, felt guilty that his brother had been injured while he had escaped unscathed.

From her sons, Jennie heard about conditions at the front. She wanted to inspect the hospitals there at first hand. Winston told her he could easily arrange something. But it was Captain Percy Scott, Commanding Officer of HMS *Terrible* in Durban, a dashing hero and inventor, later an admiral, who gave permission for her, together with Eleanor Warrender and Colonel Hensman, to go to the war zone. And it was Walter Hely-Hutchinson who lent her his own railway carriage and provided much food. It was on this trip, armed with Kodaks, field glasses and a brown holland dress – 'a substitute for khaki in case we should meet the enemy' – that she saw the 4.7 naval gun and its carriage designed by Captain Scott to which the name *Lady Randolph Churchill* was given. The gun crew gave her an empty shell as a souvenir. In her personal photograph album, which includes a portrait of Scott (as well as pages of portraits of Walter Hely-Hutchinson, General Pole-Carew and Lords Milner, Methuen, Albemarle,

Roberts and Kitchener), Jennie wrote proudly, 'After Spion Kop this gun did its best to facilitate General Buller's final advance on Ladysmith.'[47] George meanwhile, 'devouring every paragraph where your name is mentioned', had followed the story of Winston's escape from Pretoria and his account of the butchery at Spion Kop. But when he read that Jennie had been escorted to the front by Percy Scott (in fact Scott was unable at the last minute to accompany her) he was, perhaps with good reason, burning with jealousy. 'I wondered what he was like and if he was nice and good looking.'[48]

On 17 March the last of the sick and wounded were loaded as the ship was due to sail. Following the relief of the besieged town of Ladysmith there were more than 6,000 British sick and wounded to be transported back home and in that situation Jennie recognised that 'it would have been ungracious not to acquiesce' in returning to England laden with injured soldiers as quickly as possible. As she wrote to Clara after a visit she made to Ladysmith following the siege, she knew this was the right course of action. She had seen there mangled bodies, horse carcasses and wild, half-starved soldiers filled with gloom and despair. She felt gratified that she had been able to help in a ghastly situation and 'that the mission of the *Maine*, as far as I am concerned, is working out'.[49]

But when the boat docked at Cape Town there was a further change of plan. She was now instructed to unload some of the wounded and await new patients. At this point Jennie again pulled rank. She went ashore, spoke with the medical officer and told him 'that it was her intention that the *Maine* would leave at daybreak the next morning as previously arranged and that I was cabling the Minister of War in London to back me up'.[50] It is easy to see why such imperious behaviour antagonised those whom Jennie crossed. But she was in South Africa only because 'the *Maine* Committee worked with such will and fire that they carried all before them. The War Office and Admiralty were badgered and heckled: Would they supply us with this? Would they guarantee us that? We would not take "NO" as an answer.'[51] Critics accused her of wanting to return now only in the hope of acquiring glory from being the first ship to bring the wounded of Ladysmith back home.

Before the ship set sail, there was further disapproval of Jennie's behaviour voiced by several American male nurses who felt she had treated it at times as her own pleasure yacht and disliked the way she and Miss Warrender continually used their Kodaks to take pictures of wounded men. The *Maine* stopped at St Helena in the Atlantic, which thrilled Jennie 'with my American love and admiration of Napoleon',[52] an admiration shared by her elder son. This was a revealing comment; the whole project had reinforced Jennie's sense of Americanness.

But the most serious criticism levelled at her was that when the ship reached Madeira on its return, carrying seriously ill men who were anxious to reach home, she went ashore to dine and delayed the departure of the ship as she did not return until very late. One of the sick, Sergeant Grantham, died at midnight. According to one unnamed nurse's testimony: 'Lady C begged for another day; the Captain granted it but when yet another was asked for she was informed that if not back at the ship by a certain time, the ship would sail without her.'[53] In her *Reminiscences*, Jennie refers to the sergeant's death from acute phthisis, or tuberculosis, and the military funeral that she organised at Funchal. After leaving Madeira, she was, by all accounts, very charming to everybody and the nurses all had their salaries raised. Even if Jennie had returned sooner, the sergeant would still have died at sea before reaching England. But something in her behaviour must have provoked the nurse to tell the story in the way that he did and his testimony was widely quoted in Natal newspapers that November.

The voyage of the *Maine* was controversial from the start and Jennie did not accompany the ship on its subsequent voyages. This was only partly because of the political situation and the hope that the United States would at least remain neutral in the war. In her battles with the authorities that were trying to send the *Maine* back to England, Jennie Churchill usually had her way. But this resulted in some jealousy provoked by the recognition given to her as a 'Society Lady' versus the elite female nurses. When the *Nursing Record and Hospital World* described her as 'Flitting about amongst the invalids like a "ministering angel"', there was more than a touch of sarcasm in its account.[54] She wrote many accounts of her time on the ship, including a long article in the form of letters in an issue of the *Anglo-Saxon Review*, and was genuinely proud of her achievement in organising and running the ship. Doubtless she was something of a ministering angel in the eyes of many a wounded Tommy, for whom she had written letters to loved ones in her own hand that they were too ill to write. As she admitted later to the Prince of Wales: 'I am satisfied with the Mission the *Maine* has fulfilled – and if I may say so my connection with it. It has been hard work and sometimes the temptation has been great to fly off in a mail steamer for home – but I am glad I resisted . . .'[55]

In all, twenty operations were performed on board the *Maine* with just three deaths – one as a result of typhoid, one from an aneurism and Sergeant Grantham's from tuberculosis – and 300 wounded soldiers were cared for by Nurse Jennie and her team. War Correspondent Winston

Churchill wrote proudly of his mother in one of his despatches: 'Lady Randolph Churchill has been untiring in her attention to the management and I impartially think that her influence has been of real value to all on board.'[56]

When she returned to England on 23 April 1900 it was spring and a new century. As she stood on deck in a dark-blue serge suit with the *Maine* badge over her left breast and wearing a straw hat with ribbons streaming in the wind she looked radiant. George, impatient, went to Southampton to greet her.

In her absence, Sidney Low had ably looked after the *Anglo-Saxon Review* and four issues had been successfully published. But, although she was enjoying the power and status that being editor of a literary magazine gave her, she had not quite captured all those that she had hoped to. Bernard Shaw agreed to contribute an article 'A Word More about Verdi' but declined Jennie's invitation to luncheon. 'Certainly not,' he telegraphed. 'What have I done to provoke such an attack on my well known habits?' When Jennie shot back with 'Know nothing of your habits; hope they are not as bad as your manners,' he was intrigued by her wit and now replied at length. Although he still declined to dine with her he offered: 'If I can be of real service at anytime that is what I exist for: so you may command me.'[57] But sales were not as high as Jennie had hoped or needed them to be – especially in America, where they had sharply tapered off after the first issue. And she was having more arguments with John Lane, eventually removing him as publisher and putting her own name in his stead.

Absence from George had done nothing to cool his passion. Quite the reverse. In February he had told her if she did not return soon he might be well enough to be sent back to his battalion and they would miss each other. He added that if she had been ill 'and I had been obliged to leave you I wouldn't have wasted a moment in flying back to you at the earliest opportunity. But it seems you are different or have altered.'[58] He had spent the last few weeks under pressure from his parents to find a rich heiress and save the family fortunes, pressure which made him desperate to marry Jennie and she unable and unwilling to resist much longer.

But what really preoccupied Jennie in the spring of 1900 was Winston's decision to return home. 'Politics, Pamela, finances and books all need my attention,'[59] he told her. He had, before going out to South Africa, resigned his commission in the army and, with Jennie's help, fought his first unsuccessful political campaign in June 1899 at a by-election in Oldham. She knew Oldham well, having campaigned there for Randolph, and her son was fully aware what an asset she could be for him in this arena – as long as she controlled her love of gambling and extravagance. She accompanied him to all the receptions and meetings and, as the Oldham *Daily Standard* reported, 'There are thousands of true hearts in this constituency which have a warm corner for Lady Randolph Churchill.' On polling day itself she created a sensation by appearing dressed entirely in blue in a landau and pair with gaily ribboned and rosetted postilions. But even her help could not sway enough voters and in the event he lost by fewer than 1,500 votes. Jennie wrote immediately to her political friends insisting that the contest was closely fought and telling them how well Winston had done. The newspapers reported that she had borne herself proudly as she retired from the room with her talented son.

But, even as he slowly matured, he was unrelenting in his demands on his mother. While she was aboard the *Maine* she had been inveigled into using her influence once more to persuade Lord Roberts to allow Winston to accompany his forces pushing through the Orange Free State. But now her son's attention was focused entirely on political success. Winning Oldham was what really mattered. By the time he returned from South Africa on 20 July 1900 to fight another campaign at Oldham his reputation was immeasurably enhanced by his military exploits. That summer he was in great demand as a speaker, which earned him large sums of money.

Eight days later, having waited anxiously for Winston to return, Jennie, aged forty-six, married George Cornwallis-West, twenty-six, quietly, at St Paul's Knightsbridge. She wore a pale-blue chiffon gown, the skirt finely tucked and inserted with Cluny lace with a lace flounce around the hem. Her hat was a magnificent confection of tucked chiffon, Brussels lace and pale-blue osprey feathers with a diamond ornament pinned to the front. Her outfit exuded confidence, and her insistence on marrying in a church, rather than a registry office, had nothing to do with religious sensitivities. Sunny, her nephew, gave her away, but she painfully missed Jack, still abroad. 'I would give much if you were here and I could give you a big fat kiss,' Jennie told him in a moving letter she sent her younger son on the morning of the wedding. 'I could assure you with my own lips what you already know – and that is that I love you and Winston dearly and that no one can ever come in between us. I shall always remain your BEST friend and do everything in the world for you. You both can count on me and I am glad to think you know and like George. He has behaved like a brick. By the next mail I will write and tell you all about the wedding.'[60] The reception was held at Clara and Moreton Frewen's London home and the

immediate honeymoon was passed at Broughton Castle, lent by Lord and
Lady Algernon Gordon Lennox. There was an extended honeymoon for
the next two months as the pair travelled to Scotland and France. But
although the Marlboroughs and Jennie's sons put a brave face on matters,
George's own, infuriated family did not attend. 'In spite of the disparity of
their ages,' Daisy Pless wrote disingenuously in her published diaries, 'we
were all pleased with the marriage and hoped it would bring lasting happiness to them both.'[61] Daisy also recorded that Jennie had let it be known
she would not keep her title and would in future be known as Mrs George
Cornwallis-West. Jennie thought this would emphasise that this was a
love match.

Winston and Jack may not have welcomed the idea of their mother's
marriage but they tried to welcome George himself. Shortly after the
wedding George wrote a brave letter to the elder of his new stepsons:

> My dear Winston . . . I cannot impress upon you how much I appreciate the
> line you have taken as regards my marriage to your mother. I have always
> liked and admired you but I do so ten times more now. I only wish as I
> wrote and told my father that my family could have taken a leaf out of your
> book. Nothing could have exceeded the sympathy and kindness which you
> and all the Churchills have shown me. I hope always as now to be a real true
> friend to you and never to come between yourself and your mother. If I ever
> do, which God forbid, you can always refer me to this letter which is a
> record of the feelings I have in the bottom of my heart towards you and
> yours. We arrive tomorrow at 2.15. Will you order lunch for three unless
> you have another coming? À demain my dear friend.[62]

Why did Jennie agree to marry George? Certainly not for intellectual
stimulation, as he was the first to admit. A month before they were married he offered to help her with some ideas but soon gave up, admitting
defeat.[63] She knew she would be the butt of society jokes, such as the one
usually ascribed to the octogenarian Lady Dorothy Nevill, who had known
Randolph so well. Wandering in Hyde Park one day, peering into peram-
bulators, she was asked what she was doing. 'I am searching for my future
husband,' she apparently replied.[64] Jennie was even prepared for a falling out
with the Prince over her marriage. He wrote to her insisting that it had
been his:

> privilege to enjoy her friendship for upwards of quarter of a century –
> therefore why do you think it necessary to write me a rude letter – simply
> because I have expressed strongly my regret at the marriage . . . I have said
> nothing behind your back that I have not said to your face . . . you know the

world so well that I presume you are the best judge of your own happiness but at the same time you should think twice before you abuse your friends and well-wishers for not congratulating you on the serious step you are going to make! I can only hope that we shall all be mistaken.[65]

Some believed that an element of jealousy between George's mother Patsy and Jennie, both of whom had held the Prince's intimate affections at one point, may have played a part in her decision to marry.

On the other hand George was, quite simply, irresistible. But, as Jennie's grandson Randolph commented tartly in the official biography of Winston, 'The marriage was improvident and unsuitable . . . Though his sister [Shelagh] was soon to marry the Duke of Westminster, he was, after paying Lady Randolph's debts, to be very hard up.'[66] Jennie took large baskets full of papers away with her on her honeymoon and, from time to time, sorted them into piles: unpaid bills, contributions to the *Review*, translations or copyright agreements. She was working on issues six and seven but was now deeply worried that the project was running at a considerable loss, with no prospect of profitability. 'Fancy having to take bills on a honeymoon,' she joked. Randolph had done the same a quarter of a century earlier. 'But one must be businesslike.' As George told Shane Leslie: 'Of course I was eager to put her affairs in order, but I found it a bit thick when expected to pay for Lord Randolph Churchill's barouche purchased in the 'eighties.'[67]

But in the short term helping to get Winston elected was what mattered. As soon as he returned he knew that an election was imminent, although Parliament was not dissolved until 17 September. He was re-adopted as the Conservative candidate at Oldham and was determined that this time, although he knew there would be a fight, he would be successful. He immediately appealed to his mother, in Scotland with her new husband, 'to impress upon you how very useful your presence will be down here providing you really felt equal to coming down and doing some work'.[68] As he reminded her, a feminine presence in an election campaign was invaluable. Since he had no wife, unlike his opponent Mr Crisp, he relied upon her. 'I know how many calls there are on your time and from a point of view of pleasure I cannot recommend you to exchange the tranquil air of Scotland for the smoky tumult here . . . I need not say that it would be very pleasing to me to see a little more of you in that way.'[69] Tellingly, she broke off her honeymoon, left George for a few days and went to help her son.

It was a short but intense campaign. And on 1 October Winston

Churchill, aged twenty-six, was elected to Parliament as the Conservative Member for Oldham. As he would not take up his seat until the New Year, he asked his mother in the meantime to organise lecture tours for him, first in England, then in America. He had received an offer from a Major J. B. Pond and wanted her to check up on his credentials and make arrangements. But he warned her that he would not go to the United States unless he was guaranteed at least a thousand pounds a month for three months. 'I beg of you to take the best advice on these matters. I have so much need of money and we cannot afford to throw away a single shilling.' He was unforgiving. 'You must remember', he told her,

> how much money means to me and how much I need it for political expenses and other purposes and if I can make three thousand pounds by giving a score of lectures in the big towns throughout England on the purely military aspect of the war, it is very hard for me to refuse, but I should like you to ask Mr Balfour and Mr Chamberlain what they may think of such a course and whether it would [be] likely to weaken my political position if I appeared as a paid lecturer on public platforms in this connection.[70]

Pond had urged Jennie to accompany her son. 'Have you any idea how green your memory is here in New York City?' he asked her, flatteringly, recognising that her glamorous figure and romantic marriage still exerted a strong pull on the American imagination. 'It seems to me it would be a very proud day for you and your friends here would appreciate it and I need not add that it would doubly enhance the value of the lecture.'[71] Six months into a new marriage, she was not persuaded.

Churchill was fêted in North America; he was again the guest of Bourke Cockran, who, Winston believed, was particularly charming given his pro-Boer views. He also dined with Governor Theodore Roosevelt, recently elected vice president, and spoke at a meeting chaired by the novelist Mark Twain, a friend of Jennie. Twain described him as an Englishman through his father and an American through his mother, 'no doubt a blend that makes the perfect man'.[72] But to his mother Churchill groused that Pond was grasping, 'a vulgar Yankee impresario', and that he was not making as much in America as in England. 'Had I been able to foresee all this I would not have come . . . [nonetheless] I am very proud of the fact that there is not one person in a million who at my age could have earned £10,000 without any capital in less than two years.'[73]

While he was away, giving his final lectures in Winnipeg in January 1901, he heard news of the death of Queen Victoria and his thoughts immediately turned to how his mother would fare: 'So the Queen is dead . . . a great and solemn event but I am curious to know about the King. Will it entirely revolutionise his way of life? Will he sell his horses and scatter his Jews or will Reuben Sassoon be enshrined among the crown jewels and other regalia? Will he become desperately serious? Will he continue to be friendly to you? Will the Keppel [Alice Keppel, then Edward VII's mistress] be appointed 1st Lady of the Bedchamber? Write to tell me all about this to Queenstown.'[74]

Jennie was indeed, without Winston's prompting, taking stock of her own future at this point. Throughout 1900 the *Anglo-Saxon Review* had trundled on. But it was clear by now that while it may have been a literary success it was, unmistakably, a commercial failure. In January, Jennie lunched with Pearl Craigie to ask her advice and sound her out on the possibility of a new editor or of launching a new monthly title. 'Various schemes are on foot,' Craigie wrote. 'She wants me to join Winston and herself on the *St James' Gazette*. Keep this a close secret.' But Jennie's idea of buying an existing magazine came to nothing. A month later Craigie reported to her friend: 'Lunched with Jennie and Winston: the latter looks dreadfully delicate. They are going to try the *Anglo-Saxon Review* a little longer on present lines.'[75]

George, marginalised, tried to be helpful, but it was Winston whose advice and co-operation Jennie sought. In April 1901 George wrote to his wife, 'One is naturally loath to give it up, always hoping that the next number may have a larger sale . . . but in spite of the modifications you propose you cannot really afford to go on with it . . . what a pity you cannot get someone to put money into it and share any profits there may be even if you make nothing out of it. It would be an amusing source of occupation to you.'[76]

Jennie needed more than an amusing occupation. She needed an income, and the *Anglo-Saxon Review* was draining her of one. The tenth and last number was published with great sadness in September 1901. At this point, she began contemplating other literary ventures, including writing her memoirs. But a more immediate source of income was needed. As a result of marrying Jennie, George had been asked to leave his regiment. He now needed to 'seek a new profession', as he so elegantly put it in his own memoirs. He had no desire to work in the City as a stockbroker but thought that he might be suited to the management side of an electrical engineering firm. Sir Ernest Cassel, previously the financial adviser to the Prince of Wales and Jennie's friend, found him work with a firm supplying the Glasgow Corporation power station. And for a while he lived in Glasgow. 'I worked hard all week,' he wrote in his memoirs, *Edwardian*

Hey-Days, 'and every Saturday Jennie and I used to go somewhere. We were constant visitors to Blenheim.' Jennie had worked hard, too, at retaining the Blenheim connection, which became much easier after the old Duchess's death in 1899. She had a natural affinity and friendship with Consuelo, who had produced a son and heir in 1897, and Winston got on well with his cousin Sunny, Blandford's son.

Almost all the friends whom George acquired came from Jennie. One of their favourite destinations was Halton, Alfred Rothschild's home in Hertfordshire, north of London. Jennie, attracted by the eclectic mix of artistic and aristocratic guests that Alfred liked to entertain, was one of a select few invited in the months after Randolph's death to stay in Alfred's reconstructed Swiss chalet in the Halton grounds. The chalet, with just three bedrooms, was reserved for his most intimate friends. After her marriage to George the couple went to Halton together three times in the summer months of 1899 and 1900. Jennie also stayed a few times on her own. There were usually Gladys de Grey and Luiz de Soveral, but Adelina Patti and Nellie Melba were regulars, too, and were sometimes persuaded to sing. Alfred, a great collector and an eccentric, liked to entertain his friends with either his small private circus or his own orchestra (all the performers had to wear a similar moustache). But above all Alfred was extremely close to Lord Kitchener, and Jennie would have seen that as a vital link to helping Winston. Fortunately – since there was no way they could have afforded their own country-house establishment – they had a variety of friends who invited them, especially in the summer months, to stay for weeks at a time. She even had to forgo visits to her beloved Paris as she could not afford hotels there, she complained to her sisters. To economise, George had persuaded Jennie to let out her London house whenever possible and, if she had to be in London for a night or two, to stay at the Ritz. Winston moved into a flat at 105 Mount Street, one of the Duke of Marlborough's London properties.

Queen Victoria's funeral took place on 2 February 1901, the same day that Winston sailed back from New York to England. He asked his mother to have waiting for him at the quayside 'complete files' of *The Times* and other newspapers. When he took his seat on 14 February it was in a new Parliament of a new century and a new reign: Prince Albert Edward was now King Edward VII. Winston graciously wrote to his mother that day, a letter which made her weep openly, enclosing a cheque for £300: 'In a certain sense it belongs to you for I could never have earned it had you not transmitted to me the wit and energy which are necessary.'[77] Jennie, too, was now living on her wit and energy, eased by her pride in and hopes for her elder son. Four days later he made his maiden speech in the House of Commons, having rehearsed it in front of his mother, in which he pleaded for more generous treatment of the Boers. She, along with four of Randolph's sisters, was in the Ladies' Gallery to hear it, her head filled with memories and hopes of what might have been when she had been there to support Randolph. Almost all the reporters made comparisons between Winston and his late father. Some mentioned his 'inherited qualities'. Churchill himself spoke of 'a certain splendid memory which many honourable members still preserve'. But the phrase that dramatically caught the public imagination was his remark: 'if I were a Boer I hope I should be fighting in the field'.[78] While he did not agree with the Boer point of view he understood their desire to fight. Jennie told Leonie that she shared her son's views on the South African War.

A few months earlier Winston had advised his lawyers that:

> while my mother's position remains unchanged, I recognise that it is difficult for her to make me or my brother any allowance and I feel it my duty on the other hand to assist her in any manner possible without seriously prejudicing my reversionary interests. I therefore forego the allowance of £500 a year she and my father had always intended to give me. I also defray the expenses of the loan of £3,500 I contracted at her suggestion for my brother's allowance and my own from 1897–1900 amounting to £305 per annum . . . what I desire in my brother's interest as in my own is that there should be a clear understanding, necessarily not of a legal nature, that in the event of Mr George Cornwallis-West being at some future time in a superior financial position, my mother will make suitable provision for her children out of her own income; in other words that she will reciprocate the attitude I am now adopting.[79]

King Edward VII's Coronation in August 1902 marked the start of a new chapter in Jennie's relationship with the royal family. Both she and Leonie were given seats in the King's Box – a favour to his women friends who could not enter the Abbey as peeresses. Leonie's deep and longstanding relationship with the King's brother, the Duke of Connaught, had not always been easy for Jennie as Leonie was, on occasions, mildly critical of her more outspoken sister. The two men never got on and Jennie's marriage to George had led to a froideur between her and the then Prince of Wales. But the new King soon forgave her. As she told Jack: 'I had a very nice letter from the King, nicest I've had from him since I married . . .'[80] And he gave her honours, first creating her Lady of Grace of St John of Jerusalem and then investing her with the Order of the Royal Red Cross in recognition of her services on the *Maine*. But occasionally Jennie went too far, especially when she criticised Mrs Keppel, which not surprisingly offended the King. On those occasions, the Duke of Connaught had to warn Leonie to 'look out for Jennie . . . Don't think I am a gossip but I write all this simply because I am always sorry when *your* sister is in my brother's bad books. I am sure if you had been here you would have prevented Jennie's tongue running loose.'[81]

But the principal cloud on Jennie's bright horizon at the dawn of the Edwardian era was that Winston had lost Pamela to another man. On 3 April 1902 she married Victor, second Earl of Lytton. However, in a letter from Clara to her husband, ostensibly discussing Winston's sadness over Pamela, another ominous shadow creeps in: 'Leonie says Jennie seems so happy and contented so I do hope George's little flirt with Mrs Pat Campbell is nothing.'[82]

12

Haunted by the Future

~

GEORGE NOW TRIED his hand at a variety of occupations and minor inventions but, however original his ideas, he never managed to turn any of them into a fortune. Perhaps he was not serious enough. Hunting, shooting and deer stalking were what motivated him. 'Those were wonderful days,' he wrote in his memoirs. 'Taxation and the cost of living were low; money was freely spent and wealth was everywhere in evidence.' From 1902 onwards, when he became one of the first Englishmen to own a petrol-driven motor car, his escapades on the roads – how fast he could go and whether he could avoid a puncture – were what fuelled the inner man.

Jennie, contented, went along with much of this. She even took up golf, not very wholeheartedly, to accompany her sportsman husband. As they travelled around to Saturday-to-Monday parties together, George revelled in the new social life provided by his wife. Once, travelling to Knole in an eight-horse-power Panhard with George at the wheel, they had an accident when he failed to notice a corner in the dark. Jennie was thrown out, there being no side door to hold her in. 'However, she was not hurt; we reversed, and arrived home about two in the morning,' George recounted lightly.[1] But this breeziness hid a depressive streak and his awareness that his financial and social contribution to the marriage was nugatory doubtless lowered his self-esteem. Eventually he looked elsewhere to bolster that.

Compton Place, near the seaside town of Eastbourne on the south coast, home of the Duke and Duchess of Devonshire, became a favourite of Jennie's at this time. Staying here enabled her to pay regular visits to Seymour Leslie, Leonie's ill-fated youngest boy, who, after Paris, had been moved to Eastbourne with his devoted nurse Miss Tree. It was hoped that the sea air would help to cure him of his tubercular-induced paralysis. Unable to swim, ride, cycle or do anything other than read and watch, the all-seeing young boy looked forward to Jennie's visits.

She would drive over in the first motor car to see me, usually bringing someone from the house party, the Prince of Wales perhaps, who wrote Albert Edward boldly across an entire page of my Visitors Book. All were bearded and condescending, graciously extending not the hand but a fleshy index finger inquiring 'and how are you my little man?' Jennie had previously warned them that after several operations the doctors did not expect the child to reach manhood.[2]

Occasionally, she went her own way at weekends – to Blenheim, Halton or Chatsworth to visit old friends – while George went off hunting. Visits to Sandringham, sometimes for as long as a week, were still an important part of her life. But mostly she was wary of leaving her new husband on his own for too long. Nor did she want to leave Jack, who seemed vulnerable in some ways. It was for both those reasons that she declined an invitation to visit George and Mary Curzon in India. 'I suppose a too uxorious spouse has kept you at home,' the disappointed Viceroy wrote to her, after wondering precisely how to address her in future. 'I suppose you are not Lady Randolph, nor Lady Jennie. I cannot identify you as Mrs West – Dear Mrs West, no that will never do,' he wrote playfully.[3] The old silver Burmese bowl, which had been bought by the Curzons as a wedding gift, would therefore have to be sent to London.

Increasingly, it was Winston to whom she looked for intellectual stimulation. Once the *Anglo-Saxon Review* ceased publication and the financial loss was absorbed, Jennie's main attempt at generating an income focused on her own ability to write. Curbing expenditure was always too painful a nettle to grasp. Winston proffered stylistic advice when she sent him work in progress. 'There is a great lack of arrangement,' he said of one of her articles, 'which makes it hard to follow and would militate against its success.'[4] He was good at chivvying her on, and, because he, too, was self taught, at telling her how to group her ideas and make up her mind about exactly what was her intention in each paragraph before she started. This would involve rewriting, he warned her, but no new material. He enclosed a suggested outline, which he had sketched out for her. By this time, he had started work on his own monumental writing project; the act of filial homage that producing the biography of his father was to be. He had always seen this book as his prerogative: indeed his mother had been instructed some years previously to deter others, 'as I have every right and can do it much better'.[5] He started by wading through the eighteen boxes of letters, full of the most valuable and interesting material, which his father had preserved.

'There are here all your early letters which were most carefully put away,' he told his mother, suggesting that she should read through them and select anything of 'general interest for the biography, after which they should I think become your personal property again'.[6] He was encouraging and told her always to seek out the drama. He also asked her to search for the personal scrapbooks – many of which she found when she went to stay at Canford Manor, as Randolph's sister, Cornelia, Lady Wimborne, had put them together. And he asked her to stay on the look-out for ways to help him collect material. 'All is grist that comes to my mill and the more saturated I am with the subject before I begin to write the better.'[7] Any family must worry when a son takes on such a task, yet she trusted him implicitly. Jack, too, was brought into the project, but given the more menial tasks of sorting and deciphering the letters of the old Duchess.

Winston also asked his mother to write out her recollections of life with Randolph from 1874 to 1880. 'You will remember how you first began at Charles Street, entertaining Mr Disraeli, hunting at Oakham, then the row I suppose in 1877, then Ireland. Do try and give me a few ideas about this. It does not matter how few they are as long as you really try to put me into possession of the personal aspect of his life in those days.'[8] Thirty years after the events she was describing, Jennie was able to view those years with some perspective. She realised the importance of presenting her dead husband's political career in the best possible light. In the finished work, her contribution became the second chapter, 'Member for Woodstock'; unsurprisingly, Jennie supplied nothing very revelatory.

Being married to George did not stop her undertaking whatever small pieces of work for her son that she could, such as buying him presents – watches and a brooch – to send those who had helped him escape the Boers, finding him a secretary, opening a bazaar in his place when he was away, visiting his constituency – 'if you have the time and inclination'[9] – or organising supper parties, such as the one that followed a meeting at Chelsea Town Hall in December 1903. He recognised how crucial her active support was. 'I am sure those people were vy pleased at your going,' he wrote to her after the bazaar opening. 'I don't know what I should have done if you had failed me.'[10]

Some, such as Pearl Craigie, worried that Winston made too many oppressive demands on his mother. 'Your new plans are most interesting. Winston nevertheless must not tire you,' she warned.[11] But this is to miss the point. Supporting and encouraging Winston was what she lived for. It was the role in life she had chosen and been cheated of with Randolph.

Others believed that she was more relaxed than she had been for a long time. Perhaps this was the reason that she allowed herself in these years to put on weight. Her sister-in-law Daisy, seeing her at Cannes in April 1903, remarked: 'George's wife is here, as charming as usual and looking very well but SO fat, gambling and wearing lovely clothes.'[12] Jennie's figure had never been her best feature and her indulgence in sensual pleasures included a delight in food. In her youth she had kept her weight under control or under large skirts, tightly waisted. Now, as she approached fifty, she seemed not to care about her figure. She continued wearing wonderful clothes and spending freely. 'As she felt well she ate well,' Anita Leslie noted. She relied on her face, which usually appeared underneath enormous velvet hats, and her personality, so overwhelming that most diarists still chose to comment about that rather than her waistline.

There was one much publicised occasion when she was staying at Gopsall Hall, home of Earl and Countess Howe (Lady Georgina Howe was one of Randolph's sisters) in the Midlands near Nuneaton, and a favourite retreat of the new King, where the party took to playing an elaborate version of charades. There was Princess Henry of Pless, dressed as Romeo and another of Randolph's sisters, Lady Sarah Wilson 'in kilts', but the acknowledged star of the evening was Jennie, whose passion for the dramatic never waned. That evening she 'came as a roistering Spanish cavalier. She wore black silk tights, a doublet and hose, a dark crimson velvet cloak trimmed with gold, had a sword, a great diamond blazing in her black sombrero with its drooping feathers, diamond buckles on her pretty shoe and a black moustache waxed and ferociously curled like the Kaiser's.'[13] What resulted, never to be forgotten by those who witnessed the scene, was women, dressed up as men, dancing with other men. American newspapers devoted pages to such lurid shenanigans – 'ridiculous accounts of an affair that never happened', was how Jennie's sister-in-law Daisy described it later. It was at Gopsall that Jennie stood on a chair and sang brazenly:

> Ruby lips, ruby lips
> Oh who will kiss these ruby lips
> When I am far away far away?

The choruses were shouts of:

> Some other man,
> I don't care a damn
> Some other man.[14]

All three sisters were now living beyond their means in varying states of financial crisis. Clara suffered most. Her romantic distraction, King Milan, had died in 1900 and, to economise on outgoings, she had been despatched to the wilds of Innishannon, a Frewen family estate in Ireland that would eventually pass to Hugh but which, for the moment, gave her and Moreton a home of their own at last. Moreton was mostly in London still trying to win friends and finance for his latest projects, currently bi-metallism.[15] Occasionally, he sent Clara some money. 'Thank you for the fiver – it is very welcome,' she would reply gratefully, for she never shed what her son described as a 'pathetic faith' in her husband. But she longed for the day when her family could finally move to Brede Place, a beautiful if dilapidated fourteenth-century manor house on the Frewen family estate in Sussex with its own chapel and priest room. Brede, mag-nificently positioned on the Downs, fulfilled her notions of how a well-to-do English gentry family should live. The trouble was that no one had inhabited the house for the previous hundred years and it needed far more money spent on its restoration than they would ever have. Moreton and Clara had owned it since 1897 but lent it, unrestored, to Stephen and Cora Crane for three years. When Crane died in June 1900, Clara was anxious to make a family life for herself there. 'Even if you can only just get enough to do Brede simply and modestly, our being *together* here will remove my greatest worry and sadness that life is running away and we are so much apart,' she begged her errant husband.[16] She pro-ceeded to spend large amounts of money, often borrowed, transforming the house and gardens.

There was an inherited Jerome blindness to living modestly from which Clara and Jennie especially suffered. 'All those women spent money like water, without thinking; they went to money lenders, borrowed, mort-gaged, whatever, the whole time. It was quite extraordinary,' remembers Jennie's granddaughter Clarissa, Lady Avon.[17] Leonie, through the Leslies having Glaslough as their country home, appeared to have slightly more money and, through her intimate and intensely discreet association with the Duke of Connaught, more independence. In fact Leonie was enjoying great social success at this time which climaxed when she and Jack were invited to accompany the Connaughts to India in 1903 as the Duke went to represent King Edward at the Durbar.

All three sisters had heeded well the lesson from their mother – appear-ances were everything. Clara, keenly aware of her two sisters' superior social grandeur, gratefully accepted Jennie's hand-me-down clothes along with the gossip they brought. Her life, increasingly at Brede, lacked a London focus, while Leonie, who moved in overlapping circles with

Jennie, could not have contemplated wearing her cast-offs any more than any of the three women could have imagined an existence without servants. Yet in the Frewen household servants sometimes went without wages. It made them feel more like part of the family, Moreton casually and cruelly observed. In addition, the two Frewen boys, Hugh and Oswald, were educated at Eton, where fees likewise went unpaid from time to time. And there were constant dunning letters from tradesmen, who occasionally went away convinced by silver-tongued Moreton that one day things would be different. But, in spite of this hand-to-mouth existence, they managed to obtain just enough money, usually through loans and other complicated schemes, for Moreton and Clara to travel together once or twice around this time – in 1902 to America promoting bi-metallism and in 1904, when Clara also borrowed 'more privately', to enjoy themselves on the Riviera.[18]

Travelling was a constant imperative for the sisters, as it was for other women of their social standing. It was mostly around the British Isles and France but it gave their lives a searching, restless quality where otherwise there might have been calm acceptance. All three insisted that they needed a London home as well. For a while the Frewens had managed to rent a large house in Chesham Place, on the corner where today stands the noisy Cumberland Hotel. When that became too expensive they moved to a smaller one close by at 39 Great Cumberland Place. With Leonie at 10 Great Cumberland Place and Jennie at 35A, the street was known as 'Lower Jerome Terrace'. The sisters regularly dropped in at each other's homes. This was especially useful when, in 1903, eighteen-year-old Clare Frewen, the only girl among the cousins, made her society debut – an event for which a London home was *de rigueur*. Jennie, without daughters or a major focus to her life, took Clare in hand.

Both aunts (Leonie was also daughterless) fussed considerably over Clare, strikingly tall, dark-haired and fair-skinned, but quietly rebellious. But, however fond she was of them, she writhed when she heard them discussing her 'chances'. Both aunts hoped that Clare would make an important marriage, yet feared that Clara, her own mother, so overtly ambitious, might spoil this. Leonie on the whole was gentler, but even she 'could give a terrific scolding on hearing that a girl had done something likely to stop nice men from proposing marriage'. This included walking a dog alone in Hyde Park or, worse still, wearing a chiffon scarf which, according to Aunt Leonie, 'drew attention'. Aunt Jennie told Clare that she *must* pull in her waist and put up her hair, as well as getting it waved each day. Clare felt like a wild animal being tamed by Jennie. She was also desperately self-conscious about how poor she was.

That summer Clare fell in love with Wilfred Sheridan, a descendant of Richard Brinsley Sheridan. At a ball, finding him dancing with another girl, she gave voice to her hurt feelings: 'But he's mine . . . you can't have him.' She stormed off impetuously. It was Jennie who educated her. 'You must learn to hide things and to behave decorously. Never let a man see you care,' she told her revealingly. 'You've so much to learn. Don't think we haven't all been through it. But remember, Englishmen don't like these outbursts and you were very rude.'[19]

According to Clare, Jennie became her second mother. 'I grew to love Jennie as soon as I got over being intimidated by her. One had to admire her; she was resplendent. Jennie's advice was generally worldly, my mother's was sentimental, Leonie's was ethical.'[20] The worldly advice included introducing Clare to Monsieur Worth in Paris, where she bought the teenager her first Worth gown, and to Emile Fuchs, the Austrian-born artist who was then painting Jennie's portrait. Fuchs was also patronised by the King and, besides painting his portrait, had designed the new and controversial postage stamps. When Jennie took Clare to meet the artist she also brought along a blue silk sash which she tied around her niece's waist, announcing that she wanted to 'smarten her up'.

Fuchs had known Jennie since 1898 when he had had his first exhibition at the Royal Academy. On display at the exhibition was a striking bust in marble of Lady Alice Montagu, which Jennie admired. She appeared at his studio one day, introduced herself, and asked him, 'Would you care to make a similar portrait of me?' Fuchs accepted the commission eagerly, and not only because Lady Randolph was a central figure in London society at the time. He was captivated by her looks. 'Striking and distinguished in appearance with black hair and piercing eyes she had besides a remarkable feminine charm. Her colouring was high and she had dimples in her cheeks when she laughed and one in her chin. This piercing quality of her eyes . . . was enhanced by a peculiar droop of the upper eyelid.'[21] Almost every day that she came to pose, a lovestruck George Cornwallis-West came too.

Fuchs immediately became part of Jennie's artistic circle at Great Cumberland Place. 'That little house was a meeting place for all that was highest in art, science, music, political and social life. The Prince of Wales often dropped in for tea of an afternoon quite informally . . .' Fuchs recalled how intensely proud Jennie was of Winston and how she would read out some of his letters. 'When he returned from South Africa she commissioned me to make a small medal with the profiles of her two boys, one on each side, which she always wore around her neck. It was considered a novel idea and led to a sort of fashion.' Jennie introduced Fuchs to many of her friends, who went on to give him important commissions, such as the beautiful Vittoria Colonna, Duchess of Sermoneta, and took him to Blenheim to meet the Duke and Duchess of Marlborough.

For a few years, Jennie's and George's marriage trundled on in apparently blissful happiness. But George could not resist other women and some of the rumours must have reached Jennie. As early as 1902, twenty-four-year-old May Goelet, the American heiress once intended by his parents as his bride, wrote to her aunt Grace of George after the season: 'Such a dear, attractive, good-looking boy and quite the best dancer in London. Anyway he fancies himself very much in love with me. So foolish of him. I am so sorry about it – but what can one do?'[22]

Equally serious for the future was their spendthrift lifestyle. George, not without his own profligacies, wrote later that in money matters Jennie was without any sense of proportion.

> The value of money meant nothing to her: what counted with her were the things she got for money, not the amount she had to pay for them. If something of beauty attracted her she just had to have it: it never entered her head to stop and think how she was going to pay for it. During all the years we lived together, the only serious misunderstandings which ever took place between us were over money matters. Her extravagance was her only fault, and, with her nature, the most understandable and therefore the most forgivable.[23]

Four years into the marriage, Winston told his mother that he looked with very grave anxiety into the future. 'I am very sorry and startled to hear of these new financial difficulties,' he wrote. 'I don't care to think where we shall all finish up . . .'[24] Their relationship had now shifted another several degrees, beyond that of brother and sister to the point where Winston dispensed advice. They discussed both financial and emotional matters frankly and Jennie unburdened herself to her son about the continuing strained relations with George's family. 'I thought a great deal over all you said to me about yourself and feel sure you are right to concentrate on and take pains with the few people you really care about. But I have no doubt that when Papa West is at length gathered to Abraham you will be able to renew your youth'[25] – an allusion, presumably, to the hope that, after his father's death, George would eventually arrive at that 'superior financial position' which would ease matters for everyone.

It was clear by now that Jennie and George would never be able to afford to buy a country estate of their own. Although they enjoyed regular invitations to the country houses of others, they had for some time been looking around to rent a place of their own. By 1905 they had discovered Salisbury Hall, an exquisitely romantic sixteenth-century house less than an hour from London near St Albans. Salisbury Hall, which had been owned by the Martin family for the previous hundred years or so, was an ancient manor set a short way back from the main London–St Albans Road. Jennie fell in love with a house surrounded by wide fields and parklands which provided wonderful pheasant shooting for George and for their weekend friends. The pretty redbrick house was compact, not enormous, having lost the odd wing over time. It had a mere eight bedrooms, which meant that there was ample room for Winston and Jack, but not enough for too many couples to stay for long periods – something that suited a household with only a few staff. There were however secret passages and servants' quarters, and the devoted Walden, as well as his wife, followed Jennie here. Jack lived there too for a while, company for his mother during the week while George was away.

The main house, then as now, is approached via a medieval brick bridge over a moat. Just to the left stands a small flint and brick building known as Nell Gwyn's cottage; according to legend, King Charles II's mistress lived here at some point in the second half of the seventeenth century, and her ghost was said to walk the grand wooden staircase or the beautiful oak-panelled hall of the main house. George, in his memoirs, wrote that there was 'no doubt' that it had been used as a petit garconnière by Charles II and that Nell Gwyn had lived there from time to time. In fact it was there that the first Duke of St Albans was born. His mother apparently said, 'Throw the little bastard into the moat,' and the King replied, 'No, spare the first Duke of St Albans.' George recounts, however, that when King Edward VII came to stay and he repeated to him this story the King said quickly: 'You're wrong. If Charles II said anything he said, "Spare the first Earl of Burford," the title given to Nell Gwyn's child before he was made Duke of St Albans.'[26]

Previous owners of Salisbury Hall included Richard Nevill, Earl of Warwick and Salisbury the Kingmaker, as well as Sir Jeremiah Snow, banker and trusted friend of Charles II. Dominating the oak-panelled hallway was a series of bas-relief medallions, each representing a famous Roman emperor or character, set on a wide frieze above the panelling, thought to have been removed centuries ago from the nunnery at Sopwith St Albans. Leading upstairs from there was an ancient oak staircase with massive square newels and moulded handrails and balusters. Jennie adored the idea of living in a house steeped in such romance and mystery. She also loved having a garden to cultivate and being able to pick her own floral arrangements.

Part of the attraction of Salisbury Hall was having somewhere to invite Winston to stay for several days at a time to write, at speed, undisturbed. Jack never stimulated his mother in the same way. He was, as his own son perceived, 'not what I would call intelligent. Although he shared my passion for Wagner, he had no real understanding of art, and his love for his first-class library hardly went deeper than admiration for the covers and bindings . . . he seldom actually read the books.'[27] Nonetheless, once he started working in the City, he could spend weekends at Salisbury Hall relaxing and giving his mother practical advice. Jennie and George hosted many parties there with a wide variety of political, literary and artistic guests. One whose dramatic visit was never to be forgotten was the Italian-born actress Eleanora Duse. Duse, famous for her Shakespearean interpretations as much as for her tempestuous love affairs with men and women, had just severed her relationship with the Italian poet Gabriele D'Annunzio. She arrived in tears and was taken into the drawing room by Jennie, where she remained more or less weeping the whole day, and was visited at intervals by the other women guests. But mostly the family memories are of Winston, who, after an ample meal around the refectory table, would stand in front of the enormous Tudor fireplace in the dining hall, declaiming on free trade and other issues.

In the first years of his mother's second marriage Winston was entirely bound up with politics and with writing his father's biography and rather hoped that Jack, learning to be a stockbroker, would take on responsibility for his mother's investments – at least as far as share movements were concerned. To an extent this was increasingly the case. 'I often think of you and Jack,' Winston had written to his mother shortly after her marriage, 'and feel very anxious about him. Please concentrate your attention on him. He is rather untamed and forlorn.'[28] Once Jack found meaningful work, to which he was able to apply his talents, Jennie's rapport with her younger son deepened. But she never relied on him in the way she did on Winston.

As Jennie's financial situation worsened – the occasional magazine article making little dent in their deepening indebtedness – it was decided early in 1905 to hold an 'inquisition' (Winston's word), which

Winston himself was to conduct. Nothing vital seems to have been concluded and they continued much as before, with occasional crises punctuating the relative calm of books and politics. For a brief moment, George, who had set up his own small financial venture in the City, seemed poised on the edge of some business success. But any hope soon petered out.

From the beginning of the century the position of women in the body politic was becoming a key issue in England. Jennie's views on female suffrage were ambivalent, typical of many women of her class. She knew from first-hand experience what a powerful effect persuasive and attractive women could exert during an election campaign, but she believed that they had a stronger effect behind the scenes, which would be weakened if all women were actually given their own vote. However hard it seems today to explain such a frankly patrician attitude on the part of an intelligent woman, it was not unusual in the first decade of the new century – before the First World War changed the way everyone looked at the female contribution to society. Jennie's anti-suffrage position offers a deep insight into her most basic attitudes to life; she had been brought up to believe that women had more power if it was exerted gently, tactfully and with charm. Most telling is her remark scribbled in the margin of a letter inviting her to comment on the example set by Lady Beaconsfield and the influence she exercised 'through her womanly tact and study of her husband's interests'. Lady Randolph wrote: 'L[ad]y B was a most vulgar old cad & did B more harm than good!'[29]

But in the early days of the militant suffrage movement the leaders targeted as many politicians as they could, and hoped to woo Winston – who at the end of 1904 had crossed the floor to join the Liberals. Tariff reform was the issue that prompted him. But the underlying reasons drew on infinitely deeper origins. The change of party came just as he was immersed in making sense of his father's life – a crucial personal task if he was ever to come to terms with (and try to understand) Lord Randolph's cruel treatment of him. As Winston wrote in *My Early Life*, 'There remained for me only to pursue his aims and vindicate his memory.' Churchill, convinced that he too would suffer premature death, was working at phenomenal speed to achieve all that he felt incumbent upon him as the son of Lord Randolph Churchill, and writing his biography was a major milestone along the route he had mapped out for himself. He also set himself the task of cultivating as many of Randolph's friends as he could, including Lord Morley, Chamberlain, Rosebery and Balfour, many of whom remarked on the similarities between father and son – Winston seemed to have inherited his father's disregard for convention, his loathing of the tyranny of party discipline and a genuine desire to engage and listen. To many it seemed that the young orator was possessed by Randolph's spirit. But when, addressing the Commons in 1904, he stumbled over his words in mid-speech and had to abandon it, the painful memory of his father's collapse was in many minds. Jennie, who believed she knew the truth of her husband's illness, bore it stoically.

In January 1906 Winston's two-volume biography was published to widespread acclaim. Arguably, this was his greatest book. It was certainly the one that was of crucial importance in his future relationship with his mother as much as with politicians and the public. The biography sold more than 2,000 copies in the week after publication. There was, as Wilfrid Scawen Blunt noted, something deeply touching about the son's fidelity to his father's memory. His triumph was to present a sympathetic portrait of the man while evading almost all personal matters and certainly without touching on his parents' troubled marriage. Jennie's unerring faith in her thirty-year-old son's ability to present her husband's life glowingly for posterity had not been misplaced.

Just as the book was published Winston was plunged into campaigning, this time as a Liberal hoping to win North West Manchester. His drift to the left had been evident for some time, hastened by the Conservative Party's attitudes towards the Boer War and Imperialism. But the final decision to join the Liberals had been prompted by his own party's increasingly unpopular opposition to Free Trade. In addition, writing his father's life story reinforced his contempt for the party which he felt had so mistreated his father. In his own mind, the change of party and defence of his father were inextricably linked. 'This election', he wrote to his father's friend Lord James in January, six days after polling had begun, 'is the justification of my father's life and points the moral of my book. The one crowning, irretrievable catastrophe which he always dreaded has now overtaken the old gang and with them the great party they misruled.'[30]

Seymour Leslie, six at the time, never forgot his aunt's fury when she heard what had happened the day her son crossed the floor of the House to join the Liberals. 'That *detestable* Arthur Balfour – I'll *never* speak to him again – got up and walked out of the House . . . a monstrous insult from a Prime Minister.'[31] But Winston, although accused of opportunism, had sensed the mood of the country as the Liberals, led by Sir Henry Campbell-Bannerman, were returned with 400 seats as against the Conservatives' 133 – an unprecedented landslide.

And just as she had helped her husband twenty years earlier, from now on Jennie assisted her son in a very different political atmosphere where the role of women was coming under intense scrutiny. Militant suffragettes frequently heckled at his meetings, shouting, 'Votes for women!' or parading placards. It was a tense time. Feelings ran high on all sides and some suffragettes found themselves not only imprisoned for their violence but force fed if they retaliated with hunger strikes. That January, Jennie was at a meeting in Manchester with Winston when a suffragette holding aloft a 'Votes for Women' banner, demanded to know whether he was in favour of female suffrage or not. The mood was angry and Churchill, who complained later that he was being 'henpecked' into a decision, replied on the hoof: 'I utterly decline to pledge myself.' He had been specifically targeted and a manifesto, written by Christabel Pankhurst, urged constituents to 'vote and work against' him. With dramatic effect, they climbed on roofs and broke windows of buildings where he was about to speak.

Jennie, who often accompanied Winston, believed that this sort of behaviour by the 'shrieking sisterhood' indicated their unsuitability for power. In the next few years her views became more entrenched. She became one of the suffrage campaigners' most resolute opponents and felt strongly enough on the issue that at the end of 1908 she agreed to become president of the North Wales branch of the Anti-Suffrage League – a position that arose through the Cornwallis-West family seat, Ruthin Castle in Denbighshire.[32] Jennie described to Leonie the militant suffragettes she encountered as 'too odious . . . Every night they make a disturbance and shriek and rant. They damage their own cause hopelessly.'[33] Jennie's formative years on the British political scene had been spent at a time when women ran the household and exerted power behind the scenes. She had enjoyed considerable success manipulating this system, and Winston's views mirrored hers. He wrote to her about a demonstration in Manchester in the summer of 1906, which he considered was very successful because 'the suffragettes were ejected with almost incredible velocity!'[34] As the suffragettes started to behave violently his attitude towards them hardened.

But 1906 proved a difficult year in other ways. Within a year of his marriage to Jennie George had had to resort to moneylenders. Thanks to Cassel's introduction and the job in Glasgow, he had a rudimentary knowledge of engineering which, together with contacts, helped land him directorships of various companies. These earned him a reasonable income. But, in an attempt to make capital, he was soon tempted to set up a partnership – a sort of minor issuing house'[35] – with a man he barely knew called Wheater, and in the first year the firm of Wheater, Cornwallis and Co. made more than £23,000. But after this initial success the partners embarked on wilder schemes such as financing a copper-mine in Spain which had little copper, culturing black pearls off the north-east coast of Australia without knowing the method, and financing the patenting and manufacture of an automatic gas-operated rifle which was refused by the War Office's Small Arms Committee on the ground that an automatic rifle would encourage a waste of ammunition. Not surprisingly, he suffered a serious reverse in the middle of the year when he was swindled out of the massive sum of £8,000 – the same sum that Winston was being paid by Longmans for his book – by a fraudulent lawyer. All the family, including Winston, who arranged a loan for him, came to his rescue.

But such unpleasant thoughts were swept to one side in May, when King Edward and his entourage – this included Mrs Keppel and Consuelo Marlborough – honoured Jennie with a visit to Salisbury Hall, for which no expense or effort was spared. Aware that his increasing stoutness made climbing stairs a problem, Jennie created a suite of rooms for the King downstairs and converted the gentleman's cloakroom into a private bathroom.

Months later there was sad news from Blenheim. Winston wrote to his mother in October that Sunny, after much unhappiness, had separated from Consuelo, who had gone to their London home. 'I have suggested to her that you would be v. willing to go and stay with her for a while as I cannot bear to think of her being all alone during these dark days. If she should send for you I hope you will put aside other things and go to her. I know how you always are a prop to lean on in bad times.'[36] But Jennie had already heard the news. She went directly to Sunderland House and from there wrote to Winston, knowing how sorry he would be to hear that Sunny and Consuelo had separated. Their letters crossed. As she explained:

> At the last moment when I was in the train – I gave up Floors and came here as I was wanted . . . It is a terrible thing and I can't tell you how painful it all is . . . poor Consuelo is utterly miserable and dignified and quite calm . . . as far as I can, I avoid everyone for fear of being asked questions – I feel as sorry for Sunny as I do for her and I am obliged to say that he is justified in taking the course he has – it does not make it any easier that she has brought the whole thing on herself – how the women who have had 20 lovers and are kept by rich Jews et autres will be virtuously shocked.[37]

Both Winston and Jennie tried to offer comfort without taking sides, she bringing Consuelo to stay with her at Salisbury Hall while he sent presents to the young Marlborough sons at Blenheim.

But it was a messy business and malicious gossip – especially that planted by Jennie's meddling sister-in-law Lady Sarah Wilson – flourished. One of her more troublesome allegations was that George had been one of Consuelo's lovers. George, protesting his innocence, was furious and told Winston that the only reason Sarah 'had any doubt about it was because I had borrowed money from Sunny. I don't want to start a row between Jennie and the Churchill family but I am sorely tempted to go and tell Sarah what I think of her and if I did she certainly would not forget it in a hurry . . . what a liar that woman is.'[38]

Then, in early November Jennie and Consuelo had a falling out. It is not entirely clear what prompted the row, but the most likely reason was Jennie's stated view that Consuelo had 'brought the whole thing on herself' by going to Paris with Lord Castlereagh earlier in the year. Jennie, having devoted her life to discretion in such matters, disapproved of women who flaunted their extramarital liaisons. Both women considered themselves wounded in the ensuing fracas. Jennie wrote to Consuelo that 'although she made every allowance for the frame of mind you must be in during such a terrible crisis in your life [I am] hurt that you should turn on me who have . . . been a true friend to you and had you been a sister could not have shown you more loyalty or affection . . . I do not regret it – God knows you are not in a position to alienate a friend – therefore I shall still call myself one.'[39]

Perhaps it was Jennie who was suffering a crisis in her life, desperately hoping she would not have to admit that all those who had poured scorn on her marrying such an unsuitable younger man had been right. For George, while promising his wife that he would far 'sooner see you than all the others',[40] was spending much time away from her in London. But after six years of marriage even the emotionally robust Jennie needed someone in whom to confide her troubles. Pearl Craigie provided a sympathetic ear when she went to see her friend at Salisbury Hall ('a pretty little place – rather secluded!') on 11 April. Craigie thought Jennie looked well and handsome, 'but she is haunted by the future. Why did she marry a man younger than her own son? It was a piteous blunder,' she wrote candidly to her friend, Father William Brown.

> The two have nothing in common. She told me that the jealousy between West and the sons drove her nearly out of her mind: they like each other

pretty well unless *she* happens to be present or in any way involved; then they are impossible. West had gone away for a fortnight; while I was there a wire came announcing his arrival this morning! She had arranged to join friends in Paris for Easter. Of course she is still very loveable and seductive but West gets sick of 'the brilliant Winston', and women make up to West in order to enrage Jennie.[41]

Typically, Jennie tried not to reveal the cracks in her marriage to anyone else. But Daisy, George's sister, knew that all was not well. In her diary the following year she wrote that Jennie still loved George immensely, 'poor dear . . . she is uncommonly nice and still very handsome, but of course the difference in age is a sad and terrible drawback (no babies possible)'.[42] George was probably seeing girlfriends throughout his marriage to Jennie.[43]

With Clara deeply engrossed in the expensive renovation of Brede Place, it was to Leonie that Jennie turned in her unhappiness. In a letter apologising for appearing 'cross and unreasonable' a few days before, Jennie tried to explain:

The fact is when I go to London there are only 2 people I ever try to see, one is Winston, the other you – both are often sad disappointments – one on account of work – the other on account of pleasure. I go away feeling sore at heart – I snatch a few minutes of Winston's society by driving him to the Colonial Office [where he had been Under-Secretary of State since the end of 1905] and the most you can offer me are a few words, uncomfortably (for me) at the telephone – But I have made up my mind – and shall not risk it any more – You know I love you and that when you want me I am to be found. I like to think that you are enjoying yrself – your greatest excitement was to see me dress for a ball – make the most of it all while it amuses you – you looked very bright and happy last night – keep so.[44]

Such moods rarely lasted long with Jennie. She cried a lot and had a furious temper – but then she got over it. Her buoyancy as well as her vitality and energy were traits she passed on to Winston. At all events by 1907 she was writing in earnest, being pressed by her publishers to deliver a book that Edwardian society was drooling to read. According to George: 'I take it to my credit that it was I who persuaded her to write those memoirs and prophesied the success which they undoubtedly had.'[45] Perhaps. But seeing the success of Winston's account of her husband's political life was another spur, as was the need for money. In March 1907, from Paris, deeply unhappy at having to ask, she succumbed to a humiliating request, asking her son for a loan of £150 in order to complete the

"GRANDOLPH AD LEONES."

A cartoon in *Punch* of Lord Randolph Churchill at the height of his political influence shown here as a 'pesky insect'. Later, *Punch* often poked fun of him in cartoons as 'Grandolph'

Jennie with her sister in-law Lady Curzon in the horse-drawn tandem in which they canvassed the 1885 Woodstock election for Randolph. Not present when the result was announced Randolph cabled his wife: 'Brilliant success almost entirely due to you and Georgie'

Randolph Churchill towards the end of his life with his 'terror' of a beard, grown during his long visit to Africa in 1891, where he hoped to make a little money for Jennie and the boys

Above left: Moreton Frewen, who married Jennie's sister Clara, dressed as a cowboy at his cattle ranch in Wyoming around 1880

Above right: Winston as a twenty-year-old cadet at the Royal Military College, Sandhurst, in 1895 at the time his father died

Bourke Cockran in 1904, nearly ten years after he first met Jennie and after his election to Congress, which ended an eight-year absence

Jennie dressed as the sixth-century Empress Theodora of Byzantium for the Devonshire House Ball in 1897. The Empress, a former courtesan as powerful as she was beautiful, was the wife of the Emperor Justinian I. She had dozens of admirers and was generally held in low regard by respectable society. Shane commented somewhat cruelly that Jennie would have resembled Theodora even without fancy dress

Nurse Jennie, in the uniform she designed herself, seated (*centre*) among her staff aboard the expensively equipped hospital ship *Maine*, which she took to South Africa to help the wounded in the Boer War

Right: George Cornwallis-West, said to be one of the handsomest young men of his generation, who married Jennie in July 1900, ignoring severe family criticism and a twenty-year age gap

Below: Salisbury Hall, the country house George and Jennie rented near St Albans, north of London, as they could not afford to buy one

Jennie, in a large hat and fine dress, campaigning among working-class men in Oldham in 1900 on behalf of Winston. The *Oldham Daily Standard* reported, 'There are thousands of true hearts in this constituency which have a warm corner for Lady Randolph Churchill'

Jennie with Leonie and Porch on a visit to Castle Leslie, Glaslough, in 1918 where Porch planted a Glastonbury holy thorn. Ireland was deceptively quiet at the time, but the folly of British repression of the 1916 Rising had resulted in utter discredit of the Government and Sinn Fein was quietly preparing for overwhelming victory at the general election

The TATLER

Vol. LXVIII. No. 884.
London, June 5, 1918

REGISTERED AT THE GENERAL
POST OFFICE AS A NEWSPAPER

Price
One Shilling

Hugh Cecil, Victoria Street

LADY RANDOLPH CHURCHILL MARRIES AGAIN
(INSET, MR. MONTAGU PHIPPEN PORCH, THE BRIDEGROOM)

Lady Randolph Churchill's engagement to Mr. Montagu Phippen Porch was announced at the end of last week, and it is understood that the marriage will take place very shortly. Before she married the late Lord Randolph Churchill in 1874 Lady Randolph was Miss Jennie Jerome of New York. She subsequently married Mr. George Cornwallis-West, whom she divorced. Mr. Montagu Porch is the son of a Bengal civil servant. He served in the Imperial Yeomanry in the South African War and has been British Resident in Northern Nigeria

Jennie, aged sixty-four, with fashionable bandeau, makes the front cover of *Tatler* when her third marriage to Mr Montagu Phippen Porch (*inset*) was announced

Oil painting of Jennie, just before she set off on her round-the-world trip with her dying husband, by the American artist Ruth Payne Burgess (1865–1934), signed in the upper right-hand corner: 'To Lady Randolph Churchill, in fond memory, Ruth Payne Burgess Blenheim 1894'

Jennie with grandson Peregrine, Jack's son, who remembers his grandmother telling him the story of Wagner's *Siegfried* as she played the tune on the piano and ignored a luncheon party in the other room

Jennie's funeral in the small churchyard at Bladon, outside Blenheim, where her first husband, Lord Randolph, was also buried. That day, 2 July 1921, was stiflingly hot. Winston and Jack led the mourners. Oswald Frewen wrote in his diary underneath this picture: 'As Shane said, in very questionable taste for the press, but very useful for the family to have for a memento of the occasion . . .'

book. She was grateful for his prompt response. 'In my scribblings I will find my solace. God bless you, dearest. Never judge me harshly for with all my selfishness and faults I do love you.'[46]

And it was Winston, not her husband George, to whom she looked for practical advice while writing. Prompted doubtless by George's philandering, her mood in the midst of writing was one in which she felt a deep hatred of all men, 'who deceive from the cradle to the grave. They'll never change. I hate them all.'[47] She was a natural communicator and wrote as she spoke, while concealing her mood. But, untrained as a writer, she often struggled with this book. Sometimes she resorted to filling whole pages with entire letters, unedited and comment-free – a not uncommon practice at the time. 'My feelings fluctuate about it,' she admitted. 'Sometimes I think it is going to be splendid and then again I am most depressed.'[48] Her principal difficulty was ensuring that no one in her tightly controlled milieu would be offended.

'Do try and read my chapters at SH,' she urged Winston. 'The 3 will only take you an hour – if as much – I want you to add to the 5th chapter that story of your father and Goschen and the Exchequer. If told at all it must be well told – and I feel diffident – also, make a little note in the 4th as to where I can get some Irish data – that chap. is too short . . .'[49] Winston came often now to SH, as Jennie called it. He built himself a platform in a sturdy old lime tree at the back of the house where he could declaim his speeches to the birds and write undisturbed. But in the event he did not read his mother's chapters there as he was about to depart on a four-month official tour to Cyprus, British East Africa, Uganda, Sudan and Egypt with Eddie Marsh, his friend and assistant. Winston promised Jennie he would somehow find time to read her draft while away.

'I hate to think of your going off for so long – and that I shall not see you again before your departure. But you will enjoy it, and it will be a great rest and change . . . Mind you get Trevelyan's *Garibaldi* to read en route – also, *Memories and Impressions of George Broderick*,' she urged him.[50] She was, just as in old times, still the provider of his intellectual fodder. In return, he asked her to see about letting his house and sorting out other administrative chores on his behalf so that the expenses did not mount up in his absence. 'I do rely on you, dear Mamma, to help me arrange these affairs for which I am not at all suited by disposition or knowledge.'[51]

Having read the work in progress, Winston was frank in his comments. 'I do not think the Goschen story would be suitable for publication,' he advised her. 'It would cause a great deal of offence not only to the Goschens but to Jews generally. Many good things are beyond the reach of respectable people and you must put it away from your finger tips.'[52] Goschen, who had accepted Lord Salisbury's invitation to join his Ministry as Chancellor of the Exchequer when Randolph resigned, described himself as of German extraction, *not* as Jewish. But Randolph and Winston both had more finely tuned antennae than Jennie and her sisters where Jewish sensitivities were concerned.[*]

Jennie considered that her son's comments were 'a bit scathing about Chap V'. While insisting she did not mind, he was in fact the critic about whom she cared most and to whom she most wished to appear professional. 'I ought to have told you that V was quite in the rough, merely a lot of notes put together which Miss Anning typed in order that you might see them. In any case, I should never have sent the chapter to the Century [her US publishers] as you saw it. I have added a lot to Chap 4 and lead up to Ireland. The Century have now 4 chapters and I hope they will leave me in peace for a little,' she told him. 'Bless you, darling. Thank you so much for looking at my chapters and I forgive you for saying "Fie" to your loving mother.'[53]

He was soothing in reply and told her she must not take his criticisms personally. 'Literary judgements are not worth much, though they are worth nothing unless they are at once impetuous and impersonal. I am delighted to hear the political chapter was only in the rough. You have a great chance of making a charming women's book about the last 30 years and I do beg you to think . . . and banish ruthlessly anything that will hurt other people's feelings.'[54]

The Reminiscences of Lady Randolph Churchill, published first by Century in the US in 1907 and a year later by Edward Arnold in England, was politely reviewed, considered a pleasant if somewhat superficial insight into society, and went through several editions. The frontispiece pictured Jennie bare-shouldered, her hair curled and off her face, just a few pearls showing at the back of her neck, the famous dark flashing eyes looking seductive and the diamond star twinkling in her hair. The book, a bestseller, was dedicated to her two sons and she made clear in the preface that 'there may be some to whom these *Reminiscences* will be interesting chiefly in virtue of what is left unsaid'. She signed it Jennie Cornwallis-West and the story closed at the point of her marriage to George. He

---

[*] Presumably in the draft version of her memoirs, which has not survived, Jennie cast aspersions on Goschen's behaviour.

wrote that the book was 'cleverly but cautiously written, there was not a line in it to which any of her many friends could take exception'.[55]

Mostly Jennie received considerable praise. The *Morning Post* declared, 'there is not a dull page in them'. But, as she told her nephew Shane, with whom she had now established a warm and easy relationship, not everyone was happy with it. 'I received a letter the other day from an irate Irishman calling me an "antique alien" because I had said that "Paddies and Biddies" mustered strong on St Patrick's Day in New York.'[56] The reception from the critics was warm enough to convince Jennie that the literary life might provide a route which could keep her from the path of poverty. She was invited to do an American lecture tour, expanding on some of the stories in the book, and turned to the novelist Henry James for advice about this. He responded encouragingly, telling her that she should go as long as she had the stamina and was being paid adequately. But he warned her that audiences would want plenty of personal detail- material that she may have kept out of the book. 'That is really all they want and to look at you for all they are worth.'[57]

For whatever reasons, she decided not to go, although she needed the money more than ever. In the spring of 1908 Clara was enduring a further crisis as bailiffs were called in to Brede Place; all the furniture which Mrs Jerome had saved from the days of the Paris Commune was to be auctioned off. Jennie had enjoyed many a tranquil moment staying at Brede with Clara, where they comforted each other when both husbands were away. Now, as supportive as possible, she went to Sussex to bid for some of the more sentimental things, as did Leonie. Clara had pawned some of her jewellery before the sale but, as she wrote to Moreton, 'I shall see all my little treasures go one by one. Jennie says she will buy in a few small things for me if she can, but you know how hard up *they* are.'[58] A few weeks later there was intense happiness from a different quarter, probably a key reason why Jennie did not feel able to go on a lecture tour. By the summer of 1908 both her sons were married.

Jack was first. He had told his mother and George several months previously that he and Lady Gwendeline Bertie, known as Goonie, were very much in love and hoped to be married. But for the moment, until his prospects improved, he felt he could not discuss the matter with her parents. 'This is absolutely secret,' Jack wrote to his elder brother, then travelling around Africa. He asked Winston to write to Goonie, but to tell no one else. If her family suspected anything, her life at home (Whytham) would be unbearable, Jack insisted.

Goonie was the daughter of the seventh Earl of Abingdon, a Catholic family who were longstanding neighbours of the Marlboroughs at Blenheim. Nonetheless they considered themselves far more firmly rooted in the past than the *arriviste* Churchills. Goonie had known both Churchill boys for some years – indeed Jennie believed that Winston himself had had designs on her, an opinion shared by Goonie's daughter Clarissa, Lady Avon: 'It is quite clear that Winston was in love with Goonie when he was young.'[59] But, if he had been, he was the first to recognise how different he and his brother were in their ability to relate to women. Winston, lacking small talk, often appeared gauche: 'I am stupid and clumsy in that relation and naturally quite self-reliant and self-contained . . .'[60] Whatever Winston may once have thought about Goonie, he now wrote to his mother that Jack must be helped somehow in his marriage plans. 'How glad I am he had not married some beastly woman for money.'[61]

But money, or lack of it, was even more critical than usual for Jennie. As George's business failure was compounded by a financial crisis in New York, he lurched towards a physical collapse. His doctors ordered him to St Moritz to recoup. 'Unfortunately, owing to the expense, I have not been able to go with him – which is depressing for both as he feels ill and is lonely – and I hate being away from him, as you know.'[62] Of the two, Jennie was always the stronger, and her resilience at this time of crisis now made a strong impression on her future daughter-in-law. After a lunch together, Goonie described Jennie as 'a very wonderful woman and so philosophical . . . in spite of everything her spirit and vitality are wonderful. She never gives in – not for a single moment.'[63]

It was a shrewd assessment. Jennie was so short of money that she apologised that November to Winston for not being able to afford a cable for his birthday. It was, she knew, a 'strange fit of economy'. But she followed it up with another – giving up Salisbury Hall for a few months as it was so expensive to run, especially in the winter, and moving into the Ritz. On his return from Africa, Winston asked his mother to find some comfortable rooms temporarily for him there too.

And then, suddenly, everything she had worked for fell into place at once. Winston had already been rejected by three women with whom he had been in love: Pamela Plowden, Muriel Wilson (who was said to have concluded that he did not have much of a future) and the actress Ethel Barrymore (who believed she would not be supportive enough in his chosen field of politics). Now, however, encouraged no doubt by his younger brother's engagement, he met once again the beautiful if impecunious

Clementine Hozier and fell deeply in love. The pair had been introduced previously in 1904 at a ball at Crewe House. Winston, immediately struck by the young girl's luminous beauty, asked his mother who she was. Jennie was amused to tell him that she was the daughter of her old friend, Lady Blanche. But there followed a four-year silence. In March 1908 they met again, this time over dinner at the London home of Lady St Helier, the former Mrs Jeune, Clementine's great-aunt Mary and the woman who, through her friendship with Sir Evelyn Wood, had been so helpful in finally getting Winston his posting with Kitchener.

Lady St Helier's dinner at 52 Portland Place is one of those occasions which has since acquired semi-mythical status. Yet it so nearly did not happen. Clementine was invited only at the last minute because the hostess had a sudden cancellation and did not want thirteen at the table. She had had an arduous day teaching and had not wanted to accept, but her mother insisted she make the effort. Winston, overworked, had also nearly cried off, expecting the occasion to be a bore. But Eddie Marsh urged him on, reminding him of the debt he owed to Lady St Helier. Arriving late, he found himself seated between Clementine and the formidable Lady Lugard, the former *Times* journalist Flora Shaw. This time the chemistry worked between Clementine and Winston. Lady Lugard was ignored.

Clementine Hozier, although granddaughter of the Countess of Airlie, had grown up in an unconventional and austere household. Her bohemian mother had been a friend of Jennie's in the 1880s, but in 1899 Lady Blanche removed Clementine and her siblings to Dieppe when she feared her estranged husband might try and regain custody of the two elder children, whom he believed were his though they probably were not. Clementine was a stunningly beautiful young woman who had suffered loss and hardship from an early age. Her elder sister and beloved friend Kitty had died aged seventeen in 1900. Now her younger sister Nellie was suffering from tuberculosis and had gone to Germany for a rigorous cure. In these circumstances, Clementine's launch into society became a matter of the greatest concern, but there was no money for this. Lady St Helier took pity while Clementine, to make ends meet, worked as a French teacher and occasional seamstress.

Winston immediately asked his mother to follow up the meeting with an invitation to Salisbury Hall. Clementine and her mother were there the weekend of 11–12 April, the same weekend that Winston was at last given his first cabinet posting. The Liberal Prime Minister Sir Henry Campbell-Bannerman having resigned owing to ill health, Herbert Asquith formed a new government and Winston Churchill was promoted from Under-Secretary of State at the Colonial Office to President of the Board of Trade in the new Government. He was just thirty-three. As a result, according to the prevailing rules, Winston was required to fight a by-election. The contest, once again for North West Manchester, was lively from the start. Not only was Winston a target of the suffragettes, who repaired each night to a café where they plotted the downfall of Mr Churchill and determined 'to keep the liberal out'.[64] But there was competition for Jennie from the flamboyant Irish aristocrat Constance Markiewicz, who drove a coach and four white horses through the city to publicise the radical suffragists' cause. Churchill was defeated, but he was immediately offered a safe seat in working-class Dundee, which two weeks later he won with a handsome majority, enabling him to take his place in government. For Jennie, at last, her dream looked set for fulfilment.

On 8 August 1908, Jack and Goonie celebrated their wedding in Abingdon and, immediately that was over, Winston invited Clemmie, as she was always known, to Blenheim – his mother acting as chaperone. On that occasion he proposed to her and was accepted. The engagement was announced a week later on 15 August, while Winston and Clemmie were again at Salisbury Hall with Jennie. Violet Asquith, daughter of the new Prime Minister, writing to her friend Venetia Stanley, observed: 'He did not *wish* for – though he needs it badly – a critical, reformatory wife who would stop up the lacunas in his taste etc. and hold him back from blunders.' The remark was a clear indication of how uncritically adoring his mother had been.[65] Even more clearly, it showed that Violet had seen herself as that 'critical, reformatory wife' and was bitter not to have captured him.

Just four weeks later Winston and Clemmie were married, on 12 September, at St Margaret's Westminster, the parish church of the House of Commons. Guests were packed into the church and the newspapers, which had not missed an opportunity to report on every aspect of the preparations for the occasion, gave detailed accounts of the wedding itself. Jennie wore a dress of antique gold satin with wide metallic embroidery and a large hat of the same colour decorated with velvet and satin-petalled lillies. She had lost none of her ability to stun and, as she walked up the aisle on the arm of her younger son, could not have failed to hear the murmur of appreciation for her. Eddie Marsh describes her at this time as:

> an incredible mixture of worldliness and eternal childhood, in thrall to fashion and luxury (life didn't begin for her on a basis of less than forty pairs of

shoes) yet never sacrificing one human quality of warm heartedness, humour, loyalty, sincerity or steadfast and pugnacious courage. By the time I knew her the first volume of her beauty was closed but years afterwards she opened a second when she suddenly decided to let hair, waist, complexion and everything go, and became, in a day, one of the most beautiful human beings I have seen.[66]

Lady St Helier lent her London house for the reception and the honeymoon was spent in Italy and Scotland. The match may have been desperately romantic but the date had been fixed in order that Winston could be back at his ministerial desk by the time Parliament reassembled.

Winston wrote to his mother from Blenheim the day after the wedding: 'Everything is v comfortable here . . . and Clemmie v happy and beautiful. Best of love, My Dearest Mamma, you were a great comfort and support to me at a critical period in my emotional development – we have never been so much together so often in so short a time. God bless you.' He then added a postscript: 'I open this letter again to tell you that George said he could wish me no better wife and happier days than he had found in you. W.'[67] He wrote again while honeymooning to tell her: 'We have only loitered and loved, a good and serious occupation for which the histories furnish respectable precedents.'[68] He knew she would be happy to hear this.

'Worldly though she was and advantageous though it would have been for my father to marry a woman of fortune, from the beginning Jennie was quite simply delighted with Clemmie,' Winston's daughter Mary Soames declares.[69] As Jennie's friend, the Hon. Evan Charteris, told her: 'You have married your two sons in a way that wld make the mothers of most daughters green.'[70] He was right. They had each chosen two well-born, beautiful and supportive women. Goonie, in spite of her more conventional background, was the more free-spirited and artistic, Clemmie, the more serious-minded and ardent, with deeply rooted puritanical elements in her nature.

'The two sisters-in-law could not have been more different,' is how Clarissa, Lady Avon remembers it. 'My mother was much vaguer, everything flowed over her. Clemmie was basically disapproving. It's a miracle they got on so well.'[71] Both women were more Liberal than Conservative, with many friends in the Liberal establishment. At the time of their marriage, Clementine Hozier was the more politically aware, a passionate Liberal supporter, uninterested in social trivia and an excellent amateur tennis player. Later, Clarissa believed that 'Chartwell was run on what

Winston wanted and so Clemmie did not have a chance to have her own friends. Everything was centred around Winston's career. My mother was a strong character and did not subsume her life . . . my father was not friends with any of her friends.'[72]

Clemmie's mother's scandalous behaviour and reputation were, it is worth noting, of no concern to Jennie. She judged not. She viewed her daughter-in-law on her own merits as a woman of wisdom who would perfectly nurture her son's ambitions and emotional needs. She knew Winston was not easy, indeed she saw that 'he is very difficult . . . and she is just right', she told her friend Mary Crichton.[73] The Countess of Airlie, writing to thank Jennie for showing her granddaughter Clementine such a loving welcome, said, 'I hope she will be all you can desire as a wife for your son.'[74] To her daughter-in-law, Mabell Airlie, she wrote: 'Winston is his father over again, with the American driving force added. His mother and he are devoted to one another, and I think a good son makes a good husband.'[75]

But in her effusion Jennie overdid the welcome. While they were away on honeymoon she agreed to do up the small house, 12 Bolton Street, previously something of a bachelor establishment, which Winston had been sharing with his brother Jack. 'Her intentions were really kind but she wasn't very tactful and it was much taken amiss,' explains Mary Soames, who heard the story from her mother years later. She had 'set about the house with characteristic energy and perhaps rather too much zeal, and on their arrival home . . . Clementine was greatly surprised to find her bedroom completely redecorated'.[76] Jennie had, in a short time, arranged to have sateen and muslin covers made and trimmed with bows for the chairs, dressing table and bed. It was 'no easy matter, I can tell you, but I hope you will like it', she told Winston.[77] 'Mummy thought she had vulgar taste and the covers were very cheap and tawdry,' says Lady Soames, admitting that her mother's own taste was 'very simple, almost austere'.[78]

Although Clementine did her best to hide her lack of appreciation of Jennie's efforts, 'she was never to have a really close relationship with Lady Randolph', wrote Mary Soames.

> This once supremely beautiful woman was still, in her fifties, remarkably handsome; but, accustomed all her life to attention and adulation, Lady Randolph had now to accept a long, cool look from her newest daughter-in-law.
>
> As time went on Clementine came to salute her courage and her unfailing zest for life, now, in those early years of marriage, she passed (in her

heart) fairly severe judgment on her celebrated mother-in-law: she thought
her vain and frivolous and, in her marriage to . . . a man so much younger
than herself, somewhat ridiculous.[79]

Others concurred. 'I think Lady Churchill (Clemmie) thought she was
awful, to put a good face on it,' said Lady Montague Browne, who was
Clemmie's private secretary. 'I remember she was quite shocked by the
whole set-up of going for younger men and always demanding that people
were pulling strings on her behalf. She simply didn't like her and thought
she was a drain on family money.'[80]

Whatever they thought of her, Jennie was delighted with both daughters-
in-law. But her ambitious attempts to help Winston did not cease and
she was constantly inviting interesting people to dinner parties at 'little
Salisbury Hall'. In November 1908 she had Lord Crewe, Lloyd George,
Augustine Birrell and Winston – 'quite a cabinet council. In fact, they did
hold an informal one on the Irish question.'[81] Other dinners included one
to introduce Winston to John Galsworthy when the former was at the
Home Office and Galsworthy's play *Justice* a current success, and another to
introduce him to Ivor Novello, the composer.

As she took stock of her life, Jennie's natural love of drama – she had
after all grown up with a theatre in her house – spurred her on to try her
hand at playwriting. Wearing a costume and assuming another character,
thereby hiding her own feelings, was something she had done from an early
age. Ellen Terry wrote of her: 'Lady Randolph Churchill, by sheer force of
beauty of face and expressiveness, would, I venture to prophesy, have been
successful on the stage if fate had ever led her to it.'[82]

Writing a play brought her close to the theatrical world she adored.
It was not a completely new idea; in 1903, while staying at Blenheim
when George was away shooting in Wales, she had made a first attempt, but
gave up to write her memoirs. Now she was, as ever, motivated by the need
to earn money. But other factors played a part too. Pearl Craigie, possibly
Jennie's closest friend and confidante, had died in August 1906, a severe
loss. 'She had the rare faculty of making you feel at peace with yourself,
and inspiring you with unfailing hope,' Jennie wrote in a later essay on
friendship.[83] Jennie had published one of Craigie's plays in her *Anglo-Saxon
Review* and Craigie had written a novel, *The Vineyard*, whose heroine
was closely modelled on Jennie. Although Jennie set up a committee
to establish a memorial to Craigie, writing a play was in a way a more
sincere tribute.

Jennie may not have had a deep intellect but her interest in literary matters was not feigned. She engaged genuinely in the world of politics, music and letters and was constantly reading. In 1908 she was engrossed by *The War in the Air* by H. G. Wells, recommending it widely and believing it to be prophetic. 'I think of what may happen if these astronauts advance as they will.'[84] George believed she was a brilliant conversationalist because she remembered so much of what she had read. 'But she was not brilliant in the deepest sense of the word. She was not a genius.'[85]

Writing a play, if she could pull it off, would take her into a new league; it was a challenge she had been ruminating for some time. Now she had decided in earnest: she must have her work staged. She never found writing easy and in March admitted to Leonie: 'Sometimes I feel despondent and doubtful of my being able to make it a really good play. I should hate mediocrity.'[86] In May, having completed a draft, she sent it, as ever, to Winston for his comments. He was far from encouraging. He preferred the second half, telling her frankly:

> There are many criticisms I could make on detail and structure but I will keep these until the business of production has actually been undertaken, then I will give you any assistance in my power. I do not think that the work is sufficiently strong in originality of plot, in situation, in dialogue, or in characterisation to justify its public production. If a professional manager were prepared to risk his money on it I should gladly suspend my opinion in the face of such practical approval. As it is I can only wish you success, which I do in all affection.[87]

According to George, it was Jennie's idea to have Mrs Patrick Campbell, the most celebrated actress of her day, not only produce it but take the leading role. She and Randolph had been to see her in *The Masqueraders* in 1894, just as she was starting to make a name for herself. Beatrice Stella Campbell, as thickly raven-haired as Jennie, was a widow whose husband had been killed in the Boer War, leaving her with two children. She was (probably) eleven or so years younger than Jennie, beautiful and witty with a talent for playing complex and fascinating women. When Jennie told her that a London manager had offered to produce her play for £300, she was attracted to the idea of taking on the production herself because she knew that high society and royalty would take a close interest in it. But long before opening day, in spite of the professional cast, multiple weaknesses were all too apparent.

George later remarked that Mrs Pat became a constant visitor to their house in 1909 – one they had borrowed from the Asquiths in Cavendish Square – working hard at the play and, with help from the matinée idol

Henry Ainley, doing 'her best to make it a success. Had the original intention been adhered to and only four matinées given these would have paid for the whole cost of production as people flocked to see a play written by one brilliant woman and produced by another. But it was kept on and, alas, being an indifferent play, it was another instance of an unsuccessful enterprise.'[88]

His Borrowed Plumes, a play within a play, was highly autobiographical. Fabia Sumner, the heroine, is an authoress who leads a busy social life and needs to write to make money. Her husband, Major Percival Sumner, a comparatively unsuccessful author, is jealous of her success. But as Fabia admits: 'I feel I don't enter into Percival's plans and amusement. I believe my writing so much bores him.' She is finding it impossible to write under the strain. Bored and resentful, Percival begins an affair. Fabia is aware of her rival and of the subterfuge in which she is indulging, but hopes it will die a natural death. A friend warns her: 'You're so occupied you don't see what all your world does. Among snakes, that woman is a puff-adder.' Fabia replies: 'Are you so sure that I do not see – that I don't know?'

In the play everything ends happily, with Fabia and her husband declaring undying love for one another. In life, however, George was 'seriously attracted by me', Mrs Pat was to claim, and everything did not end happily. In her memoirs, Stella Campbell was scathing about the intrinsic merits of the play. 'Jennie, I fancy, imagined producing her play would be of some social advantage to us all: I was intolerant of what I thought was nonsense and showed it quickly.'[89]

Just before the play opened, as the pace of rehearsals quickened, Jennie allowed herself to feel – briefly – optimistic. She wrote to Leonie that 'Mrs Pat has really been an angel and the play would not exist without her – I can't understand why I feel so calmly about the play . . . perhaps I do not know the horrors before me.' She cannot have known that some of the cast had started calling it 'His Sorrowful Blooms'. She also told her sister that the Duke and Duchess of Connaught were coming to watch it in a few days' time. 'I am rather surprised that they have not invited me to tea or to come and see me. But, you know, I always thought that they did not like me overmuch. One in the family is enough.'[90] She was right. Jennie's loose tongue had often caused the deeply respectable Duke to fear for Leonie's connection to her more volatile sister. 'One of your greatest attractions to me', he had written to his 'Dearest Leo', 'is that you don't gossip.'[91]

Tempting fate, Jennie gave a small supper party at the Ritz. 'Too successful for words,' was her euphoric verdict. The party was a mixture of friends and actors, including Mrs Pat and her leading man, C. Matthews Milward, as well as Jennie's old adversary Gladys de Grey. Relations between the two women had improved by this time, and George and Jennie were frequent visitors to Coombe House, Gladys de Grey's home on Wimbledon Common where she held magnificent musical soirées. 'We kept it up till 2.30 – even Gladys staying – wild dances and fandangos, everyone taking the floor.'[92] If the play was a success, she told Leonie, it would come on again in the autumn.

His Borrowed Plumes opened on 6 July 1909 at the Hicks Theatre (later the Globe, now the Gielgud) in Shaftesbury Avenue. The house was packed with a glittering mixture of celebrities and aristocrats, including Earl Howe, Lord Elcho, Grand Duke Michael of Russia, Prince Francis of Teck and the young Lady Diana Manners. Winston sat in a box with his mother and stepfather looking, apparently, profoundly nervous – nervousness which only increased when it became clear that the acoustics were faulty. Despite the excitement surrounding the gala opening, it survived two weeks – not bad for the time – but was not strong enough to return in the autumn. It was not a bad play, indeed it was quite entertaining, as the critics agreed. But it revealed more about Jennie than about life. Max Beerbohm described it as 'very good entertainment . . . a story conceived and set forth clearly, without halting, with a thorough grasp of dramatic form. From the standpoint of a critic who desires an illusion of real life, it does not pass muster. The characters have been sacrificed to the story.'[93] Plays challenging traditional views of marriage and divorce and even female sexuality had been around for a decade or so and, compared with the scandalous reactions to Henrik Ibsen dramas,* His Borrowed Plumes seemed rather tame.

In the play Fabia says of her husband that, to ease his conscience, he likes to dwell on her shortcomings, and Stella would say later that her affair with George developed because 'I believed his life was unhappy and warmly gave him my friendship and affection.'[94] George was, as Jennie/Fabia understood, resentful of his wife's constant involvement in social, literary and philanthropic schemes that did not involve him. He felt at once dominated by Jennie and worried by her lavish spending.

Slowly, as it dawned on Jennie that writing plays, however much fun, operated as yet another drain on her resources, there emerged that year one more way of adding to them that capitalised on something she was unquestionably good at: spending money. She took to buying up houses

---

* Hedda Gabler was first performed in London in 1891.

and redecorating them with great panache. It was something she stumbled on almost by accident when the lease of the house next door in Great Cumberland Place became available. Winston encouraged her, commenting tartly that he did not believe in writing books which did not sell or plays which did not pay. 'The only exceptions to the rule are productions which can really claim to be high art appreciated only by the very few.'[95] He told her that he thought it 'very creditable indeed that you should be able to turn over as large a sum as a cabinet minister can earn in a year . . . there are lots of other houses in London and you will have learned a great deal more than you knew before of the latest methods of furnishing. I really think it would be well worth your while to look about for another venture of the same kind.' Finally, he said once again how sensible he thought she was to 'prefer a mind free from money troubles and petty vexations to the mere possession of a particular house. Not being a snail you can get on quite well without it.'[96]

In spite of her daughter-in-law's view, most of her contemporaries considered that Jennie had exquisite taste. As the observant Seymour Leslie recalled, she mixed this with an original approach to entertaining:

> Jennie's drawing room never has the chairs arranged except *en cercle*, the lighting is dramatic but one can't read by it, luncheon is usually late and one is half asphyxiated beforehand by the parlour maid burning incense in a large spoon. She has lovely bookcases but no readable books . . . indeed Jennie's 'interiors' were not adapted for cosy confessions but, in her perfect taste, set the fashion for houses fit to be photographed. Before the days of professional interior decorating . . . it was Jennie who swept away England's tablecloths and substituted mats on gleaming mahogany.[97]

Further bright news was that she was now a grandmother twice over. In May, Jack and Goonie had a son, John, and invited George to be godfather. Six weeks later, Winston and Clemmie celebrated the birth of their first child, Diana. But the happiness of becoming a grandmother, traditionally a time for reflection, forced Jennie to recognise with sadness the increasingly evident failure of her second marriage. And she was reminded of the pain of what might once have been by a brief exchange of letters she had at this time with Charles, now Prince, Kinsky following the premature death of his wife Elisabeth. Kinsky's had by all accounts been an unhappy marriage. But he replied coolly to her condolences, insisting, 'I should feel small before her indeed . . . if I was to give way,' and promised Jennie he would read her *Reminiscences*, which had by then been out for nearly a year.[98]

Ethel Smyth, the composer, was one of the few who understood how sharply Jennie felt the loss of this man's love. Jennie had introduced her to Kinsky when she had gone to work and study in Vienna, hoping that he might influence the right people on her behalf. 'I wish she had married Kinsky,' Ethel told Shane.[99] Had she done so, the real loser would unquestionably have been Winston. Her primary love would have found its outlet elsewhere.

13

Courage Enough to Fight my own Battle in Life

~

JENNIE HAD ONE final attempt to make money. From the depths of her private anguish she conceived her most grandiose scheme. It was the project that best defined her identity as a lover of English culture and history, yet perhaps it could only have been driven by an American. That she rose above the drama in her private life to create a magnificent public pageant drawing on English history and literature is a tribute to her enormous personal courage as well as to her love for her adopted land. Financially, it was a spectacular failure.

In May 1910, Edward VII died. Although king for only nine years, his influence had marked the parameters of Jennie's adult life. She had, with one notable interruption, always been an important and privileged part of his most intimate circle. From the moment he had first espied her at Cowes they had had an understanding with and of each other. She offered a heady mixture of daring and discretion, to which he responded. When he craved simple friendship towards the end of his life, she offered him that too. Few women understood him so well. On one occasion, when a hostess handed round hot soup at midnight, Jennie complained loudly: 'My dear girl, if you feed him on condiments he will never go.'[1]

As soon as the King's death was announced, the entire nation went into official mourning, and every social event of the London season was immediately cancelled. His body lay in state in Westminster Hall until the funeral on 20 May. Jennie wrote to Queen Alexandra with truly heartfelt pain of the 'terrible calamity which has befallen not only the Royal Family but the whole nation. Personally, I can never forget that for 35 years the King showed me and mine the greatest kindness and I look back on many pleasant memories. He was a great King and a loveable man.'[2] And then she and Leonie went to pay their respects in person, first to the Queen and then to Mrs Keppel, the ideal Edwardian mistress.

As London society closed down out of respect for the former monarch, George and Jennie were living mostly apart, their future uncertain. George had not yet taken up permanently with Mrs Pat, and Jennie was involved in various schemes. In April 1911, when the errant husband wrote offering to return, Jennie, following Winston's advice, told him he was welcome if he came back freely of his own will. But, as Clemmie pointed out, 'Unless he is going to be really nice and make your Mamma happy one wld think there might be little advantage in his coming back . . . if he does return after such a public desertion he will have to behave properly I suppose? . . .'3

However embarrassing his mother's marital difficulties must have been, Winston remained calmly supportive throughout this domestic crisis. Not only was he Home Secretary dealing with momentous issues of state but, during those months of 1911, he was called upon more and more by a Prime Minister (Asquith) often incapacitated by drink or other distractions, to introduce Parliamentary Bills or conduct negotiations. He never complained, never resented his mother's actions. Somehow he found the time to sort out her separation. 'I have advised my mother', he told George, 'not to seek by any means to renew relations with you after the way you have treated her for the last two years.' He insisted that, although she harboured no resentment against him, 'the public manner in which you advertised your desertion has created serious difficulties for both of you, quite apart from the unnecessary affront to her.'4 He told George there were various complex financial issues to be discussed, including the disposal of property, and offered to meet him when he was next in London.

He wrote to his mother the same day: 'I am quite sure it would not accord either with your dignity or happiness to seek by any promise of relations or circumstances to induce G to return to you. You would not wish to hold him in thralldom and such a condition could not last and would only be cruel to both of you.' An immediate disentanglement and rearrangement of her affairs before any further details leaked out about the rupture was in everybody's best interests. In the meantime he advised her not to write to George. 'There is great strength in silence and that strength is often proportionate to the difficulty of preserving silence.'5

Winston suffered for his mother. 'My heart bleeds for you and I am only trying to guide you upon the course which will secure the peace and honour of your life.' As ever, the immediate question was how Jennie would fund her living expenses. Winston reminded her: 'You cannot keep even the smallest household under £1,000 a year. This will leave you almost nothing for all the things you want to do. On the other hand if you can, at any rate for the present, abolish household expenses you will have more pocket money and more freedom than you have had for many years.'6

Clementine, then nursing her second child – a son Randolph, nicknamed Chumbolly and born in May 1911 – struck a mildly disapproving note. 'She believed Lady Randolph had been a bad mother and now she resented the way she leant so heavily on her elder son,' Lady Soames explains. 'It's no good pretending she did not feel that. They never had a classic falling out. It's just that [my mother] never joined in the chorus of praise for her mother-in-law.'7 One of the minor irritations felt by both daughters-in-law was Jennie's habit of buying herself designer gowns with magnificent hats whenever she went to Paris and bringing them each a cheap little concoction from Bon Marché. 'More suitable for the young,' she maintained. 'She never treated them as grown-up women as important as herself,' Anita Leslie observed.8 It was a strange lapse of sensitivity given the harsh treatment she had suffered from her own mother-in-law.

As Winston increasingly idolised his mother, Clemmie was slightly embarrassed by her and, as she saw it, by the way she tried to jockey herself into a better position:

> Your Mama came to see me yesterday . . . She is rather fussed about whether you can take her in my place (as I am going in the King's Box) to the Coronation [of George V]. She wanted to write and ask Lord Beauchamp about it; but I asked her to write and ask you about it first as I am sure it will be better if you arrange it. The Connaughts have offerred [sic] her a seat but I think she is waiting before answering in case the one you could get for her should be better.9

As Mary Soames comments drily, 'One notices veiled criticism of Lady Randolph's seat-bargaining tactics.'10

But Jennie's desire for a better seat was not mere snobbery. Her response to the crisis in her own life was to keep busy and, in the weeks before the Coronation, she was working frantically to organise a Shakespearean Ball on 20 June. This was part of an appeal she was helping to launch to raise money to build a National Theatre in London where high-quality productions, not necessarily dependent on box-office popularity, could be mounted. 'As things are in London the establishment even of a permanent repertory theatre is really next-door to impossible without official and national status,' she explained. 'The more I see of our theatres the more I am convinced of the need for a National School of Acting.'11 She was aiming to raise at least £10,000 to go towards buying a site opposite the Victoria and Albert Museum in Kensington, and she understood how crucial it was to have the royal family on her side.

Several noted hostesses were giving balls to welcome the new era, but none was as original or magnificent as Jennie's, nor inspired by such a purpose. 'She seems to be doing it very well but the work is prodigious and very thankless,' Clemmie wrote to Winston.[12] Jennie had persuaded Edwin Lutyens to transform the Albert Hall into a beguiling Elizabethan–Italianate garden where the six hundred or so guests, in the costumes of Shakespearean characters, could dance from 11 p.m. until 5.30 the following morning. Jennie herself went as Olivia and George as Sebastian from *Twelfth Night*, both of them trying for this event to put a brave face on their disintegrating marriage. Even King George V and Queen Mary graced the occasion, forty-eight hours before the Coronation.

Like everything Jennie did, no expense was spared to make the event compellingly authentic. The Albert Hall, under a fake blue sky replacing the dark redbrick Victorian roof, became a faithful reincarnation of Tudor England. 'Here were no tawdry stage costumes, no mere imitations of reality. Here was the real thing,' wrote the critic H. Hamilton Fyfe. 'Real satins and ermines, real silk and brocades, real gold and silver embroideries, real lace of the finest periods were cunningly employed to set off the beauty of the fairest women in England.'[13] There was clipped yew in the shape of topiary birds, twirling grapevine on the marble terrace and a balcony where supper was served. The night was a dramatic success. But it was only one night. The country's aristocracy and wealthy elite had enjoyed themselves, treating the high prices they had paid for a box as a donation to a good cause. Now Jennie was dreaming up something on a far greater scale with much wider appeal but with the same goal of promoting a Shakespeare Memorial and a National Theatre.

Coronation day, overcast and wet, came and went. In the event, Jennie sat with Mrs Keppel in the King's box, laughingly dubbed by many 'the King's loose box'. But for a moment in Westminster Abbey it seemed that Edwardian excess might continue in a different guise and that mumbled mentions of war with Germany might remain just that. Shortly after the Coronation Winston and Jennie went to stay with the American actress Maxine Elliott, who had recently moved to Hartsbourne Manor, near Salisbury Hall, and was a friend of both mother and son. Maxine not only fuelled Jennie's theatrical passions but she entertained a wide swathe of society in great style. 'Maxine is so nice,' Winston told Clemmie, who had stayed behind. 'She has a new bullfinch – arrived only last night and already it sits on her shoulder and eats seeds out of her mouth.'[14]

And so that summer Jennie devoted herself to thinking seriously about an ambitious scheme to stage an enormous exhibition at Earl's Court, a generally derelict area of west London, which boasted a large stadium but little else, to be called 'Shakespeare's England'. Again she engaged Edwin Lutyens, this time to rebuild Earl's Court 'into a wonderful OLD London of the Elizabethan period with the picturesque wooden houses of the time, the same quaint old streets – some of them only a few feet wide – and the same curious old world atmosphere of that epoch of chivalry and romance'.[15] Once again she hoped it might be financially profitable for her personally, as well as an important gift to posterity.

Rivalry with her old and formidable adversary Gladys de Grey, now Ripon, continued to work like a knife in an old wound. The day after Jennie's ball and the day before the Coronation, Gladys had staged the first performance of the Russian Ballet in London. On 21 June, Nijinsky made his debut on the London stage. He and his Russian troupe were a phenomenal success, magically lifting the spirits of the bored upper classes with every leap. Each performance of the Ballets Russes was a personal triumph for Gladys Ripon, but none more than the one given four days after the Coronation in front of the King and Queen, at which she swept up and down the aisle at the Opera House personally greeting as many members of the audience as she could.

In this atmosphere of torrid excitement for the new, Jennie immediately set about establishing an Organising Committee as well as an Executive Committee to speed up her own enterprise. But, as she wrote to remind her friend Edith, the Hon. Mrs Alfred Lyttelton, known as D.D., 'The fact that the scheme is mine in its entirety, and if it takes place I run it and am prepared to give four months of hard work, places me in a very different position than it would be if the exec or organising committees had originated it and merely asked me to manage it and accept a certain percentage.'[16] She knew the enterprise would involve a colossal amount of work and that a premium should be put on her creativity in initiating the idea and her ability, through her contacts, to see it through. 'Ten percent of the profits and not less than £500 in case of failure' did not seem exorbitant to Jennie.[17] All she wanted of the two Committees was their co-operation and goodwill while she ran the whole thing on her own and arranged her own guarantors.

D.D. was ten years younger than Jennie but moved in the same aristocratic circles and was especially close to many of the Souls. She harboured ambitions to write herself, although her first novel was not published until 1926, and she was a friend of both George Bernard Shaw and Mrs Patrick Campbell. In 1909 she had lobbied them and other theatrical friends suggesting that a National Shakespeare Theatre Association be formed and that members should contribute £1 a year. As the tercentenary of Shakespeare's death was approaching in 1916, various rival committees were being set up, each favouring their own pet scheme which would serve as a suitable memorial. Some proposed the erection of a statue, others an ill-defined Shakespeare temple.

Jennie was not the first to recognise the need for a National Theatre in the capital linked to the country's greatest dramatist – there had been one at Stratford, the Bard's birthplace in Warwickshire, since 1879. But in those days that was a rural outpost and a long distance to travel. It was Jennie who, in late 1911, following on from her successful ball, dreamed up a brilliantly imaginative idea to raise funds for a National Memorial Theatre, and she had enough experience of committees by this time to recognise the importance of running it herself. She now proposed an event that would last several months and cater for the public at popular prices. 'It could be run for the benefit of the . . . tradesman who hires his shop . . . to advertise and sell and the man who pays one shilling to come in and expects to get his shilling's worth. Neither, I expect, will be influenced by the fact that it is for the benefit of the National Theatre.'

D.D., with advice from her husband Alfred, kept pulling Jennie back to earth and reminding her that she must get estimates for the building works as well as for the wages of the employees and performers. Even so, she was 'convinced' that there was a lot of money in the scheme and told Jennie: 'I think if it is a success you ought to make arrangements at once to take it to America. It might go round to three or four big towns if you yourself would work it up – going beforehand and getting the people together . . . you would, of course, have your percentage on all these exhibitions and you might make a lot of money for yourself as well as for the fund.'[18]

Taking it to America was a step beyond Jennie's immediate thoughts. For the moment she needed to raise some £55,000 to build replicas of Tudor houses, the Globe Theatre and the Mermaid Tavern, all designed by Lutyens. She approached wealthy friends and her own bank, Cox and Co., which, after serious investigations, agreed to back the project up to £35,000. But another £15,000 was necessary and so Jennie asked a favour from George. She asked him to approach Mrs W. B. Leeds, widow of an American millionaire who had left her everything he possessed and who adored George. There were rumours that the couple were about to elope.

'I was loath to do so as I knew that money transactions between friends are, to say the least of it, undesirable,' George recounted. 'However I thought it over, studied the figures carefully, and came to the conclusion that, although there was an undoubted risk, if it was good enough for the bank with whom it was arranged that she [Mrs Leeds] should stand upon an equal footing, she might be justified in assisting my wife, whose friend she also was.' George went to Paris and Mrs Leeds came up with the cash. 'I am sorry to say', George added, 'she lost every penny but she paid her liabilities without a murmur and never once did she reproach me for the part I had played.'[19]

The day before the exhibition opened Jennie, who had worked unstintingly for the previous few months, hosted a vast luncheon party. 'She drew upon her friends from all classes of society,' wrote George; 'the idle rich, the Corps Diplomatique, the bar and the stage were all represented.' But no amount of grand luncheons could improve the wet weather that summer. The exhibition opened at the beginning of May 1912 with great élan and advertising; the sideshows were interesting and the restaurants good, the sixteenth-century dancing was lively and the sixteenth-century orchestral concerts, under the conductorship of Sir Henry Wood, authentic. The Banqueting Hall, where 'Queen Elizabeth' could be seen dining in state with her favourites and lovers, was imaginative and amusing. In spite of all this, 'Shakespeare's England' flopped. The event attracted few visitors, and, disappointingly, there was no question of sending it to North America, and no profit from which Jennie could take her 10 per cent.

'The Mermaid Tavern in the gardens was run as a club and Jennie roped in all her friends and her friends' friends to become members,' George explained. 'It contained a very good restaurant and a room where one could read the papers and write. It was well patronised and ought to have been a great success but, like everything else connected with this ill-fated exhibition, it seemed cursed by bad luck and resulted in a heavy loss.'[20] George, feeling excluded, was harsh in his criticisms and maintained that far too much money was lavished on the project, resulting in inevitable financial failure. Others concluded that the show was too sophisticated.

The high spot of the exhibition came on 11 July, when a re-enactment of a medieval tournament was held in the big hall, now laid out as the courtyard of a medieval castle. The jousting and revels, it was promised, would rival in every way the famous Eglington Tournament of 1839, while the costumes and armour of the competitors and the trappings of their horses would be historically accurate to the minutest detail. The lances, however, were made of papier mâché to ensure there were no casualties. The entire scene was advertised as outdoing in splendour and magnificence Henry VIII's Field of the Cloth of Gold. First there was a procession headed by trumpeters, Elizabethan courtiers and dozens of beautiful women, including Lady Georgiana Curzon, Lady Diana Manners, Violet Keppel, Mrs Raymond Asquith, Muriel Wilson and Victoria Sackville-West.

George and his two sisters all played a part, with Shelagh riding in the Ballet des Chevaux, Daisy leading the Parade of the Princess Errant and George in the train of Baron Ashby St Ledgers, Cornelia's son and Jennie's nephew, who was created baron in 1910 while his father Lord Wimborne was still alive. Among the many dukes, princes, counts and barons taking part was the widower Charles Kinsky, there for Jennie's sake. But even for this magnificent and truly historic event, given enormous advance publicity, the great arena was nearly empty. Afterwards, there was another ball, 'at which I regret to say there was more than enough room to dance', George concluded sourly.[21]

There was a small postscript indicating the sort of prank that exercised society at the time. The ninth Duke of Marlborough was ultimately declared winner of the Gold Cup at the 'Jousting the Tilt' competition, even though on the day itself the cup was presented to another knight, believed to be Lord Ashby St Ledgers. It was later discovered that an ineligible proxy, his younger brother Freddie Guest, had competed in his place.

The newspapers all gave the tournament extensive coverage, but that event alone, hugely expensive to stage, could not prevent the exhibition losing money overall. It also, finally, lost her her husband. She had brought in the enterprising producer C. B. Cochran, but even his professional touch could not staunch the flow. Jennie had thrown herself into the venture, thinking of little else for four months. It won her plaudits but no financial rewards. George, already estranged, now felt totally emasculated and, immediately after 'Shakespeare's England', gave up the marriage for good. Encouraged by Stella, he decided that he, too, could make money by writing.

But the protracted separation was proving painful for both Jennie and George. At the beginning of the year he had written that he had been on the verge of ringing her up once or twice – he was worried about the size of the household drinks bill – 'but honestly I don't think I could bear to hear the sound of your dear old voice just now'.[22] The next letter between them that survives comes almost a year later, in December 1912, when with great difficulty he wrote formally agreeing to part from Jennie. He added that 'neither of us wish to go through the terrible ordeal of parting and as, after all that has happened, we cannot go back . . . I can honestly say I have never done anything in my life that I so hated doing.' It was a pathetic letter. Describing Jennie as 'a splendid woman', he told her: 'If I have ever done or am likely to do anything in the world it has been and will be through your good influence. So far as the past is concerned it sounds silly to write this as I have done nothing beyond trying to make an honest living, still I know some of my best endeavours, thoughts and ideals have emanated from you.'[23]

Jennie replied from Coombe Abbey in Coventry, where she was spending New Year's Eve: 'Dearest George, I am glad that I was prepared for your letter – the blow falls hard enough as it is – but if this thing is to take place it can't be done too quickly now and we shall both be happier when it is over. Thank God I have the physical and mental strength and courage enough to fight my own battle in life.' Jennie, now almost fifty-nine, reminded him what a sacrifice she was making in giving him up, 'for I have loved you devotedly for twelve years . . . and this love will only die with me'.[24]

In 1913 the desperate letters started up again. Jennie had filed a petition for divorce on 20 January and the case was heard six months later on 15 July. Newspapers went to town, describing this American mother of a cabinet minister whose eyes were 'still sparkling with fire' and whose lips were 'full of character'. The grounds on which she sought divorce were that George had refused her her conjugal rights. The petition was undefended. But gossip was rife. The novelist Edith Wharton was one of many who wrote Jennie letters saying how sorry she was to hear of her troubles.

Sometimes Jennie found the wrangling overwhelming and, insisting that she was not unsympathetic, asked her solicitor to reply to her husband's letters. George, responsible for his wife's debts, found that with his business tottering he could barely afford to pay rent for himself. He told Jennie that he had given up his own rooms and was living with his sister Shelagh. 'Things are pretty black,' he told her. Nonetheless, he had paid all her bills with the exception of about £1,300, 'which was almost entirely for furniture and objets d'art bought comparatively recently. I had always understood from you that the lacquer furniture, Queen Anne settee and some other things were paid for by an exchange of furniture. Such I fear was very far from the case. I am in a very difficult position. I have nothing practically to live on except about £450 a year.'[25] Jennie was asking for £2,000 a year, which George balked at. 'Supposing £4,000 a year was the most I was making then you would be receiving, with your American income and the remnant of your English, more than twice as much as me, which is hardly a fair proportion.'[26]

By the end of 1913, with matters still unresolved, George warned that her demands were quite impossible for him. To comply would make him certainly a bankrupt unless he could raise a further sum within the next few weeks. But he promised her that 'if, as time goes on, I found myself in a position to make you a suitable allowance either through marriage or success in business, you know I would do so, but don't ask me to commit financial suicide. I will drink a silent toast to you tonight, dear Jennie . . .'[27]

Within a few days of receiving this, Jennie decided she could stand the tawdry squabbling no longer. Staying in the South of France with Winston and Clemmie at the villa of Bend'or, Duke of Westminster, George's former brother-in-law, trying unenthusiastically to write another play, she admitted she preferred letter writing instead. 'There's a piano and lots of books . . . we lead the simple life and don't indulge in much.'[28] She told Leonie that Charles Kinsky had sent her a Cartier clock as a Christmas present. She now instructed her solicitor to reach a compromise. She agreed not to issue any proceedings against George for alimony. In return he agreed to pay her, out of his net income, after first retaining the annual sum of £2,000, an annual sum of £1,000.

Even so George was, in March 1914, declared bankrupt with liabilities of £15,000 and assets of £900. The sad newspaper paragraph announcing that his creditors had met in the bankruptcy court that day was cut out by Jennie, dated, and kept among her papers. As well as losses in speculation on the stock exchange, George blamed the personal extravagance of his wife for his situation. According to some notes prepared by Seymour Leslie for Anita in September 1964, Leonie maintained that Jennie spent £5,000 a year on clothes. 'I find this incredible even for an Elizabeth Taylor,' he remarked.[29]

Throughout all of this Winston tried to be as supportive as ever. But, since his appointment as First Lord of the Admiralty in October 1911 his enormous workload and burgeoning responsibilities meant that he scarcely had time to see his own wife and two children. He and Clemmie did what they could to be with Jennie. When she accompanied them to the theatre in London that year, all three were attacked by suffragettes. Lady Randolph responded by telling the protesters that they ought to be 'forcibly fed with common sense'. Winston and Clemmie also invited her to join them on a marginally less fraught outing in May cruising in the Mediterranean on the battleship *Enchantress* with the Asquiths – H.H. himself, his wife Margot, and his daughter Violet. Watching naval exercises at sea provided a brief respite from haggling with George and from threatened bankruptcy proceedings at home.

From this point on it was largely Jack, now a successful stockbroker, who took over Jennie's financial affairs, adopting a more severe, matter-of-fact line with his mother. 'We have begged you so many times to live within your income, which is not a very severe demand,' he maintained.

Your income is larger than mine in most years and you have nothing whatever to keep up. Unless you are able to do so and if you start running up bills again then there is nothing that can save you from a crash and bankruptcy . . . if you will keep within bounds all these worries will pass and you will live in perfect comfort. Lots of others whom you know are in much worse positions than you,' he chided.[30]

There were further disagreeable and humiliating letters from her younger son discussing the minutiae of any likely action against George as there were several outstanding bills and writs taken out against him which could trigger his bankruptcy. Jack wanted to know whether a piece of jade, which he believed she had bought after the final separation, should be returned. 'You must decide all this yourself,' he wrote to her in France, 'but as it stands they will sue G and he will deny liability. If he loses the case I should think his bankruptcy will shortly follow. If he wins, the shops will sue you. I am not at all sure that your name is not already in . . . the only course open to the shops is to sue you both. You have the goods and both you and G deny liability. It is no good saying that he promised to pay. He has not got the money and his promises are of no value.'[31] Jack told her he thought she should come home and try to settle matters. Or at the very least go to Paris where letters could reach her. But he warned her that the most important thing was to keep these matters out of the papers.

Jack realised now that the sooner the decree was made absolute the better – although he still worried about how the outstanding bills would be paid. He repeatedly begged her to return to London, proposing that she might stay at the Admiralty, Winston's official residence, where they could then clear up the last of these tiresome things. 'Winston is writing to you,' he promised, 'but what with aeroplanes and estimates, which come on about the 17th, one can hardly get a word in edgeways with him.'[32] On 17 March 1914 Winston made a key speech in the House lasting two-and-a-half hours in which he defended the increase in Britain's naval expenditure by pointing to the upsurge in German and Austro-Hungarian naval construction. He was also busy taking flying lessons, a highly dangerous activity at this time. With tensions in Europe mounting, his ability to divert his thoughts to his mother's problems as much as he did, is impressive.

On Sunday, 4 April Jennie wrote with characteristic stoicism to George from the Ladies' Athenaeum Club, having learnt that the decree nisi would be made absolute on the Monday:

and I hear that you are going to be married on Tuesday. You must not fear what I say for I shall not willingly speak of you and we are not likely ever to meet. This is the *real* parting of the ways but for the sake of some of the happy days we have had together should you ever be in trouble and wanted to knock at my door it would not be shut to you. In returning to you my wedding and engagement rings, I say goodbye. A long, long goodbye.[33]

And on 6 April George married the forty-nine-year-old Stella at Kensington Register Office. She insisted that the speed was necessary because she was about to appear in Shaw's *Pygmalion*, written with her in mind. She also insisted that she was rescuing George from a very unhappy marriage. Yet both George's sisters were full of sympathy for their former sister-in-law. The divorced Shelagh wrote: 'Dear Jennie, I must write you a little line as I feel so much for you during this last year and especially by the announcement of last week. George must have been absolutely driven or, out of a sense of honour to you and us, he would never have acted with the indecent haste he did. Believe me, Jenny [sic], I knew all the time what you were going through and I admire what you did for him more than I can say. I hope we shall meet in the summer.'[34] Even Daisy wrote, predicting that George would regret his actions. Jennie had already made an announcement in the Court Circular that she would in future be known once again as Lady Randolph Churchill. That April she changed her name by deed poll.

But in 1914 Jennie's private grief had to be subsumed into the much greater tragedy of a nation at war. On 3 August Germany invaded Belgium; the next day Britain declared war on Germany. Jennie, having been kept in the know by her son, was hardly surprised. Jack was the first to be called up, into the Queen's Own Oxfordshire Hussars, and posted abroad with the rank of major. Just before he sailed, Winston organised a family photograph. Jennie, careworn, is seated between her two daughters-in-law, the four grandchildren Diana, Randolph, John and Peregrine, dotted among them. She had started to let her hair go grey and was looking her sixty years. She still had her admirers, but, at a sixtieth-birthday dinner, had admitted it was difficult to enter a room knowing that she was no longer the most beautiful person there.

Within weeks of war, the family was hit by tragic news. In October, Leonie's second son Norman Leslie, aged twenty-eight, was killed by a sniper's bullet in France. 'He could not have died more nobly and his name will live on forever,' his elder brother Shane wrote bravely to his father.[35] Leonie, who was in London when she heard the news, never fully recovered from the loss. Norman was her best friend, while Shane, suffering from mental instability, was always a source of great concern. But dignity in coping with grief was part of her Jerome inheritance. In those early days of the war, society was not yet accustomed to the heavy toll that would follow and the deluge of condolence letters indicated the devastation that greeted Norman's death. Shane set out on a pilgrimage to find his brother's body. Having identified him by touching a tooth he had broken on a billiard ball as a child, he put his remains in a coffin and ensured that he was given a proper burial. He cut off a lock of his hair for Leonie. Then he joined the ambulance brigade.

All three sisters suffered in different ways during the war. Clara's sons, Hugh and Oswald, enlisted in the Royal Navy; Hugh, returning home on leave, found that his marriage had collapsed and Moreton, short of money as ever, ranted and raged. Their daughter Clare had married Wilfred Sheridan in 1910 and was the mother of two children. In May 1915, Wilfred, at thirty-four, volunteered and was sent to France. Four months later he was killed, leaving Clare a widow with two small children.

Jennie helped her sisters, as well as her niece, through their problems. She took Clare to concerts and slipped her small presents and gave Leonie some clothes when she took Shane, who had suffered a second nervous breakdown in 1915, back to America. Leonie admitted that the journey home to England would be grim and lonely. 'However, I'm like you, luckily, and can always summon up courage.'[36] Jennie and Leonie had always supported each other in times of crisis. She had tried her hardest to give Leonie strength to understand her son Shane's conversion to Roman Catholicism and Irish nationalism in a positive light. He was 'quite delightful', Jennie told her sister, 'full of political ardour. My belief is you will find him in the House ere long. After all it's better for him to be a nationalist than a priest.'[37] Now, after a bitter and public divorce, it was Jennie who was left lonely and, unusually, lacking in courage to face the future without money or a husband. She hated having no one to accompany her to the theatre and sometimes resorted to taking her maid, Gentry. 'I wish we could see more of each other,' she wrote to Leonie,

> life is so short and we both so down the wrong side of the ladder! The fact is that we are both 'Marthas' instead of 'Marys' and allow things which do not really count to take up our time and keep us apart. We pander to the world which is callous and it only wants you if you can smile and be hypocritical. One is forever throwing away substance for shadows. To live for others sounds alright – you do, darling!! But what is the result? You are a very unhappy woman all round! As for me, every effort I make to get out of my natural selfishness meets with a rebuff. My sons love me from afar, and

give me no companionship even when it comes their way. The fault is undoubtedly with me. Every day I become more solitary and prone to introspection, which is fatal.[38]

Anita Leslie noted that Jennie was having 'a fit of the blues'. Others, less charitable, saw it as self-pity. Even her nephew Seymour, fond as he was of his aunt, was not impressed to find her often in tears when he called. 'No husband, no lover, she has become a trial,' he wrote ungenerously.[39] But Jennie's vitality needed others around her for it to flourish. She loved being *de toutes les fêtes* – a characteristic she recognised herself. She was very much 'up' in company and very low if alone. After Randolph's failure had become apparent, what kept her buoyant most of the time was the vicarious thrill and excitement she derived from Winston's political career.

Vittoria Sermoneta, the Italian duchess befriended by Leonie as well as Jennie, believed she took an interest in politics only for her son's sake, whereas her own tastes were 'frankly worldly'. But that is to overlook the much more turbulent years she had spent nurturing Randolph. For both mother and son there was a seamlessness in transposing the support from the one to the other. Jennie's immediate response in 1895, when asked for the return of the robes Randolph had worn as Chancellor of the Exchequer, was to insist that she was saving them for her son. Her unwavering support for him was to be tested constantly in the next decade. The way that support descended in a straight line from father to son is seen most clearly through the years of Irish Home Rule debates.

As a Tory, Churchill had opposed Home Rule. Yet by the time he spoke in Belfast in 1912 as a Liberal he said he supported it. He claimed to be doing this in the name of Gladstone and, at the same time, saluting the memory of his father, who had opposed Home Rule saying famously, 'Ulster will fight and Ulster will be right.' Winston was always keen to give the impression that he and his father were at one on this issue, although, as Jennie must have known, they were not. But he understood that Home Rule, as long as it remained subservient to Westminster, was not only possible it was essential for his own political survival. He favoured limited Home Rule for pragmatic reasons – to contain the powerful Irish voice abroad. He recognised that the Irish overseas, if allowed to remain an enemy, were a serious obstacle to his most treasured goal, Anglo-American friendship.

As soon as war broke out, the vital issue of Home Rule was postponed in order to deal with the more urgent task of fighting the Germans, even though the Irish nationalists raged at this. Jennie, who understood Ireland

from years of first-hand experience, was, as ever, completely behind her
son, even when his political opportunism threatened to bring her into conflict with the Protestant Leslies. She wrote to Leonie from her house in
Brook Street:

> Dearest Sniffy, I suppose you will have been following the Home Rule
> debate in the House. I can't see that putting the two bills on the statute book
> is going to make any difference if they are not in operation until after the
> War and then only after an amending bill and a General Election. I had
> Winston for a moment yesterday and asked him what he thought about it.
> All he said was that Bonar Law's speech made him 'sick' and that 'They',
> meaning the opposition, were so stupid it was incredible.[40]

Sporadically, for much of the war, Jennie corresponded with Shane about
the Irish situation. She told him she believed the Catholics were going to
play the right game. 'I believe Sinn Feinism will give Home Rule to
Ireland. How I wish we could collar those 200,000 well drilled young S.F.'s
and send them to the front. I must write to you again on the Irish situation.
There is so much that can be done but not complete separation – that
would be folly and ruin.'[41]

As a former editor of the Washington-based journal *Ireland*, Shane was
well placed to give his aunt, who he hoped would be a conduit to his
cousin, information about the views of American Catholics and the
Church, 'which here is more than a sect, it is a section of the country. It
counts one sixth of the population and one third of the forces so the car-
dinals tell me. Tell Winston', he wrote in December 1917, 'the Irish
convention *MUST* be a success. It would be fatal for Parliament to tinker
with any result they reach . . . a success . . . will certainly improve the war
outlook here.'[42]

But the real tragedy of the war for Jennie was Winston's treatment over
Gallipoli. In the spring and early summer of 1915, Britain and its Allies,
in response to a request from Russia, decided to attempt to push through
the Dardanelles and reach their troubled ally in the east. Control of the
Dardanelles would allow the Allies to get supplies to Russia's Black Sea
ports; it was also hoped that the attack would lead to an assault on the
Turkish capital, Constantinople, and so force Turkey out of the war and
attract new allies in the Balkans. But the Dardanelles operation proved
a bloody disaster, a tragedy for which the First Lord of the Admiralty had
to take responsibility and which was to haunt him ever after. The Turks were
better prepared than expected for the assault landings, however daring,
and the Allies were unable to push inland. By the end of the year Allied

casualties were so heavy for no conceivable advantage that the decision was taken to evacuate.

The failure of the campaign sparked enormous criticism, much of it directed personally at Churchill, a verdict history has tended to support. He was removed from office in May, and given the token post of Chancellor of the Duchy of Lancaster (a ministerial position without responsibility for a government department). There survives a graphic account of Winston at this time, showing his absolute conviction, unstintingly supported by his mother, that the battle had never been fought to the finish. Jennie invited the influential war correspondent Ellis Ashmead-Bartlett to dinner at her house on 10 June to meet Churchill, who then insisted that he brief the Prime Minister at No. 10. Ashmead-Bartlett wrote of how Churchill 'suddenly burst forth into a tremendous discourse on the expedition and what might have been, addressed directly across the table in the form of a lecture to his mother, who listened most attentively. Winston seemed unconscious of the limited number of his audience.'[43]

When Winston left the Admiralty, looking ill and worn, Clemmie, quietly supportive, was worried that the strain might break him. 'I thought he would die of grief,' she said later.[44] Jennie, on the other hand, reacted with fury on her son's behalf. 'I went yesterday to the Farm [Hoe Farm in Surrey, rented by the Churchills at this time] to see the family. I motored Winston down. I'm afraid he is very sad at having nothing to do. When you have had your hand at the helm for four years it seems stagnation to take a back seat and for why? NO fault can be found with his work at the Admiralty yet they give him the sack . . . it makes my blood boil!' she wrote to Clara.[45] There is no clearer indication of the intimacy in their relationship than the way Jennie immediately and fiercely rallied to her son's defence at this low point in his life. She had defended him before, but this time was different. Although he needed Clemmie's support too, there is a sense that he really needed to know the strength of his mother's bitterness and to realise that she, above all, saw how cruelly he had been treated. It was not so different from his need to make his mother suffer from his perceived neglect as a schoolboy.

In July he was asked by Kitchener to visit the Dardanelles and give an up-to-date assessment. But the proposal was vetoed. Jennie, again, was 'furious about his being prevented from going there – so am I . . .' Jean Hamilton, wife of Major-General Sir Ian Hamilton, in command of the Allied Expeditionary Force, confided to her diary. 'Winston is Gallipoli's best friend and I fear some devilry is afoot.'[46] To Leonie a few weeks later in October, Jennie wrote:

This slow and supine government are now beginning to realise what Winston has preached for the last six months. If they had made the Dardanelles policy a certainty, which they could have done in the beginning, Constantinople would have been in our hands ages ago. In confidence, it is astounding how Winston foresaw it all. There is a minute of his written at the beginning of June in which he warned the Government that Germany will not bring back troops from Russia to the West but will [be prepared to] lose them to march through Serbia, having reduced Bulgaria. But nothing will make them listen. Winston is on the warpath.[47]

When on 11 November, Asquith formed a new inner War Committee of five members, Winston, who was not included in it, offered his resignation from the Government. He said he did not feel able in times like these 'to remain in well paid inactivity'.[48] Had he stayed, as Jennie clearly understood, he would have been directly responsible for the conduct of the war. He wanted to get out of England. And so, later that month, he decided to join his regiment at the front and, as Major Churchill of the Oxfordshire Yeomanry, sailed for France, widely condemned. One or two voices were heard to support him, such as the *Daily Mirror* of 16 November, which commented: 'He is not afraid of much.' A dramatic picture of Jennie just before Winston left is given by Max Aitken (later Lord Beaverbrook), the Canadian newspaper proprietor. He called on the Churchill household to find it 'upside down while the soldier statesman was buckling on his sword. Downstairs Eddie Marsh was in tears. Upstairs Lady Randolph was in a state of despair at the thought of her brilliant son being relegated to the trenches.'[49]

Yet, in spite of this moment of weakness, Jennie was never lost for courage as far as Winston's physical safety was concerned – believing, as he did, that it was his destiny to survive. 'Please be sensible,' she wrote. 'I think you ought to take the trenches in small doses after ten years of more or less sedentary life – but I'm sure you won't "play the fool." Remember you are destined for greater things ... I am a great believer in your star.'[50] In December 1915, with Jack and Winston both away at the front, Jennie went to live temporarily with her daughters-in-law at 41 Cromwell Road. Clemmie and her children had already moved in with Goonie and her two sons and a couple of servants. For Jennie it was an economy measure, but, given that she would have required at the least her own sitting room as well as a bedroom, it was a good illustration that they could all get on if they had to. Clemmie, now that Winston's salary had been halved, was grateful for the 'generous' contribution Jennie made, of £40 a month. 'I am so glad my Mother has contributed to Cromwell upkeep,' Winston told her. 'She has a heart of gold.'[51]

Jennie survived such difficult moments through pride in her son's abilities and a fury against the Government. Winston, however, urged her to moderate this anger, telling her that she was 'quite right to keep in touch with our friends, also with our pseudo-friends'. But he added a cautionary note: 'My attitude towards the Government is independent, not hostile, & yr tone shd be salt not bitter.'[52] She admitted to Leonie that she was 'jumpy' when she heard that Winston had been offered a battalion, the 6th Royal Scots Fusiliers, which would be in the fighting line, and that his orderly had been killed when a shell exploded in their trench as they stood near to one another. But then she could not resist bragging to her sister that a paper on trench warfare Winston had written was so good that it had apparently been circulated to all the officers at the front.

All Jennie's friends remember how she used to speak glowingly of Winston's achievements and to walk arm in arm with him even after his marriage to Clemmie. 'She had unswerving faith in his capacities and was absolutely certain that everything he did was right,' according to Vittoria Sermoneta. 'I remember her saying once "Winston's shoulders are broad enough to bear any burden."'[53] Nonetheless Winston's resignation and what she perceived as his subsequent shabby treatment by the Government were all too painfully reminiscent of what had happened to Randolph, for whom it had signified the end. It was in both their minds.

Winston wrote to his mother that he had thought a lot about his father on 24 January, the anniversary of his death, wondering what he would think about it all, but concluded: 'I am sure I am doing right.' He assured her that he faced only the ordinary chances of war and that 'she should not worry at all at the dangers when they come. I only fret when I think of the many things that ought to be done and my real powers lying unused at this great time.'[54]

Churchill remained in France until March 1916, when he asked to be released from the army and returned to Westminster. As ever, Jennie put on a brave face. 'Winston is writing a lot and painting very well in his leisure moments,' she reported to Shane.[55] But she knew only too well that he was in despair, a despair she shared totally with him, convinced that the Government would never employ him again. As she admitted to her nephew: 'I grieve to have him out of office in these strenuous times. He has been sacrificed to the jealousies and ineptitudes of the third class intelligences which compose the majority of the coalition government.' She reserved most of her fury for 'the disloyalty of Asquith. I do not hold a brief for Haldane* but the cowardly way he was abandoned by the G[overnment] is only equalled by his throwing Winston to the wolves. History will get at the truth and Asquith will be judged as he deserves. Meanwhile to stay in at any cost is his sole consideration . . .'[56]

Clemmie slowly began to modify her earlier view of Jennie. She came to admire her mother-in-law in these difficult years when she saw at first hand her brave response to the myriad worries that beset her. 'Your poor Mama is ill,' Clemmie wrote to Winston in April. 'She has had a toe (which was much inflamed) cut off and she is in great pain. So write and comfort her. Also, burglars have stolen all her pretty trinkets, valuable and personal things she had collected all her life. It is cruel.'[57] Her new house, 8 Westbourne Street (Brook Street had been sold for a good profit and she was in the process of getting rid of this one too), had been burgled. She responded philosophically, telling Seymour that 'that burglar relieved me of an obsession. For years I've had to take houses big enough to hold all these bibelots; I am almost grateful to him.'[58]

Doing up and selling houses had become an occasional but helpful source of income for her. Some of her most successful interior-design schemes relied, like her, on a mixture of good taste and effervescent personality. She liked yellow curtains, unusual in those days, to harvest the light, and her use of place mats on highly polished mahogany tables no longer covered with old-fashioned lace tablecloths, was considered revolutionary. But she was best known for her suggestion in a letter to the newspapers at the outbreak of the war that male household staff must be released to join up, declaring her preference for parlour maids – 'footwomen' as Winston called them – 'never before seen in Mayfair but henceforward carrying no social stigma'.[59] She could be very funny when she wanted, and these women – dressed in a bizarre uniform of smart swallow tails and evening waistcoats with white shirt fronts and collars and black ties – certainly provided her with material for jokes. She liked to tell the story of how Winston, gazing at one, asked, 'Does that *glorious* creature bring in the beef?'[60]

Like everyone, she found the air raids disturbing. But not everyone managed to continue with a social life in the way Jennie did, albeit in reduced circumstances. She often went to classical music concerts which continued defiantly in the war-torn capital, and still dined at the Ritz. When

---

* Lord Haldane, a close friend of Asquith, had been forced to resign as Lord Chancellor in 1915 after being falsely accused of pro-German sympathies.

bombs fell on the square near Cromwell Road her thoughts flew to her daughters-in-law but the grandchildren were, mostly, safe in the country. Writing to Shane when she was in Dorset visiting her former sister-in-law Lady Wimborne, she felt a need to explain that she was not there to escape London raids, 'although having been in them all up to now I have had enough of them . . . I was at the opera one night when the [anti-aircraft] guns overpowered the orchestra and the bombs fell quite close but no one moved and the music and the singers went on calmly.'[61] Sir Thomas Beecham was conducting 'better than ever', she coolly observed.

Another time, when she went to stay with Claude Lowther, an eccentric collector, at his 'divine old Palace', Herstmonceux Castle in Sussex, she admitted that she was avoiding the bombs. She heard about the Zeppelin raid from her maids, who telephoned her. That particular visit was special because Winston and Clemmie were also there and because Winston had taken up painting. It is generally agreed that, after his departure from the Admiralty, Goonie was the one who encouraged him to paint. Winston himself writes of 'the muse of Painting' coming to his rescue 'out of charity and out of chivalry, because after all she had nothing to do with me – and said "Are these toys any good to you? They amuse some people."[62] But Jennie, too, had always painted and had found it a solace in the long days of worry over Randolph. When Winston was a small boy he had accompanied his mother to her painting lessons with Mrs E. M. Ward. Jennie discussed his talent with John Lavery, the fashionable Belfast-born artist also married to an American beauty, the former Hazel Martyn. According to Jennie '[Lavery] says that if Winston cared to take painting up as a profession he could, but of course he uses it as an opiate.'[63] Goonie may have been the catalyst, but the muse was a more complex being.

Another of Lowther's guests on that occasion was Violet Asquith, who left a vivid record of Winston's gloom and Jennie's liveliness. At dinner it was Jennie who was 'chattering briskly' after they had all recovered from the shock of a vast ram with muddy hooves roaming through the rooms of priceless furniture and objets d'art. As it broke into a sudden canter and nearly knocked her down, she screamed, 'What is this animal doing here?'[64]

It would be easy to give the impression that the First World War was nothing more than a series of inconveniences for Jennie. But she and Leonie wanted to be of service, on their own terms, and applied to the War Office to undertake 'War Work'. They hoped their fluent French might make them useful as translators for generals. But women of their age and

social class were not in demand. The only vacancies were for women prepared to wash dishes in the soldiers' canteen at Victoria Station. Leonie, at
first, found that handing out cups of tea to men just leaving for the trenches
was a good way to sublimate the pain of Norman's loss. 'This was the real
thing. The back breaking work helped me,' she said.[65] Then she ran a
Belgian refugee camp in Ireland. Maxine Elliott similarly organised a relief
barge from which she gave food and clothing to refugees.

Jennie was different. When Eleanor Warrender, who had been such a
stalwart support on the *Maine*, lunched with her at the beginning of the
war on her way to do nursing in Belgium, Jennie realised how lacking in
purpose was her own life. While Eleanor, who never married and was
to be awarded the Croix de Guerre, devoted herself to a life of service,
Jennie turned to what *she* did best: organising others. She threw herself into
raising money for the American Women's War Relief Fund and became
chairman of the Executive Committee. She also became honorary head
matron of a hospital in London at Lancaster Gate near her home, where
she went regularly. Then she helped to persuade the millionaire Paris
Singer, of the sewing-machine dynasty, to allow his magnificent home,
Oldway House at Paignton in South Devon, a building modelled on the
Palace of Versailles, to be used as a 250-bed hospital. Even the rotunda was
converted to house rows of beds for the wounded soldiers being brought
back to England from the trenches. The fund also provided motor ambu-
lances for the front, clothes for refugees, employment for women and
famine relief for Belgium. Jennie toured barracks and hospitals hoping to
entertain the troops by accompanying her friend the soprano Lady Maud
Warrender (the sister-in-law of Hugh and Eleanor) on the piano and was
scornful of the 'pseudo-benevolence' of various Lady Bountifuls who liked
to offer rides only to soldiers with visible bandages.

What she enjoyed best most days was writing, but she had to scratch
around to find work. 'Here we are anticipating a dreary and hard winter,
taxed out of existence,' she wrote to Shane at the beginning of the war.
'Out of the fullness of your literary knowledge can't you find me a review
or newspaper which would pay me well for a few idle remarks?' She
explained to him that she was trying not only to sell her house but to 'li-
quidate generally. I am disappointed that my contract with Harpers came
to an end. It meant a good deal to me.'[66] She sent him a collection of her
recent articles written for *Pearson's Weekly*, appealingly confusing her title,
'Great Talks on Small Subjects – no, Small Talks on Great Subjects'. And
in 1916 *Pearson's* also published *Women's War Work*, a book of essays which
she edited and for which she wrote the preface. 'One of the best forms of

excitement known by all who do good work is to see it grow out of their labour and their inspiration,' she concluded. It was a maxim she lived by.

Jennie's views on women's suffrage, like those of hundreds of others, matured during the war. She now praised the way the suffrage societies called a halt to campaigning for the vote and threw themselves into active service for their country. She told a *New York Times* reporter in 1916 that the war would advance the position of women in society by making many women unwilling to return to a sense of 'uselessness' and 'pleasure-loving lives'. She believed that relations between the classes had improved during the war as all mothers waited with anguish for vanished sons. She recognised that war work had brought to an end lower-class women's tolerance for serving as domestics and that after the war they would seek higher-paid factory work. 'It is my opinion', she said, 'that after the war women will be given the vote without much opposition and dozens of men who in the past opposed the idea agree with me upon this subject.'[67]

She declared in the book that 'it is a source of pride to me personally that the women of America have proved . . . "that their hearts are always ready to respond to the call of suffering humanity". The record of what they have done not only in England, but in other countries, speaks for itself.' But privately, to Shane and others, she was deeply critical of America, which she wished had been prepared militarily and emotionally to enter the war sooner. Her patriotism by now was entirely English. England, she believed, would be 'the greatest nation in the world when the War was finally over. Yes, I'm not excepting America for she missed her chance of coming out as a nation. Not that I really blame the US for keeping out of the war but the consequences will not tend to glorify the state.'[68]

Jennie had not lived in America since she was a child. She used occasional American expressions such as referring to a male friend as a 'beau'. But over the years she had rarely felt American other than when it suited her, at the head of a committee of other American women. Winston also had ambivalent feelings about the country at this time. It had, from the first, thrilled and excited him. He recognised that it was a 'very great country . . . Not pretty or romantic but great and utilitarian,' and always urged the closest co-operation militarily with the United States. When America finally entered the war in April 1917, he wrote to fellow MP Sir Archibald Sinclair that America, 'dear to your heart and mine, is please God, a final makeweight'.[69] But a few years later he said to Clemmie that he found it 'uphill work to make an enthusiastic speech about the United States . . . when so many hard things are said about us over there'.[70]

Meanwhile Jennie was again corresponding regularly with Eleanor's brother, her old friend Hugh Warrender, who had been posted to the front. She had been knitting him a muffler, until he asked her not to bother. There had been rumours for some time that Warrender, who was to end the war as a lieutenant colonel, wanted to marry Jennie. According to the *New York World*, She had paid him so many visits at his house in Pinner, Middlesex that friends believed an engagement was imminent.[71] Winston, the article claimed, opposed the marriage, fearing that it would give 'an air of levity' to the family which might interfere with his own prospects as a serious politician. Warrender's surviving letters to Jennie reveal deep friendship but lack passion. They are full of details about the horrors of trench warfare, and express his sadness at the death in January 1917 of his brother, Vice-Admiral Sir George Warrender, husband of Jennie's friend Maud, and the losses suffered by his own battalion.

14

Putting My Best Foot Forward

~

JENNIE DID, HOWEVER, have a new young male admirer at this time, Montagu Phippen Porch. She had met Porch before the war in 1913 at the wedding in Rome of her nephew Hugh Frewen – a meeting for which Winston was, inadvertently, responsible. Hugh, in desperation at the way his father had used up his inheritance, had written to Winston, then Colonial Secretary, for help in getting a job. Winston introduced him to Sir Percy Girouard, who took him to Nigeria as his private secretary, where he met Porch. After the wedding, Jennie spent a happy few days in the Italian capital, showing her new friend her favourite Roman sights. Twenty-three years younger than she, he was immediately love struck.

Porch, known to the family as Porchy, came from a family of landed gentry in Somerset with private means. After Oxford he joined the Imperial Yeomanry as a trooper and served in the South African War. But in 1906, when his future stepson was Under-Secretary of State for the Colonies, he applied to join the Foreign Service and was sent out to Nigeria. He was not highly thought of in London, having been blamed for using unnecessary military force to collect tribute from the natives. The Resident reported that he was 'excitable, highly strung, disliked by the natives and unpopular with brother officers'.

Brought back to London in 1908, he convinced the authorities that he had acted in good faith and persuaded them to allow him to go back once more to Nigeria. But his career was damaged and from now on he merely oversaw construction projects. However, when war broke out in 1914, he found himself involved in military activity as an intelligence officer in Africa. When he next had leave, in 1916, he determined to seek out Jennie and ask her to marry him. The letters continued and in early 1918 Jennie took him to meet Leonie at Glaslough. He planted a Glastonbury holy thorn in the grounds which he had brought from his home, proposed once again and Jennie agreed. She was lonely and knew she could not rely on her sons to fill the vacuum. Her exuberant spirit required that she still engaged with life. She was not ready to sink into grandmotherly obscurity.

Jennie always made clear that she would not take Porch's name nor would she live in Africa; perhaps he hoped she would change her mind in due course. She was certainly considering a visit as several of her friends warned her of the dangers of mosquitoes. The most important thing was to win over her two sons, and as soon as she had decided to marry Porch she wrote to them. Jack was shocked. He had never met the man and could not recall his mother ever mentioning his name. 'Whenever I go to a war you do these things.' But then he softened and, writing from British Headquarters in France, told her he was sure she had thought it out carefully, that he recognised how lonely the last few years had been and that as long as he made her happy 'we shall soon be friends'. He added warmly that nothing she did could 'make any change in our love for one another'.[1] Winston too, according to Porch, said he was 'very surprised' at having such a young stepfather for the second time.[2] But he made no public comment.

Jennie and Porch were married on 1 June 1918 at Harrow Road Register Office. Porch knew how important it was for Jennie at this time to marry a soldier, partly to please her two sons. The situation in Europe was still causing anxiety and the outcome of the war far from certain. As she had written in the preface to *Women's War Work*: 'When the world is convulsed by war, the most violent of human activities, it is only natural that the soldier, the embodiment of that activity, should occupy the foremost place in people's minds, and that patriotism, which takes the form of fighting, should make the most direct and universal appeal to sympathy and help.'

Porch found an officer's uniform and signed the register as 'Lt – West African Frontier Force'. Next, Winston signed as a witness and, turning to the groom, said warmly, 'I know you'll never regret you married her.' ('I never did,' Porch declared many years later.)[3] When photographs of the happy couple reached Porch's superiors in Nigeria, there were threats that he might be prosecuted for wearing a uniform to which he was not entitled. Porch defended himself by saying that Jennie had insisted, which was probably true. She had a weakness for men in uniform. He took Jennie to Bath to meet his mother, who had not attended the wedding. He also wrote to his new stepson, Winston, saying how incredible he found it that he should be allowed so much happiness when the world was in such turmoil. 'I love your mother,' he went on. 'I can make her happy – her difficulties and obligations from henceforth will be shared by me – so willingly.'[4]

Montagu Porch was a beautiful man. But that does not begin to explain why Jennie for the second time married a man young enough to be her son. One possible explanation is that she wanted to show Winston that he would always be the number-one man in her life. Thus she could never marry anyone who would threaten his dominant position. Perhaps also, however unconsciously, she was searching for a lost youth, compensating for the disappointing relationship she had endured with Randolph. Although she would have been prepared to lavish all her love on Winston, he was increasingly in demand elsewhere and not available to her. With Winston so preoccupied, at least she would not be alone.

London society – as well as embassies around Europe – made much sport out of the marriage. Lady Cynthia Asquith, daughter-in-law of the former Prime Minister, wrote in her diary for Sunday, 2 June that she had heard Jennie 'was not in love with him but suffers very much from loneliness and wishes for a companion. He apparently had been madly in love with her for five years.' She quoted Jennie as saying 'he has a future and I have a past so we should be all right'. Lytton Strachey, who met her within weeks of her wedding, found her an 'amazing character, tremendously big and square'. After chatting 'for hours', he described her as 'a regular old war horse, sniffing the battle from afar. She was dressed in a very shabby grey dress, which she from time to time rearranged with an odd air of detachment.'[5]

Sunny Marlborough wrote to his lover and future wife, the American Gladys Deacon, more revealingly at the same time. 'It is said that Jennie looked worn out after 3 days of Porch. Th [Theresa?] Londonderry met the Porches at the opera, seized on the man, gave him ½ hour of her chatter, explained to him Jennie au fond . . . then said but why the ring? How furious these old cats must be to find that the eldest of their gang can get hold of a ring.'[6] Two days later he wrote confirming that 'Porch is physically in love with Jane and she shows signs of his attentions. Apparently at 67 she can still create carnal desires among several men.'[7]

Years later, long after Jennie's death, Ethel Smyth was to write:

> that she should again have married a young man and this time pulled off happiness *enchants* me! No one but she would have dared fate to do its damnedest in such a way once more . . . I believe that till her untimely end she was as happy as one of the most delightful and loveable of women deserved to be . . . what I so deeply admired in her – the impossibility of squashing her spirit, her resilience. Who but she would pluck the flower, safety, out of that nettle, danger?[8]

Others, too, noticed how contented Jennie was with her third marriage.

Jean Hamilton thought she was 'at the top of her form . . . looking so handsome, quite twenty years younger', Jennie had confided in her: 'I am 65 [sic] and am going to marry the handsomest man in London whom all the girls envied.' When she added that she felt quite young and had just bought herself three lovely gowns, Jean recorded: 'I quite understood his infatuation last night for her joy was infectious.'9 A part of Jennie was to remain forever the confident nineteen-year-old who had captivated Randolph all those years before. Shane wrote unkindly to his daughter Anita at the time she was writing Jennie's biography: 'She told her close friend Olive Guthrie (Leonie's sister-in-law) that Monty was the best lover of all her experience. But she must have been grateful for any mercies at 63.'10 Clearly Jennie's precise age was also a subject of gossip.

While she and Monty revelled in their romance, George and Stella were miserable and soon separated. But she refused him a divorce and it was only after her death in April 1940 that George, 'who was known as "the old wives' tale"',11 married for the third time, Mrs Georgette Hirsch, née Seligman, a woman four years younger than him. With supreme irony the marriage took place on 15 April 1940, not only the day of his second wife's funeral but the same day that his first wife, Jennie, had married Randolph in 1874. Or perhaps he was just insensitive to dates. Stricken with Parkinson's disease, he committed suicide on April Fool's Day, 1951.

Jennie always retained her dignity in respect of George, but shortly after he married Stella they met at a party. Chips Channon recalled the event. 'I was with Lady Randolph, "Aunt Jenny" as I called her, and at the door we met the newly married couple, Mrs Pat and her husband face to face . . . There was a tense moment and we passed on; no word of greeting was exchanged.'12 Jennie never resorted to rancour, may even have felt pity towards him. Two years before she died she wrote:

> My dear George,
> I heard about you from Clare . . . I am glad you wrote . . . and in your heart of hearts you must know that I never could have any but kindly feelings towards you. I never think of you but to remember all those happy days we spent together . . . I have forgotten everything else. I do wish you all that is best . . . Peace is an essential to life and if you have that you are on a fair way to happiness. Life is frightfully hard. One's only chance is within oneself. Bless you, always your best friend, Jennie.13

Jennie's life took on a calmer tone after the war. But since Porch was often away in Africa, building himself a house in the Gold Coast, she did not entirely give up her traditional summer manoeuvres, staying at one country house after another. Porch was partly trying to make some money and partly embarrassed by the reception he received in London drawing rooms. Even Leonie and Clara made fun of 'Poor Porch in his new and unaccustomed role of *homme monde* [sic]'.[14] But, deeply in love with Jennie, he intended to return home as soon as possible.

There was a flurry of excitement in the family when Clare Sheridan, now a successful sculptress and independent woman, visited Moscow in September 1920 as a guest of the Bolshevik Government. Her brother Oswald believed the trip 'will be a 9 days scandal to Aunt Jane's friends and the rest of the world won't even know or care that she has gone'.[15] Oswald recounted in his diary, with heavy sarcasm, how shortly after Clare's departure Jennie arrived for tea one day 'an hour and ten minutes late . . . her dear heart bleeding' for Puss (the pet name for Clare).[16] Another time, when Jennie hosted a lunch, Oswald recounted how, by turns, 'the Aunts relieved each other alternately blackguarding the Bolshies and soothing Puss'. Oswald defended his sister, who he maintained 'doesn't preach Bolshevism. She will just tell you what happened without ramming tenets down your throat.'[17] But when the aunts kept interrupting with '"that vile creature" or "the horrible assassins"', then she gets pink and restive and the appropriate aunt pacified her and starts her off again and then interjects more abuse and . . . the other aunt has to do the pacifying. It was highly electrical. Poor Puss she might know that a family (hers above all) are the first to ostracise.'[18]

It was a particularly sensitive situation for Winston, who had expressed the most vehement opposition to the new regime in Russia, believing it should be strangled at birth. David Lloyd George, Prime Minister since 1916, had brought him back into the Government as Minister of Munitions in July 1917. In this position Churchill argued at the end of the war in favour of military intervention to bring down the Bolshevik regime, which had betrayed the Allies by making peace with the Germans at Brest-Litovsk in March 1918. But the intervention failed – a failure for which he paid a heavy political price.

Clare herself was bemused, although given this background cannot have been surprised. 'I do not gather on what basis the family [by which she meant her mother, Jennie and Leonie] is so upset,' she wrote to cousin Shane. 'I am 35 and a working woman. I have come where there is work. I could work here all winter but I am hurrying to get back to the children.'[19] She was not especially interested in politics, she had to earn a living. Having Trotsky sit to her was an opportunity she found impossible to turn down. Yet the criticism neatly underscored the attitudes of the last century from which the Jerome sisters all suffered. They wanted money but knew not how to earn it, only how to spend it.

Jennie continued to engage with life until the end. In her last months, she embraced two of the century's most exciting discoveries: flying and movie making. She persuaded an RAF officer she met at a party to take her up in his tiny plane and fly over Kent at ninety miles an hour. 'An extraordinary experience . . . right above the clouds in a little coupé,' she told friends. And she had a small part in a film. She was forty years older than the rest of the cast but, as one of the other actresses said: 'We never gave it a thought; she was just one of us. Jennie was so young.'[20] Literally and metaphorically, Jennie never stopped travelling, going to the opera or visiting friends and grandchildren, of whom in 1920 she had six.[21]

Now in her mid-sixties, she still did what she could for Winston, who in 1919 was made Secretary of State for War as well as Air Minister. But by this time Clemmie was his primary source of support. Although never interested in dieting, Jennie was concerned to keep herself as youthful as possible. This, she insisted was not for herself, 'it's for Monty's sake . . . he is so sweet to me and will be waiting for me now', she told Jean Hamilton.[22] In February 1921, Jennie managed to sell for £35,000 a house she had bought in Berkeley Square – 'a clear profit of £15,000', as Winston told Clemmie with relief. 'She has already taken a little house in Charles Street. No need to go abroad. All is well. I am so glad.'[23] The coincidence of life's circularity cannot have been lost on Jennie: Charles Street was where she and Randolph had started their married life.

And so, in the spring of 1921, as Porch had gone to Nigeria to explore investment opportunities, she went off to spend the profit from the sale of the house, staying with her old friend Vittoria Colonna, Duchess of Sermoneta, in Rome. The Palazzo Caetani, where she had often stayed before the war, was being refurbished and Jennie loved giving her friend advice on interior decoration. 'In my library I still have the cretonne she subsequently chose for me in London and had sent out to Rome,' the Duchess wrote. 'The green background is faded now and the birds and fruit have lost their brilliancy but I always put off the day of changing the chair covers for they remind me of my lost friend.' The two women enjoyed going to balls together – 'she was full of vitality and determined never to miss a trick. She danced the tango, then the latest craze, with great energy and ability' – and going shopping together – 'we ransacked all the old curiosity shops and Jennie bought profusely; her zest in spending money was one of her charms'.[24] Jennie and Leonie had known Vittoria Sermoneta for many years, since first meeting her at Cowes. 'I have never forgotten the kindness of those two smart and popular women towards the shy girl of seventeen I was when I first met them . . . They spoke to me in a gay friendly way . . . I can see them now, dressed alike in white serge tailored suits with the sailor hats made fashionable by Queen Alexandra.'[25]

One day during this visit she went off for a picnic with Winston and Clemmie and the Laverys at Cap d'Ail. But most of the time was spent shopping. Jennie bought some dainty slippers at the best Roman shoe-makers – she always prized her slim feet and had a weakness for beautiful shoes with dangerously high heels. Soon afterwards, back in England, she went to visit another friend, Lady Frances Horner, at her Elizabethan manor, Mells, in Somerset. Coming down for dinner in a rush, she slipped on an oak staircase. It was later stated that she was wearing new shoes when she fell. A local doctor was summoned, who said it was a bad fracture of the left leg near the ankle, weakened years before by a fall on a grouse moor. She remained at Mells for a couple of days but, when the pain did not subside, was brought back to London by ambulance.

Two weeks later, although the swelling had gone down, a portion of the skin blackened and gangrene set in. The doctors hurriedly prepared to amputate the leg above the knee. Afterwards Jennie courageously insisted that the amputation should not be discussed, maintaining that she did not want a great fuss made. Leonie, distraught, blamed the maid for not rubbing the slippery leather soles of her beautiful Roman shoes with sandpaper to make them grip, though this was to ignore the height of the heels. Porch sent telegrams and wrote desperate letters full of love, but was always behind with the news. He told her sweetly when he first heard the bad news: 'I shall love you very much to make up for all the pain and anguish you have suffered.' Then he described his plans to return to England as soon as possible as his business had gone so well.[26]

By mid-June, the two sisters with their 'jagged nerves' were in more or less constant attendance. Clara, 70 per cent distraught, and Leonie, 95 per cent prostrated, according to Oswald Frewen, came and went in the blisteringly hot summer weather – 84 degrees in the shade. Jack Churchill was the 'only element of imperturbable sanity in the place'. Clara, for whom 'there was no calming her nerves . . . had been frantically sitting up at Aunt Jane's for two nights and gotten her a hospital bed from Heal's', wrote Oswald. He explained that 'Aunt J has had her left leg amputated above the knee; wherefore the Churchills announce the loss of a *foot* – so Churchillian!'[27] Adding to the sense of crisis was the fact that Shane and his wife Marjorie were expecting a baby at any moment and Shane was, not surprisingly, 'bubbling like a cauldron'. When his father-in-law, Governor

Ide, who had come over to be with Marjorie, collapsed and died suddenly, Leonie complained to Shane that he was not helping her because he had gone home to be with his wife and tell her of her father's death.

Towards the end of June, Jennie seemed to recover strength, agreed to see visitors and made some jokes. Grimacing with pain, she admitted that she had not realised until now how the soldiers she had tended in hospitals had suffered. 'The more it hurts, the more those devils of doctors like it,' she said.[28] She told Eleanor Warrender that she was 'putting her best foot forward'. Winston telegraphed Porch: 'danger definitely over. Temperature going down.' Clara and Leonie felt able to resume a more normal life.

But on 29 June, after breakfast, an artery well above the point of amputation suddenly gave way. She started haemorrhaging blood but just managed to say: 'Nurse, I'm feeling faint.' Then she fainted and never recovered. She was sixty-seven. Like everything she did in life, her leaving of it was highly charged and dramatic. Winston, in the midst of a crisis over Turkey, came rushing round in his pyjamas from Sussex Square and arrived at the same time as Jack. Jennie was already unconscious. Clara was in Brede in Sussex and by the time she arrived at the Porches' matrimonial home, 8 Westbourne Street, she had seen headlines on posters in Trafalgar Square announcing 'Death of Lady Randolph Churchill'. In a foolhardy attempt to lessen the shock, Leonie had sent her a telegram, 'Jennie suddenly ill better come immediately,' when Jennie was already dead. Within minutes of her death, Marjorie Leslie produced a nine-pound baby boy. Leonie was with her.

Shortly before her third marriage Jennie had confided to Jean Hamilton that Leonie, who felt a twinge of jealousy about her ability to attract such a handsome young man as Montagu Porch, had given her some sisterly advice, suggesting that she should associate more with her contemporaries. Jennie's response was that 'on the contrary she meant to continue to fly at [her contemporaries'] approach as they depressed her to the last degree, they were all blind or deaf or lame'.[29] When Jennie asked Leonie if she thought that she and Porch looked very absurd together, the reply was a cool 'Oh, you look as if you might over lay him at any moment.'[30] Jennie, for whom life in a wheelchair would have been insupportable, was at least to be spared that. As Winston wrote to Lady Islington, 'she suffers no more pain nor will she ever know old age, decrepitude, loneliness . . . I wish you could have seen her as she lay at rest – after all the sunshine and storm of life was over. Very beautiful and splendid she looked. Since this morning, with its pangs, thirty years have fallen from her brow. She recalled to me the countenance I had admired as a child when she was in her heyday . . .'[31]

Oswald Frewen recalled how the family trooped up to the bedroom, one by one, to pay their last respects. He himself found Jennie in death quite unlike herself in life. Gone was the vivacity, the flashing eye. In its place he remarked on the mouth 'drooping grim as a warrior chief . . . the brow noble . . . the only woman it called to mind was my formidable grandmother who died in 1896. We all saw the likeness. Ma, Aunt Leonie and Winston.'[32] Eleanor Warrender, downstairs, was a calming influence on the near hysterical Clara Frewen.

One of Jennie's last letters had been to her old friend George Curzon. In characteristic good humour she declared, 'My poor departed leg served me well for 67 years and led me into some very pleasant walks. I am not to be pitied – now that my grand pain is over.'[33] Curzon sent a quick reply. But almost as soon as it was despatched, he heard she had died. Still in shock, he wrote to Winston extolling her amazing courage and spirit and describing his memories of the early days when she was 'the brilliant wife of a brilliant statesman, then rising to fame . . . since then I have found her – quite apart from the attraction of her radiant personality – to be a true, constant and loyal friend, ever warm hearted and generous'.[34]

'My dear George,' Winston replied immediately. 'I found yr letter lying on the table downstairs. In a few minutes it wd have been taken up to her . . . I do not feel a sense of tragedy, but only of loss. Her life was a full one. The wine of life was in her veins. Sorrows and storms were conquered by her nature and on the whole it was a life of sunshine.'[35]

Jennie's funeral was on 2 July, a hot Saturday. She was buried in Bladon, next to Randolph, and the family had a special reserved coach on the 9.30 a.m. train from Paddington. Porch could not get home in time, but sent a wreath. 'I think Aunt Jennie was in another saloon in which we had tea on the return journey,' Oswald wrote. As well as the immediate family, the mourners on the train included Hugh and Eleanor Warrender, Lord Randolph's brother-in-law Lord Howe (representing Queen Alexandra), the doctor whom the family considered was responsible for her demise, and the devoted family butler, Walden. Clara was relieved that Winston had invited her to lead the procession – 'the honour due to the elder sister'. Oswald was gleeful that with the Frewens in the vanguard 'the Leslies and Churchills were eating our dust instead of we theirs'.[36]

The sun blazed down the whole day on the quiet country church in the shadow of the great estate of Blenheim where the whole adventure had begun more than forty years before. The service was conducted by a sympathetic parson, with a small choir of boys' and women's voices, and the grave was lined with white roses and pale mauve orchids. Winston threw some red roses into the open grave, the sexton dropped a handful of friable dust on to the coffin and altogether it was 'quite a bright little service'. Clara, in a fit of abstraction, referred to it as a 'quiet country wedding'.[37]

Afterwards the family, swollen by Lord and Lady Abingdon (Jack's parents-in-law) and Lady Sarah Wilson, walked over to Blenheim itself for a picnic lunch in the grounds as there were no servants available in the Palace. After lunch, Winston took Hugh and Eleanor and Clara and Oswald for a tour around the grounds before returning on the 4.15 train, which pulled in to London at 6 p.m. There had been a memorial service in London at St Margaret's Westminster at the same time. The next day Clara and Leonie, bereft without the lynchpin of their relationship, paid a final visit to Westbourne Street. Porch, 'poor fellow', returned to London a month later to a denuded house, a lonely land and a sea of debts. He treasured the note Jennie had written him just before her final trip, in which she told him, 'I love you better than anything in the world and shall try to do all those things you want me to in your absence.'[38] He retired to the country and in 1926 married again, Donna Giulia Patrizi, a daughter of the Marchese Patrizi della Rocca. He did his best to avoid all discussion of his life with Jennie up to his own death in 1964.

Jennie died intestate. Her last will had been made in 1915, before her final marriage and was therefore invalid. She left a mountain of debts. The bills for couture clothes, antique furniture, tapestry and bric-à-brac as well as the transport and insurance costs, which Jennie tried to avoid paying, to ship them home, were piling up as she lay in bed, seriously ill. With Winston preoccupied with affairs of state, it fell to Jack Churchill, and, once he returned, to Porch, to settle the claims for payment and see off those who threatened to commence proceedings against her. As Seymour wrote to Anita: 'when she died intestate leaving awful debts (couture and antiques) Leo remarked: "It is Winston who weeps copiously but it is Jack, his brother, and poor Porchy who are paying off her debts."'[39] One of the last cheques she had written before her accident had been for £1,041 14 s and 3d to the long-suffering Hugh Warrender, a guarantor of the large loan she had needed after her divorce to buy herself a house. But her income had declined so much during the war that she could barely afford to pay her super-tax bills in the last few months of her life. It was only thanks to Porch's regular £60 cheques – and her eternal optimism – that she kept afloat.

The invoices for unpaid luxuries vied with the unbelieving condolence letters for priority. Soveral, Bourke Cockran, Ernest Cassel, many Rothschilds, princes and friends wrote of their grief and vivid memories. Clare Sheridan sent a telegram from Mexico describing Jennie as her 'second mother'.[40] Asquith said, 'She lived every inch of her life up to the edge.'[41] Lloyd George spoke of her as 'the life and delight of the party'.[42] The obituaries almost all made reference to Jennie's American wit and vivacity, energy and tact. She was remembered for her influence in creating the Primrose League and for founding the *Anglo-Saxon Review*. As the *New York Evening Post* put it, when she married Randolph in 1874 American wives of British husbands were a rarity; that was no longer so in 1921. 'But of the whole list, there probably has been no one with just Lady Churchill's charm and influence and there certainly has been none who, like her, could count both a husband and son of the first importance in British public life.'[43] In 1921 the scale of Winston's importance could only be guessed at by most. He himself feared that his career might already be over. It took another thirty years before he was hailed as 'The Greatest Briton'. Jennie already knew it.

Epilogue

Remember that a Son Should Always Seek and Find Extenuating Circumstances for his Mother

~

There is a story told of Churchill when he was a young soldier on the North West Frontier. He was one day accosted by a fellow officer who said: 'Churchill, your politics are as rotten as your mother's morals.' Lieutenant Churchill apparently replied: 'No man says that to me and lives.' A duel was fought, but the fate of the other man is not recorded. There is no known death announcement from the regiment which would correspond with this story.

Apocryphal? Maybe. But the story has sound credentials. Shelagh, Lady Montague Browne heard it from her grandfather, himself a soldier of repute on the North West Frontier. She later worked for Lady Churchill as her private secretary, who encouraged her to find out more. 'I once asked Churchill well into his dotage, "Did you ever fight a duel?" Lady Montague Browne recounts. "Why do you ask?" he replied. Duels were illegal. "I think you're the sort of person who would – you're a romantic . . ." Silence. He looked down at his hands. He finally broke the silence to mumble: "Hmmm. No idea."'

Lady Montague Browne did further research among the family but could never prove her grandfather's account. But she insists that her grandfather was a reliable witness and had recounted the story long before she went to work for the Churchills. What is interesting is not necessarily the 'truth' of such a tale. The truth lies in the way that such an account gains credence by its very credibility. What it reveals about both mother and son is valid whether or not the events actually happened. 'He was always very reverential towards his mother and treated her with extreme kindness. One of the stories he was fondest of telling was how he ran through the streets when he feared she was dying. It was quite clear he loved her and that this love required he disregarded certain aspects of her.'[1]

Not everyone, however, was prepared to disregard them in the same way. As the historian John Lukacs explains, Churchill's enemies often referred to him as a 'half-breed' or 'mongrel' on account of his mother having been an American and a woman with more than one past.[2] Thus

Churchill's opportunism was inextricably linked with his mother's morals. It behoved the man, if he was to defend the whole nation, first to defend the woman who was his own mother. But to defend his mother to the point where he was prepared to kill another man demands a rare form of filial duty. Such devotion also indicates an unusual mother. Jennie was that.

There is a scene in the film *Young Winston* where Jennie, played by Anne Bancroft, in her most vivid finery visits a butcher to ask him for his vote. This is based on a line in her *Reminiscences* where she writes that he gave her his vote and 'some time after the election I was the proud recipient of half a sheep'.[3] In the film, the butcher becomes much more suggestive. He asks her where her husband is. 'Still in bed,' she replies, although it is the middle of the morning. 'If I were him I wouldn't rush to get out of bed either,' the butcher responds, at which Jennie smiles dangerously – the assumption being, quite clearly, that she was the sort who would keep a man in bed all day.

Two hundred lovers, according to Roy Jenkins, discussing Jennie in his impressive biography of Churchill (2001), seems 'too round' a figure to be believable. Yet the mythical mud has certainly stuck in this case. Those who know, or think they know, only one thing about Jennie Jerome seem to know that she had two hundred lovers. George Moore, the unreliable Irish novelist, planted the seed for that dubious figure in a teatime conversation quoted by Cynthia Asquith in her *Diaries*, not published until 1968 but doubtless tittered over privately long before that. Moore's spitefulness is easily explained. He was a man who 'told but never kissed', a man who claimed that he spanked the bottom of Jennie's friend, the writer and editor Pearl Craigie, when she declined his overtures, an incorrigible liar at the best of times but, as a spurned lover, a slimy troublemaker at the worst.

On 1 June 1918 this storyteller, along with the artist Wilson Steer, took tea with Lady Cynthia Asquith. Moore was in a witty, expansive mood and, having first laid down the law in very technical art criticism, proceeded to be 'rather funny' about Lady Randolph. Cynthia suggested that perhaps her newly married friend liked the idea of being known as the 'one white woman in Nigeria instead of the one black one in London', a rather out-of-date joke since Jennie had not been raven-haired for many years now, having made a small concession to wartime austerity by allowing her thick hair – always considered one of her finest attributes – to remain grey. 'He [Moore] said he could only account for how they would spend their evenings by a reapplication of the Arabian nights. She regaling him with the recital of one of her amours (Moore claimed two hundred lovers for her) nightly – and the collection would be known as the Nigerian Nights.'[4] 'What cat's paws these women are,' remarked Seymour Leslie in some notes written for his niece Anita.[5]

How could one possibly quantify such a figure, and who were all these men? The eminently readable William Manchester in *The Last Lion* gave a list of her lovers – numbering fewer than twenty – but no sources. He stated categorically: 'Her lovers are *known* [italics added] to include Kinsky, Henri Breteuil, Thomas Trafford, Baron Hirsch, Sir Edgar Vincent (later Viscount D'Abernon), Lord Dunraven, Herbert von Bismarck, Henri le Tonnelie [sic], Norman Forbes Robertson, Hugh Warrender of the Grenadier Guards, a cavalry officer named Kinkaid Smith, the American Bourke Cockran, [Paul] Bourget, William Waldorf Astor, Harry Cust, a soldier named Taylor, a man called Simon, an Italian named Casati, and Albert Edward of the house of Saxe-Coburg . . . later King Edward VII.'[6]

It's an arbitrary list. Breteuil and Le Tonnelier are one and the same man. Major Caryl Ramsden – a source of amusement for the Prince of Wales – is not mentioned, nor is the shadowy John Delacour, named by Randolph in a threatened divorce case who flitted in and out of their lives, nor is 'Star' Falmouth, believed by the Leslies to be the father of Winston's brother Jack, nor is Marion Crawford, the American author who lived mostly in Italy. Crawford's name has not survived in the gossipy letters between the sisters, but Clare Sheridan knew about her aunt's attraction for him. Writing to her cousin Anita she said: 'Here is the Aunt Jennie letter. It will amuse you.' The letter itself seems to have disappeared but was obviously from around 1894 because Clare adds: 'Lord Wolverton was the man she was in love with at the time . . . but she's suddenly got a mad pash for Marion Crawford and wants to lure him to accompany them to Japan!!'

Crawford, playwright and novelist, was a ladies' man of legendary and irresistible charm, a romantic in his life and writing who personified the American dream of escape. There were frequent rumours of a rift in his marriage. He was a friend and admirer of Vittoria Sermoneta, who may have introduced him to Jennie. Clare went on:

> Wonderful description of Marion Crawford (moustache and all) . . . what a pity, what a thousand pities, Jennie and Mama were so frivolous and really so superficial. Instead of telling us what Marion C looked like why not have told us of anything interesting he said . . . if only Mama, instead of describing the tulle dresses, had described the conversations she had with some of the interesting people there . . . what surprises me is that the three sisters gave birth to brilliant children. I don't know where we get it from.[7]

Perhaps Jennie, in spite of her legendary discretion, encouraged belief in the myth. As her friend Daisy Warwick, once the Prince of Wales's beautiful mistress, wrote to her a few years before she died: 'We have both lived our lives and gathered more experiences than most women.'[8] If so, one begins to see why history has treated the mother so badly and the son so well. Jennie lived a remarkably free life for the time. She did not have absolute freedom, of course, but she could do almost anything as long as she obeyed the rules, such as making sure that revealing private letters were tucked into the public ones. The sisters often used the French term, *Cache ton jeu* (never explain), discretion above all, but at the same time pushed acceptable boundaries to the limit. It is only the rare indiscreet letter that has survived and found its way into the Churchill Archives at Cambridge. How significant is the Marquis de Breteuil's request in 1889 that Jennie find him a hotel 'à côté de chez vous, of which you have spoken, because I want to be as close as possible'?[9]

That Jennie attracted men, and mostly much younger men, there can be no doubt. She married two of them and clearly had relationships with others such as Rossmore and Ramsden, Warrender and Wolverton, Flower and Falmouth. Perhaps in the end the only person who kept count was Jennie herself. Even Leonie, occasionally jealous and always more controlled, may not have known all the details of her liaisons. For a woman to have a strong libido was not a subject of discussion in polite society, perhaps not even recognised. And unquestionably the family tried to control the stories. Shane painstakingly copied out some of the letters in the family archive, yet careful examination indicates a protective attitude towards his aunt. There is one letter for which no copy exists. In the autumn of 1894 Jennie wrote to Leonie, Shane's mother, several letters about her desperate sadness and fears for the future without Charles Kinsky. 'I know you didn't like him much but I loved him,' Jennie admitted. 'I really think I have been paid out for all my own iniquities.' It was on these iniquities, perceived or real, that the myth was based. Clearly her contemporaries believed that she was a woman with a past – her own phrase – an impression which slowly gathered pace after her death.[10]

Jennie's effervescent personality and lust for life were not shared by all other American women who married Englishmen. Yet wealthy American wives of impoverished British aristocrats did provide rich fodder for novelists. While Henry James and Edith Wharton wrote novels about the cultural impact on individual Americans, Anthony Trollope and Frances Hodgson Burnett were more interested in the effect on English society. All four understood the bracing, but sometimes painful, effect of the clashing cultures. But the general view of American women who came to England in search of titles or adventure was that they were big spenders as well as being brash, fast, wild and probably over-sexed buccaneers, as Wharton saw them. 'Give up that fast lot,' the elderly Duchess had begged her daughter-in-law in 1886. This view persisted well into the twentieth century when Edward VIII wanted to marry the American divorcee Mrs Simpson. All the negative aspects of American womanhood seemed to culminate in her. She was not even rich.

Jennie was much more than just another American wife with a voracious sexual appetite. Her myth derived from a particular set of circumstances and characters. In 1912 Lord Rossmore published his memoirs entitled *Things I Can Tell*. This book, according to Eveleigh Nash's list of new books, 'abounds in amusing anecdotes and there are few people in society who will not be tempted to read it – if only in self-defence – for in dining out this Autumn there is one question which is sure to be asked and that is, "Have you read the Rossmore Recollections?"'[11] Jennie, albeit with some significant alteration of dates, featured in those recollections. But a more serious account, contributing to an unfavourable interpretation of Jennie's behaviour, was the publication in 1924, three years after her death, of Frank Harris's *My Life and Loves*. Not only does Harris give a detailed account, uncorroborated yet impossible to refute, of Randolph sleeping with an old hag and thereby contracting syphilis. He is also slyly critical of Jennie, whom he describes as tactless and imperious. Humiliated by her husband one day in front of Harris, the journalist claimed he pointed out to Randolph at the time: 'Your wife will always hate me.'

Harris writes that 'ever afterwards Lady Randolph missed no opportunity of showing me that she disliked me cordially. I remember some years later how she got into the express train for the south in Paris and coolly annexed an old man's seat. I spent ten minutes explaining who she was and pacifying the old Frenchman but she scarcely took the trouble to thank me. She showed her worst side to me.' Some years later, over dinner with Lady Randolph, when he discussed with her how she had taken Randolph around the world before he died, he claims she said, 'At first, when he was very strong, it was bad enough but as soon as he became weak I didn't mind.'[12] Such unprovable stories may have no place in a serious biography. But awareness of how friends and contemporaries viewed Jennie sheds light on how reputations harden into reality. Was she really 'more panther than woman' – the animal imagined by two contemporaries, Violet Asquith and Lord D'Abernon, when describing Jennie?

In 1930, almost ten years after Jennie's death, Winston wrote his own account of his childhood, now the accepted version of events. His mother scarcely features in his earlier two-volume biography of his father. *My Early Life* is an exquisite piece of writing which sets in stone the notion that his mother was beautiful but distant, an object of admiration for other men. It is her picture that adorns the frontispiece, not his, nor a family portrait. But how fair is the suggestion that Jennie neglected her brilliant but wayward son in his early years until his talent made him interesting – the considered belief of her daughter-in-law Clementine? *My Early Life* was, after all, the version of events Winston wanted for posterity. The book contributed to the idea that here was a man who against the odds was singled out by fate for great leadership, ironically a view Jennie herself encouraged. Jennie was torn between supporting a difficult and frequently sick husband, who for what ever reasons often rebuffed her, and maintaining a sparkling social and cultural life which on the surface appeared successful. Her behaviour towards her young sons was scarcely different from that of many mothers of her day, especially those who married as young as she with husbands – and sons – as demanding as hers. The most serious criticism might be not that she neglected Winston, but that she failed adequately to criticise him, thereby keeping him in one sense forever a child. Clementine inevitably suffered from this. As their friend Lady Diana Cooper (née Manners) observed:

> I never heard Winston nagged. All great men are more childish than good women and there must have been behind the scenes . . . some of the scolding that a nanny gives her charge for childishness, showing off, over excitement, obstinacy or sulks, some promise extracted that such behaviour would not happen again. I can hear this Prime Minister's professed penitence, the vow made and never kept by the incorrigible schoolboy.[13]

After 1930 there was largely a silence about Jennie, in print at least, until the late 1960s, shortly after Winston's own death on 24 January 1965, the seventieth anniversary to the day of the death of his father. Suddenly a plethora of books, a television series, as well as the feature film *Young Winston*, based on *My Early Life*, appeared. These taken together are what have contributed to most people's views of Winston Churchill's American mother. *Jennie: The Life of Lady Randolph Churchill* by Anita Leslie, a greatniece, daughter of Shane, appeared in 1969, the first of the biographies to be published in England. Anita maintained that she had been thinking about writing it for years, inspired by stories that her grandmother Leonie, who lived until Anita was fifteen, had told her. Leonie – 'a little mouse but she had more charm and wit than Jennie', according to Anita[14] – was a repository for many family stories. Anita's version of Jennie's life is lively and portrays a woman of charm, warmth and daring, a leader among the three sisters.

But, much to Anita's chagrin, she was beaten by the appearance in America of a two-volume biography by Ralph Martin. Martin, the son of Polish immigrants, a School of Journalism student and a former combat correspondent, spent years researching his more detailed and revealing biography. It was his nineteenth book. But although it sat at the top of the US bestseller lists for at least a year, it was not welcomed by all the family. Martin was threatened with legal action by Peregrine Churchill, son of Jack, grandson of Jennie, who objected to the suggestion that his father might not have been Lord Randolph's son. 'There was an attempt to prevent anything I said which hinted at syphilis,' said Martin. 'But in the end, although it cost me a lot of money, the US version was unexpurgated.'[15] There were, however, text changes made to future editions, as well as an apology, as part of the compromise settlement.

Anita said at the time of publication: 'I don't mean to attack the American version of the book, only to tell the correct version.'[16] She said there were four main areas of contention. She believed that Jennie was not pregnant at the time of her marriage to Randolph, that she did not have a love affair with the Prince of Wales, that Lord Roden was not the father of Jack, and finally (while not denying that Randolph died of syphilis) that he caught the disease not from an old whore in Oxford but from a French actress in Paris.

The Leslie family rallied round. Anita's uncle Seymour provided pages of corrections, lamenting that Martin's 'long book is marred by absence of any sense of period, inaccuracies in every chapter and much quotation from such silly gossip columns as 'Town Topics' and the notoriously incorrect Frank Harris . . .'. Seymour took Martin to task for his Americanisms and wrote 'untrue story' or 'nonsensical statements' against much that the author had written. In particular he did not like Martin's comment that Jack and Winston were 'brothers separated by personality'. 'NOT TRUE,' he stated.[17]

Shortly after these two books appeared came a third. *Jennie – A Portrait with Letters* was published in 1974 in association with Thames Television and was written by Peregrine Churchill, who owned many of Jennie's letters, together with playwright Julian Mitchell. Peregrine had known his grandmother as a small child and said he had fond memories of her. This book was the basis for a lavish TV series costing more than £500,000 which took two years to film and starred Lee Remick, then aged thirty-eight, who played Jennie from the ages of twenty to sixty-seven, Ronald

Pickup as Randolph and Siân Phillips as Mrs Patrick Campbell. Jeremy Brett was Kinsky. Much of the filming was done on location at Blenheim and Salisbury Hall.

But by this time there was a different person being discussed. Jennie had now morphed from an American adventuress and would-be editor into the Mother of the Great British Prime Minister, the man who, virtually single-handed, had stood up to Adolf Hitler. All subsequent works would have to look at her through the prism of world events and her son's role in shaping them. Where did his courage and determination originate? How important was it for him that he was half American? Goebbels maintained that being half American meant he was not a proper Englishman. What exactly was the mother's role, beyond the practical tasks of acting as a superior social secretary and book supplier, crucially important though these were, in creating Winston Churchill, the war leader?

Throughout her life Jennie was the biggest single influence on Winston. They wrote to each other constantly, advised each other, encouraged each other and supported each other. They were deeply and emotionally involved in each other's lives, even at times of national crisis. With marriage, Winston turned increasingly for emotional support to Clemmie, but he needed always the unwavering love and support of a woman. Even in old age he kept a replica of his mother's sculpted hand on his desk, now on display at Chartwell. It is rich in symbolism. The votive hand is an ancient sculptural form, a metaphor for giving. For Winston it was the hand that first led him into the world, now outstretched across the years, still there to lend support. She gave him his drive, his energy and his tenacity. Above all she inspired him to believe in his destiny. When the bullets whistled past him in South Africa, when he charged the Dervishes at Omdurman and saw friends and brother officers killed, as when he fought the bloody battle at Spion Kop, he did not, as others might, cower and give thanks for being spared. Certain of survival, he felt a sense of elation at being one stage further along the road of destiny. In particular, when he was out of power from 1929 to 1939, the so-called Wilderness Years, his sense of purpose that he was being kept for something greater never deserted him entirely. Much of this confidence and courage was inherited from his mother's Jerome genes and American patrimony.

Of course, it is easy to see why, in his youth, Winston believed that his English aristocratic lineage and descent from the first Duke of Marlborough was what mattered most in his genetic make-up. He was educated as a deeply patriotic Englishman and, as he grew up, his passionate belief in the myths that contributed to English history only grew stronger. The accident that his birth took place at Blenheim, not in a London townhouse as intended, served to contribute to this, and his criticisms of his mother's proposed subtitle for her *Anglo-Saxon Review*, 'Blood is Thicker than Water', shows that his American inheritance meant far less to him then. However, opportunism was not the only motive guiding him towards a rapprochement with the United States from the 1930s onwards. He had a genuine love for all his relations, including obscure Jerome cousins, and a deep interest in and understanding of the American Civil War. At the end of the First World War, addressing a large gathering in London of the Anglo-Saxon Fellowship, he declared: 'When I have seen during the past few weeks the splendour of American manhood striding forward on all the roads of France and Flanders I have experienced emotions which words cannot describe.'[18] What he hoped Britain would gain as a reward for answering the appeals of Belgium and France in 1914 was 'supreme reconciliation' with the United States.

In 1929 he made a long tour of the Civil War battlefields and announced that President Lincoln and General Lee were two of the five most influential people in his life. But by 1939 there is no doubt that he was exploiting his American ancestry. Around this time he commissioned his cousin Shane to write an account of his grandfather Jerome's life – an episode that ended unhappily and in controversy.

There exists in the collection of the Frewen family today a pale-brown book entitled 'Scurril'. According to a note inside it signed 'Oswald Frewen, Sheephouse Brede, 1949', this is all that remains from a commission which Winston gave to Shane in the summer of 1941 to research Leonard Jerome's background, as there were 'clouds on his memory'. According to Oswald, when Shane wrote up his research and handed it over:

> Winston ran through the first 15 pages, turned it over to [his son] Randolph in great doubt, who made a few corrections to it and then confirmed his father's damnation of it. Clare Sheridan visited Winston about then, to whom he entrusted the proof with a message that he would pay the author all out of pocket expenses to date but the book was not to be published. Clare returned with the book to Sheephouse and at my suggestion duly delivered the message to Shane, but the book to me. I renamed it ('for cover') and had it bound. It is an unique copy and may be even of value to bibliophiles, scandalmongers or pornographists. O.F.[19]

Plainly Shane had not produced the book that Winston had hoped for. But it is not clear exactly what he had unearthed that his cousin found so offensive. And yet by 24 December 1941, lobbying for US support in Washington, Winston spoke unashamedly of 'the ties of blood on my mother's side', as well as of the friendships that he had developed in America over many years of active life and 'the commanding sentiment of comradeship in the common cause of great peoples who speak the same language, who kneel at the same altars and, to a very large extent, pursue the same ideals'. Two days later he made a stronger, more emotional address to both houses of Congress in the Senate Chamber at Washington. This time, his American mother was the centrepiece of the speech. He spoke of:

> the fact that my American forebears have for so many generations played their part in the life of the United States and that here I am, an Englishman, welcomed in your midst . . . I wish indeed that my mother, whose memory I cherish across the vale of years, could have been here to see.
>
> By the way, I cannot help reflecting that if my father had been American and my mother British, instead of the other way round, I might have got here on my own. In that case . . . I should not have needed any invitation, but if I had, it is hardly likely it would have been unanimous. So perhaps things are better as they are.

And perhaps indeed they were.

So why does Jennie matter? Certainly not just for her risqué jokes, the loose Japanese clothes she sometimes wore or the (reputed) tattooed serpent on her wrist.[20] Yet these were vital symbols of personal freedom which she insisted on claiming for herself. Nor does she matter merely for her courage and daring in standing on a table and singing, for dancing the tango or the can-can and revealing her ankles, or for claiming the right to smoke in public, which few women dared. Yet these, too, were important in showing that an individual can steel their nerves and do what others can only imagine. Nor for the originality of her ideas in interior design, starting up a literary magazine or sailing a hospital ship to South Africa, all of which required the determination and vision on a grand scale that were her trademarks. Among her contemporaries it is not the wives of Gladstone, Disraeli, Curzon or Salisbury who are remembered for their political savvy and ability to wield power discreetly behind the scenes. It is Jennie. It is she, marked out from childhood by her father who knew she was special, whose many witticisms and bons mots are recorded in the diaries and memoirs of others. It was her opinion which was sought on current issues and her ideas on fashion which were closely watched. And it is she who, crucially, first enabled her son to believe in his powers of persuasion as he wrote to her heartbreakingly from school. Soon afterwards she acted as his agent, ensuring that he was published and noticed, and sent him books to feed his late-developing, questing intelligence, now acting as both tutor and mentor. Jennie Jerome is and must be remembered for being more than simply the mother of Churchill. Yet my own belief is that he would not have been the same statesman and leader, nor would he have provided the same level of national and international leadership, without Jennie as his mother.

In 1943, as Britain sank into the depths of Second World War gloom, Winston was in America discussing strategy with Roosevelt when his aunt Leonie died. He could not return for the funeral but requested twice that the memorial service be delayed until he could be there, so anxious was he to attend. In the event he returned a day or two after it was over. He went immediately to the House of Commons, delivered his report, which was rapidly translated around the world, and then left the chamber and went to the smoking room. Here he saw an old friend, Sir Archibald James, and immediately begged him to tell him all about Leonie's memorial service. Who was there, where had everyone sat and what had been said? Within minutes there were tears streaming down Winston's face as he delivered his own funeral oration for his departed aunt. 'The last link with my youth severed,' he concluded, and then fell silent, head bowed and hunched with grief. Then he got up to go. When he reached the door he straightened again and went on to fight the battle for the living.[21] Winston believed that on balance Jennie won her own battle of life, and that it was a life with more sunshine than sorrow or storms.

Notes

Abbreviations

AE PoW	Albert Edward, Prince of Wales
BL	British Library
Char	Chartwell Trust Papers, Churchill College Archives, Cambridge
CF	Clara Frewen
CJ	Clara Jerome (Mrs Leonard Jerome)
CJ2	Clara Jerome (later Mrs Moreton Frewen)
CSC	Clementine Spencer Churchill
FM	Frances, Duchess of Marlborough
FMC	Fitzwilliam Museum, Cambridge
FP	Frewen papers, in the possession of Jonathan Frewen
GCW	George Cornwallis-West
JJ	Jennie Jerome
JRC	Jennie Randolph Churchill
JSC	Jack Spencer Churchill
LHJ	Lewis Harcourt Journal, Harcourt Mss, Bodleian Library, Oxford
LJ	Leonard Jerome
LL	Leonie Leslie
LP	Leslie Papers, National Library of Ireland, Dublin
LRC	Lord Randolph Churchill
MF	Moreton Frewen
MFP	Moreton Frewen Papers, Washington Library of Congress
MP	Montagu Porch
NLI	National Library of Ireland, Dublin
NYPL	New York Public Library
RCP	Royal College of Physicians
RLRC	Mrs George Cornwallis-West, *Reminiscences of Lady Randolph Churchill*
TKP	Tarka King Papers (letters and photographs and other documents, mostly Leslie family papers), in the possession of Tarka King, Anita Leslie's son
WSC	Winston Spencer Churchill

Where the origin of the information is obvious from the context I have not given a source note. I have sometimes quoted from existing works about Jennie and her family – principally the two-volume biography by Ralph Martin, the biography of Jennie by her great-niece Anita Leslie, and *Jennie: A Portrait with Letters* by Peregrine Churchill and Julian Mitchell – without always seeing the original documents. Occasionally the authors of these books have used letters to support their conclusions, some of which are published in their books or which may be in the family possession, but have not always identified these by date or location. In some cases, letters have been transcribed by family members and thus appear in different places in a slightly different form. Some undated letters have been stuck into scrapbooks: there is no proof that the envelope near by is the one that contained that letter.

PREFACE

1. Seymour Leslie, *The Jerome Connexion*, p. 13.
2. Robert Rhodes James, ed., *Chips: The Diaries of Sir Henry Channon*, p. 465.
3. 1882, quoted in R. F. Foster, *Lord Randolph Churchill: A Political Life*, p. 127.
4. Julian Osgood Field, *Uncensored Recollections*, p. 294.
5. Jennifer Leslie, conversation with author, 18 May 2004.
6. Quoted in Martin Gilbert, *Churchill: A Life*, p. 102.
7. According to Allen Packwood, the present Keeper of the Churchill Archives, the letters between Jennie and Randolph found their way into the possession of Winston Churchill, no doubt as a result of his own work on his father's biography and, subsequently, his early life, and were catalogued by the Public Record Office as part of his archive and therefore part of the material owned by the Chartwell Trust between 1961 and 1964. After Sir Winston's death the letters passed to Randolph Churchill at East Bergholt and then to Martin Gilbert at the Bodleian to inform work on the official biography, before being deposited in the Churchill Archives centre in 1995. They formed part of the material that was purchased for the nation from the Chartwell Trust using a heritage lottery fund grant of £12.5 million.

1: JUST PLAIN JENNIE

1. Address by Winston Churchill in accepting an honorary doctorate of laws from the University of Rochester, June 1941.
2. Anita Leslie, *The Fabulous Leonard Jerome*, p. 30.
3. Churchill scholar Elizabeth Snell maintains that, while there were certainly Iroquois Indians in upper-state New York where Anna Willcox (née Baker) moved as a thirty-five-year-old wife and mother, there were no Iroquois in

Nova Scotia where she appears to have spent much of her earlier life. While admitting the possibility that Clarissa may have been an illegitimate half-Indian whom the Willcoxes brought up as a daughter, Snell adds, 'this is harder to believe than the simple forthright facts as recorded by her colonial family in their probate records'.

4. Winston S. Churchill, 'Churchill's American Heritage', *Finest Hour* (Journal of the International Churchill Society), no. 104 (Autumn 1999).

5. See W. D. Rubinstein, ed., *Wealth and the Wealthy in the Modern World*, pp. 189–226.

6. Quoted in Leslie, *The Fabulous Leonard Jerome*, p. 41.

7. Quoted in Anita Leslie, *Jennie*, p. 42.

8. Ibid.

9. Jan Morris, *Trieste*, p. 30.

10. Information based on notes by Shane Leslie, LP.

11. Mrs George Cornwallis-West, *The Reminscences of Lady Randolph Churchill*, hereafter *RLRC*, p. 3. I have used the second Century edition published in New York in 1908.

12. Personal correspondence courtesy of Tarka King, TKP.

13. Passenger lists of Baltic, quoted in Ralph Martin, *Jennie*, vol. 1, p. 342.

14. There was for years confusion about the place as well as about the date of Jennie's birth. It used to be thought that she was born at 426 Henry Street and a plaque was erected there to commemorate the birth at a ceremony in 1952. That was the house where her parents had lived with her uncle prior to her birth. But without contemporary documents – the street maps are the best available – it is impossible to prove. The reason number 426 was chosen in 1952 could have been that at least this house had some connection to Jennie, while 197 Amity Street is a less imposing house to be linked to the mother of the British Prime Minister.

15. *New York Times*, 5 March 1891.

16. Quoted in Martin, *Jennie*, vol. 1, p. 8.

17. *RLRC*, p. 5.

18. Grenville Moore, *Memories of an Old Etonian*, quoted in Leslie, *Jennie*, p. 13.

19. Leslie, *The Fabulous Leonard Jerome*, p. 103.

20. Quoted in Martin, *Jennie*, vol. 1, p. 14.

21. Minnie Hauk to LJ, 17 Aug 1866, TKP.

22. Minnie Hauk to LJ, 24 Oct 1866, TKP.

23. *RLRC*, p. 4.

24. *New York Times*, 22 Mar 1867.

25. 'Scurril', quoted courtesy of Jonathan Frewen.

26. From *Memoirs of Frank Griswold*, quoted in Martin, *Jennie*, vol. 1, p. 11.

27. Quoted in Martin, *Jennie*, vol. 1, p. 18.

28. 'Scurril'.
29. Ibid., and Shane Leslie notes.
30. Leslie, *The Fabulous Leonard Jerome*, p. 99.
31. LJ to CJ, quoted in ibid., p. 279.

2: I LOVE HER BETTER THAN LIFE ITSELF

1. *RLRC*.
2. Quoted in Martin, *Jennie*, vol. 1, p. 22.
3. Ibid.
4. *RLRC*, p. 31.
5. Ibid., p. 6.
6. Quoted in Leslie, *The Fabulous Leonard Jerome*, p. 131.
7. Ibid., p. 128.
8. In *Ocean Notes for Ladies* by Katherine Ledoux (1877) readers were advised to dress sensibly and respectably as 'accidents too and loss of life are possible at sea and I have always felt that a body washed ashore in good clothes would receive more respect and kinder care than if dressed in those only fit for the rag bag'.
9. *RLRC*, p. 18.
10. It is hard to be precise about the cost of a Worth gown, although his top prices would equate with today's most expensive couture pieces at around $100,000. However, according to Phyllis Magidson, Curator of Costumes and Textiles at the Museum of the City of New York, the cost of a day toilette would have been equal to a year's salary for a middle-class household. All the gilded-age families, each of which was estimated to own at least a million dollars in the currency of their day, were dressed by Maison Worth. The cost of these pieces was a factor in Worth's reputation as the father of couture.
11. Quoted in Ann Thwaite, *Waiting for the Party: The Life of Frances Hodgson Burnett*, p. 192.
12. Quoted in Christopher Hitchens, *Blood, Class and Nostalgia*, p. 122.
13. *RLRC*, p. 24.
14. Ibid., p. 35.
15. Ibid., p. 37.
16. Montague Guest and William Boulton, *The Royal Yacht Squadron: Memorials of its Members*, p. 287.
17. Quoted in Leslie, *The Fabulous Leonard Jerome*, 7 Aug 1873, p. 166.
18. Winston S. Churchill, *Lord Randolph Churchill*, quoted in ibid., p. 169.
19. Lord Rosebery, *Lord Randolph Churchill*, p. 32.
20. Quoted in Foster, *Lord Randolph Churchill*, p. 11.
21. Jennie's letters contain few allusions to books she was reading, but her conversation was full of references to classical works and made clear she was

widely read. Her library, many hundreds of books now in the possession of a descendant, gives a clear indication of her preference for works of memoir and history, but also includes fourteen volumes of the works of De Quincey, five volumes of the Dialogues of Plato, four volumes of the essays of Montaigne. Many first editions are signed by the author to Jennie. As well as the expected collected volumes of novels by Jane Austen and Walter Scott, she had an unusually large collection of poetry, including Yeats's *Love Poems, Some Greek Love Poems, The Love Books of Ovid*, fourteen volumes of Byron's *Poems* as well as six volumes (1779) of *Trials for Adultery* (Anon) and two volumes of *Journal d'une femme de cinquante ans* (de la Tour), two volumes of *Anna Karenina* and, alone among Hardy novels, *Tess of the d'Urbervilles*.

22. Quoted in Anthony Montague Browne, *Long Sunset*, p. 192.
23. LRC to JJ, Char 28 2 1, 16 Aug 1873, quoted in Peregrine Churchill and Julian Mitchell, *Jennie*, p. 20.
24. JJ to LRC, quoted in ibid.
25. LRC to JJ, quoted in ibid., p. 21.
26. LRC to Duke of Marlborough, quoted in Churchill and Mitchell, *Jennie*, pp. 23–5.
27. Ibid., p. 25.
28. Blenheim Papers, quoted in Randolph S. Churchill, *Winston S. Churchill*, companion vol. 1, part 1, p. 11.
29. Duke of Marlborough to LRC, 31 Aug 1873, quoted in ibid., p. 12.
30. LJ to JJ, Char 28 1 25–6, 8 Aug 1873, quoted in ibid., p. 9.
31. See Roland Quinault, entry for seventh Duke of Marlborough, *New Dictionary of National Biography*, http//www.oxforddnb.com/view/article/5403.

3: I HAVE PLACED ALL MY HOPES OF FUTURE HAPPINESS IN THIS WORLD ON YOU

1. WSC to JRC, Char 28 27 2–3, 15 Aug 1902.
2. Quoted in Churchill and Mitchell, *Jennie*, p. 50.
3. Leonie produced generations of writers; Shane and Seymour, and Shane's daughter Anita, between them mined the family seam which has helped with the preservation of some letters, in either family or university archives, but others have been cut and pasted for use in books or quite simply lost in life's inevitable randomness.
4. Shane Leslie to Anita Leslie, 22 Aug 1967, TKP.
5. LRC to JJ, 4 Sept 1873, Blenheim, quoted in Churchill and Mitchell, *Jennie*, p. 32.
6. JJ to LRC, 16 Sept 1873, quoted in ibid., p. 44.
7. LRC to JJ, Char 28 2 23, 18 Sept 1873, quoted in ibid., p. 47.
8. Quoted in Churchill and Mitchell, *Jennie*, p. 49.

9. LRC to JJ, 19 Sept 1873, Blenheim, quoted in ibid., p. 50.

10. LRC to JJ, Char 28 2 45–7, 24 Sept 1873.

11. LRC to CJ, 30 Sept 1873, quoted in Churchill, *Winston S. Churchill*, companion vol. I, part I, p. 15.

12. LJ to JJ, 7 Oct 1873, quoted in ibid., p. 17.

13. Ibid. (LJ's italics).

14. LRC to JJ, 23 Sept 1873, quoted in Leslie, *Jennie*, p. 29.

15. Ibid.

16. Ibid.

17. JJ to LRC, Char 28 92 10, 26 Sept 1873.

18. Eddie Marsh, private secretary to Winston, quoted Jennie saying this after Randolph's death. Ulterior motives cannot be discounted. As Marsh concluded: 'It would be a glozing matron who would say that now.' Sir Edward Marsh, *A Number of People*, p. 155.

19. JJ to LRC, Char 28 93 89, 26 Dec 1873.

20. LRC to JJ, Char 28 3 68–9, 13 Dec 1873.

21. JJ to LRC, Char 28 93 89, 26 Dec 1873.

22. JJ to LRC, Apr 1874, quoted in Churchill and Mitchell, *Jennie*, p. 70.

23. LRC to JJ, Char 28 2 66, 19 Oct 1873.

24. LRC to JJ, Char 28 2 92, 30 Oct 1873.

25. LRC to JJ, Char 28 3 36, 30 Nov 1873.

26. JJ to LRC, Char 28 92 106, Oct 1973.

27. LRC to JJ, Char 28 3 43, 4 Dec 1873.

28. LRC to JJ, Char 28 41, 24 Oct 1873, quoted in Foster, *Lord Randolph Churchill*, p. 18.

29. Rev. Damer to FM, 19 Mar 1867, Blenheim, quoted in ibid., p. 30.

30. LRC to JJ, Char 28 3 72, 16 Dec 1873, quoted in Foster, *Lord Randolph Churchill*, p. 30.

31. LRC to JJ, Char 28 3 100, 26 Dec 1873.

32. LRC to JJ, Char 28 3 103, 27 Dec 1873.

33. LRC to JJ, Char 28 3 107, 28 Dec 1873.

34. FM to JJ, Char 28 42 1, 7 Jan 1874.

35. Quoted in Foster, *Lord Randolph Churchill*, p. 24.

36. LRC to JJ, Char 28 4 19–25, 1 and 5 Feb 1874.

37. LRC to JJ, Char 28 4 27, 5 Mar 1874.

38. LRC to JJ, Char 28 4 30, 6 Mar 1874; also LRC to JJ, Char 28 4 32–3, 7 Mar 1874.

39. Field, *Uncensored Recollections*, p. 299.

40. JJ to LRC, Char 28 94 50, Mar 1874.

41. My grateful thanks to Jane Ridley for details about the role played by Francis Knollys in persuading HRH to write to Blandford, a letter Randolph showed his parents to good effect.

42. JJ to LRC, Char 28 94 67, 16 Mar 1874.

43. JJ to LRC, Char 28 94 54, n.d.

44. LRC to JJ, Char 28 3 97, 26 Dec 1873.
45. LRC to JJ, Char 28 4 27, 5 Mar 1874.
46. LRC to JJ, Char 28 4 71, 25 Mar 1874.
47. Blenheim Papers, no longer available at Blenheim, whereabouts unknown, quoted in Churchill, *Winston S. Churchill*, companion vol. 1, part 1, p. 19.
48. Ibid.
49. Ibid.
50. Cf. Reuben S. Vanderpoel's enlightened attitude towards his daughters in *The Shuttle* by Frances Hodgson Burnett (Persephone, 2007), as well as the treatment of Mary Leiter (later Lady Curzon) by her wealthy entrepreneur father.
51. LJ to Duke of Marlborough, Paris, 9 Apr 1874, quoted in *Winston S. Churchill*, companion vol. 1, part 1, p. 20.
52. Quoted in Foster, *Lord Randolph Churchill*, p. 18.
53. LRC to FM, 14 Apr 1874 quoted in Churchill, *Winston S. Churchill*, companion vol. 1, part 1, p. 21.
54. Duke of Marlborough to LRC, n.d., quoted in Churchill, *Winston S. Churchill*, companion vol. 1, part 1, p. 18.
55. LRC to FM, 14 Apr 1874, quoted in ibid., p. 21.
56. FM to LRC, quoted in ibid., p. 22.
57. LL to unidentified friend, TKP.
58. Ibid.
59. LRC to FM, 14 Apr 1874, Churchill, *Winston S. Churchill,* companion vol. 1, part 1, p. 21.

4: JENNIE IS QUITE SATISFIED WITH RANDOLPH JUST NOW

1. *RLRC*, p. 75.
2. Ibid., p. 81.
3. Ibid.
4. Ibid., p. 77.
5. JRC to CJ, 21 Oct 1874, quoted in Leslie, *Jennie*, p. 42.
6. CJ2 to CJ, n.d., stuck into scrapbook, TKP.
7. CJ2 to CJ, 14 Jul 1874, TKP.
8. Ibid.
9. *RLRC*, p. 49.
10. CJ2 to CJ, 30 May 1874, TKP.
11. Letter partially transcribed in 'Scurril', courtesy of Jonathan Frewen.
12. CJ2 to CJ, 14 Jul 1874, TKP.
13. Undated letter, empty envelope pasted into scrapbook near by postmarked 1 Jul 1874, TKP.

14. Partially transcribed in 'Scurril', n.d., courtesy of Jonathan Frewen.
15. CJ2 to CJ, 30 May 1874, TKP.
16. JRC to CJ, n.d., postmarked 1 Jul 1874, TKP.
17. CJ2 to CJ, 30 May 1874, TKP.
18. CJ2 to CJ, 14 July 1874, TKP.
19. CJ2 to CJ, n.d., 48 Charles Street, TKP.
20. JRC to CJ, n.d., TKP.
21. *RLRC*, p. 49.
22. Ibid., p. 61.
23. Quoted in Gail McColl and Carol McD. Wallace, *To Marry an English Lord*, p. 82.
24. Quoted in Martin, *Jennie*, vol. 1, p. 98.
25. *RLRC*, p. 61.
26. Quoted in Elizabeth Eliot, *They All Married Well*, p. 68.
27. JRC to JC, n.d., 48 Charles Street, TKP.
28. CJ2 to CJ, letters June 1875, quoted in Leslie, *Jennie,* p. 47. See also TKP.
29. Unnamed daughter of Sir William Gordon Cumming to Anita Leslie, 10 Jul 1969, TKP.
30. Quoted in Foster, *Lord Randolph Churchill*, p. 28.
31. Quoted in Leslie, *Jennie,* p. 41.
32. Quoted in Martin, *Jennie*, vol. 1, p. 102.
33. LRC to CJ, Char 28 41, 30 Nov 1874, quoted in ibid., p. 107.
34. LRC to CJ, 30 Nov 1874, quoted in Churchill and Mitchell, *Jennie*, p. 75.
35. FM to CJ, Char 28 41 1a, 30 Nov 1874.
36. LRC to CJ, 4 Dec 1874, quoted in Randolph S. Churchill, *Winston S. Churchill*, vol. 1: *Youth 1874–1900*, p. 4.
37. Quoted in Stanley Weintraub, *Edward the Caresser*, p. 131.
38. FM to CJ, Char 28 41 4–5, 3 Dec 1874.
39. Winston S. Churchill, *My Early Life*, p. 19.
40. Ibid.
41. Quoted in Martin, *Jennie*, vol. 1, p. 113.
42. Ibid.
43. FM to JRC, Char 28 42 4, 5 Nov 1875.
44. FM to JRC, Char 28 42 51, n.d.
45. LRC to JRC, 16 Jan 1876, quoted in Churchill and Mitchell, *Jennie*, p. 82.
46. LRC to JRC, 17 Jan 1876, quoted in ibid., p. 83.

5: I QUITE FORGET WHAT IT IS LIKE TO BE WITH PEOPLE WHO LOVE ME

1. Quoted in Churchill, *Winston S. Churchill*, companion vol. 1, part 1, p. 34.
2. LRC to fifth Earl of Hardwicke, quoted in ibid., p. 33.
3. *The Times*, 12 May 1876.
4. JRC to LRC, 20 Apr 1876, quoted in Churchill and Mitchell, *Jennie*, p. 92, and in Churchill, *Winston S. Churchill*, companion vol. 1, part 1, p. 39.
5. Ibid.
6. LRC to JRC, 17 Apr 1876, quoted in Churchill, *Winston S. Churchill*, companion vol. 1, part 1, p. 39.
7. *The Times*, 4 May 1876.
8. Quoted in Churchill and Mitchell, *Jennie*, p. 92.
9. Quoted in ibid., p. 100.
10. LRC to JRC, Char 28 5 38, 5 Jul 1876, and ibid.
11. Undated cutting from *New York Times*.
12. *RLRC*, p. 93.
13. LJ to JRC, Char 28 1 34, 13 Nov 1876.
14. *RLRC*, p. 97.
15. JRC to LRC, Char 28 96 18, n.d.
16. LRC to JRC, Char 28 6 39, Apr 1877.
17. JRC to LRC, Char 28 96 35, 1877.
18. Churchill, *My Early Life*, p. 18.
19. All these letters from JRC to LRC are in Char 28 96, n.d.
20. JRC to LRC, Char 28 96 39, n.d.
21. JRC to LRC, Char 28 96 39, n.d.
22. Leslie, *Jennie*, p. 69.
23. JRC to LRC, Char 28 96 1, n.d.
24. JRC to LRC, Char 28 96 3, n.d.
25. Quoted in Celia Sandys, *From Winston with Love and Kisses*, p. 31.
26. JRC to LRC, Char 28 96 21, n.d.
27. FM to JRC, Char 28 96 44, n.d.
28. JRC to LRC, Char 28 96 14, n.d., quoted in Churchill and Mitchell, *Jennie*, p. 107.
29. JRC to LRC, Char 28 96 33, n.d.
30. Quoted in Earl of Rossmore, *Things I Can Tell*, pp. 104–5.
31. *RLRC*, p. 99.
32. Ibid.
33. Margot, Countess of Oxford and Asquith, *Autobiography*, vol. 1, p. 8.
34. Quoted in Richard Davenport-Hines, entry for Sir Edgar Vincent, Viscount

D'Abernon, *New Dictionary of National Biography*, http//www.oxforddnb.com/view/article/36661.

35. Churchill, *My Early Life*, p. 19.
36. Quoted in Sandys, *From Winston with Love and Kisses*, p. 31.
37. Ibid.
38. Churchill, *My Early Life*, p. 17.
39. Ibid., p. 18.
40. Churchill, *My Early Life*, p. 16.
41. These letters are in Char 28 96.
42. FM to LRC, Char 48 51, n.d.
43. LRC to JRC, Char 28 5, 20 Jan 1876.
44. LRC to JRC, Char 28 6, 16 Dec 1877, quoted in Foster, *Lord Randolph Churchill*, p. 46.
45. LRC to JRC, Char 28 6, 24 Jan 1879, quoted in ibid.
46. LRC to JRC, Char 28 6 65, n.d.
47. LJ to JRC, Char 28 1 35, 30 Nov (no year).
48. In October 1889 Moreton's shares in De Beers, on which he had been counting, plunged. The losses suffered by his brother Stephen proved catastrophic and he had to resign his commission in the 16th Lancers as a result. It was the regiment that came up with the nickname, which soon stuck.
49. Quoted in Martin, *Jennie*, vol. 1, p. 151.
50. JRC to CJ, 12 July 1880, quoted in Leslie, *Jennie*, p. 70.
51. Ibid.
52. Charlie Fitzwilliam to LL, 1 Jan 1882, TKP.
53. JRC to LRC, Char 28 96, n.d.
54. LRC to JRC, Char 28 5 11–12, n.d. (Jan 1876).
55. Quoted in Winston S. Churchill, *Lord Randolph Churchill*. vol. 1, p. 109.
56. LRC to JRC, Char 28 5 55, May 1877.
57. LRC to JRC, Char 28 6, 22 Jan 1879.
58. LRC to JRC, Char 28 11 42, 7 Nov 1891.
59. Deborah Hayden, *Pox, Genius, Madness and the Mysteries of Syphilis*, p. 51.
60. Shane Leslie to Anita Leslie, Jutland Bay, 1966, TKP.
61. Undated fragment, JRC to CJ, 29 St James's Place, TKP.
62. Charles Higham, *Dark Lady: Winston Churchill's Mother and her World*, p. 67, recounts this on the basis of a letter apparently written by Anita Leslie, which he does not cite nor give a location reference for.
63. Undated notes prepared for Anita Leslie, TKP.
64. Countess of Airlie, *With the Guards We Shall Go*, p. 17. The Countess also describes how on one occasion Strange Jocelyn, as a young man in Paris, having stayed out too late found the hotel entrance closed and so climbed up a water pipe to get into his bedroom through a window, hoping to avoid his parents' wrath. The story has been retold in other places as evidence that such

a man could easily make his way, unnoticed, into a woman's bedroom.

65. Baron Moran, *Winston Churchill: The Struggle for Survival 1940–1965*, 22 Feb 1947, p. 318.

66. JRC to CJ, TKP, quoted in Leslie, *Jennie*, p. 77.

6: RATHER A RELIEF TO GET WINSTON OFF MY HANDS

1. JRC to CJ, Nov [1880?], TKP.
2. Ibid.
3. Quoted in Martin, *Jennie,* vol. 1, p. 143.
4. See *Oxford Times*, 30 Mar and 3 Apr 1880.
5. Quoted in Martin, *Jennie,* vol. 1, p. 138.
6. Quoted in ibid., p. 143.
7. Quoted in ibid., p. 149.
8. *Diary of Sir Edward Walter Hamilton, 1880–1885*, quoted in Leslie, *Jennie,* p. 79.
9. *RLRC*, p. 125.
10. Quoted in Leslie, *Jennie,* p. 73.
11. *RLRC*, p. 126.
12. Ibid.
13. JRC to T. H. S. Escott, 10 Feb (1882), British Library, Escott Papers Add 58793.
14. Quoted in Martin, *Jennie,* vol. 1, p. 149.
15. See 'Diary Extracts', *Finest Hour*, no. 98 (Spring 1998), p. 13 (issued devoted to JRC). Diary of JRC in possession of family of Peregrine Churchill.
16. LRC to Sir Henry Drummond Wolff, quoted in Leslie, *Jennie,* p. 83.
17. Foster, *Lord Randolph Churchill*, p. 97.
18. LRC to JRC, Char 28 7 2, 15 Aug 1881, quoted in Elisabeth Kehoe, *Fortune's Daughters*, p. 86.
19. *RLRC*, p. 117.
20. Wilfrid Scawen Blunt, 'Secret Memoirs, 22 Jun 1892, FMC, vol. XV, ms 32-1975, quoted in Mary Soames, *Clementine Churchill*, p. 6.
21. *RLRC*, p. 139.
22. JRC to LRC, Char 28 98 14, n.d. (1883).
23. LRC to JRC, Char 28 7 3–7, 1–5 Jan 1883.
24. Quoted in Leslie, *Jennie,* p. 83.
25. JRC to LRC, Char 28 98 24, 3 Jan 1883.
26. JRC to LRC, Char 28 98 35, 11 Jan 1883.
27. JRC to LRC, Char 28 98 24, 3 Jan 1883.
28. JRC to LRC, Char 28 98 34, 10 Jan 1883.
29. JRC to LRC, Char 28 98 9–10, n.d.

30. JRC to LRC, quoted in Churchill, *Winston S. Churchill*, vol. 1: *Youth 1874–1900*, p. 49.
31. Quoted in ibid., p. 50.
32. Churchill *My Early Life*, p. 20.
33. LRC to JRC, Char 28 6 72, 21 Apr 1880.
34. Winston S. Churchill, *Marlborough: His Life and Times*, quoted in Jon Meacham, *Franklin and Winston*, p. 11.
35. Churchill, *Winston. S Churchill*, vol. 1: *Youth 1874–1900* p. 48.
36. Mary Soames, interview with author, 6 Nov 2004.
37. Quoted in Meacham, *Franklin and Winston*, and Mary Soames, interview with author, 16 Nov 2004.
38. Jennifer Leslie, interview with author, 18 May 2004.
39. Leslie, *Jennie*, p. 82.
40. JRC to LRC, quoted in Churchill, *Winston S Churchill*, vol. 1: *Youth 1874–1900*, p. 49.
41. Blunt, 'Secret Memoirs', 29 May 1891, FMC, vol. XIV, ms 31-1975.
42. Memorandum of Captain R. V. Briscoe RN (retd), written at Rome, 8 Mar 1913, at Balfour's request, quoted in Foster, *Lord Randolph Churchill*, p. 127.
43. I am grateful to Professor David Dilks for making this comparison.
44. Quoted in Virginia Woolf, *Roger Fry*, p. 27.
45. Maurice Baring, *The Puppet Show of Memory*, p. 71.
46. JRC to LRC, Char 28 98 8, 1883, quoted in Kehoe, *Fortune's Daughters*, p. 110.
47. Lady Dorothy Nevill, *Life and Letters*, p. 284.
48. *Pall Mall Gazette*, 23 Nov 1885.
49. Quoted in Foster, *Lord Randolph Churchill*, p. 132.
50. *RLRC*, p. 136.
51. Quoted in Natalie Adams, 'Lady Randolph and Winston's Political Career', *Finest Hour*, no. 98 (Spring 1998), pp. 14–15 (issue devoted to JRC).
52. Hon. George Lambton, *Men and Horses I Have Known*, p. 64.
53. Austrian Staatsarchiv, Vienna, shelfmark HHStaF4. Thanks to Professor Otto Rauchbauer, biographer of Shane Leslie, for help with locating and reading this.
54. CF to CJ, n.d., TKP.
55. Quoted in Manchester, *The Last Lion*, p. 138.
56. See letters pasted into scrapbook, TKP.
57. Notes prepared for Anita Leslie by Prince von Clary und Aldringen at the time she was researching *Jennie*, TKP.
58. See Lambton, *Men and Horses I Have Known*, p. 173.
59. Manchester, *The Last Lion*, p. 138.
60. Winston S. Churchill, *Savrola*, p. 30.

61. LJ to JRC, Char 28, 30 Jul 1883.

62. 14 Aug 1783, Blenheim Mss, quoted in Foster, *Lord Randolph Churchill*, p. 127.

63. Blunt, 'Secret Memoirs' as above.

64. JRC to LRC, Char 28 98 8, n.d., quoted in Kehoe, *Fortune's Daughters*, p. 110.

65. In October 1883 Lord Randolph was considering an investment with Sir Henry Drummond Wolff of £20,000–£25,000 in the new Woodstock railway. When that fell through he raised the loan five months later. Wolff to LRC, 23 Oct 1883, RCHL i/189, quoted in Foster, *Lord Randolph Churchill*, p. 125.

7: LORD RANDOLPH CHURCHILL WILL PROBABLY ALWAYS RETAIN A GREAT POWER OF MISCHIEF

1. Quoted in Anita Leslie, *Edwardians in Love*, p. 192.

2. Quoted in Foster, *Lord Randolph Churchill*, p. 159.

3. Quoted in Churchill, *Winston S. Churchill*, vol. 1: *Youth 1874–1900*, p. 57.

4. *RLRC*, p. 152.

5. *Pall Mall Gazette*, 7 May 1884.

6. Quoted in Foster, *Lord Randolph Churchill*, p. 161.

7. See Hansard, 3 ccxiii 356 ff., quoted in ibid., p. 163.

8. WSC to JRC, 24 Feb 1884, quoted in Churchill, *Winston S. Churchill*, companion vol. 1, part 1, p. 87.

9. WSC to JRC, 8 Jun 1884, in ibid., p. 88.

10. Ibid, p. 94.

11. Quoted in Sandys, *From Winston with Love and Kisses*, p. 64.

12. George Smalley, *Anglo-American Memories*, p. 89.

13. Quoted in Kehoe, *Fortune's Daughters*, p. 120.

14. Quoted in ibid.

15. LJ to CJ, n.d., Mic 606/L 1–5 1886, NLI.

16. CJ to JRC, 22 Dec 1884, quoted in Churchill, *Winston S. Churchill*, vol. 1: *Youth 1874–1900*, p. 61.

17. Quoted in *RLRC*, p. 112.

18. WSC to JRC, Char 28 13 47, 21 Jan 1885.

19. Field, *Uncensored Recollections*, p. 288.

20. LJ to LRC, 26 Feb 1885, Union Club, quoted in Churchill, *Winston S. Churchill*, vol. 1: *Youth 1874–1900*, p. 65.

21. JRC to LRC, 13 Feb 1885, quoted in Sandys, *From Winston with Love and Kisses*, p. 69.

22. WSC to LRC, 20 Oct 1885, quoted in Churchill, *Winston S. Churchill*, companion vol. 1, part 1, p. 113.

23. Quoted in *Finest Hour*, no. 98 (Spring 1998), p. 15.

24. Char 28 45, 2 Jul 1885.
25. *RLRC*, p. 167.
26. Ibid., p. 171.
27. LHJ, vol. 369, p. 58, 1885.
28. Blunt, 'Secret Memoirs', 4–5 Jul 1885, FMC, vol. IV, ms 28-1975.
29. Quoted in Foster, *Lord Randolph Churchill*, p. 271.
30. BL, India Office Library, Mss Eur B 152.
31. BL, India Office Library, 27 Oct 1885, DVPF 130/3 no. 77.
32. *Spectator*, 15 May 1885.
33. 19 May 1885; see Foster, *Lord Randolph Churchill*, p. 177.
34. BL, India Office Library, Mss Eur B 151.
35. Field *Uncensored Recollections*, p. 309.
36. Frank Harris, *My Life and Loves*, p. 472.
37. Quoted in Foster, *Lord Randolph Churchill*, p. 123.
38. Henry Labouchère to Joseph Chamberlain, 25 Dec 1885, Chamberlain Mss 5/50/54, quoted in ibid., p. 216.
39. Harris, *My Life and Loves*, p. 477.
40. *Punch*, 30 July 1887.
41. Henry Labouchère to Lord Rosebery, 25 Nov 1885, quoted in Foster, *Lord Randolph Churchill*, p. 217.
42. *RLRC*, p. 180.
43. Churchill, *Lord Randolph Churchill*, vol. 2, p. 61.
44. LJ to LRC, Char 28 1, 28 Feb 1886.
45. *Vanity Fair*, 13 Mar 1886.
46. *Vanity Fair*, 6 Mar 1886.
47. Undated cutting from *New York Times*.
48. *New York Times*, 18 Apr 1886.
49. Undated cutting, Ford Collection, NYPL.
50. *Brooklyn Daily Eagle*, 12 Jul 1885.
51. Dr Robson Roose to JRC, 17 Mar 1886 quoted in Sandys, *From Winston with Love and Kisses*, p. 80.
52. MF to JRC, quoted in ibid.
53. Quoted in Robert Rhodes James, *Lord Randolph Churchill*, p. 249.
54. Quoted in Foster, *Lord Randolph Churchill*, p. 270.
55. Quoted in Leslie, *Jennie*, p. 108.
56. FM to JRC, Char 28 42, 7–8, 8 Sept (no year).
57. Ibid.
58. FM to JRC, Char 28 42, 7–8 Sept (no year).
59. FM to JRC, Char 28 42, 26 Sept 1886.
60. FM to JRC, Char 28 42, 10 Sept 1886.
61. Marie, Duchess of Edinburgh to JRC, Char 28 46 11, 11 Apr 1886.
62. Marie, Duchess of Edinburgh to JRC, Char 28 46 9, 4 Apr 1886.

63. Marie, Duchess of Edinburgh to JRC, Char 28 46 11, 11 Apr 1886.

64. LJ to JRC, Char 28 1, 16 Jan 1886.

65. LJ to JRC, Char 28 1 46–7, 28 Feb 1886.

66. FM to JRC, Char 28 42, 9–10 Sept 1886.

67. LL to CF, n.d. 1886, Mic 606/L, LP, quoted in Leslie, *Edwardians in Love*, p. 198.

68. LL to CF, n.d. 1886, Mic 606/L, LP.

69. Neil McKenna, biographer of Oscar Wilde, to whom I am grateful for pointing out this episode, concludes: 'So Randolph Churchill was certainly gay friendly if not actually gay himself.'

70. Churchill, *Winston S. Churchill*, vol. 1: *Youth 1874–1900*, p. 80.

71. See Foster, *Lord Randolph Churchill*, p. 271.

72. WSC to JRC, Char 28 13 104, 14 Dec 1886.

73. *RLRC*, p. 184

74. Quoted in Andrew Roberts, *Salisbury*, p. 412.

75. Lord Salisbury to Lord Hartington, 24 Dec 1886, quoted in ibid., p. 414.

76. *RLRC*, p. 184.

77. LHJ, vol. 380, p. 4, 23 Dec 1886.

78. Ibid., 31 Dec 1886.

79. Quoted in Roberts, *Salisbury*, p. 416.

80. Rhodes James, *Lord Randolph Churchill*, p. 311.

81. LHJ, vol. 380, p. 107, 6 Jan 1887.

82. Earl Dunraven, *Past Times and Pastimes*, vol. 1, p. 183.

83. LHJ, vol. 380, p. 189, 1886.

84. Quoted in Martin, *Jennie*, vol. 1, p. 227, and Rhodes James, *Lord Randolph Churchill*, p. 312.

85. Martin, *Jennie*, vol. 1, p. 228.

86. Quoted in Foster, *Lord Randolph Churchill*, p. 319.

87. LHJ, vol. 380, p. 189, 1886.

88. JRC to LRC, Char 28 96 59, 1877.

89. LHJ, vol. 381, p. 153, 1887.

8: ALL THAT YOU ARE TO ME

1. *RLRC*, p. 188.

2. Quoted in Dunraven, *Past Times and Pastimes*, vol. 1, p. 183.

3. *RLRC*, p. 197.

4. Ellen Terry, *The Story of my Life*, p. 352.

5. Quoted in Leslie, *Jennie*, p. 117.

6. Anita Leslie to Robin Mackworth-Young, 3 Jul 1969, TKP.

7. AE PoW to JRC, Char 28 49 10, n.d. Most correspondence from Albert

Edward, Prince of Wales to LRC can be found in Char 28 48, 49 and 50 and is rarely dated.

8. AE PoW to JRC, Char 28 50 36.

9. Rosa Lewis to Mary Lawton, quoted in Anthony Masters, *Rosa Lewis*, p. 27.

10. Frances, Countess of Warwick, *Afterthoughts*, p. 81.

11. LRC to JRC, Char 28 8 9–10, 16 Feb 1886.

12. JRC to LRC, Char 28 100 17, Jan 1886.

13. JRC to LRC, Char 28 100 19, 21 Feb 1886.

14. LRC to JRC, Char 28 8 20, 12 Mar 1887.

15. Quoted in Kehoe, *Fortune's Daughters*, p. 150, and Martin, *Jennie*, vol. 1, p. 299.

16. JRC to LRC, Char 28 100 8–9, 8 Feb 1886.

17. JRC to LRC, Char 28 100 12, 15 Feb 1886, quoted in Churchill and Mitchell, *Jennie*, p. 160.

18. JRC to LRC, Char 28 100 19, 21 Feb 1886.

19. JRC to LRC, Char 28 100, 5 Mar 1886, quoted in Churchill and Mitchell, *Jennie*, p. 162.

20. JRC to LL, Feb 1887, quoted in Leslie, *Jennie*, p. 122.

21. Quoted in letter from JRC to LRC, Char 28 100 23–27, 27 Feb 1886.

22. LJ to CJ, July 1887, Shane Leslie Papers, Georgetown University, Washington DC, Box 46.

23. LRC to Nawab of Hyderabad, copy in MFP.

24. Notes prepared for Anita Leslie by Hugh Frewen, n.d., TKP.

25. MF to CF, 23 Nov 1887, MFP.

26. N.d. 1887, MFP.

27. MF to CF, n.d. 1887, MFP.

28. LJ to Joseph Pulitzer, n.d. 1887, Pulitzer Papers, Rare Books and Manuscript Library, Columbia University.

29. LJ to Joseph Pulitzer Union Club, 1 Apr (1887), Pulitzer Papers, Rare Books and Manuscript Library, Columbia University.

30. Notes prepared for Anita Leslie, 1969, by Hugh Frewen, TKP.

31. Martin, *Jennie*, vol. 1, p. 184.

32. Margot, Countess of Oxford and Asquith, *Autobiography*, vol. 1, p. 229.

33. Quoted in Leslie, *Jennie*, p. 144.

34. MF to CF, 21 Dec 1887, MFP.

35. MF to CF, 25 Feb 1888, MFP.

36. *RLRC*, p. 177.

37. Quoted in Lambton, *Men and Horses I Have Known*, p. 185.

38. Ibid., p. 187.

39. *RLRC*, p. 211.

40. WSC to LRC, Char 28 14 37–9, Oct 1887.

41. WSC to JRC, Char 28 14 53–4, 26 Dec 1887.

42. *The Times*, Berlin, 21 Dec 1887.

43. LRC to JRC, Char 28 8 51, 10 Dec 1887.

44. WSC to JRC, Char 28 14 55, 30 Dec 1887.

45. FM to LL, 27 Dec 1887, quoted in Leslie, *Jennie*, p. 129.

46. FM to LRC, quoted in Leslie, *Jennie*, p. 130.

47. Quoted in Leslie, *Jennie*, p. 133.

48. *RLRC*, p. 214.

49. *The Times*, St Petersburg, 22 Jan 1888.

50. *RLRC*, p. 255.

51. LRC to JRC, Char 28 8 84, 20 Oct 1888.

52. George W. Smalley to JRC, Char 28 43, 4 Mar 1888.

53. Lloyd Brice to JRC, Char 28 43, 19 Oct 1889.

54. Shane Leslie, obituary of JRC, undated cutting, *Observer* (June 1921).

55. LL to CF, 24 Dec 1888, MFP.

56. LL to CF, 27 Dec 1888, MFP.

57. LJ to CF, 28 Oct 1888, from Union Club, TKP.

58. LL to CF, n.d., MFP.

59. LL to CF, 8 Feb 1889, MFP.

60. LL to CF, n.d. 1889, MFP.

61. N.d. 1887, MFP.

62. 30 Jan 1889, MFP.

63. *RLRC*, p. 271.

64. Quoted in Joseph Epstein, *New Criterion*, vol. 9, no. 3 (Nov 1990).

65. LL to CF, 5 Feb 1889, MFP.

66. LL to CF, 13 Feb 1889, MFP.

67. Ibid.

68. LL to 'Dear Little Jane', n.d. 1889, MFP.

69. *RLRC*, p. 266.

70. JRC to LRC, Char 28 101 17–19, 27 Nov 1890.

71. Charles Kinsky to CF, 27 Jan 1890, MFP.

72. JRC to LRC, Char 28 101, 15–16, 8 Jan 1890.

73. JRC to LRC, Char 28 101 11, 26 Jan 1891.

74. Quoted in Leslie, *The Fabulous Leonard Jerome*, p. 298.

75. This sentence crossed out but still decipherable in 'Scurril': LJ to LL, courtesy of Jonathan Frewen.

76. Undated notes by Shane Leslie, copy in TKP.

77. JRC to LRC, Char 28 101 9–11, 26 Jan 1891.

78. Undated notes by Shane Leslie, TKP.

79. MF to CJ, 21 Jul 1891, MFP.

80. *New York Times*, 6 Sept 1891.

9: DYING BY INCHES IN PUBLIC

1. LRC to JRC, Char 28 12, 25 Jan 1892.
2. LRC to MF, 13 Mar 1891, MFP.
3. Charles Kinsky to MF, n.d. 1891, MFP.
4. *Clarion*, 16 Jan 1892.
5. *Clarion*, 26 Dec 1891.
6. LRC to JRC, Char 28 11, 2 April 1891.
7. Quoted in Churchill and Mitchell, *Jennie*, p. 164.
8. See Foster, *Lord Randolph Churchill*, p. 374.
9. JRC to CF, July 1891, MFP.
10. MF to CF, July 1891, MFP.
11. JRC to CF, n.d. 1891, MFP.
12. Blunt, 'Secret Memoirs', 4 Aug 1885, FMC, vol. IV, ms 28-1975.
13. AE PoW to JRC, Char 28 48, 19 Sept 1894.
14. John H. Mather MD, 'His Father Died of Syphilis: Lord Randolph Churchill: Maladies et Mort', *Finest Hour*, no. 93 (Winter 1996–7), pp. 23–8.
15. Ibid.
16. Dr Chris Clough, Medical Director, Joint Committee on Higher Medical Training, letter to author, 9 Sept 2005.
17. Foster, *Lord Randolph Churchill*, p. 377.
18. Undated notes by Peregrine Spencer Churchill for Dr J. H. Mather, and also Manchester, *The Last Lion*, p. 203.
19. LHJ, vol. 387, 1 Nov 1892.
20. Foster, *Lord Randolph Churchill*, p. 377.
21. LRC to FM, 14 Feb 1893, courtesy of Dr J. H. Mather photocopies.
22. LRC to JRC, Char 28 11 45–6, 23 Nov 1891, quoted in Martin, *Jennie*, vol. I, p. 302; see also 1891 transcript in Dublin from LRC to JRC.
23. Quoted in Martin, *Jennie*, vol. I, p. 299.
24. JRC to LRC, 18 Dec 1891, quoted in Churchill, *Winston S. Churchill*, vol. I: *Youth 1874–1900*, p. 167.
25. Quoted in Martin, *Jennie*, vol. I, p. 301.
26. Quoted in Sandys, *From Winston with Love and Kisses*, p. 167.
27. Frances, Countess of Warwick *Afterthoughts*, p. 81.
28. Quoted in Sandys, *From Winston with Love and Kisses*, p. 168.
29. Quoted in Martin, *Jennie*, vol. I, p. 298.
30. LRC to JRC, Char 28 12 3, 13 Feb 1892.
31. LRC to JRC, Char 28 12 5, 17 Mar 1892.
32. LRC to JRC, Char 28 12 7, 20 Mar 1892.
33. Quoted in Mitchell and Churchill, *Jennie*, p. 165.
34. Ibid.

35. JRC to LRC, quoted in Churchill, *Winston S. Churchill*, companion vol. 1, part 1, p. 268, 25 Sept 1891.

36. Ibid.

37. Quoted in Churchill and Mitchell, *Jennie*, p. 166.

38. LHJ, vol. 384, pp. 107–8, Aug 1892.

39. LRC to JRC, Char 28 12 14, 4 Aug 1892.

40. Ibid.

41. Quoted in Martin, *Jennie*, vol. 1, p. 303.

42. MF to CF, Mar 1893, LP.

43. JRC to LRC, Oct 1892, quoted in Martin, *Jennie*, vol. 1, p. 299.

44. LRC to JRC, Char 28 12 25, 4 Oct 1892.

45. LRC to JRC, Char 28 12 26, 9 Oct 1892.

46. LRC to JRC, Char 28 12 28, 10 Oct 1892.

47. Dr Thomas Keith to Dr Robson Roose, quoted in Churchill, *Winston S. Churchill*, companion vol. 1, part 1, p. 340, 12 (?) Oct 1892.

48. Char 28 11 45–6, quoted in ibid., p. 343.

49. LRC to FM, 31 Oct 1892, courtesy of Dr J. H. Mather photocopies.

50. LHJ, vol. 387, 27/31 Oct 1892.

51. LRC to 'Dearest Winston and Jack', 25 Oct 1892, quoted in Churchill, *Winston S. Churchill*, companion vol. 1, part 1, p. 344.

52. LRC to FM, 31 Oct 1892, courtesy of Dr J. H. Mather photocopies.

53. Churchill, *My Early Life*, p. 44.

54. JRC to WSC, from Kissingen, 7 Aug 1893, quoted in Sandys, *From Winston with Love and Kisses*, p. 181.

55. LRC to WSC, from Kissingen, 9 Aug 1893, quoted in ibid., p. 181.

56. WSC to JRC, Char 28 19 16, 20 Sept 1893, quoted in ibid., p. 189, and Churchill, *Winston S. Churchill*, companion vol. 1, part 1, pp. 413–14.

57. WSC to JRC, Char 28 19 24, 29 Oct 1893.

58. LRC to JRC, Char 28 12, 6 Oct 1893.

59. *Brooklyn Daily Eagle*, 26 Nov 1893.

60. LRC to Dr Thomas Buzzard, papers at RCP, 8 July 1893.

61. Ibid.

62. LRC to JRC, Char 28 12, 10 Dec 1893.

63. LRC to JRC, Char 28 12 66, 3 Feb 1893.

64. Ibid.

65. LRC to JRC, Char 28 12 73, 21 Apr 1894, quoted in Churchill, *Winston S. Churchill, vol. 1: Youth 1874–1900*, p. 469.

66. JRC to WSC, Char 1 8 59, 17 May 1892, quoted in ibid., p. 490.

67. JRC to WSC, Char 1 8 37, 3 May 1892.

68. Shane Leslie review of Rhodes James, *Lord Randolph Churchill*, undated newspaper cutting. Leslie took the phrase used by Lord Rosebery in his *Lord Randolph Churchill*, p. 72, without attributing it.

69. Earl of Rosebery, *Lord Randolph Churchill*, p. 181.

70. Dr Thomas Buzzard to Sir Richard Quain, n.d. Dec 94, RCP.

71. LRC to Dr Thomas Buzzard, 5 June 1894, RCP.

72. Ibid.

73. Dr Thomas Buzzard to JRC, 25 June 1894, RCP.

74. JRC to CF, 8 Nov 1894, TKP.

75. Dr G. E. Keith to Dr Thomas Buzzard, 11 Sept 1894, Grand Hotel, Yokohama, RCP.

76. Dr G. E. Keith to Dr Thomas Buzzard, report no. 13, 3 Oct 1894, RCP.

77. Dr G. E. Keith to Dr Thomas Buzzard, report no. 15, 30 Oct 1894, RCP.

78. Dr G. E. Keith to Dr Thomas Buzzard, report no. 16, 4 Nov 1894, RCP.

79. LRC to FM, 8 Oct 1894, Churchill Archives, Marb 1/17, marked 'Very Private'.

80. FM to LRC, Char 28 109, 20 Nov 1894.

81. JRC to LL, 31 Oct 1894 Singapore, TKP.

82. JRC to CF, 8 Nov 1894, TKP.

83. JRC to LL, n.d., letter transcribed by Shane Leslie, LP (see Epilogue).

84. JRC to LL, 30 Nov 1894, Singapore, TKP.

85. JRC to LL, n.d., letter transcribed with some censorship by Shane Leslie, LP (see Epilogue).

86. JRC to LL, postmarked London, 30 Nov 1894.

87. JRC to CF, 8 Nov 1894, TKP.

88. Typed notes prepared by P. S. Churchill for Dr J. H. Mather, n.d.

89. WSC to JRC, Char 28 20 45–6, 2 Nov 1894.

90. WSC to JRC, Char 28 20 50, 25 Nov 1894.

91. Montague Browne, *Long Sunset*, p. 122.

92. JRC to LL, 10 Dec 1894, P&O Carthage, TKP.

93. JRC to LL, 31 Oct 1894, Singapore, TKP.

94. FM to LRC, Char 28 109 10, 11 Sept 1894.

95. JRC to LL, 18 Jan 1895, TKP.

96. AE PoW to JRC, Char 28 48 30, 27 Dec 1895.

97. JRC to LL, Jan 1895, TKP.

98. Ibid.

99. CF to LL, Jan 1895, TKP.

100. Shane Leslie, *Long Shadows*, p. 25.

101. Shane Leslie review of Rhodes James, *Lord Randolph Churchill*, undated newspaper cutting.

102. Quoted in Rhodes James, *Lord Randolph Churchill*, pp. 369–70.

103. JRC to Lord Justice FitzGibbon, Churchill Archive, 4 Jan 1895. (Letters to JRC on the death of LRC are in Char 28 56–60.)

104. AE PoW to JRC, Char 28 48 35, 27 Jan 1895.

105. Murray Guthrie to JRC, Char 28 58 40, 26 Jan 1895.

106. Lord Curzon to JRC, Char 28 58 53, 10 Feb 1895.

10: ALL MY AMBITIONS ARE CENTRED IN YOU

1. JRC to Lord Justice FitzGibbon, 18 Feb 1895, quoted in Foster, *Lord Randolph Churchill*, p. 379, as 'The very last letter in the huge Churchill archive'.
2. LRC to JSC, quoted in Leslie, *Jennie*, p. 178.
3. Seymour Leslie, *The Jerome Connexion*, p. 10.
4. Unidentified cutting. Remarks by Judge Daniel F. Cohalan on the late W. Bourke Cockran.
5. Anita Leslie, *Jennie*, p. 185.
6. Ibid.
7. William Bourke Cockran Papers, Mss col. 582, Manuscripts and Archives Division, NYPL.
8. 24 Feb 1895, quoted in Churchill and Mitchell, *Jennie*, p. 171.
9. WSC to JRC, 3 July 1895, quoted in Churchill, *Winston S. Churchill*, vol. 1: *Youth 1874–1900*, p. 255.
10. WSC to JRC, Char 28 21, 31 Aug 1895, quoted in Martin, *Jennie*, vol. 2, p. 58.
11. WSC to JRC, quoted in Churchill, *Winston S. Churchill*, companion vol. 1, part 1, p. 572.
12. Quoted in Leslie, *Jennie*, p. 189.
13. Ibid.
14. *Brooklyn Daily Eagle*, 8 Dec 1895.
15. WSC to JSC, 15 Nov 1895, quoted in Churchill, *Winston S. Churchill*, companion vol. 1, part 1, pp. 599–600.
16. Quoted in Gilbert, *Churchill: A Life*, p. 62.
17. Quoted in Churchill, *Winston S. Churchill*, companion vol. 1, part 1, p. 676.
18. JRC to WSC, Char 1 8 64, 1 Oct 1896, quoted in ibid., p. 691.
19. JRC to WSC, Char 1 8 81, 24 Dec 1896, quoted in ibid., p. 717.
20. JRC to WSC, Char 1 8 73–4, 19 Nov 1896, quoted in Churchill, *Winston S. Churchill*, companion vol. 1, part 2, p. 710.
21. JRC to WSC, Char 1 8 75–6, 27 Nov 1896, quoted in Martin, *Jennie*, vol. 2, p. 97.
22. Quoted in Martin, *Jennie*, vol. 2, p. 86.
23. JRC to WSC, Char 1 8 77–8, 11 Dec 1896, quoted in Churchill, *Winston S. Churchill*, companion vol. 1, part 2, p. 710.
24. Quoted in Leslie, *Jennie*, p. 202.
25. Quoted in Leslie, *Long Shadows*, p. 16.
26. See WSC to Lumley and Lumley, 17 Dec 1901, quoted in Churchill, *Winston S. Churchill*, vol. 2: *Young Statesman 1900–1914*, p. 2.
27. WSC to JRC, Char 28 24 20, 19 Jan 1898, quoted in Churchill, *Winston S. Churchill*, companion vol. 1, part 2, pp. 859–63.

28. Quoted in Gilbert *Churchill: A Life*, p. 65.

29. JRC to WSC, Char 1 8 81, 24 Dec 1896, quoted in Churchill, *Winston S. Churchill*, companion vol. 1, part 2, pp. 717–18.

30. Quoted in Consuelo Vanderbilt Balsan, *The Glitter and the Gold*, p. 57.

31. JRC to WSC, Char 1 8 91, 1897, quoted in Churchill, *Winston S. Churchill*, companion vol. 1, part 2, pp. 740–1.

32. Ibid.

33. JRC to WSC, Char 1 8 94, 5 Mar 1897, quoted in Churchill, *Winston S. Churchill*, companion vol. 1, part 2, p. 743.

34. JRC to WSC, Char 1 8 96, 11 Mar 1897, quoted in ibid., p. 744.

35. *Brooklyn Daily Eagle*, 26 Nov 1893.

36. AE PoW to JRC, Char 28 50 42, n.d.

37. Leslie, *Long Shadows*, p. 15.

38. *RLRC*, p. 386.

39. Marie, Queen of Roumania, *The Story of my Life*, vol. 1, p. 81.

40. JRC to WSC, Char 1 8 99, 18 Mar 1897, quoted in Churchill, *Winston S. Churchill*, companion vol. 1, part 2, p. 7.

41. Ibid.

42. Quoted in Gilbert, *Churchill: A Life*, p. 71.

43. JRC to WSC, 7 Oct 1987, quoted in Churchill, *Winston S. Churchill*, vol. 1: *Youth 1874–1900*, p. 355, and Martin, *Jennie*, vol. 2, p. 116.

44. JRC to WSC, Char 1 8 118, 25 Nov 1897, quoted in Churchill, *Winston S. Churchill*, companion vol. 1, part 2, p. 8.

45. WSC to JRC, Char 28 24 79, 13 Apr 1898, quoted in Manchester, *The Last Lion*, p. 261.

46. Quoted in Churchill, *Winston S. Churchill*, vol. 1: *Youth 1874–1900*, p. 351.

47. JRC to WSC, Char 1 8 125–6, 20 Jan 1898, quoted in Churchill, *Winston S. Churchill*, companion vol. 1, part 2, p. 874.

48. Quoted in Churchill, *Winston S. Churchill*, vol. 1: *Youth 1874–1900*, pp. 378–9.

49. JRC to WSC, Char 1 8 127–8, 27 Jan 1898, quoted in Churchill, *Winston S. Churchill*, companion vol. 1, part 2, p. 880.

50. Quoted in Martin, *Jennie*, vol. 2, p. 126.

51. WSC to JRC, Char 28 24 74, 31 March 1898.

52. JRC to WSC, Char 1.8 122, 13 Jan 1898, quoted in Churchill, *Winston S. Churchill*, companion vol. 1, part 2, p. 866.

53. Quoted in Martin, *Jennie*, vol. 2, p. 121.

54. Ibid.

55. WSC to JRC, Char 28 24 10, 5 Jan 1898.

56. WSC to JRC, Char 28 24 11, 6 Jan 1898.

57. JRC to WSC, Char 1 8 125, quoted in Churchill, *Winston S. Churchill*, companion vol. 1, part 2, pp. 874–5.

58. WSC to JRC, Char 28 24 40, 16 Feb 1898.

59. Adolphus Liddell to Constance Wenlock, 5 Dec 1887, University of Hull, Brynmor Jones Library, DDFA 3/5/3 – with thanks to Richard Davenport-Hines.

60. WSC to JRC, Char 28 24 32, 28 Jan 1898, quoted in Gilbert, *Churchill: A Life*, p. 65.

61. Ibid.

62. Quoted in ibid., p. 88.

63. Quoted in Eliot, *They All Married Well*, p. 73.

64. Quoted in Frances, Countess of Warwick, *Life's Ebb and Flow*, p. 141.

65. R. B. Haldane to JRC, 15 July 1898, quoted in Churchill, *Winston S. Churchill*, vol. 1: *Youth 1874–1900*, p. 396.

66. Quoted in Gilbert, *Churchill: A Life*, p. 92.

67. Quoted in Martin, *Jennie*, vol. 2, p. 150, and Churchill, *Winston S. Churchill*, companion vol. 1, part 2.

68. Quoted in Gilbert, *Churchill: A Life*, pp. 96–100.

69. Quoted in ibid., p. 98.

70. Quoted in Eileen Quelch, *Perfect Darling*, p. 144.

71. AE PoW to JRC, Char 28 48 57, 31 Oct 1896.

72. AE PoW to JRC, Char 28 64 19, 30 Mar 1898.

73. George Cornwallis-West, *Edwardian Hey-Days*, p. 102.

74. GCW to JRC, Char 28 34 1, 4 Jan 1898.

75. Letter from Daisy, Princess of Pless (writing under a pseudonym) to the Marquis de Soveral, 17 Jan 1899. Private information, thanks to Christine Rickards Rostworowska.

76. GCW to JRC, Char 28 34 6, 9 July 1898.

77. Quoted in Ethel Smyth, *What Happened Next*, p. 285.

78. Quoted in Martin, *Jennie*, vol. 1, p. 146.

79. JRC to GCW, Char 28 34 53, 9 Nov 1898.

11: THE VERSATILITY OF LADY RANDOLPH IS QUITE UNUSUAL

1. *RLRC*, p. 361.

2. WSC to JRC, Char 28 26, 1 Jan 1899, quoted in Churchill, *Winston S. Churchill*, companion vol. 1, part 2, pp. 997–8.

3. Quoted in Martin, *Jennie*, vol. 2, p. 159.

4. JRC to William Bourke Cockran, William Bourke Cockran Papers, Manuscript and Archives Division, NYPL.

5. JRC to William Bourke Cockran, n.d., William Bourke Cockran Papers, Manuscript and Archives Division, NYPL.

6. Quoted in Michael McMenamin and Curt Zoller, *Becoming Winston Churchill:*

The Untold Story of Young Winston and his American Mentor, p. 115.

7. Email from Michael McMenamin to author, 7 Feb 2007.

8. Quoted in Martin, *Jennie*, vol. 2, p. 162.

9. Quoted in ibid., p. 164.

10. Lady Randolph Spencer Churchill, ed., *Anglo-Saxon Review: A Quarterly Miscellany*, introductory essay.

11. Major Desmond Chapman-Huston, *The Lost Historian: A Memoir of Sir Sidney Low*, p. 101.

12. Quoted in Martin, *Jennie*, vol. 2, p. 165.

13. *RLRC*, p. 367.

14. Quoted in Chapman-Huston, *The Lost Historian: A Memoir of Sir Sidney Low*, p. 103.

15. Warwick, *Life's Ebb and Flow*, p. 138.

16. Undated newspaper cutting, Churchill Archives, Aug 1899.

17. Lord Rosebery to JRC, 28 Sept 1901, quoted in *RLRC*, p. 366.

18. GCW to JRC, Char 28 35 4, 5 Jan 1899.

19. GCW to JRC, Char 28 35 22, 16 Mar 1899.

20. Quoted in Manchester, *The Last Lion*, p. 320, and in Eliot, *They All Married Well*, p. 74.

21. GCW to JRC, Char 28 35 48, 11 Aug 1899.

22. GCW to JRC, Char 28 35 50, 14 Aug 1899.

23. GCW to JRC, Char 28 35 57, 20 Aug 1899.

24. GCW to JRC, Char 28 35 50, 14 Aug 1899.

25. GCW to JRC, Char 28 35 67, 16 Sept 1899.

26. WSC to JRC, quoted in Martin, *Jennie*, vol. 2, p. 193.

27. Ibid.

28. Ibid.

29. Mrs Pearl Craigie to Father Brown, 4 Oct 1899, Reading University Manuscript Papers.

30. Correspondence between Stephen Crane and LRC, 1899 Crane Papers, Rare Books and Manuscript Library, Columbia University.

31. Quoted in Leslie, *Jennie*, p. 234.

32. Lady Randolph Churchill, 'Plans of American Women in London', *New York Times*, 27 Oct 1899.

33. Quoted in Leslie, *Jennie*, p. 235.

34. *RLRC*, p. 409.

35. Quoted in Leslie *Jennie*, p. 238.

36. Ibid.

37. JRC to LL, 24 Dec 1899, Hospital Ship *Maine*, TKP.

38. *Natal Witness*, 8 June 1900.

39. *Natal Witness*, 20 Nov 1900.

40. Quoted in Johan Wassermann and Brian Kearney, eds, *A Warrior's Gateway: Durban and the Anglo-Boer War 1899–1902*, p. 226.

41. JRC to CF, 16 Jan 1900, MFP.

42. Ibid.

43. *Natal Witness*, 20 Nov 1900.

44. Lady Randolph Churchill, 'Letters from a Hospital Ship', *Anglo-Saxon Review*, vol. V (Jun 1900), p. 218.

45. JRC to LL, 3 Feb 1900, TKP.

46. Quoted in Martin, *Jennie*, vol. 2, p. 223.

47. Churchill Archives, 'The American Ladies Hospital Ship' photograph, ROCH 9/1/8.

48. GCW to JRC, Char 28 36 8–9, 8 Feb 1900.

49. JRC to CF, 12 Mar 1900, MFP.

50. Quoted in Richard J. Kahn, 'Women and Men at Sea: Gender Debate Aboard the Hospital Ship *Maine*', *Journal of History of Medicine*, vol. 56 (2001), pp. 111–39.

51. *RLRC*, p. 403.

52. Lady Randolph Churchill, 'Letters from a Hospital Ship', *Anglo-Saxon Review*, vol. V (Jun 1900), p. 218.

53. *Natal Witness*, 20 Nov 1900.

54. *Nursing Record and Hospital World*, 10 Feb 1900.

55. Quoted in Martin, *Jennie*, vol. 2, p. 231.

56. Undated newspaper cutting, quoted in ibid., p. 230.

57. Quoted in Martin, *Jennie*, vol. 2, p. 187.

58. GCW to JRC, Char 28 36 5–7, 2 Feb 1900.

59. WSC to JRC, 9 June 1900, quoted in Churchill, *Winston S. Churchill*, vol. 1: *Youth 1874–1900*, p. 530.

60. JRC to JSC, 28 July 1900, quoted in Leslie, *Jennie*, p. 253.

61. Daisy, Princess of Pless, *From my Private Diary*, p. 47.

62. Quoted in Tim Coates, *Patsy*, p. 35.

63. GCW to JRC, Char 28 36 24, 2 May 1900.

64. Quoted in Lady Maud Warrender, *My First Sixty Years*, p. 194.

65. AE PoW to JRC, Char 28 49 28, quoted in Leslie, *Jennie*, p. 253.

66. Churchill, *Winston S. Churchill*, vol. 1: *Youth 1874–1900*, p. 532.

67. GCW in conversation with Shane Leslie, quoted in Leslie, *Jennie*, p. 254.

68. WSC to JRC, 21 Sept 1900, quoted in Churchill, *Winston S. Churchill*, vol. 1: *Youth 1874–1900*, p. 536.

69. Ibid.

70. Ibid., pp. 540–1.

71. James Pond to JRC, Char 28 66 80, 2 Nov 1900.

72. Quoted in Churchill, *Winston S. Churchill*, vol. 1: *Youth 1874–1900*, p. 543.

73. WSC to JRC, 1 Jan 1901, quoted in ibid., pp. 544–5.

74. WSC to JRC, Char 28 26, 22 Jan 1901, quoted in ibid.

75. Mrs Pearl Craigie to Father Brown, 21 Feb 1901, Reading University Manuscript Collection.

76. GCW to JRC, Char 28 36 37, 28 Apr 1901.

77. WSC to JRC, 14 Feb 1901, quoted in Churchill, *Winston S. Churchill*, vol. 2: *Young Statesman 1900–1914*, p. 2.

78. Quoted in Gilbert, *Churchill: A Life*, p. 140.

79. WSC to Lumley and Lumley, 17 Dec 1901, quoted in ibid.

80. JRC to JSC, quoted in Martin, *Jennie*, vol. 2, p. 275.

81. Duke of Connaught to LL, 1 Jan 1904, LP.

82. Quoted in Leslie, *Jennie*, p. 264.

12: HAUNTED BY THE FUTURE

1. Cornwallis-West, *Edwardian Hey-Days*, pp. 128 and 234.

2. Leslie, *The Jerome Connexion*, p. 9.

3. Lord Curzon to JRC, Char 28 66, 25 Dec 1900, quoted in Martin, *Jennie*, vol. 2, p. 267.

4. WSC to JRC, Char 28 27 1, 3 Apr 1902.

5. WSC to JRC, Char 28 24 20, 19 Jan 1899.

6. WSC to JRC, Char 28 27 2, 15 Aug 1902.

7. Ibid.

8. WSC to JRC, Char 28 27 35, 9 Feb 1905.

9. WSC to JRC, Char 28 27 20, 18 Sept 1903.

10. WSC to JRC, 19 Dec 1902, quoted in Martin, *Jennie*, vol. 2, p. 289.

11. Feb 1901, quoted in ibid., p. 272.

12. Daisy, Princess of Pless, *From my Private Diary*, 9 Apr 1903, p. 84.

13. Ibid, p. 99.

14. Celia Lee, ed., *A Soldier's Wife: Diary of Jean, Lady Hamilton*, 2 Dec 1903.

15. Hugh wrote later, 'On 9 October 1904, my father [Moreton] came up to Trinity to "celebrate" my majority and to raise some thousands of pounds on my Innishannon inheritance on the plea that if I did not agree he would go bankrupt. It was not until long after that he admitted to me that this had been a deliberate mis-statement.' 'Hugh's grand letter', 18 Aug 1956, remarked Shane. LP.

16. CF to MF, 2 Jun 1901, MFP, quoted in Kehoe, *Fortune's Daughters*, p. 222.

17. Clarissa, Lady Avon, interview with author, 2 Feb 2005.

18. 'Hugh's grand letter', 18 Aug 1956, LP.

19. Quoted in Anita Leslie, *Cousin Clare*, p. 36.

20. Quoted in Martin, *Jennie*, vol. 2, p. 284.

NOTES

21. Emile Fuchs, *With Pencil Brush and Chisel: The Life of an Artist*, p. 49.
22. May Geolet letter, autumn 1902, from Bad Homburg, quoted in Marian Fowler, *In a Gilded Cage: From Heiress to Duchess*, p. 280.
23. Cornwallis-West, *Edwardian Hey-Days*, p. 119.
24. WSC to JRC, Char 28 27 23, 26 Mar 1904.
25. WSC to JRC, Char 28 27 24, 22 Aug 1904, quoted in Churchill, *Winston S. Churchill*, companion vol. 2, part 1, pp. 450–1.
26. Cornwallis-West, *Edwardian Hey-Days*, p. 147.
27. Quoted in John Churchill, *Crowded Canvas*, p. 20.
28. WSC to JRC, Char 28 27 10, quoted in Churchill, *Winston S. Churchill*, companion vol. 2, part 1, pp. 176–7.
29. Quoted in Natalie Adams, Churchill Archives Centre, 'An Ardent Ally: Lady Randolph and Winston's Political Career,' *Finest Hour*, no. 98 (Spring 1998), pp. 14–16.
30. WSC to Lord James, 18 Jan 1906, James Mss m 45/1432, quoted in Foster, *Lord Randolph Churchill*, p. 386.
31. Leslie, *The Jerome Connexion*, p. 9.
32. See Elizabeth Crawford, *Women's Suffrage Movement of England and Ireland: A Reference Guide, 1866–1928*, p. 220.
33. Quoted in Adams, 'An Ardent Ally'.
34. WSC to JRC, Char 28 27 52, 24 Jun 1906, quoted in Churchill, *Winston S. Churchill*, companion vol. 2, part 1, p. 409.
35. Quoted in Quelch, *Perfect Darling*, p. 83.
36. WSC to JRC, Char 28 27 63, 13 Oct 1906, quoted in Churchill, *Winston S. Churchill*, companion vol. 2, part 1, p. 588.
37. JRC to WSC, Char 28 78 44, quoted in Amanda Mackenzie Stuart, *Consuelo and Alva*, p. 270.
38. GCW to WSC, Char 1 57 9, 21 Oct 1906, quoted in ibid., p. 272.
39. JRC to Consuelo Vanderbilt, Char 28 78 45, quoted in ibid., p. 273.
40. Quoted in Churchill and Mitchell, *Jennie*, p. 227.
41. Mrs Pearl Craigie to Fr William Brown, 12 Apr 1906, The Papers of Mrs Pearl Craigie, Special Collections, University of Reading.
42. Daisy, Princess of Pless, *From my Private Diary*, 14 Apr 1907, p. 163.
43. When George's marriage to Stella broke down she discovered that he had been visiting a lady friend in Hampshire with whom he had been on close terms since before his marriage to Jennie. Private information.
44. JRC to LL, from Salisbury Hall, 15 May 1907, quoted in Churchill and Mitchell, *Jennie*, p. 228.
45. Cornwallis-West, *Edwardian Hey-Days*, p. 119.
46. JRC to WSC, Char 1 65 27, 22 Mar 1907.
47. JRC to unidentified correspondent, Char 28 78 53–4, Mar 1907.
48. Quoted in Martin, *Jennie*, vol. 2, p. 310.

49. JRC to WSC, Char 1 66 10, 22 Aug 1907, quoted in Churchill, *Winston S. Churchill*, companion vol. 2, part 1, pp. 670–1.

50. Quoted in Martin, *Jennie*, vol. 2, p. 310.

51. WSC to JRC, Char 28 27 67, 21 Aug 1907.

52. WSC to JRC, Char 28 27 64–6, n.d.

53. Quoted in Martin, *Jennie*, vol. 2, p. 311.

54. WSC to JRC, Char 28 27 72, 26 Sept 1907.

55. Cornwallis-West, *Edwardian Hey-Days*, p. 119.

56. JRC to Shane Leslie, 14 Nov 1908, TKP.

57. Char 28 78 63, 5 Oct 1908, quoted in Churchill and Mitchell, *Jennie*, p. 229.

58. Quoted in Kehoe, *Fortune's Daughters*, p. 256.

59. Clarissa, Lady Avon, interview with author, 2 Feb 2005.

60. Quoted in Martin, *Jennie*, vol. 2, p. 312.

61. Ibid.

62. Quoted in ibid., p. 313.

63. Ibid.

64. Quoted in Jill Liddington, *Rebel Girls*, pp. 186–7.

65. Violet Bonham Carter, *Lantern Slides: Diaries and Letters 1904–1914*, p. 162.

66. Marsh, *A Number of People*, p. 154.

67. WSC to JRC, Char 28 27 86, 13 Sept 1908, quoted in Churchill, *Winston S. Churchill*, companion vol. 2, part 2, p. 819.

68. WSC to JRC, Char 28 27 86a, 20 Sept 1908.

69. Mary Soames, interview with author, 16 Nov 2004.

70. Evan Charteris to JRC, Char 28 78 70, 1908.

71. Clarissa, Lady Avon, interview with author, 2 Feb 2005.

72. Ibid.

73. Quoted in Martin, *Jennie*, vol. 2, p. 319.

74. Ibid.

75. Quoted in Mary Soames, *Clementine Churchill*, p. 51.

76. Quoted in ibid., p. 57.

77. 29 Sept 1908, quoted in Leslie, *Jennie*, p. 284.

78. Mary Soames, interview with author, 16 Nov 2004.

79. Quoted in Soames, *Clementine Churchill*, p. 57.

80. Lady Montague Browne, interview with author, 29 Jun 2005.

81. JRC to Shane Leslie, 18 Nov 1908, TKP.

82. Terry, *The Story of my Life*, p. 352.

83. Quoted in Martin, *Jennie*, p. 376.

84. JRC to Shane Leslie, 18 Nov 1908, TKP.

85. Cornwallis-West, *Edwardian Hey-Days*, p. 119.

86. Quoted in Churchill and Mitchell, *Jennie*, p. 230

87. WSC to JRC, Char 28 27 87, 16 May 1909.

88. Cornwallis-West, *Edwardian Hey-Days*, p. 264.
89. Quoted in Quelch, *Perfect Darling*, p. 110.
90. JRC to LL, 27 Jun 1909, copy transcribed by Shane Leslie, TKP; also quoted in Churchill and Mitchell, *Jennie*, p. 231.
91. Duke of Connaught to LL, 31 Jan 1904, LP. The correspondence between Leonie and the Duke of Connaught was willed to Seymour Leslie, who returned it to the Royal Family. It is now in the Windsor Archives, but was not available to this biographer.
92. JRC to LL, 27 Jun 1909, copy transcribed by Shane Leslie, TKP; also partly quoted in Churchill and Mitchell, *Jennie*, p. 231.
93. Max Beerbohm, *Around Theatres*.
94. Quoted in Margot Peters, *Mrs Pat: The Life of Mrs Patrick Campbell*, p. 290.
95. WSC to JRC, Char 28 27 88, 4 Aug 1909.
96. Ibid.
97. Leslie, *The Jerome Connexion*, p. 14.
98. Charles Kinsky to JRC, Char 28 78, 23 Apr 1909.
99. Ethel Smyth to Shane Leslie, 17 Mar 1940, TKP.

13: COURAGE ENOUGH TO FIGHT MY OWN BATTLE IN LIFE

1. Quoted in Lee, ed., *A Soldier's Wife*, p. 42.
2. JRC to Queen Alexandra, Char 28 78 73, 9 May 1910.
3. CSC to WSC, 20 Apr 1911, quoted in Mary Soames, ed., *Speaking for Themselves*, p. 42.
4. WSC to GCW, 13 Apr 1911, copy transcribed by Shane Leslie, LP L/4/15.
5. WSC to JRC, 13 Apr 1911, copy transcribed by Shane Leslie, LP L/4/15.
6. Ibid. By comparison, Mrs Keppel in 1918 had investments yielding around £20,000 a year, which she considered necessary for her clothes, flowers and general lifestyle.
7. Mary Soames interview with author, 16 Nov 2004.
8. Leslie, *Jennie*, p. 305.
9. CSC papers courtesy of Lady Soames, n.d. probably 3 Jun 1911, to WSC.
10. Soames, ed., *Speaking for Themselves*, p. 45.
11. Unidentified cutting, quoted in Martin, *Jennie*, vol. 2, p. 342.
12. CSC to WSC, n.d. (probably 3 Jun 1911), courtesy of Lady Soames.
13. H. Hamilton Fyfe, *Shakespeare Memorial Souvenir of the Shakespeare Ball*, ed. and with an introduction by Mrs G. Cornwallis-West.
14. WSC to CSC, 25 Jun 1911, quoted in Soames, ed., *Speaking for Themselves*, p. 48. Maxine Elliott introduced Churchill to fellow MP Archibald Sinclair,

who also had an American mother. As early as 1905 Sinclair and Churchill discussed the possibility of drawing closer to the US, which both men favoured.

15. Undated press release, Churchill Archives Papers.
16. JRC to Mrs Alfred Lyttelton, Char 28 78 83, 5 Aug 1911.
17. Ibid.
18. Mrs Alfred Lyttelton to JRC, Char 28 78 80, 2 Aug 1911.
19. Cornwallis-West, *Edwardian Hey-Days*, p. 163.
20. Ibid., p. 164.
21. Ibid.
22. GCW to JRC, Char 28 39 3, 7 Jan 1912.
23. GCW to JRC, Char 28 39 4, 29 Dec 1912.
24. JRC to GCW, Char 28 39, 5, 31 Dec 1912, in draft, quoted in Martin, *Jennie*, vol. 2, p. 352.
25. GCW to JRC, Char 28 39 9, 15 Oct 1913.
26. GCW to JRC, Char 28 39 8, 13 Jun 1913.
27. GCW to JRC, Char 28 39 10–11, 31 Dec 1913.
28. JRC to 'Sniffy,' 30 Dec 1913, copy transcribed by Shane Leslie, TKP.
29. Seymour Leslie notes, TKP.
30. JSC to JRC, Char 28 33 4-5, 14 Feb 1914.
31. JSC to JRC, Char 28 33 8-9, 3 Mar 1914.
32. JSC to JRC, Char 28 33 12, 7 Mar 1914.
33. JRC to GCW, Char 28 39 19, 4 Apr 1914.
34. Shelagh Grosvenor to JRC, Char 28 39 20, 15 Apr 1914.
35. Shane Leslie to Jack Leslie, 23 Oct 1914, LP L/2/9, quoted in Kehoe *Fortune's Daughters*, p. 294.
36. LL to JRC, Char 28 136 20, 1915, quoted in ibid., p. 305.
37. JRC to LL, 28 Oct 1905, TKP.
38. Quoted in Leslie, *Jennie*, p. 307.
39. Quoted in ibid., p. 331.
40. JRC to LL, 15 Sept 1914, copy transcribed by Shane Leslie, TKP.
41. JRC to Shane Leslie, 4 Nov 1917, Shane Leslie Papers, Georgetown University, Washington DC.
42. Shane Leslie to JRC, Char 28 129, 12 Dec 1917.
43. Quoted in Leslie, *Jennie*, p. 318.
44. Quoted in Martin Gilbert, *Winston S. Churchill*, vol. 3: *1914–1916*, p. 473.
45. Quoted in Leslie, *Cousin Clare*, p. 78, 4 Jul 1915.
46. Lee, ed., *A Soldier's Wife*, Jul 1915, p. 130.
47. Quoted in Leslie, *Jennie*, p. 321.
48. Quoted in Gilbert, *Churchill: A Life*, p. 328.
49. Quoted in ibid., p. 324.
50. Quoted in Kehoe, *Fortune's Daughters*, p. 309.

51. WSC to CSC, 1 Dec 1915, quoted in Soames, ed., *Speaking for Themselves*, p. 124.

52. Char 28 120 3–4, 1 Dec 1915, quoted in Gilbert, *Winston S. Churchill*, companion vol. 3, part 2, p. 1301.

53. Vittoria Colonna, Duchess of Sermoneta, *Sparkle Distant Worlds*, p. 12.

54. WSC to JRC, 29 Jan 1916, LP.

55. JRC to Shane Leslie, 3 Sep 1916, Herstmonceux, TKP.

56. Ibid.

57. CSC to WSC, 6 Apr 1916, quoted in Soames, ed., *Speaking for Themselves*, pp. 197–8.

58. Leslie, *The Jerome Connexion*, p. 54.

59. Quoted in ibid., p. 14.

60. Quoted in Lee, ed., *A Soldier's Wife*, p. 121.

61. JRC to Shane Leslie, 4 Nov 1917, TKP.

62. Quoted in Violet Bonham Carter, *Winston Churchill as I Knew Him*, p. 464.

63. Quoted in Martin, *Jennie*, vol. 2, p. 373.

64. Bonham Carter, *Winston Churchill as I Knew Him*, p. 463.

65. Quoted in Leslie, *Jennie*, p. 313.

66. JRC to Shane Leslie, n.d., from 72 Brook Street, TKP.

67. Interview quoted by C. Kay Larson in her Introduction to Jennie Spencer Churchill, *Women's War Work*. This undated introduction was specially prepared for the internet and is a New York Military Affairs Symposium document available at http://libraryautomation.com/nymas/jenniechurchill.html

68. JRC to Shane Leslie, 3 Sept 1916, TKP.

69. Quoted in Martin Gilbert, *Churchill and America* (Thurso Papers, 11 Apr 1917).

70. Quoted in Soames, ed., *Speaking for Themselves*, 14 Feb 1921, p. 229.

71. Char 28 84 13, 26 July 1914.

14: PUTTING MY BEST FOOT FORWARD

1. JSC to JRC, Char 28 121 71, 25 May 1918.

2. Quoted in Martin, *Jennie*, vol. 2, p. 387.

3. Quoted in ibid. Ralph Martin interviewed Montagu Porch while researching his biography of Jennie published in 1971.

4. MP to WSC, quoted in Martin, *Jennie*, vol. 2, p. 390.

5. Lytton Strachey to Dora Carrington, 20 Jun 1918, quoted in Lytton Strachey, *Letters*, p. 400.

6. Sunny, Duke of Marlborough to Gladys Deacon, 22 Jun 1918, courtesy of Hugo Vickers.

7. Sunny, Duke of Marlborough to Gladys Deacon, 24 Jun 1918, courtesy of Hugo Vickers.

8. Letter from Ethel Smyth to Shane Leslie, 17 Mar 1940, TKP.

9. Lee, ed., *A Soldier's Wife*, p. 186.

10. Shane Leslie to Anita Leslie, n.d., TKP.

11. Rhodes James, ed., *Chips: The Diaries of Sir Henry Channon*, p. 295.

12. Ibid.

13. JRC to GCW, 17 Jun 1919, quoted in Leslie, *Jennie*, p. 338.

14. Oswald Frewen Diary, 12 Mar 1920, courtesy of Jonathan Frewen.

15. Ibid., 24 Sept 1920.

16. Ibid., 30 Sept 1920.

17. Ibid., 22 Nov 1920.

18. Ibid.

19. Clare Sheridan to Shane Leslie, Moscow, 17 Oct 1920, TKP.

20. Newspaper cutting quoted in Martin, *Jennie*, vol. 2, p. 239.

21. Two months after Jennie's death one of them, Marigold or 'the Duckadilly', Winston and Clemmie's youngest, died suddenly after catching a fever. She was aged two years nine months. Mary was born almost a year later on 15 September 1922 and so never knew her grandmother Jennie.

22. Quoted in Lee, ed., *A Soldier's Wife*, p. 246.

23. WSC to CSC, 6 Feb 1921, quoted in Soames, ed., *Speaking for Themselves*, p. 225.

24. Vittoria Sermoneta, *Sparkle Distant Worlds*, p. 11.

25. Ibid., p. 12.

26. MP to JRC , Char 28 133 1–3, May 1921.

27. Oswald Frewen Diary, 13 Jun 1921, courtesy of Jonathan Frewen.

28. Ibid., 28 Jun 1921.

29. Lee, ed., *A Soldier's Wife*, p. 185.

30. Quoted in Lady Cynthia Asquith, *Diaries 1915–1918*, 2 Jun 1918, p. 445.

31. WSC to Lady Islington, 1 July 1921, quoted in Manchester, *The Last Lion*, p. 760.

32. Oswald Frewen Diary, 29 Jun 1921, courtesy of Jonathan Frewen.

33. Quoted in Martin Gilbert, *Winston S. Churchill*, vol. 4: *1917–22*, p. 601.

34. Lord Curzon to WSC, in ibid., p. 602.

35. WSC to Lord Curzon, in ibid.

36. Oswald Frewen Diary, 2 Jul 1921, courtesy of Jonathan Frewen.

37. Ibid.

38. JRC to MP, quoted in Martin, *Jennie*, vol. 2, p. 393.

39. Undated notes prepared by Seymour Leslie for Anita Leslie, TKP.

40. Quoted in Kehoe, *Fortune's Daughters*, p. 345.

41. Lord Oxford and Asquith to WSC, Char 1 140 5, 29 Jun 1921.

42. David Lloyd George to WSC, Char 1 141 71, 29 Jun 1921.
43. *New York Evening Post*, 2 Jul 1921, obituary. See Char 1 140 for JRC obituaries.

EPILOGUE

1. Sir Anthony and Lady Montague Browne, interview with author, 29 Jun 2005.
2. John Lukacs, *Five Days in London: May 1940*, p. 22.
3. *RLRC*, p. 174.
4. Lady Cynthia Asquith, *Diaries 1915–1918*, 1 Jun 1918, pp. 444–5. An indication of Lady Cynthia's propensity to believe the worst of Jennie may be found in an account she gives in the diaries of an 'ugly story' involving Black Jane falling in love with a private and insisting that General Cowans give the man a commission. In fact the woman involved in that story was another Mrs Cornwallis-West, George's mother Patsy. Ibid., 8 Aug 1916, pp. 201–2.
5. Seymour Leslie to Anita Leslie, 16 Jun 1968, TKP.
6. Manchester, *The Last Lion*, p. 137.
7. Clare Sheridan to Anita Leslie, 24 Aug 1951, TKP.
8. Frances, Countess of Warwick, to JRC, Char 28 136 62–3, *c.* 1915.
9. Marquis de Breteuil to JRC, Char 28 43 8.
10. JRC to LL, 31 Oct 1894, Singapore, TKP.
11. Reproduced in Rossmore, *Things I Can Tell*, p. 1.
12. Harris, *My Life and Loves*, p. 490.
13. Quoted in *Atlantic Monthly*, 27 Mar 2002.
14. Anita Leslie, interview with *Washington Post*, undated cutting, TKP.
15. Ralph Martin, telephone conversation with author, 16 Dec 2005.
16. Anita Leslie, interview with *Washington Post*, undated cutting, TKP.
17. Undated notes, TKP.
18. Quoted in Gilbert, *Churchill and America*, p. xxii.
19. Courtesy of Jonathan Frewen.
20. There are no references in the Churchill Archive which could prove the existence of Jennie's tattoo. Yet it has been taken for granted by a number of social commentators not only that she had one, but that she was one of the first to adopt the craze. 'Lady Randolph Churchill had for some time hidden the tattooed snake which encircled her arm under a broad bracelet,' states one such authority. The fashion for tattooing at the end of the nineteenth century probably derived from the number of gentlemen and sailors who visited the Far East and returned to England with a small animal on their hand or shoulder. Smart society mostly visited Mr Sutherland Macdonald, a former British Army Royal Engineer, who set up a tattoo studio called the Hamman in

Jermyn Street in the 1890s. Many European aristocrats were believed to have tattoos, including the Prince of Wales, King Edward VII, the Duke of Clarence, King George V and Tsar Nicholas II. Pictures of Jennie in her last years where her arm is visible would indicate that there was no tattoo on her wrist.

21. Letter from Sir Archibald James to Anita Leslie, TKP.

Select Bibliography

Thousands of books have been written about Winston Churchill and dozens more continue to appear each year. Listed below, with a number of related titles, is a small selection of those which I have found most helpful. The place of publication is London unless otherwise stated.

Airlie, Mabell, Countess of, *With the Guards We Shall Go*, Hodder & Stoughton, 1933

Andrews, Allen, *The Splendid Pauper*, Harrap, 1968

Asquith, Lady Cynthia, *Diaries 1915–1918*, Hutchinson, 1968

Auerbach, Nina, *Ellen Terry*, W. W. Norton, 1987

Balfour, Arthur, *Chapters of an Autobiography*, Cassell, 1930

Balsan, Consuelo Vanderbilt, *The Glitter and the Gold*, Maidstone, George Mann Books, 1973

Baring, Maurice, *The Puppet Show of Memory*, Heinemann, 1922

Beerbohm, Max, *Around Theatres*, Simon & Schuster, 1954

Belmont, Mrs August, *The Fabric of Memory*, New York, Farrar, Straus & Giroux, 1957

Berger, Meyer, *The Story of the New York Times 1851–1951*, New York, Simon & Schuster, 1951

Bibesco, Princess Martha, *Sir Winston Churchill: Master of Courage*, Robert Hale, 1957

Bonham Carter, Violet, *Winston Churchill as I Knew Him*, Eyre & Spottiswoode, 1965

Bonham Carter, Violet, *Lantern Slides: Diaries and Letters 1904–14*, ed. Mark Bonham Carter and Mark Pottle, Weidenfeld & Nicolson, 1996

Brandon, Ruth, *The Dollar Princesses*, New York, Knopf, 1980

Brendon, Piers, *Winston Churchill: A Brief Life*, Pimlico, 2001

Brett, Reginald, Viscount Esher, *Cloud-capp'd Towers*, John Murray, 1927

Brown, Malcom, *George Moore: A Reconsideration*, Seattle, University of Washington Press, 1955

Burchett, George, *Memoirs of a Tattooist*, Oldbourne, 1958

Campbell, Mrs Patrick, *My Life and Some Letters*, Hutchinson, 1922

Carey, Agnes, *Empress Eugénie in Exile*, Eveleigh Nash & Grayson, 1922

Chapman-Huston, Major Desmond, *The Lost Historian: A Memoir of Sidney Low*, John Murray, 1936

Chapman-Huston, Major Desmond, ed., *The Private Diaries of Daisy, Princess of Pless 1873– 1914*, John Murray, 1950

Churchill, Jennie Spencer [Lady Randolph Churchill], *Women's War Work*, C. A. Pearson, 1916

Churchill, John, *Crowded Canvas*, Odhams Press, 1961

Churchill, Peregrine and Mitchell, Julian, *Jennie: A Portrait with Letters*, Collins, 1974

Churchill, Lady Randolph, *Small Talks on Big Subjects*, C. A. Pearson, 1916

Churchill, Lady Randolph Spencer, ed., *The Anglo-Saxon Review: A Quarterly Miscellany*, 10 vols, London and New York, John Lane, 1899–1901

Churchill, Randolph S., *Winston S. Churchill*, vol. 1: *Youth 1874–1900*, Heinemann, 1966 (and companion volumes)

Churchill, Randolph S., *Winston S. Churchill*, vol. 2: *Young Statesman 1900–1914*, Heinemann, 1967 (and companion volumes)

Churchill, Randolph S., *What I Said about the Press*, Weidenfeld & Nicolson, 1967

Churchill, Winston S., *Savrola*, Longman, 1900

Churchill, Winston S., *Lord Randolph Churchill*, 2 vols, Macmillan, 1906

Churchill, Winston S., *My Early Life*, Macmillan, 1930

Churchill, Winston S., *Painting as a Pastime*, Odhams Press, 1948

Churchill, Winston S., *The Second World War*, 6 vols, Cassell, 1948–1954

Churchill, Winston S., *Marlborough: His Life and Times*, ed. Henry Steele, New York, Commager, 1968

Churchill, Winston S., *A History of the English-Speaking Peoples*, one-volume abridgement by Christopher Lee, Cassell, 1998

Churchill, Winston S., *The Dream,* republished by The Levenger Press, 2005

Clark, Barrett H., *Intimate Portraits*, New York, Dramatists Play Service, 1951

Coates, Tim, *Patsy: The Story of Mary Cornwallis-West*, Bloomsbury, 2003

Colby, Vineta, *The Singular Anomaly*, University of London Press, 1970

Cornwallis-West, George, *Edwardian Hey-Days*, London and New York, Putnam, 1930

Cornwallis-West, George, *Edwardians Go Fishing*, Putnam, 1932

Cornwallis-West, Mrs George, *The Reminiscences of Lady Randolph Churchill*, New York, Century, 1907; and London, Edward Arnold, 1908

Cornwallis-West, Mrs George, *His Borrowed Plumes*, British Library Manuscript Collections, LCP 1909/16

Cowles, Virginia, *Edward VII and his Circle*, Hamish Hamilton, 1956

Crawford, Elizabeth, *The Women's Suffrage Movement in Britain and Ireland: A Reference Guide*, Routledge, 2005

Davis, Elmer, *History of the New York Times*, New York, New York Times, 1921

Davis, Richard Harding, *About Paris*, New York, Harper & Brothers, 1895

Dilks, David, *Curzon in India*, 2 vols, Hart-Davis, 1969

Dilks, David, *Neville Chamberlain*, Cambridge, Cambridge University Press, 1984

Dilks, David, *The Great Dominion: Winston Churchill in Canada 1900–1954*, Toronto, Thomas Allen Publishers, 2005

Dunraven, Wyndham Thomas, fourth Earl of, *Past Times and Pastimes*, 2 vols, Hodder & Stoughton, 1923

Eade, Charles, ed., *The Unrelenting Struggle: War Speeches by the Rt Hon. Winston S. Churchill*, Cassell, 1942

Eliot, Elizabeth, *They All Married Well*, Cassell, 1960

Field, Julian Osgood, *Uncensored Recollections*, E. Nash, 1924

Fielding, Daphne, *The Duchess of Jermyn Street*, Eyre & Spottiswoode, 1964

Forbes-Robertson, Diana, *My Aunt Maxine: The Story of Maxine Elliott*, New York, Viking Press, 1964

Foster, R. F., *Lord Randolph Churchill: A Political Life*, Oxford, Clarendon Press, 1981

Foster, R. F., *Paddy and Mr Punch: Connections in Irish and English History*, Penguin Press, 1993

Fowler, Marian, *In a Gilded Cage: From Heiress to Duchess*, Random House, 1993

Frankland, Noble, *Witness of a Century: Life and Times of Prince Arthur Duke of Connaught 1850–1942*, Shepheard Walwyn, 1993

Frewen, Moreton, *Free Grazing: A Report to Shareholders of Powder River Company*, Steel & Jones, 1883

Frewen, Moreton, *Melton Mowbray and Other Memories*, Herbert Jenkins, 1924

Frewen, Oswald, *Sailor's Soliloquy*, Hutchinson, 1961

Fuchs, Emile, *With Pencil, Brush and Chisel: The Life of an Artist*, Putnam, 1925

Gilbert, Martin, *Winston S. Churchill*, vol. 3: *1914–16*, Heinemann, 1971 (and companion volumes)

Gilbert, Martin, *Winston S. Churchill*, vol. 4: *1917–1922*, Heinemann, 1975 (and companion volumes)

Gilbert, Martin, *Winston S. Churchill*, vol. 5: *1922–39*, Heinemann, 1976 (and companion volumes)

Gilbert, Martin, *Churchill: A Life*, Heinemann, 1991

Gilbert, Martin, *Churchill and America*, New York, Free Press, 2005

Gilmour, David, *Curzon*, John Murray, 1994

Guest, Montague and Bolton, William, *The Royal Yacht Squadron: Memorials of its Members*, John Murray, 1903

Haffner, Sebastian, *Churchill*, Haus Publishing, 2003

Hambly, W., *The History of Tattooing and its Significance*, Witherby, 1925

Hamilton, E., *The Halcyon Era*, John Murray, 1933

Hamilton Fyfe, H., *Shakespeare Memorial Souvenir of the Shakespeare Ball*, ed., and with an introduction by Mrs G. Cornwallis-West, Frederic Warne, 1911

Harris, Frank, *My Life and Loves*, unexpurgated edition, New York, Grove Press, 1963

Harris, Luther S., *Around Washington Square: An Illustrated History of Greenwich Village*, Baltimore, Johns Hopkins University Press, 2003

Haslip, Joan, *The Lonely Empress*, Weidenfeld & Nicolson, 1965

Hayden, Deborah, *Pox, Genius, Madness and the Mysteries of Syphilis*, New York, Basic Books, 2003

Higham, Charles, *Dark Lady: Winston Churchill's Mother and her World*, Virgin, 2006

Hitchens, Christopher, *Blood, Class and Nostalgia: Anglo-American Ironies*, Chatto & Windus, 1990

Hobbes, John Oliver (Mrs Pearl Craigie), *The Vineyard*, Unwin, 1904

Holmes, Richard, *In the Footsteps of Churchill*, Cambridge, Mass., Basic Books, 2005

Homberger, Eric, *Mrs Astor's New York: Money and Social Power in a Gilded Age*, Yale University Press, 2002

Jenkins, Roy, *Churchill*, Macmillan, 2001

Kehoe, Elisabeth, *Fortune's Daughters*, Atlantic Books, 2004

Kinvig, Clifford, *Churchill's Crusade: The British Invasion of Russia (1918–20)*, Hambledon Continuum, 2006

Kraus, René, *Young Lady Randolph: Life and Times*, Jarrolds, 1944

Lambton, the Hon. George, *Men and Horses I Have Known*, Thornton Butterworth, 1934

Langtry, Lillie, *The Days I Knew*, Hutchinson, 1925

Lee, Celia, ed., *A Soldier's Wife: Diary of Jean, Lady Hamilton*, Celia Lee Publications, 2001

Lee, Christopher, *This Sceptred Isle: 55 BC–1901*, BBC Publications, 1997

Lee, Christopher, *This Sceptred Isle: Twentieth Century*, BBC Publications, 1999

Leslie, Anita, *The Fabulous Leonard Jerome*, Hutchinson, 1954

Leslie, Anita, *Jennie: The Life of Lady Randolph Churchill*, Hutchinson, 1960

Leslie, Anita, *Mr Frewen of England*, Hutchinson, 1966

Leslie, Anita, *Edwardians in Love*, Hutchinson, 1972

Leslie, Anita, *Cousin Clare: The Tempestuous Career of Clare Sheridan*, Hutchinson, 1976

Leslie, Anita, *The Gilt and the Gingerbread*, Hutchinson, 1981

Leslie, Seymour, *Glaslough in Oriel*, The Donagh Press, 1913

Leslie, Seymour, *The Jerome Connexion*, John Murray, 1964

Leslie, Shane, *The End of a Chapter*, Constable, 1916

Leslie, Shane, *Studies in Sublime Failure*, Ernest Benn, 1932

Leslie, Shane, *American Wonderland*, Michael Joseph, 1936

Leslie, Shane, *Men were Different: Five Studies in Late Victorian Biography*, Michael Joseph, 1937

Leslie, Shane, *The Film of Memory*, Michael Joseph, 1938

Leslie, Shane, *Long Shadows*, John Murray, 1966

Liddington, Jill, *Rebel Girls*, Virago, 2006

Longford, Elizabeth, *A Pilgrimage of Passion: The Life of Wilfrid Scawen Blunt*, Weidenfeld & Nicolson, 1979

Lukacs, John, *Five Days in London: May 1940*, Yale University Press, 1940

MacAllister, Ward, *Society as I Have Found It*, Cassell, 1890

MacColl, Gail and Wallace, Carol McD., *To Marry an English Lord*, New York, Workman Publishing, 1989

Mackenzie Stuart, Amanda, *Consuelo and Alva Vanderbilt*, HarperCollins, 2005

McMenamin, Michael and Zoller, Curt, *Becoming Winston Churchill: The Untold Story of Young Winston and his American Mentor*, Portsmouth, New Haven, Greenwood Publishing, 2007

Marie, Queen of Roumania, *The Story of My Life*, Cassell, 1934

Marsh, Sir Edward, *A Number of People*, Heinemann, 1939

Martin, Ralph G., *Jennie: The Life of Lady Randolph Churchill*, vol. 1: *The Romantic Years 1854–1895*, Prentice Hall, 1969

Martin, Ralph G., *Jennie: The Life of Lady Randolph Churchill*, vol. 2: *The Dramatic Years 1895–1921*, Prentice Hall, 1971

Mason, Michael, *The Making of Victorian Sexuality*, Oxford University Press, 1995

Masters, Anthony, *Rosa Lewis: An Exceptional Edwardian*, Weidenfeld & Nicolson, 1977

Meacham, Jon, *Franklin and Winston: A Portrait of a Friendship*, Granta Books, 2004

Montague Browne, Anthony, *Long Sunset: Memoirs of Winston Churchill's Last Private Secretary*, Cassell, 1995

Moore, George, *Memoirs of my Dead Life*, Heinemann, 1921

Moran, Charles McMoran Wilson, Baron, *Winston Churchill: The Struggle for Survival 1940–1965: Taken from the Diaries of Lord Moran*, Constable, 1966

Morley, John, Viscount, *Recollections*, Macmillan, New York, 1917

Morphet, David, *Louis Jennings MP, Editor of the New York Times and Tory Democrat*, Notion Books, 2001

Morris, Jan, *Trieste and the Meaning of Nowhere*, Faber & Faber, 2001

Morris, Lloyd, *Incredible New York*, Random House, 1951

Nevill, Lady Dorothy, *Reminiscences*, ed. Ralph Nevill, Edward Arnold, 1906

Nevill, Lady Dorothy, *Under Five Reigns*, ed. Ralph Nevill, Methuen, 1910

Nevill, Lady Dorothy, *Life and Letters*, Methuen, 1919

Newsome, David, *The Victorian World Picture*, John Murray, 1997

Nicolson, Juliet, *The Perfect Summer: Dancing into Shadow in 1911*, John Murray, 2006

O'Connor, Richard, *Courtroom Warrior: The Combative Career of William Travers Jerome*, Boston, Little Brown, 1963

Oxford and Asquith, Margot, Countess of, *Autobiography*, Butterworth, 1920

Pearsall, Ronald, *The Worm in the Bud: The World of Victorian Sexuality*, Penguin, 1969

Pearson, John, *Citadel of the Heart*, Macmillan, 1991

Peters, Margot, *Mrs Pat: The Life of Mrs Patrick Campbell*, The Bodley Head, 1984

Pless, Princess Daisy of, *From my Private Diary*, ed. Major Desmond Chapman-Huston, John Murray, 1928

Pless, Princess Daisy of, *By Herself*, John Murray, 1929

Pless, Princess Daisy of, *Better Left Unsaid*, New York, Dutton, 1931

Pless, Princess Daisy of, *What I Left Unsaid*, Cassell, 1936

Quelch, Eileen, *Perfect Darling: The Life and Times of George Cornwallis-West*, Woolf, 1972

Reynolds, David, *In Command of History: Churchill Fighting and Writing the Second World War*, Allen Lane, 2004

Reynolds, K. D., *Aristocratic Women and Political Society in Victorian Britain*, Oxford, Clarendon Press, 1998

Rhodes James, Robert, *Lord Randolph Churchill*, Weidenfeld & Nicolson, 1939

Rhodes James, Robert, ed., *Chips: The Diaries of Sir Henry Channon*, Weidenfeld and Nicolson, 1967

Roberts, Andrew, *Salisbury: Victorian Titan*, Weidenfeld & Nicolson, 1999

Rode's New York City Business Directory for 1854–55, Being a Supplement to the New York City Directory for 1854–55, New York, Rode, 1854

Rose, Kenneth, *Curzon: A Most Superior Person*, Macmillan, 1985

Rosebery, Archibald Philip Primrose, Earl of, *Lord Randolph Churchill*, Humphreys, 1906

Rossmore, Lord, *Things I Can Tell*, G. Bell, 1912

Rubinstein, W. D., ed., *Wealth and the Wealthy in the Modern World*, Croom Helm, 1980

Sandys, Celia, *Churchill: Wanted Dead or Alive*, New York, Carroll & Graf, 2000

Sandys, Celia, *Chasing Churchill*, New York, Carroll & Graf, 2004

Sermoneta, Vittoria Colonna, Duchess of, *Things Past*, Hutchinson, 1929

Sermoneta, Vittoria Colonna, Duchess of, *Sparkle Distant Worlds*, Hutchinson, 1947

Seward, Desmond, *Eugénie: The Empress and her Empire*, Sutton, 2004

Sheridan, Clare, *Nuda Veritas*, Thornton Butterworth, 1927

Sheridan, Clare, *My Crowded Sanctuary*, Methuen, 1945

Sheridan, Clare, *To the Four Winds*, André Deutsch, 1957

Smalley, George W., *Anglo-American Memories*, Duckworth, 1912

Smyth, Dame Ethel, *Impressions that Remained*, Longman, 1919

Smyth, Dame Ethel, *Streak of Life*, Longman, 1921

Smyth, Dame Ethel, *What Happened Next*, Longman, 1940

Soames, Mary, *Family Album*, Houghton Mifflin, 1982

Soames, Mary, ed., *Speaking for Themselves: The Personal Letters of Winston and Clementine Churchill*, Black Swan, 1999

Soames, Mary, *Clementine Churchill: Revised and Updated*, Doubleday, 2002

Stott, Rebecca, *The Fabrication of the Late Victorian Femme Fatale*, Macmillan, 1992

Strachey, Lytton, *Letters*, ed., P. Levy and P. Marcus, Viking, 2005

Terry, Ellen, *The Story of my Life*, Hutchinson, 1908

Vickers, Hugo, *Gladys Duchess of Marlborough*, Weidenfeld & Nicolson, 1979

Walkowitz, Judith, *City of Dreadful Night: Narratives of Sexual Danger in Late Victorian London*, Chicago, University of Chicago Press, 1992

Warrender, Lady Maud, *My First Sixty Years*, Cassell, 1933

Warwick, Frances, Countess of, *Life's Ebb and Flow*, Hutchinson, 1929

Warwick, Frances, Countess of, *Afterthoughts*, Cassell, 1931

Wassermann, Johan and Kearney, Brian, eds, *A Warrior's Gateway: Durban and the Anglo-Boer War 1899–1902*, Pretoria, Protea Book House, 2002

Wecter, Dixon, *The Saga of American Society – A Record of Social Aspiration 1607–37*, New York, Charles Scribner's Sons, 1970

Weintraub, Stanley, *Edward the Caresser*, Simon & Schuster, 2001

Wharton, Edith, *The Buccaneers*, New York, D. Appleton-Century, 1938

Woolf, Virginia, *Roger Fry*, Hogarth Press, 1940

Acknowledgements

In 2001 I read Roy Jenkins's biography of Winston Churchill. Jenkins may not have unearthed much in the way of new material but I admired his narrative powers and his skill in bringing a politician's eye to bear on the long and distinguished life. At the same time I was also struck by how little space he devoted to the mother of Winston Churchill, a woman about whom I was convinced there must be much more to know. And so my first debt is to the late Roy Jenkins for setting the hare.

No one who researches Churchill lives can go far without the Churchill College Archives in Cambridge and its unfailingly helpful archivists. I should particularly like to thank the Director Dr Allen Packwood, Natalie Adams, Sandra Marsh, Andrew Riley and all the staff for going out of their way to locate material and make researching there such a happy (if necessarily cold) experience. I should also like to thank Gillian Dickinson, the accommodation staff and porters who all became friendly, welcoming faces over several years.

I have also researched at Durban Reference Library, South Africa, and would like to record my thanks to the late, incomparable David Rattray who brought South African history alive. In Washington at the Library of Congress I thank Daun van Ee, Historical Specialist, Manuscript Division, and his courteous staff; at Georgetown University, I am grateful to Nicholas Scheetz, Manuscript Librarian, for his scholarship as well as much friendly encouragement. In New York, staff at the New York Public Library, the New York Historical Society, the American Irish Historical Society, Columbia University Library and Brooklyn Public Library, where I would particularly like to mention Lisa de Boer and Joy Holland, all deserve thanks. In London I have found useful material at the Rothschild Archive, where I am most grateful to Melanie Aspey and Michael Hall, and at the Westminster Archives, thanks to Janice West. Paul Cartwright and Oliver House in the Modern Papers Reading Room of the New Bodleian Library, Oxford, have also been extremely helpful, as have Kathy Woollett at the East Sussex Record Office, staff at the Fitzwilliam Museum in Cambridge, especially Nick Robinson, and archivists at the King's Royal Hussars Museum in Winchester. I cannot imagine being without the rich facilities of the London Library, the British Library, the Newspaper Library at Colindale or the National Archives in Kew. Staff at my local library in Richmond upon Thames have also, as ever, been most helpful. Jeff Roth at the *New York Times* has performed useful research services, for which I thank him profusely. I should also like to thank Helena Calleta at the Open Book in Richmond, the sort of bookseller no writer should be without.

I would particularly like to thank Sir Martin Gilbert, official biographer of Sir Winston Churchill, to whom all Churchill historians owe a huge debt, as well as Mrs Yvonne Churchill for granting me permission to quote from copyright material. My heartfelt thanks to a number of individuals either for pointing me in a direction I had not thought of or for drawing my attention to diaries and letters. Some have generously offered me hospitality, making the research an extremely happy process, others have kindly read parts of the manuscript or lent me books, papers or photographs from their collections, including Randolph and Catherine Churchill, and Jonathan and Anita Frewen in Kent, Michael Kelion in London, Tarka and Jane King in Wiltshire, Jack and Carol Levin in Brooklyn Heights, Andrew and Kate Lluberes in Washington, Dr John Mather in Maryland and Nicola and Chris Beauman in London. Above all I realise my good fortune in being able to discuss Jennie with her two surviving granddaughters: Dame Mary Soames, who generously shared her memory and some private correspondence with me, and Clarissa, Countess of Avon. Others have produced information I was unaware of, not least Richard Davenport-Hines, Christopher Lee and Amanda Mackenzie Stuart, for which I am deeply grateful.

At Blenheim, I am grateful to His Grace the Duke of Marlborough, for allowing me to see the private apartments where Jennie stayed, as well as to the Archivist, John Forster. At Chartwell I should like to thank Carole Kenwright, Judith Seaward and Vicky Stubbs. For allowing me to see inside Rosetta Cottage at Cowes I would like to thank Anne Hammond and her hard-working staff at the National Trust.

There are many people who have shared their thoughts and insights with me or pointed me in directions I would not necessarily have thought of, provided useful books and generally buoyed me along the Churchill road. I am most grateful to them all and hope they will forgive this alphabetical thank-you list: Erika Bard, Correlli Barnett, Alison Baverstock,

Caroline Bradbeer, Dr Piers Brendon, Owen Byrne (the Jockey Club of America), Catherine Calvert, Dr Chris Clough, Tim Coates, David Coffer, Mark Coghlan (Durban), Phyllis Connerty, Paul Courtenay, Russ Craig (Salisbury Hall), Elizabeth Crawford, Professor David Dilks, Oliver Everett, Olivia Fane, Christina Farr, Doucet Fischer, Professor Roy Foster, David Freeman, Debbie Gabbie (Bourne Partnerships, Salisbury Hall), the late Jean Goodman, Jonathan Goodman, Veronica Franklin Gould, Michael Hall, Biddy Hayward, Tim Hely-Hutchinson, Richard Hoare, Elisabeth Kehoe, Andrew Kerr, Alastair Laing, Lee Langley, Richard Langworth, Celia and John Lee, Jennifer Leslie, Sir John Leslie, Samantha Leslie, Andrew Lownie, Joseph McCarthy (Brooklyn), Neil McKenna, Michael McMenamin, Phyllis Magidson (Curator of Costumes and Textiles at the Museum of the City of New York), Ralph Martin, Michael Meredith (Eton College Library), Julian Mitchell, Valerie Mitchell (Director of the English-Speaking Union), Sir Anthony and Lady Montague Browne, David Morphet, Jan Morris, Professor James W. Muller, the late Nigel Nicolson, Professor Otto Rauchbauer, Dr Jane Ridley, Kenneth Rose, Jeff Roth, Christine Rickards Rostworowska, Professor William Rubinstein, Desmond Seward, Richard Slowe, Elizabeth Snell, Michael Sternberg, Daniel Topolski, Amanda Vaill, Hugo Vickers, Lord Watson of Richmond, Camilla Watson, Andrew and Tessa Wells, Hugh Whitemore, Gordon Williams, Lynn Williams, Gordon Wise and Lindy Woodhead.

My agent, Clare Alexander of Aitken Alexander, has always seen Jennie as the key figure I believe she is from the moment I first mentioned my idea. I am grateful for her friendship, professional support and creative input whenever I have needed it. My publishers, John Murray in London and W. W. Norton in New York, have also been exemplary and indulged me with extra time in which to write this book. There are many people in both houses to whom I owe thanks but I single out especially Roland Philipps, Caroline Westmore and Angela Vonderlippe. I have been blessed with an editor who is spoken of in reverential terms as the prince among editors: Peter James. He knows what a valuable task he has performed and how much I owe to his textual vigilance. Once again, I have been extremely fortunate that Douglas Matthews, the world's favourite indexer, has compiled my index.

Finally, anyone who has lived with a biographer knows only too well the pressures that an obsessive subject brings in its wake. My daughter Imogen has been with me to Chartwell and Blenheim and many other sites of Churchill interest more than once, and all my family, Mark, Adam and Amy, came with me to South Africa, took numerous photographs, climbed Spion Kop in silence and stood in front of the wreck of the train from which Winston Churchill escaped. I thank them all for sharing this and much more, for listening to me, offering their own valuable perspective and for sporadic technical as well as constant emotional support. To all the above mentioned I am grateful. Myself alone I blame for any errors or omissions.

Index

NOTE: The initials WSC refer to Sir Winston (Spencer) Churchill